BOXING
CONFIDENTIAL

BOXING CONFIDENTIAL

*Power, Corruption and the
Richest Prize in Sport*

Jim Brady

MILO BOOKS LTD

First published in December 2002 by Milo Books Ltd

ISBN 1 903854 06 7

Typeset by e-type, Liverpool

Printed and bound in Great Britain by
Cox & Wyman Ltd, Reading, Berkshire

MILO BOOKS LTD
10 Park Street
Lytham
Lancs
FY8 5LU
info@milobooks.com

Contents

Preface

WHEN I WAS a kid, I picked up a copy of a book called *Jim Norris and the Decline of Boxing*. I was in school, and had gone to the library during lunch. I was so excited to read it, I put a copy of my world history textbook in front of it, and devoured the exploits of Joe Louis, Max Schmeling and other boxing heroes. The hell with Alexander the Great.

I flunked world history, but Barney Nagler's book was a great awakening. It told a side of boxing that you never read in *Ring* magazine, the so-called Bible of the sport. This was really the way this racket worked. *Ring* editor Nat Fleischer was a fan who idealized the fight game; Nagler explained the human side.

My dad was a fighter, and he always told me it was a rotten business. He was the finest person I ever met, so I believed him. But I grew up on televised boxing, and I still remember my dad telling me, "Boy, did you miss a great fight." Archie Moore had just got off the deck three times to knock out Yvon Durelle in the eleventh. For the next fifteen years, I said to my dad, "I sure wish you'd have woken me up." Ironically, I would eventually send both fighters their films. Archie wrote me one of the most beautiful letters I ever got. Durelle was very appreciative in his impossibly accented French-Canadian way.

I eventually came to meet a lot of fighters, and to this day, I'm struck by their pre-ordained rendezvous with tragedy. I talked to Jerry Quarry, the "Great White Hope" of the 1960s, when he was young and hungry in Los Angeles' Main Street Gym. I remember how lonely he sounded thirty years later, tragically suffering from dementia. I saw Howie Steindler in the Main Street Gym; he was the inspiration for Burgess Meredith's grizzled trainer in *Rocky*. Steindler would be found with his brains blown out. I still remember the crummy bathroom that stunk with the sweat of the poor. Davey Moore had left some grafitti – the featherweight champ had been recently beaten to death in the ring. Steindler was a funny little guy, with signs like "Your dues are the backbone of this gym. Please pay them. We are getting curvature of the spine."

I remember talking to Willie Besmanoff, who fought all the great heavy-weights of the fifties and sixties. His young daughter shrieked to me, "He's crazy!" Willie, who faced Sonny Liston and a young Cassius Clay, confessed, "That's what really hurts." Willie called his daughters "my zree lovely angels," in his German-English. Yet they didn't want to take care of him, though he had sweat and bled so they could live.

I remember a guy named Nap Mitchell, who boxed Archie Moore in his last time in the ring. It was just an exhibition, and I think Archie had fought him once for real in 1944. The "Ol' Mongoose" couldn't pull his left hook, and this time Mitchell went down like he was dead. Five years later he was. He killed himself, and his girlfriend.

I still recall the old "Windy City Gym" at 1154 East 63 Street in Chicago. I was one of the few white guys who'd go there. One time I had been working out, and my long blond hair was wet and stringy. I suddenly felt somebody touching it, and looking with awe. It was a little black child about six, named Montell Griffin. One day he'd grow up to be a champion and beat the great Roy Jones.

Johnny Williams was another kid who trained there. He was a country boy from Mississippi, and the gym owner Clarence Griffin let him sleep on site. In 1981, Johnny won almost every national amateur title at light-heavyweight, but Griffin loved the kid too much and was afraid to turn him pro. In 1983, "Griff," a father figure to a lot of black youngsters, dropped dead in a fighter's corner. He was still chasing his dream at fifty-seven. He once told me, "My autobiography should be: 'From rags to even raggedier.'" Poor Johnny Williams got destroyed by a young amateur named Tyson. He had no trade and began selling drugs. He was a nice kid who had staked his future on boxing, and was devastated by the loss of Griffin. A couple of years later he was blown away on the streets.

I did a couple of movies, and was a "stand-in" for the actor Tom Berrenger in a terrible flick called *Flesh and Blood*. I punched a heavy bag, and a week later, I held a bag for another bad movie. Griff started calling me Laurence Olivier.

There was a big heavyweight up there named Maine Miller. He refused to play the fall guy, because nobody "knocks me out."

Whatever happened to the Windy City Gym? What became of my youth? Who is this aging man who looks back in the mirror? Somehow, all these guys are a still a part of me, and I wrote this book for them.

I'd like to thank Mel Peabody, a fine trainer from Lawrence, Massachusetts, who not only is the most ethical man I ever met in boxing, but in his own, rough-hewn, unpretentious way, one of the most moral people I've ever met in my life. Peabody loves boxing, and protects fight-ers. He is just a working man, but he's constantly going into his own pocket so that his fighters, and the troubled kids who come to his gym, have a chance. It's big mouths like Don King that are synonymous with boxing, but it's guys like Peabody who are really its heart and soul.

In 2001, Peabody's fighter, Edwin Santana lost to Joel Casamayor for the WBA 130 pound championship. Santana was a huge underdog, but he said beforehand, of Peabody, who had guided him since he was twelve, "I want to win, but not for me. For Mel. I love Mel."

I also want to thank Mark Cannata, for his computer expertise. Mark is also a "champ" in his own right.

And I want to thank the people who shared the memories with me. Many have passed on since I first began jotting down decades ago. The legendary Nat Fleischer was only ten months away from his death, and he was tired and terribly old, yet he spent an hour with me, when he was certainly entitled to some privacy. I'm also indebted to many fine reporters who helped plough the field that I cultivated. Legends like Jimmy Cannon, who first called boxing, "the red light district of sports," and Dan Parker, who fought the gangsters in the 1950s when others "took their envelope" and looked away, are two that never should be forgotten. Jack Newfield is another great writer with a social conscience who all journalists should try to emulate. So is Thomas Hauser, who says, "We're only here for a short period of time, so we should try to do good."

I hope I have "done good" with this book, but any failures are all mine.

Introduction

IT WAS A stiflingly hot August day in Chicago in 1977. A few young people roamed Rush Street, the glittery mecca of clip joints and topless bars. As they talked and laughed in the heat, nobody paid much attention to the forlorn creature trying to work up the courage to panhandle a meal.

"Hello Johnny," said Clarence Griffin, a dapper black man, pulling out a dollar from his almost empty wallet.

The derelict barely nodded. A dishevelled figure of about fifty with a glazed look in his eyes, he still clung to some semblance of dignity. He wore a thin, dirty suit. His smooth, slightly furrowed, caramel-coloured face was covered with a layer of grime. His Afro was unruly and in need of a comb. As the sun beat down, he sweated fiercely. It was four o'clock in the afternoon, and he smelled, but he'd been run out of the gas station where he used to wash. What he really needed was a good night's sleep.

Once, Johnny Bratton had been the welterweight champion of the world, and chants of "Honey Boy, Honey Boy," resounded from the cheap seats at Chicago Stadium, just a few miles away.

He was just a boy from Chicago's South Side who had a dream, and quit Dusable High School when he was sixteen. By eighteen, he was boxing main events before thousands. While his former classmates were still in school, Johnny fought the great Ike Williams in New Orleans, and at twenty, though still too young to buy a drink, he slugged it out with the great Beau Jack.

"Man, that's some sweet fighter," sighed Hymie "the Mink" Wallman, the first time he saw this sinewy young panther claw his way to victory under the hot arc lights. Wallman was so smitten, he begged $20,000 from the millionaire sportsman Jim Norris to buy Bratton's contract. Wallman was a front for mobster Franke Carbo, the bloodsucker who ran the fight game.

"Johnny just had so much charisma," recalled Clarence Griffin, blissfully retreating into the past. "Griff," who bore a striking resemblance to the actor Morgan Freeman, grew up in the same Southside black ghetto, where graffiti was scrawled on soot-stained walls and police sirens howled into the night. He now ran the old "Coulon's Gym" on 63rd Street, where Johnny used to train.

Griff smiled sadly as he remembered Johnny's big-finned Cadillac, the one with "Honey Boy" inscribed on the side. Bratton also had a sporty Jaguar, inscribed with his initials. At a time when blacks couldn't even eat downtown, Bratton was quite the dandy, with his hair straightened, and wore a greasy, slick-backed "Conk" and sported a slew of sharp zoot suits with military creases. The little black kids, in their ragged clothes, would tear after him whenever he roared through the blighted neighbourhood. Even the street hustlers used to say, "Johnny, you sure is looking fine."

As black and white television descended on black and white America in the early fifties, Johnny Bratton's face became a staple of the old *Wednesday Night Fights*. His slick box-punching sold a lot of TVs, but he had been moved too fast, and developed brittle hands. By the time Bratton was twenty-one, he'd already had forty-four professional fights. By 1949, when he was just twenty-two, the South Side phenomenon was rated fourth in the world by *Ring* magazine. All-time greats Sugar Ray Robinson and Kid Gavilan were one and two.

On 14 March 1951, Bratton trounced Charley Fusari at the Stadium to win the vacant NBA world championship after Robinson had moved up and destroyed Jake LaMotta a month earlier for the middleweight title. But it wasn't till 21 February 1976, that Johnny got a chance genuinely to appreciate his own artistry. That night, downtown at the posh Sheraton-Chicago Hotel, along the Magnificent Mile, Jack Cowen promoted a fight show, and the old broadcast of Bratton's fight with Fusari was shown. Hundreds of people actually waited anxiously for the decision, until 2:00 in the morning, on a fight that happened twenty-five years earlier.

As the ballroom crowd loudly cheered Bratton's victory, they had no idea that the shabby, middle-aged man, standing all by himself, vacantly staring at the big screen, was actually *the* Johnny Bratton. For Johnny, seeing himself in his prime was like a drowning man watching his life flash by.

In May 1952, Bratton got whipped in fifteen by bolo-punching Kid Gavilan for the world crown. There was another title fight loss in 1953. Johnny began hearing strange voices. He finally was carted off to Manteno, an infamous state mental institution, in 1957. The *Chicago Tribune*, which once chronicled his victories, now had a sad shot of Johnny gazing out of a padded cell. He was thirty years old.

After shock treatments, brutal hosings by the guards, and few attempts at therapy, Bratton was back on the street again by 1961. Though he had scored fifty-nine wins inside the ring, mental illness was one opponent he couldn't beat. He survived the "Swinging Sixties" by sleeping in abandoned cars.

By 1977, as the icy fingers of a Chicago winter closed in, the old champ sought refuge in the Del Prado Hotel. He couldn't afford a room; he slunk off into a corner just to stay warm. Twenty-five years earlier, when Johnny Bratton was champion, the Del Prado had been the place to stay. Now, like Johnny, it was on its last legs. There were complaints from some residents, though others would say, "Do you know who that is? That's Johnny Bratton. Why, he used to be as famous as Joe Louis."

Bratton tried living in the past. He was a buff on movie trivia. He loved Edward G. Robinson and Errol Flynn. He would kibbitz with the old pensioners, then suddenly break into strange laughter, and have loud, animated conversations with people no one could see. "Johnny could really hurt you when he wasn't on his medicine," recalled former Chicago cop Tony Fosco who confronted him a couple of times.

In the wee hours one morning, when all was quiet and no one else could see, Johnny slowly unfurled himself from the couch where he'd been sleeping, and creakily begin to shadow box in front of the big hallway mirror. Maybe his mind was gone, but Johnny Bratton could still be the champion of the world.

* * *

Boxing is the "sweet science," said one writer. *Professional* boxing is the "red-light district of sports," said another. There's no racket so full of excitement, glamour, or tragedy, as the fight game. "The boxing public, generally, are a bloodthirsty lot," reckoned Henry Cooper, one of Britain's most beloved fighters. "They like to see a good hard fight, and if there's plenty of gore and snot flying around they love it," Cooper came a long way, from a plasterer to a knighthood. Freddie Mills, however, one of the most courageous men ever to enter a ring, somehow ended up dead in an alley in Soho, central London, fifteen years after losing the light-heavyweight championship of the world. Randy Turpin of Leamington blew his brains out in 1966, a decade and a half after upsetting the incomparable Sugar Ray Robinson. For sixty-four glorious days, Turpin breathed the rarefied air of a national icon, but once the cheering stopped, both Turpin and Mills tumbled deeper and deeper into the abyss. To be a professional fighter demands a great deal of courage and self-discipline, but the aspect of self-destructiveness can't be denied.

Long before political correctness, "boxing ... was the most acceptable way to toughen a boy ... make a man of him," claims British writer and broadcaster Melvyn Bragg. "Perhaps I am of the last generation that regarded boxing as young men today cleave to football. We liked football in the 1940s and 1950s, we loved cricket, but boxing was up there and for some, like my father and many of his friends, it vaulted over all sports. It was the raw truth of conflict within the rules. It was character building. It was man to man."

Professional boxing has been called "showbusiness with blood," and modern man's answer to the old Roman Circus. Whatever it is, there just aren't many happy endings in the fight game. Sure, Wilbert "Skeeter" McClure won a gold medal in the 1960 Olympics, and became a top pro. He's now a Boston psychologist. Fifties trialhorse Bert Whitehurst twice lasted the distance with Sonny Liston, en route to becoming a PhD. Vitali Klitchko is WBO heavyweight champ, and also holds a doctorate. The late Nat Fleischer, boxing's preeminent historian, figured Warren Barbour might've beaten Jack Johnson, had the young "White Hope" turned pro, but this millionarie's son opted for politics, and became a United States senator from New Jersey.

But for every miracle, there are tragedies like Del Fontaine, the globe-trotting American middleweight of the 1930s, who lost to the hangman at the Old Bailey. Anthony "Two Guns" Fletcher, a tough fighter from Philadelphia, sits on Pennsylvania's Death Row. In London, former WBC super middleweight champion Gerald McClellan suffered brain damage, blindness, and lost almost all of his hearing, after being halted by Nigel Benn in February 1995. On 19 September 1980, in Los Angeles's Olympic Auditorium, a cadaverous Johnny Owen, a homely, big-eared Welshman who would blush at the sight of a woman because he had never slept with one, was flattened by WBC bantamweight champ Lupe Pintor. Delirious Mexicans threw cups of urine on the pale little Owen as he was carried out. Johnny never got up again.

By 1998, Jerry Quarry, a "Great White Hope" who might have been a king were it not for Joe Frazier and Muhammad Ali, couldn't even find his way back home when he went for a walk. Jerry's doctor said he had the deteriorated brain of an eighty-year-old man. Quarry had earned millions but was subsisting on just $540 a month disability. Still, he'd shuffle toward young boys and in his soft voice he'd say, "Son, do you know, I was nearly heavyweight champion of the world."

One day Quarry lapsed into a coma. His family took him off life support.

* * *

Boxing is man's basic sport. It's brutal, often barbaric, and the way fighters are robbed of their blood money is scandalous, but prize-fighting will always be with us. It is the one sport that sanitizes man's blood lust, and inspires him to be courageous. Man will always need heroes.

One of America's greatest presidents, Teddy Roosevelt, who donned the gloves, thought boxing was a brilliant metaphor for life. "It's not the critic who counts; not the man who points out how the strong man stumbled, or where the doer of deeds could've done better. The credit belongs to the man who is actually in the arena; whose face is marred by dust and sweat and blood; who strives valiantly; who errs and comes short again and again; who knows the great enthusiasms, the great devotions; who spends himself in a worthy cause; who, at the best, knows in the end the triumph of high achievement, and who, at the worst, if he fails, at least fails while daring greatly, so that his place shall never be with those timid souls who know neither victory or defeat."

Floyd Patterson, the former heavyweight champion, spent twenty years in the ring, and described boxing this way: "It's like being in love with a woman. She can be faithful, she can be mean, she can be cruel, but it doesn't matter. If you love her, you want her, even though she can do you all kinds of harm."

By March 1998, Patterson, then aged sixty-three, was making $76,421 a year as the head of the New York State Athletic Commission, but was forced to testify in a court case after promoters of the ghastly "Ultimate Fighting Championships" challenged his ban.

Opposing lawyer David Meyrowitz asked him who he had fought for the heavyweight championship in 1956.

Patterson: "I'd have to think about that. I can't remember the opponent I fought, but I wound up beating him to become heavyweight champion of the world."

"Where did the fight take place?"

"I really don't know, I think it was New York." (It was Chicago, against Archie Moore.)

"Do you know the name of your predecessor?"

Patterson, still looking very much like he did as champion, frantically began to search his pockets. "Yes, I am going to get that out. Just a minute … I have it here." (It was Rocky Marciano. Floyd never found the name.)

"Mr. Patterson, do you know the name of your predecessor, chairman of the New York State Athletic Commission?"

"Yes, I do know, but, uh …"

"What's the secretary's name?"

"Oh boy … I see her quite often, I know her very well. I just forgot her name."

It went on this way for three horrible hours. After the video transcript was leaked, Patterson was forced to resign as chairman. Finally, he confessed, "Sometimes, I can't even remember my own name."

Patterson had once held the richest prize in sport.

CHAPTER ONE

An Alternative History
Of The Heavies

THE NAMES ARE now shrouded in mist: Sullivan, Corbett, Fitszimmons, Jeffries, Johnson, Dempsey, lost forever in a more glorious time. They gave us the Solar Plexus Punch, the Massacre in the Sun, the Battle of the Long Count. But behind the glamour and glitz is a very different story of what really happened when men competed for the ultimate sporting prize.

The Marquess of Queensberry had no idea what he was starting when he and John Graham Chambers published the first rules for boxing with gloves in 1867. Thirteen years later, Madison Square Garden was built; it would become, along with the National Sporting Club in London, the mecca of prize-fighting. But the transition from bare fists to gloves was hardly smooth. In May 1883, heavyweight champ John L. Sullivan halted Charley Mitchell of England in three when police jumped into the ring and stopped the fight. In November 1884, the cops broke up another bit of fisticuffs with Alf Greenfield "for tending to corrupt public morals" in round two. Sullivan, the Boston-Irish champion, would straddle the era when the new sport of boxing replaced old-fashioned pugilism.

On 11 September 1899, a twelve-year-old New Yorker named Nathaniel Fleischer saw his first professional fight: Terrible Terry McGovern destroyed Pedlar Palmer, the British champ, to win the vacant world bantamweight title in just a round. For years, Fleischer relived that night, and by 1904 he had become a correspondent for the old *Morning* and *Sunday World*, and the *New York Press*. The tiny Fleischer had been a good all-around athlete, a fine collegiate broad jumper who was fast on his feet. Though he actually covered the sinking of the Titanic, it was boxing that thrilled him like nothing else. Fleischer would come to epitomize everything good about boxing, though he was hardly the fierce protector whom gangsters feared, as legend would later have it. That's just one more myth. Fleischer simply loved the sport, the way a mother loves a wayward son, terrible imperfections and all.

On 1 September 1900, the Horton Act, which had allowed legal prize-fighting, expired in New York State. The night before, "Gentleman" Jim Corbett had taken on Kid McCoy at the Garden. Corbett had recently been smashed into defeat in twenty-three rounds by his old sparring partner Jim Jeffries when trying to regain the heavyweight championship. That clash drew the biggest gate of the Horton era, $60,000. Rumours raced that the McCoy fight would be fixed, but it still drew $50,000. The match turned into an apparently fierce brawl. McCoy was knocked out in the fifth, which made believers of the *New York Times*, but a few days later, after Corbett ran off to London with a stunning vaudeville singer, his furious wife went straight to the *New York World* and accused her handsome husband of running out because he'd didn't want to face the consequences of a fixed fight. Proving that hell hath no fury like a woman scorned, she claimed that Gentleman Jim had made an agreement for McCoy to win, then double-crossed him. She filed for divorce. Corbett never won another fight but did return to New York, and earned a living in vaudeville. Gentleman Jim, with his regal pompadour, was a dashing figure, and would pull up at the theatres in a beautiful motorcar. They were such novelties, people would gather around just to touch.

Prize-fighting, however, had reverted to back rooms and barges. With the Horton Act's expiration, nearly all the New York fight clubs went out of business. But enforcing a permanent ban on prize-fighting proved to be impossible. By 1908, the sport had sputtered to life and sixteeen clubs were holding weekly cards in New York City and nearby Brooklyn. By 1911, there were thirty fight clubs in New York City alone, and by 1913, when Nat Fleischer was in his mid-twenties, there were eighty-nine boxing clubs in New York State, while New York City saw an average of twenty shows a week, more than you have in the whole of Britain or America on a weekly basis today. As gaslight gave way to electricity, and the horse and buggy were replaced by the backfiring motor car, boxing was still a Darwinian rite of survival for the poor, dirty faced youngsters who tried to claw their way from up from New York's teeming underbelly.

Papers like the *New York World* loved the excitement of prize-fighting and gave it front-page coverage, while still self-righteously demanding that police stop this "gathering of a disorderly conduct which attracts the worst ruffians and criminals in the city."

"Before Tex Rickard took the helm," recalled Fleischer in his 1958 autobiography, *50 Years at Ringside* , "the old Garden was a haven for crooks. Pick pockets flourished there, and the safety of the patrons at a bicycle race or a fight was entirely a matter of luck. Rickard changed all that by ousting the objectionable characters and making the Garden what it is today – an arena where men, women, and children may go without fear of being molested."

As much as he loved boxing, Fleischer wasn't naive about what was going on. "Boxing on a whole was ruled by ruffians, gangsters and politicians," he wrote. "The many fixed fights that soured he public on the sport were engineered by politicians with headquarters in Tammany Hall ... They made the odds, brought about the fixes and collected the bets."

Once, during a six-day bicycle race in 1909, Fleischer recalled that the scum of the city had descended on the Garden, forking over fifty cents just to get out of the bitter cold. As pickpockets, streetwalkers and muggers worked the corridors, Martin Sheridan, a cop who headed the city pickpocket squad, was planning a big raid for eleven o'clock. Fleischer was then a police reporter, and Sheridan invited Nat to have dinner with him and six other detectives, who were going to make the pinch. Sheridan was also celebrating payday. After everyone dined, and had a couple of beers, Sheridan magnanimously went for the bill.

Suddenly, he bellowed, "Those bastards! They picked *my* pocket!"

When Sheridan and his squad descended on the Garden, Sheridan not only rounded up the thieves, he shook down everybody to recoup his pay cheque, than had them taken to the Garden basement, where he taught them the majesty of the law, to the accompaniment of billy clubs and rubber hoses.

* * *

Race, not politics or legality, became the dominant theme of boxing when the controversial Jack Johnson became the first black heavyweight champion. Johnson came from a poor Southern background but was an articulate, well-read man, with a beautiful bass voice reminiscent of the singer Paul Robeson. Gaby Deslys, the French actress, best described his appeal, which went beyond animal magnetism: "His great staring eyes simply devoured one. His wit ... *enchantement!*" He was also a magnificent defensive boxer.

On 4 July 1910, Johnson humiliated the great former champion, Jim Jeffries, in Reno, Nevada, and sparked a national clamour for a "Great White Hope." Jeffries, a symbol of white might, had been smashed to the canvas several times before he was rescued in the fifteenth round. "I thought you said this fellow could hit," Johnson sneered to John L. Sullivan, who watched in horror from ringside. Race riots broke out all over the country. Ten people died, but Johnson revelled in the controversy.

"It will probably be the last big fight in the country," lamented John L. Sullivan.

Johnson didn't fight for two years but the US media did not soften its opinion of him. When he travelled to Britain in 1911, the *New York Times* asked, "Was it Jack Johnson's pompous ways in England and the flashiness the coloured champion displayed with his white wife that caused such a reversal of feeling in the land of King George against the man who defeated Jim Jeffries?

"Colored boxers always liked to visit England, because they were placed almost on an equality with the Briton. Jack Johnson has suddenly changed this order of things. It is given out pretty straight that it was not the fact that Johnson was to box Bombardier Wells [the leading British heavyweight] that caused the great outcry, although it had considerable to do with it, but simply the forward methods adopted by the champion and putting himself too high on a pedestal to suit even the mild-tempered Britons."

There's no question that the ever-smiling Johnson, with his flashing gold teeth, was an arrogant sonofabitch, but it was his way of coping with a lifetime of racism. When he went to the National Sporting Club, trying to get a match with Wells, he was rudely told, "Servants entrance, Johnson!" As a kid in Galveston, Texas, Johnson had been forced to use the dusty "coon walk" which bordered the streets. As heavyweight champion, it still was no different.

According to boxing historian John D. McCallum, Johnson had three white wives. One killed herself just eleven months after marrying him. "He was a bum, a dead loss," bristled the not-so-gentlemanly Jim Corbett years later. "He hated everybody: his manager, Tex Rickard, who made him rich, (and) his women. He even hated himself. It isn't generally known, but three times Johnson tried to commit suicide, but couldn't pull the trigger."

Two years to the day he destroyed Jeffries, he easily vanquished another white boxer, Fireman Jim Flynn. But Johnson, *bon vivant* and connoisseur of white women, had scandalized America, and was finally indicted under the Mann Act for allegedly taking women across state lines for "immoral purposes." Though Johnson was married to this particular woman, she was white, and this black son of ex-slaves was forced to flee the United States because the Mann Act had been designed simply to railroad him into prison.

Though the public viewed Johnson's lust for white women as the act of an "uppity nigger," Johnson later said, "The public fails to understand my feelings toward different kinds of women. I didn't court white women because I thought I was too good for others. It was just that they always treated me better. I never had a coloured girl that didn't two-time me."

By 1913, he was on the run and boxed Battling Jim Johnson in Paris in the first all-black heavyweight championship encounter in history. He managed only a draw with Battling Jim, a mediocre heavyweight who managed to hurt him in the final round. That December, the *New York Times* concluded, "Negro's Supremacy in Ring Near End." But in the summer of 1914 he was too crafty for Frank Moran, a hard-hitter from Pittsburgh. Moran couldn't land his big right, which he called "Mary Ann."

By 1915, with World War One devouring Europe, Johnson was desperate to make a deal to return to America, even though Bruno Bielaski, chief of the US Bureau of Investigations, told him he would still be prosecuted even if he was no longer champion. By now, the high-living Johnson was also desperate for money. Promoter Jack Curley kept trying to entice him back into the ring. "Your mother in Chicago wants to see you," he told the thirty-seven-year-old champion. Finally he accepted a contest in Havana, Cuba, against a towering white cowboy, Jess Willard. Even before a punch was thrown, the *Chicago Herald* claimed that the bout would be "a frame-up."

Jack Johnson's long, tortuous odyssey as heavyweight champion came to an end under a broiling Havana sun on 15 April 1915. Though Johnson later said that Curley offered him a $20,000 bonus if he threw the fight, the amazing movie footage – that wasn't obtained until 1967, by Bill Cayton – shows Johnson fighting hard and hurting the gigantic Willard in the seventh and eighth. He carried his mocking, familiar smile till then, but finally began to slow down, and Big Jess sent him crashing with a murderous right hand to the jaw.

The *New York Times* reported:

'It was a clean knockout and the best man won. It was not a matter of luck. I have no kick coming.'

Such were the words of ex-champion Jack Johnson when he had recovered from Jess Willard's terriffic left to the heart and right swing to the jaw in the twenty-sixth round of the championship fight that restored pugilistic supremacy to the white race.

From the tenth to the twentieth round, Johnson exercised every art in his power to put out the challenger. After the twentieth round there was little doubt among those at the ringside as to how the fight was going. It was too plain that once more youth was showing. Johnson was tiring so fast that he tried to hold Willard in clinches, but ... Willard always got the best of the infighting, continually landing terrific blows to the body.

Johnson's wife, Lucille, was at ringside, and years later – when he again was broke – Johnson claimed in an article that she sat there only until receiving the pay-off money for him to take his dive. This swag, Johnson claimed, came from spectators who had carried $500 bills. In 1915, when a man was lucky to make $10 a week, how many people carried $500 bills? Top admission was only $20.

The myth of Johnson throwing the fight, and his title, exists to this day. But referee Jack Welsh swore that he saw Johnson bet $2,500 on himself. And after getting knocked out, Johnson was observed in the box office hovering over Curley to make sure he got every dime of his $30,000 purse. The *New York Times's* man at ringside claimed, "Johnson realized in the twenty-second round that his hold on the championship was growing short and asked for Jack Curley. The latter was at the gate at the time, but appeared shortly before the last round. 'Tell my wife, and I'd wish you see her out,' said Jack. Curley understood and carried out Johnson's wish." Johnson didn't want his wife to see him get knocked out.

After Jack finally hit the canvas, a famous photo showed him flat on his back, but his legs weren't outstretched on the canvas. Johnson always claimed that proved he'd taken a dive, and hadn't been knocked out. What Cayton's film showed - but the photo doesn't – was Johnson's legs falling slowly to the hot canvas.

Johnson subsequently surrendered to the American authorities and served a year in Leavenworth for his alleged breach of the Mann Act. The warden had his picture taken with him. At his trial Johnson claimed that prizefights were "all crooked." By 1928, Johnson was broke again, and sold his outrageous "confession" to Nat Fleischer and *Ring* magazine for $250. Fleischer, who saw the fight, never believed it, but he did print it.

"If Johnson was going to throw that fight, I sure wish he'd have thrown it sooner; it was hotter than hell down there," bristled Willard, who never got the credit he deserved for flattening a legend.

★ ★ ★

In 1916, a rugged Colorado saloon brawler named Jack Dempsey went to New York to try his luck in the ring. He'd come to "Big Time" in search of fame and fortune, and wound up with a manager: John 'The Barber" Reisler. "Many said he would have sold his mother's blood if the price was right," Dempsey growled years later. "I had never come up against such a vicious person before."

On Independence Day, 1919, the young ex-hobo challenged Jess Willard in a hastily-erected wooden arena in Toledo, Ohio. Dempsey, whose taut skin was the colour of rawhide, was a 5-4 underdog. Even his own father bet against him. The *New York Times* noted that the twenty-four-year-old challenger had looked "slightly worried" before the bell, while Willard "seemed most at ease. He waved his hand to friends near the ringside and shouted greetings to some of them."

As Big Jess lumbered across the ring to greet the tigerish Dempsey, he gingerly shook hands and said, "Hello Jack. How are you? All right?"

Dempsey grinned without mirth and replied, "You bet."

At 4:07, on a blistering afternoon, the fighters went to the centre of the ring. Temperatures at ringside had tipped 120 degrees.

Dempsey later admitted he was scared before the fight. Once it began, he was a savage. Nothing like it had ever been seen in a prize-fight. About a minute into the first round, Dempsey, who looked a child compared to the champion, slammed home a thudding left-right, and Willard went down so hard that the roar from the outdoor crowd could have been heard all the way to Canada.

The 245-pound champion stumbled up at "six," only for the 187-pound Dempsey to smash him to the canvas five more times. As poor, hulking Jess grabbed the ropes on his haunches, Dempsey, like a murderous beast, stood over him, belting him down again. He hit him on the back of the head as Jess dazedly turned away, and gave him no chance to regain his senses. It was an absolutely barbaric spectacle. Willard went down for the seventh time in the first round and referee Ollie Pecord count him out amid bedlam. He didn't hear a whistle blow in lieu of the bell.

Dempsey rejoiced, thinking he'd won, and left the ring. Suddenly his manager, Jack Kearns – who had bet $10,000 of his $27,500 purse on a first-round knockout – started screaming, "Jack, come back! Jack, come back!" Ringsiders had heard the whistle signalling the end of round one, and the brutal contest was still on.

Between rounds, the bloody Willard slumped on his stool. "I've got a hundred thousand dollars … and a farm in Kansas … a hundred thousand dollars … and a farm in Kansas," he gasped, so he could keep going. But his ribs were broken. A cheekbone was shattered in seven places. His face was coated with blood. His wife, watching her first prize-fight, looked on in horror.

By round two, Dempsey had actually punched himself out and Big Jess nailed the crouching, malevolent demon with a good right hand, but thirty seconds after round three ended, Willard's seconds finally threw in the towel. Willard's grotesque face was a mass of red; Dempsey was splattered with Jess's blood. Willard's right eye was completely closed, and there was another fresh bleeding cut beneath his right eye. His jaw was shattered. Six teeth were knocked out, and the entire right side of his face was swollen to almost double its normal size. In just nine minutes, Willard had taken the most hideous beating in the history of modern boxing. To watch the film eighty years later is still a shock.

That night, Dempsey awoke in his hotel room and thought it was all a dream. He couldn't believe he was heavyweight champion. He threw on some clothes, ran outside and grabbed a newsboy selling papers.

"Who won?" he asked.

"You did, you damn fool," snapped the wise kid, giving Dempsey a paper.

Hardened sportswriters were shocked at Dempsey's two-fisted savagery. Lore had it that his gloves were "loaded." In the late 1950s, when Kearns was busted, the convicted ex-pimp claimed he sprinkled Plaster of Paris on Dempsey's hands, which hardened into lethal weapons. Kearns, who had bitterly broken with Jack in 1926, sold his story to *Sports Illustrated* in the early 1960s, and even gave the mag his "recipe." When *Boxing Illustrated* tried to duplicate it with Cleveland Williams in 1964, his loaded bandages started crumbling immediately once he hit a heavy bag.

Dempsey won a hefty lawsuit against *Sports Illustrated*. Then, with everyone long dead and libel no longer possible, fight doctor Ferdie Pacheco claimed that there was no way that Willard could have sustained such a beating had Dempsey just used his fists. Drawing on his experience as Muhammad Ali's long-time cornerman, and what he had seen as a physician, he said it was impossible to leave dents in a man's skull like Dempsey left in Willard's with just gloved fists.

In 1970, Nat Fleischer told what supposedly had happened. He had covered the fight as a a young New York newspaperman. Before the carnage, he was in Dempsey's dressing room. "I was very friendly with Dempsey and Jack Kearns, his manager, and his trainer Jimmy DeForrest," he told the BBC on film, in 1970. "What happened ... the heat was so terriffic, he (Kearns) had Jimmy DeForrest pour some cool water over the hands of Jack. Naturally, Jack already had the bandages on his hands ... (and) it will tighten. That's what happened with Jack.

"Some of the people came out with the story that he had Plaster of Paris on his gloves. It was simply the hardening of the bandages, due to the fact that a little water had been placed on his hands. With the sweat brought about when the gloves were put on his hands, made it like an iron fist."

Anyone who has ever boxed knows sweat makes the tape limp, and the inside of the gloves soggy. That July 4, Toledo was a furnace. It was even hotter at ringside, since 40,000 people surrounded the fighters. It was so damn hot, spectators in their straw hats actually had towels draping their heads, like Lawrence of Arabia.

In a rare, revealing photograph (now in the Robert Shepard Collection) of Dempsey entering the ring, Jack's taped left fist is very visible. Not only is there no sign of Plaster of Paris, Dempsey's left hand doesn't even seem excessively taped, unlike so many fighters today.

Dempsey had something inside his gloves alright – his murderous fists. Willard, a bitter, cantankerous man, went to his grave believing he'd been cheated. Before he died in 1967, Dempsey simply told him, "Okay Jess, you won."

★ ★ ★

In London, Frenchman Georges Carpentier faced British hope Joe Beckett. The Armistice had ended World War One a year earlier and, as punters pushed their way along the narrow, congested streets, fierce national pride was on the line as they rooted for the broad-backed Beckett. Carpentier was a war hero, and the idol of France. H.G. Wells and George Bernard Shaw were at ringside. So was the Prince of Wales. As the frail Carpentier slipped through the ropes, writer/essayist Arnold Bennett felt the Frenchman "might have been a barrister, a poet, a musician, a Foreign Office attache, a Fellow of All Souls, but not a boxer."

Yet within seconds, a roar had gone up – and Beckett had gone down, felled as cleanly as a bull in a slaughterhouse. "Nothing less than winning the greatest war could have interested and moved (the English crowd) more profusely," felt Bennett.

But for the most part, British boxing was a dark, dingy, hole-in-the wall affair. Maybe the National Sporting Club, in Covent Garden, reeked of upper class gentility, but the "Ring" at Blackfriars was really the soul of British boxing. It was a renovated octagon that had once been a chapel. Now pale young lads beat the holy hell out of each other there. Britain had thousands of fighters at that time, and it was almost impossible to slug your way to the top.

"My earliest memories of boxing started when I was a schoolboy," recalled Teddy Waltham, who later refereed and headed the Board of Control. "When I was seventeen, I went to the old National Sporting Club … I won a competition there. Everyone called Mr. (Peggy) Bettinson, 'Guvnor' … I never fought for a championship, but I was in the top grade, you might say.

"One fight I had with Laurie Raiteri, he was a small welter. He was short and kept jumping in, and Old Man Gutteridge, the chief second at the old National Sporting Club, said, 'Look Teddy, just step back a bit, and he's bound to get disqualified.' In the third round, Old Man Douglas (the referee), bellowed, 'Raiteri, that will do. *Bettinson, not a penny!*' "

At the glorious old National Sporting Club, Waltham routinely fought ten-rounders: "It was nine pounds, win, six pounds, lose, and you had to be pretty good to box ten-threes at the National Sporting Club. You have to remember, a miner or a labourer was getting about twenty bob a week to keep a family on. So, those extra two or three quid he got for boxing were a godsend. There'd be thirty or forty boys waiting. When the whip said, 'I want a six-rounder,' there'd be a fight among themselves to see who got the job, and they were probably getting a pound."

★ ★ ★

In 1920, the Walker Law fully legalized boxing in New York State. Jimmy Walker, the sponsor, later turned out to be one of the most corrupt mayors in New York City's history, and was run out of town shortly after Franklin D. Roosevelt was elected president in 1932. But the Walker Law ended the bogus "club memberships" and deceptive "exhibitions." On 14 December 1920 Jack Dempsey retained the heavyweight title at Madison Square Garden by knocking out Bill Brennan in the twelfth round. A former Klondike gold prospector called Tex Rickard got a ten-year lease on the Garden, at $400,000 a year, and the "Golden Age of Sport" began.

At the same time, the Volstead Act had been passed, banning the sale of alcohol. The same self-righteous zealots who had tried to stamp out prize-fighting had succeeded in prohibiting booze. America would be officially dry until December 1933, but the country wasn't about to give up spirits. Prohibition gave birth to the bootleggers and to organized crime.

Fleischer, a Victorian, patriotic man, claimed that virtually every fight club eventually had bootleggers' dough behind it. "Dutch" Schultz and Owney Madden ran New York. "Boo Boo" Hoff ran Philadelphia, while the infamous Al Capone ruled Chicago. In Chicago alone, an estimated 1,000 people were murdered from 1920-30 as mobsters battled over turf. Capone bragged that at least fifty percent of the cops were on his payroll. He owned a succession of corrupt mayors.

The day after he destroyed Willard, Jack Dempsey announced he was "drawing the colour line" and would "pay no attention to negro challengers, but will defend against any white heavyweight." Outstanding black fighters like Sam Langford, Harry Wills, George Godfrey and Joe Jeannette would never get a chance at the title. Dempsey himself wasn't a racist. He had fought blacks before and boxed exhibitions with them, even in the Deep South. "Every thinking white man," claimed an irate editorial in the *Baton Rouge State Times* after Dempsey had sparred with the black Bill Tate, "knows the importance of absolute separation of the races in everything approaching social contact." Dempsey bailed out Tate financially during the Depression, even though he had fallen on hard times himself.

The reason he wouldn't fight blacks as champion was because Tex Rickard had been so shaken by the race riots after Jack Johnson humiliated Jeffries that he vowed, "I'll never promote a black-white heavyweight title fight again." Some historical revisionists have claim that Dempsey was afraid of the powerful Harry Wills. "I wasn't afraid of Wills," Dempsey said, later. "The only person I was afraid of was Kearns, who was always saying, 'I can put you back in the gutter.'" Nat Fleischer, in the third issue of *Ring*, a magazine he had launched devoted to boxing, took a bold stance and pleaded that Wills be given his chance.

Jack Sharkey, who began his own march to the heavyweight title in 1924, recalled in 1987, "We called 'em niggers in those days, and that's not a very nice word. Dempsey wasn't afraid of Wills. Oh, he'd have beaten Wills. I beat Wills. I was whipping Dempsey, too, but he hit me in the nuts all night long. I turned and complained to the referee, and he hit me on the chin. With him," recalled Sharkey, with a shudder, "you had to *fight.*"

By 1922, Rickard had a lot more to worry about than Wills. Three young girls showed up at New York's infamous Bellvue Hospital with a shocking tale. Alice Ruck, aged fifteen, Elvera Renzi, twelve, and Anna Hess, eleven, claimed they had been enticed into a taxi and forced to breathe iodine as they were sexually assaulted. After the girls awoke, they claimed they found themselves on the banks of the Hudson River.

After an extensive examination, doctors found no trace of iodine. The young girls admitted the whole story was a lie: they were afraid of getting in trouble for being out late. But how could such young girls concoct such a sexually sordid tale? *Something* had happened, and cops questioned them further. This time they told a tale that was even more shocking. They had met a well-dressed man at the Madison Square Garden swimming pool. He was nice and gave them money. Eventually, as time passed, he even invited them up to his Garden Tower apartment, on 47th Street, where they laughed and drank wine. Soon this man was touching their breasts and removing their clothes. It was allegedly Tex Rickard, the most powerful promoter in boxing.

A warrant was issued for his arrest. Rickard loudly protested his innocence, but how was it that young kids from New York's poverty-stricken East Side could describe with chilling accuracy the layouts of Rickard's Tower bedroom and other apartments, if he hadn't taken them there?

Despite his money and influence, Rickard was in big trouble. The plot thickened when another girl, Mary Hornbetch, who was eleven, told investigators that she knew what was going on but had not participated herself. Sarah Schoenberg, another eleven-year-old, corroborated the first three girls' stories with the damning claim that she had engaged in sexual intercourse with the millionaire promoter. She was so immature that she didn't have front teeth. She even spoke with a lisp. When the children finally appeared before the Grand Jury, they couldn't be shaken by vigorous cross-examination. With magistrate George W. Simpson admitting that their statements "bore the imprint of truth," Rickard, ever the gambler, was facing the biggest crapshoot of his life.

But he wasn't through. Nellie Gasko, another girl who had confessed involvement with Rickard, was kidnapped by Nathan Pond, a former pug who was a flunky of the promoter. Pond was charged with "bribing and deceiving a witness in a pending criminal action." An employee of Madison Square Garden, Walter Field, whose testimony was also critical, suddenly blew out of New York City. He was the lessee, on paper, of the apartments where Rickard allegedly had his deviant trysts.

With five different, young girls telling the same sordid story, the evidence against Rickard was damning. Then one night the huckster got a phone call telling him to go to bar in the notorious Hell's Kitchen district. Rickard took a private eye with him, and met two men, William Kelleher and D.J. Supple. They were from the Society for the Prevention of Cruelty to Children, and told Rickard that if he didn't come up with $50,000, he was going to prison.

Rickard didn't pay off. Instead, he used their approach to imply there was a blackmail conspiracy against him. It's questionable what the two men could have done to help him, but both were were fired. Rickard was formally indicted on two counts of assault and abduction, and days later, two more counts of abduction were added.

Rickard's celebrity was bound to be a big factor at his trial. And, in a hypocritically prurient time, women were excluded from the jury and even the courtroom. As lisping Sarah took the witness stand, followed by Nellie Gasko, Rickard's high-priced mouthpiece, Max Steur, couldn't shake her testimony. By the third day, however, he mounted a vicious counter-attack that tore at the young girls' character. If they were so innocent, thundered Steur, why was it that Sarah was having sexual relations with a boy her own age, while Nellie was a forger, burglar, robber and truant?

Though the prosecution case was still overwhelming, an all-male jury incredibly acquitted the promoter in just ninety minutes. Rickard had been given sterling character references by Major Anthony Drexel Biddle, the Philadelphia sportsman, and Kermit Roosevelt, son of ex-president Teddy Roosevelt. Rickard nearly collapsed when the verdict was read. Though the courtroom erupted in loud cheers, Rickard's *celebrity* is what beat the rap. He was also "smart" enough to victimize poor children.

★ ★ ★

The Jack Dempsey-Tex Rickard combination helped to define a sporting era. "DEMPSEY KNOCKS OUT CARPENTIER IN THE FOURTH ROUND," screamed the *New York Times* of 3 July 1921, after 90,000 people had crammed into a makeshift stadium in Jersey City to watch the so-called "Battle of the Century." Dempsey's defence against the French heart-throb was, said the *Times*, a "fight which had aroused more interest, in all probability, than any other in all of history."

Two year later came another extraordinary epic. "DEMPSEY WHIPS FIRPO IN SECOND ROUND OF FIERCEST OF HEAVYWEIGHT BATTLES; 90,000 IN POLO GROUNDS, 25,000 RIOT OUTSIDE," bellowed the *New York Times* again. In an incredible fight – like two starving Neanderthals doing battle over a piece of meat – Dempsey smashed Luis Firpo of Argentina to the canvas ten times, while the "Manassa Mauler" hit the deck twice. Firpo even belted Dempsey out of the ring, where he would have been counted out had sportswriters not pushed him back in. The *Times* gasped:

> No champion ever had a closer call. In the first round, after Firpo had gone down seven times, one of his long smashing rights caught Dempsey fairly and knocked him clear through the ropes. The champion's head disappeared over the edge of the ring, his white-clad legs shot up in the air, and it seemed that a new world's champion was about to enter his glory. On the count of nine, Dempsey managed to stagger back into the ring, but the end of the round found him obviously badly shaken, and staggering as he had never staggered before. To the spectators at the ringside, it looked as if Dempsey was all gone …

Dempsey roared back to knock out Firpo. The fight lasted all of three minutes and fifty-seven seconds.

With Prohibition on, gangsters were heavily involved in the fight game. "They were nice people," claimed Johnny Wilson, middleweight champ from 1920 to 1923. Bill Brennan, who gave Dempsey one of his toughest fights, disagreed. He was gunned down in his own New York speakeasy. "I guess Bill bought the wrong beer," shrugged Dempsey.

With boxing the most glamorous of sports, bootleggers and mobsters were involved because of the celebrity. Excitement and money of course, were also big factors, and mobsters like Tommy McGinty (Cleveland), Max "Boo Boo" Hoff and Nig Rosen (Philadelphia), Dan Carroll and Phil Buccola (Boston), Al Capone (Chicago), and Owney Madden, Dutch Schulz, and Lucky Luciano in New York, controlled the sport. Tommy Loughran, the marvellous light-heavyweight champ, later claimed, "They wanted to have a prize possession, like a fellow with a race horse or a baseball team. Money meant nothing to them." They had so much because of the illegal booze.

Mickey Cohen, gangster Bugsy Siegel's Los Angeles henchman, started his career as a fighter in the 1920s, and claimed: "The boxing world and the racket world were almost one and the same. Most boxers were owned by rackets people. And at one time six of the boxing titles [there were only eight then] belonged to guys in the so-called racket world."

In 1926, in Philadelphia, the top bootlegger was Boo Boo Hoff, a bald, undistinguished gent who started out as a newsboy, hawking papers on a street corner. Then he worked in a cigar store, but got into the rackets and promoted fights with a partner named Charlie Schwartz. He ran gambling and provided industrial alcohol, which was still, lauaghably, legal though it was unquestionably diverted into the speakeasies. In 1926, Quaker Industrial Alcohol produced 1.5 million gallons, and Hoff and Schwartz ran the entire scam behind the respectable façade of the Franklin Mortgage and Investment Company. Benjamin M. Colder, Hoff's lawyer, was a US congressman, and filed the corporate papers. By 1928, bootlegging was so out of control, a Grand Jury was convened. After seven months and 748 witnesses, the final report concluded that there were 1,170 illegal saloons and thousands of speaks. The Grand Jury estimated that Philadelphia cops were getting $2 million a year in bribes, and Hoff had hundreds of corrupt public servants on his payroll. Evidence revealed that cops, who were lucky to have a $2,500 a year job, somehow had $5,000 to $20,000 in the bank, with no other source of income. The outraged citizenry declared Hoff, who was just thirty-three, the leading bootlegger and corrupter in the city, but he was so smart that he was thoroughly insulated from criminal prosecution. Hoff piously proclaimed he "was never connected with liquor in any way shape or form," but earned his wealth through promoting and managing fighters.

On 23 September 1926, just hours before Gene Tunney was to face Jack Dempsey, Tunney's wily manager Billy Gibson brought Hoff and his attorney in to see Gene. Gibson told his handsome, clean-cut fighter that he needed his signature on an agreement. Tunney, who later served on numerous corporate boards and fathered a son, John, who became a United States Senator, wisely signed "Eugene Joseph Tunney." His real name was James Joseph Tunney. Hoff later tried to claim that he loaned Tunney and Gibson $20,000 before the fight, but this was obviously a shakedown. Hoff later had to sue, claiming he was owed twenty per cent of Tunney's massive championship purses. The suit crept along at a snail's pace. Ultimately Hoff died broke in 1941, and Gibson expired from *syphllis*.

Jack Dempsey, who sportswriter Grantland Rice called "half savage," had gone Hollywood and married gorgeous starlet Estelle Taylor. He was bitterly estranged from Jack Kearns, and failed to defend his title for three years. He'd even had his nose remodelled. Yet his drawing power was undimished. In September 1926, a total of 135,000 spectators paid more than $2 million on a rain-soaked night to watch him fight Tunney. Millions listened raptly to a new thing called radio. This time the *Times* headlines did not proclaim a crushing Demspey victory: "TUNNEY WINS CHAMPIONSHIP IN 10 ROUNDS; OUTFIGHTS RIVAL ALL THE WAY, DECISION NEVER

IN DOUBT." Jack Kearns was sitting at ringside crying. "At the finish," wrote reporter James P. Dawson, "Dempsey was a sorry, pitiful sight, the object of sincere sympathy ... His mouth and nose spouted blood, his left eye bruised and battered, was closed tight and bleeding."

Dempsey had once been branded a "slacker" for evading service in World War One and for allegedly lived off the earnings of a prostitute, but when he prepared for the inevitable rematch in Chicago, there were 8,000 fans at his training camp. The Manassa Mauler had come to symbolize the Roaring Twenties. Radio even broadcast his sparring sessions live. But with Jack's marriage coming apart, Estelle Taylor in bed with a "nervous condition" and Kearns constantly filing court orders to harrass the ex-champ, Dempsey began collapsing under the pressure.

Three days before the Tunney-Dempsey rematch in Chicago, then a synonym for gangsterism, the *Chicago Herald-Examiner* published a sensational letter from Dempsey in which he charged that Tunney had conspired with Boo Boo Hoff, the gangster, and Abe Attell, the former featherweight champ, to try to fix their first fight in Philadelphia (Attell had been implicated in fixing the 1919 baseball World Series, under the direction of gambler and Mob titan Arnold Rothstein). According to Dempsey, Hoff and Attell had tried to fix the first fight by "getting to" referee Tom Reilly of Philadelphia, and one of the judges. "I was to lose the decision," Dempsey claimed, "and if I hit you (Tunney) at any point lower than the top of your head and dropped you ... somebody would yell, 'Foul.'"

Although Jack admitted the plan fell through, and the judges did their job well, these charges cannot just be ascribed to ballyhoo or sour grapes. Dempsey was risking his life in publicly questioning Hoff. Dempsey also demanded that Tunney explain his relationship with Hoff, and the corrupt Attell. Now, the story was that Tunney had supposedly "borrowed money" from Hoff before their first fight, though the $200,000 Tunney supposedly paid back sounds a lot more like a shakedown than any loan. Dempsey later claimed, "I was more afraid of who sat at ringside than of who was waiting for me inside the ring."

On 23 September 1927, the day after their memorable "Long Count" battle, the *New York Times* told the world, "GENE TUNNEY KEEPS TITLE BY DECISION AFTER TEN ROUNDS; DEMPSEY INSISTS FOE WAS OUT IN THE SEVENTH, AND WILL APPEAL; 150,000 SEE CHICAGO FIGHT, MILLIONS LISTEN ON RADIO."

Three-quarters of a century later, lore has it that referee Dave Barry was bribed: Dempsey supposedly got jobbed after he unleashed a furious burst of punches and put Tunney down in round seven. The champion was on the deck for fourteen seconds but was not counted out. Barry didn't begin the count because Dempsey was standing over Tunney, just like he'd done to

Willard and Firpo, and wouldn't go to a neutral corner. A new rule that a boxer must retire to a neutral corner once his opponent was on the floor had had been brought in precisely because of Dempsey's habit of hovering over a fallen foe and then belting him the second he rose, and had been explained at the rules meeting (Tunney always maintained that he could have got up anyway). Reporter Dawson contended, "His refusal to observe the boxing rules of the Illinois State Athletic Commission, or his ignorance of the rules, or both, cost Jack Dempsey the chance to regain the world's heavyweight championship." Strangely, when Tunney later knocked Jack down for a brief count, Barry counted immediately, though Gene was nowhere near a neutral corner.

Did anyone get to Barry? The referee was certainly familiar with the underworld: he ran a speakeasy. Chicago's Al Capone remarked, "I should've known better than to bet against a kid from New York," after he reportedly lost $500,000 betting on Jack. Dempsey did his best to stay away from Capone, who liked basking in Jack's presence, as Capone wasn't above fixing sports events. Dutch Reuther, who pitched for the notorious "Black Sox," the team that threw the World Series, told his son that Capone had come to him earlier about a proposal to dump ball games.

Dempsey eventually became a fight promoter in Chicago with Capone's backing. "I quit because I was being used as a front, a promoter in name only. Capone's mob wound up telling me who was going to fight and how much I had to pay them. When they started giving orders who was going to win…naming the round – I got out."

In July 1928, an era came to an end when Rickard, who had become the greatest promoter since P.T. Barnum, lost $600,000 on Tunney's easy defence against New Zealander Tom Heeney, the so-called "Hard Rock from Down Under." Within months, Rickard was selling his office furniture. He died shortly after. On 24 October 1929 came "Black Friday." The stock market crashed, and the Great Depression began.

* * *

He was a ruggedly handsome man with blunt features, a round face, dark, swept-back hair and animated, caterpillar eyebrows. He bore a striking resemblance to Jack Dempsey, had an impish grin and was liked by everyone who knew him. Yet he became a reviled symbol of Hitler's Third Reich, and is still one of the most unfairly maligned men in the history of sport.

"The Fuhrer takes a deep interest in (Max) Schmeling's career," reported the London *Daily Telegraph* in March 1937. "After he knocked out Joe Louis in New York last summer he was received in the chancellory by Herr

Hitler, who told him how delighted he was about the triumph of Nordic over negro blood." Just eight days after transforming the "Brown Bomber" to rubble, Max Schmeling, his beautiful blonde Czech actress wife Annie Ondra, and his mother, were Hitler's lunch guests.

Though Schmeling strongly praised Louis to the German papers, and called it the hardest fight of his career, *Angriff*, the Nazi rag, ignored that and portrayed Schmeling's 10-1 upset as a blow for German nationalism and white supermacy.

> Schmeling, the German, did that for the Americans, for the same people who did not want to give him a chance, who mocked him (and) derided him. He succeeded against world opinion. And he says he would not have had the strength if he had not known what support he had in his homeland. He was allowed to speak with the Fuhrer and his ministers, and from that moment his will for victory was boundless.

Maximilian Adolph Otto Siegfried Schmeling was born on 26 September 1905 in Klein Luckaw, Germany. He grew up in a farming community in the midst of World War One. His father was a seamen, his mother worked for the postal service. Young Max was an indifferent student but a fine all-around athlete, and bought a pair of secondhand boxing gloves at sixteen after seeing an American fight film at a cinema. By 1919, he was working as a messenger boy, delivering advertisements to Hamburg newspaper offices, and was encouraged in his love of sport by his bosses. Max was two months shy of his nineteenth birthday when he knocked out Bans Czapp in Dusseldorf in August 1924, in his pro debut. Max had ten pro fights over the next four months. He was halted in four by Max Dieckman and bashed to defeat by British-Canadian Larry Gains. He came back to win first the German and then the European light-heavyweight titles. He was on a twenty-fight winning streak when Welshman Gypsy Daniels belted him out in the first round in 1928.

Germany was being ravaged by political instability and depression. Inflation was so steep that it took a bushel full of marks to buy a loaf of bread. Berlin, once a haven for artists and writers, was plagued by violent street demonstrations. Nat Fleischer, editor and founder of *Ring* magazine, spied the hard-hitting youngster in Germany and helped to launch him on an American campaign. Schmeling sailed to New York, where he decisioned Joe Monte in ten. Fleischer was supposed to get ten per cent of his purses but, in a world suddenly caught in the grips of the Great Depression, he never did.

The stock market crash left wealthy champions like Jack Dempsey and Benny Leonard broke. Business tycoons threw themselves out windows.

Wall Street was brought to its knees. Through the financial panic, Schmeling kept fighting. He beat Spain's Paolino Uzcudun in New York and then met Jack Sharkey in the finals of a tournament for the vacant heavyweight championship on 12 June 1930, after Gene Tunney had given up the crown.

As the erratic, highly-strung Sharkey entered the ring garbed in an American flag, he was roundly booed by the Yankee Stadium crowd of 80,000. Sharkey outboxed Max, but in the fourth unleashed a very low left hook that dug into the German's groin. Max groveled on the canvas, like a sparrow with a broken wing, gesturing to referee Jim Crowley, who looked to judge Harold Barnes. Four times the indecisive Crowley was told that Sharkey had fouled, but only after Schmeling was carried to his corner writhing in agony, was he reluctantly declared the new heavyweight champion.

"I never fouled him," spat Sharkey, in 1987, by then an embittered recluse living in Epping, New Hampshire. But films prove that he did. The doctor who examined Schmeling in his dressing room found physical evidence. Schmeling became the first continental European to win the crown, and the only man ever to win sport's loftiest prize on the floor.

He went back to Germany and was accorded a hero's welcome, but he never let it go to his head. Max always loved children, and his greatest regret was that he never had any, but he did a lot of charity work with youngsters. However, he had to cancel an American exhibition tour after he won the title, because he couldn't draw.

On 21 June 1932, Sharkey, who was known as the "Boston Gob" ("gob" was US slang for a sailor), took the title off him with an unpopular decision in their rematch at the "Graveyard of Champions," New York's Long Island Bowl. According to the *Times*, the "majority of experts favor (ed) (the) loser."

"We wuz robbed," shrieked Max's manager, Joe Jacobs, coining a famous phrase.

"Sharkey just wasn't popular," recalled Herb Skellett, now an eighty-one-year-old Massachusetts man who had sparred with some of the top fighters around Boston when he was a kid and had actually met ancient Jake Kilrain, the bareknuckler who fought John L. Sullivan. "I used to go see Sharkey fight," remembered Herb, "but mostly, people came just to boo him."

"I never understood why the fans soured on me," Jack rued sixty years later.

* * *

In Europe, a giant Italian heavyweight named Primo Carnera had become a big attraction. "Primo was a nice guy and a very sensitive guy," said Harry Markson, the old publicity man who later headed up the Garden.

He was born in Sequals, Italy, on 26 October 1906. Carnera had a poverty-stricken childhood, and during World War One his parents were forced into slave labour in Germany. Primo, a shy, lonely boy, was very sensitive about his size, but as Europe tried to dig itself out of the rubble, the young gargoyle became a circus strongman. His circus folded in Paris in 1928.

As Carnera sprawled morosely on a park bench, wondering where his next meal was coming from, an old fighter spied him and took him to Leon See. "I taught him speed ... then defence," claimed See, who had an Oxford degree. He denied that Carnera's earliest fights were fixed. "Definitely not. But I had to choose the opponents carefully. Some of his bouts were quite hard."

Carnera's first matches were in the Salle Wagram, a legendary fight club in Paris. In his third pro bout Salvatore Ruggirello was vanquished. This fight was almost certainly fixed; Carnera's win is too hard to believe. According to the 1930 *Everlast Boxing Record Book*, Ruggirello halted Britain's Jack Stanley twice, won and lost ten-rounders with Charlie Smith, who eventually became British heavyweight champ, and also had a victory in Chicago over fringe contender Les Kennedy. According to this record book, Ruggirello lost a six-rounder to Carnera, while the *Ring Record Book* has Salvatore halted in three. Either way, it defies belief that a good heavyweight like Ruggirello could lose to a clumsy novice who had been a pro six weeks.

Legend has it that many of Carnera's fights were "in the bag." The question is, after viewing many films, and looking at things in historical prespective, which ones?

In January 1930, the circus really began when Carnera had his first fight in the States, beating Big Boy Peterson in New York. Elziar Rioux went out in forty-seven seconds just one week later in Chicago. This sham drew 18,000 fans, who paid 59,625 scarce Depression dollars, but nobody saw a punch land, and outraged sportswriters dubbed Carnera's opponent "Rioux the Rug" for going down so fast. The Illinois commission, under a lot of pressure, fined Rioux $1,000.

After Carnera faced Leon "Bombo" Chevalier on April 14, the California commission revoked Carnera's license, and his manager's, for the "suspicious" sixth-round stoppage. Supposedly Chevalier was belting the hell out of "Da Preem" until his own handlers rubbed something in his eyes.

Carnera boxed twenty-six times in 1930, appearing everywhere from Boston to Barcelona. One opponent was George Godfrey, who had been denied a shot at the heavyweight championship because he was black. According to the 1930 *Everlast Boxing Record Book,* which was published before the Carnera fight, Godfrey, who was its third-ranked contender, "occupied third place despite some unsatisfactory performances. There is a rather general impression that the big black man generally wears invisible handcuffs when he steps into the ring to do battle with a leading white contender." Godfrey was chucked out in the fifth against Carnera in Philadelphia. The fight was so bad, according to the *New York Times*, that "it cost Godfrey his boxing license, half his purse and his status as a heavyweight contender."

That same year, Carnera faced Ace Clark in Philadelphia. According to the *Encyclopedia of Crime*, Clark had also changed his mind about diving after battering Carnera and nearly closing his eyes. Between rounds, as Clark plopped on his stool, his manager supposedly beckoned Ace to look towards a gentleman at ringside. It was a gangster brandishing a pistol.

By now, Leon See, the enterprising Frenchman who had discovered Carnera, was long gone. Carnera was handled by Louis Soreci, Bill Duffy and Walter Friedman. They were fronts for the New York gangsters Owney "Killer" Madden, Dutch Schultz, and Vincent "Mad Dog" Coll. According to *Blood And Power*, a compelling history of organized crime written by the brilliant scholar Stephen Fox and drawing heavily on government reports and private archival papers, "All through the 1920s, while other gangsters flirted with Dempsey and Tunney, Owney Madden supervised his own stable of fighters, including titleholders in the bantamweight and light-heavyweight division. The biggest man in the biggest town, he still could not claim the heavyweight champion, the real prize in boxing. He got his chance after Tunney retired and vacated the title. From 1930 to 1937, Madden controlled four of the five heavyweight champs, only Max Baer escaped his grasp."

In October 1931, Sharkey decisioned Carnera in Brooklyn, New York. Though lore has it that Sharkey handled Carnera easily, the full film of the fight shows Sharkey, nearly half a foot shorter, lunging and falling in, though he did knock Carnera down and get the decision. "He was just too big," Sharkey remembered with a sad, weary exasperation.

★ ★ ★

On 29 June 1933, Sharkey supposedly became the Judas who dumped the heavyweight championship and took a dive to lose his crown to the giant Carnera. "Don't they realize that he just got better?" Sharkey said years later, emitting a sigh.

By 1987, Sharkey was an ancient eccentric living in a drab farmhouse in the picture-postcard town of Epping, New Hampshire. An old, blue-green Chevrolet station wagon sat forlornly, nose-down, on his spacious front yard. It had been that way for years. Sharkey was no longer allowed to drive.

Though it was just September, and the New England leaves were a marvellous red, yellow and green, Sharkey's house was so cold, so barren, it was like someone had everything packed and was waiting for the moving van to arrive.

On one wall there were pictures, glorious memories from a far distant time: a handsome young Sharkey, with his black patent leather hair and premature widow's peak. His beautiful wife. There were loads of old glossies: Sharkey with a smiling Franklin Delano Roosevelt, then President of the United States. Sharkey with movies stars, clad rakishly in knickers, balloon-legged pants. But to look at this doddering old man, fifty-five years later, it was hard to believe. Heavyweight champions are mystical beings. They don't become senile. They don't suffer from depression. Their kidneys don't go. Their mangled old hands don't shake as they sputter indignantly, "Being heavyweight champion ... ain't worth a pisshole in snow."

Sharkey's grandfatherly voice cracked. "I coulda licked any sonofabitch who walked on shoe leather, any sonofabitch," he finally said, even if it was so faint.

A week earlier, he had suffered a terrible fall, crashing to the pavement in Epping and hitting his face hard on the concrete. As onlookers raced over to him, and called for an ambulance, the eighty-five-year-old ex-champ struggled to his feet, and roared, "No, no, goddamnit! When I got knocked down, I always got up!"

That was not always true. His life had been poisoned by cancerous rumours surrounding his title loss to Primo Carnera, and he spent the last sixty years trying to hide from a "crime" he swore he didn't commit. "You just feel devalued, you just wanna hide," he muttered, thinking out loud, remembering what he felt like, the first day he woke up and was no longer champion.

"Why, that New York mob," he hissed, alluding to people like Owney Madden, the weazel faced gangster who controlled him through Johnny Buckley, and writers like Paul Gallico and Budd Schulberg, who convicted him, without evidence.

Sharkey did admit to this writer, for the first and only time, that an offer had been made for him to dump the heavyweight championship – but it was to his stablemate Ernie Schaaf, not Carnera. "Certain people wanted me to lose to Schaaf," he said slowly, picking his words very carefully. "They told me I'd still have a piece (since Sharkey was also Ernie's co-manager). I'd never do that," he suddenly said, his pale, parchment face recoiling in disgust. "I was raised a Catholic."

If Sharkey was lying, he could have won an Academy Award. Those "people" were obviously "Fat John" Buckley, his manager, who Sharkey spoke bitterly of one moment, then lovingly of the next, and Killer Madden, the Leeds-born gangster who once shot a man to death on a jammed trolley car, then cheekily rang the bell as he got off. Though Sharkey never mentioned Madden, who was arrested fifty-seven times in New York City alone, the Kefauver investigation in 1960 proved that Madden was pulling strings behind Buckley.

Obviously, it would have been in Sharkey's financial interest to dive to Schaff, his good friend, but this, he says, he would not do. In February 1933, Schaaf died after fighting Carnera. Cries of "Fake!" and "Fix!" resounded when Schaaf collapsed in the ring, but fell silent when he failed to recover consciousness. Sharkey was in Ernie's corner.

Five and a half months later, on 29 June 1933, Carnera knocked out Sharkey with a right uppercut in round six. Though Nat Fleischer later intimated that he thought Sharkey took a dive, his actual report of the fight in *Ring* said, "Under the impact of the blow, Sharkey was stretched motionless on his face. Not a quiver of the body could be noted as the count was completed, a new world heavyweight king was crowned."

Dawson wrote in the *New York Times*, "A terrific right hand uppercut to the chin which almost decapitated Sharkey brought Carnera the title."

Grantland Rice reported, "The shot had enough force to sink a battleship," while Arthur Donovan, who was the referee, said, "There was terrific force behind the final blow, and Sharkey was as clearly knocked out as any fighter I've ever seen."

A film of the full fight, which critics never bothered to look at, shows Sharkey getting staggered by a monstrous left hook about a minute before finally going down. If Sharkey was in the tank, that was the time to go, but he actually fought back and rocked Carnera before he was finally felled. The right uppercut that supposedly did the damage is unclear, but how do you battle an insidious myth?

Budd Schulberg's book *The Harder They Fall* was loosely based on Carnera's life, and Primo, an amiable sort, supposedly said later, "It's all true." It can't be. What Schulberg did was create a marvellous piece of fiction, and the myth makerss projected their own prejudices, misconceptions and half-truths. Even Schulberg wrote recently in *Boxing Digest* that Carnera "may or may not have thrown the fight."

Gallico, who was one of the most influential sportswriters of the 1920s and '30s, later claimed that Carnera "never could fight," and "one hard tap to the chin and he fell down goggle-eyed." If Carnera couldn't fight, how did he get off the canvas twelve times and actually outbox Max Bear, who hit so hard, legend has it he used to knock down bulls with his right hand when he worked in a slaughterhouse?

Baer did eventually knock him out, in round eleven, to win the title on 14 June 1934. All the over-heated hyperbole, all the purple prose, can't disprove what films actually show. According to Dawson, who covered Baer-Carnera for the *New York Times*, "Max Baer, the new Jack Dempsey in every respect save seriousness," finally "battered Carnera into a figure of abject helplessness with a piteous, furious assualt.

"In defeat Carnera crowned himself with the glory of the vanquished fighter who sticks to his guns until he is helpless ... No heavyweight title defender in the modern history of boxing has been a victim of so many knockdowns in a championship struggle. Even the beating that Jess Willard took at the hands of Dempsey in Toledo back in 1919 paled against that absorbed by Carnera."

Carnera was controlled by Madden, and Baer wasn't. If Carnera was a just a circus act, a third-rater, stage-managed to the championship, why would the most powerful gangster in the sport put his boy in to lose? How did Carnera last nearly six horrific rounds with young Joe Louis, whom Dawson rightly called, "one of the greatest fighters of modern times"?

When you look *objectively* at the evidence, and the lengthy films of Carnera's fights with Louis, Tommy Loughran, Ernie Schaaf, Jack Sharkey and others, there is just one conclusion you can draw. "Carnera was a pretty good fighter," remembered Sharkey. "He just didn't take it too good here," said the gnarled old man, as he pointed to his whiskered chin.

Jack Sharkey was a proud, brutally honest man, and his life was destroyed by the rumours he had thrown the world title. He won only two of his last seven fights, before he finally retired after being annihilated by young Joe Louis in 1936. He became such a hermit that when he appeared on the TV show *I've Got A Secret,* in 1955, nobody knew who he was.

Carnera ended up far worse. He never got the credit he probably deserved for winning the most revered title in sport. Poor Primo, one of the biggest draws in boxing, got just $360 – after Baer had him down twelve times when he won the championship. Primo even had to plead bankruptcy.

Owney Madden retired to Arkansas in 1940 with more than $3 million, and died there in 1964. But on May 27, 1936, after being halted for the second time by "the second Joe Louis," big Leroy Haynes, Trevor Wignall, the great British sportswriter, finally found the oversized Carnera in a tiny hospital bed, after looking for two days. "He was paralyzed down one side, his face was a still mask, he wept for the greater part of the two hours I was with him, and all he asked for was a chance to get back to Italy."

* * *

On 13 June 1935 Max Baer lost the heavyweight title to Jim Braddock, "the Cinderella Man," who had been on relief, with his gas and electricity shut off, just two years before. This was Madden's last heavyweight champion.

The Associated Press called it "the most startling upset since John L. Sullivan went down before Jim Corbett." Baer looked so bad against Braddock that even Jim implored him, "C'mon Max, pick it up. They'll think it's a fix."

On September 24, Baer was slaughtered by Joe Louis, who had been a pro only fourteen months. There were 95,000 fans in Yankee Stadium. "Sure, I quit," admitted Bear, who had loved bludgeoning Carnera but found an escape hatch against Louis. "If anyone wants to see the execution of Max Baer, he's going to pay a lot more than $25 for a ringside seat."

Louis was the new phenomenon of boxing. In 1935 Mike Jacobs brought Louis into prominence, after promising his black managers, John Roxbury and Julian Black, that Joe would, "Never have to lay down, or fight with handcuffs on." In a revolutionary idea, Louis would go as far as his ability would take him." Less than a year later, Max Schmeling, who had been even money not to last till the fifth, smashed him into defeat before 45,000 at Yankee Stadium. "Louis, hailed as the king of fighters entering the ring, was counted out, his invincibility as a fighter a shattered myth," concluded Dawson, who figured this was a bigger upset than when Braddock whipped Bear.

In December, 1936, Schmeling signed to fight Braddock for the title, but with Nazism on the rise, and Schmeling a certainty to take the title back to Hitler's Germany, there was no way that could happen. While Hitler persecuted the Jews, Fleischer, whose grandparents had suffered the bloody pogroms of Russia, pleaded in a *Ring* editorial that the United States boycott the 1936 Olympics in Berlin.

America's Jesse Owens was the hit of the games. The German crowd actually chanted, "Oh-vens, Oh-vens," remembered American runner Marty Glickman, who at the last minute, wasn't allowed to compete. He was Jewish. Meanwhile Hitler stormed out rather than salute the brilliant black American.

On June 3, 1937, a dour Schmeling showed up at the "weigh-in" for his fight with Braddock that was supposed to take place in New York's Garden Bowl. Braddock wasn't there; he was training in Michigan to fight Joe Louis on June 22. Schmeling abided by his contract and stepped on the scales, but it was a "phantom" fight. As reporters scribbled furiously, Major General John J. Phelan, who headed the New York commission, solemnly read a statement: "This body, after due and lengthy consideration of the matter, find James J. Braddock, and his manager, Joe Gould, in violation of the commission's orders and hereby imposes a civil fine of $1,000 apiece … In addition, this board suspends Braddock from fighting in this state, or in any state affiliated with the New York commission … also, any fighter meeting Braddock will be suspended."

Schmeling immediately left for the Hotel Commodore. Normally polite and smiling, Max's face was a mask of fury: "This ruling is a joke. It practically legalizes the (Louis-Braddock) fight in Chicago and leaves me out in the cold. What does it mean to suspend Braddock? He gets to fight Louis anyway, and certainly the title will pass to Louis."

Before Louis could get the fight, his co-manager John Roxborough was snatched on a New York sidewalk. "We're going for a ride," some gangsters told him. Roxborough thought he was going to be murdered, but they finally pulled up in back of a nightclub and sat him down in front of Joe Gould, who managed Braddock.

"Look, Louis is going to whip Braddock," Gould explained, "and we want fifty per cent of Louis – or no fight." Gould was partners with Owney Madden.

"No," said Roxborough, a tough guy himself in the black rackets.

Gould was shocked. No "nigger" turned down Madden. He sputtered, "Twenty-five per cent."

"No," said Roxborough.

"Twenty per cent?" asked Gould, almost pleading.

Roxborough, "slow and easy," as Louis later told it, got up and left. He headed uptown and had a double scotch on the rocks. The myth is that Gould was so worried about Braddock's future that he got ten per cent of all Louis's future purses so that he'd leave Braddock set. In reality, Braddock ended up working on the docks when he was in his sixties. Mike Jacobs did, however, pay ten per cent of Louis's purses to Gould. Madden must have got the money.

On June 22, in Chicago's Comiskey Park, Louis became the first black man since Jack Johnson to win the title when he knocked Braddock out in the eighth round. "Every punch was like getting hit with a crowbar," Braddock said. Louis had gotten off the deck in the first round to win, but the Brown Bomber said, even as there was Mardi Gras-like rejoicing all over black America, "I won't feel like I'm the champ till I beat S'mellin'."

* * *

In December 1937, Schmeling was back in the ring against Harry Thomas, a fringe contender from Eagle Bend, Minnesota. Three years later, Arch Ward, sports editor of the *Chicago Tribune*, would charge that the Schmeling-Thomas match was "one of the biggest swindles in the history of boxing." The Illinois State Athletic Commission began an investigation, but found no evidence to support the allegation. The State Attorney General not only rejected charges of a fix but claimed that Thomas was

punch drunk. But how badly did he want to be involved? The fight hadn't
even happened in Illinois. Thomas faced Schmeling in Madison Square
Garden, New York. Still, Illinois chairman, Joe Triner, who'd sanctioned
Louis-Braddock over New York's protest, contacted promoter Mike Jacobs,
to see what he thought. Obviously, there had been "fix" rumours going
around for some time. Jacobs wrote back to him on January 4, 1939, long
before Ward's column ever appeared.

According to Jacobs, a homely ex-ticket scalper who had got into boxing
and helped to bankroll Tex Rickard, "All the press reports on this bout were
highly favorable. It was the unanimous opinion of every newspaper representative present as well as the opinion of the spectators at said bout that
they witnessed a great bout. Each of the contestants fought honestly. Harry
Thomas made a courageous and heroic effort to win. In the eighth round
his mouth was bleeding profusely, and the referee stopped the bout while
Thomas was still on his feet fighting."

According to *Ring* magazine, Thomas was down eight times. But seventeen years later, *Sports Illutrated*, a new magazine backed by Henry Luce's
millions that would change forever how sports was covered in America,
came out with Thomas's sensational charges about the fight.

According to Thomas, he had come under the management of the
fabulously wealthy Jim Norris. This was the same Jim Norris whose
father James had taken him to the Dempsey-Willard fight in 1919,
when he was just thirteen, and whetted his appetite for prize-fighting.
Though Norris was Thomas's real manager, Nate Lewis was Norris's
"front." Lewis was also promoting at the Chicago Stadium, which
Norris and his partner Arthur Wirtz had picked up for ten cents on the
dollar a couple of years after it was built. It had gone bankrupt during
the Depression.

If you believe Thomas, Lewis got a telegram from Joe "We Wuz
Robbed" Jacobs, Schmeling's manager, to meet him in the posh Drake
Hotel in downtown Chicago. Lewis phoned Thomas, and met the big,
battle-scarred heavyweight in a bar. Then they took a cab to the Drake.
Lewis told Thomas to wait for Norris in the lobby, which he did for quite
some time. Finally, a flunky came down and Thomas was ordered up to a
room. When Thomas lumbered in, there was the dapper Norris, Lewis, and
Joe Jacobs. Thomas flipped his fedora on the bed. "Don't do that," yelled
Jacobs. "It's bad luck!"

They got down to business. Joe Jacobs was there to sign Thomas for
Schmeling, but Thomas claimed that Joe Jacobs told him, "You got that farm
up there in Minnesota. You can make more money on this one fight that
you can make on that farm for the rest of your life." Thomas, who normally
would have been freezing in arctic-like Minnesota, was all ears.

"You do business with us, and you'll be taken care of," Joe Jacobs supposedly said.

"What do you mean, 'business'?" Thomas asked, suspiciously.

Norris quickly jumped in: "You have to take a dive."

Thomas vigorously protested. He'd never been off his feet. He didn't want to get counted out.

"All you got to do is keep going down," Norris said, trying to placate him.

Joe Jacobs quickly promised Thomas that he'd make at least $65,000. He was such a liar, he swore that Thomas and Schmeling would split the gate. Promoter Mike Jacobs (no relation) didn't get his own private bank vault by splitting gates with fighters. But as Joe Jacobs tried to convince him, he told Thomas that Norris and Thomas would split his share 50-50. Finally, Thomas signed for the Schmeling fight.

Part of the deal was that Thomas would face Jimmy Adamick in Madison Square Garden in February, and carry him. The entire plan, according to Thomas was: he'd lose to Schmeling, carry Adamick, and then fight Joe Louis for the heavyweight championship, which would be an honest fight. If Thomas beat Louis, he'd be able to face Schmeling in a rematch, with this fight on the level. Obviously, the terms of the fix weren't in the contract, but the contract for the three bouts was notarized by Wirtz's secretary.

After Thomas finally got in the ring with Schmeling, he fought hard for the first three rounds, but later claimed Nate Lewis, his front manager, told him, "Take it easy, Harry. You're too rough." Schmeling had him down eight times and stopped him in the eighth.

Next day, Thomas and Lewis reportedly went to Norris's New York hotel room to divide up the pay-off. Despite the fact that Thomas could've whipped all three men at the same time, he was ordered, "Wait outside," while Joe Jacobs, Lewis and Norris huddled. Finally, Thomas, black and blue from the night before, was greeted by Norris, who handed him a bunch of money.

Thomas kept looking at the first thousand-dollar bill he'd ever seen in his life. As he kept fondling it, wondering if it was real, he finally counted his end, but snapped, "Jim, where's all that money we talked about *before* the fight?"

"That's the pay-off," Norris said, flippantly. "What can we do about it?"

Norris was light by two-thirds, but Thomas was used to being abused. Like a small kid, he kept babbling about showing his thousand-dollar bill to his father. Thomas finally got five grand. Norris got five, (at least in front of Thomas), and expenses were another $5,000, which obviously Norris and Lewis had padded. It was a long way from the $65,000 Joe Jacobs had promised.

In January 1938, Thomas stopped Unknown Winston in Minnesota. A month later, Thomas "carried" Jimmy Adamick so well in the Garden that he lost two rounds for low blows, as well as the decision. Though that should have blown Thomas's chance for a shot at the heavyweight championship, that April he faced the murderous Louis at the Chicago Stadium (owned by Norris and Wirtz). Thomas was despatched in the fifth.

Thomas's "confession" was hard to believe, but there was a witness. Sig Hart, who was eighty-two years old in 1954, confirmed that "Norris admitted to me that they were arranging for Thomas to lose the [Schmeling] fight." Though Norris had paid Hart's rent and had been a friend for twenty years, the broken-down old bantam refused to go into the Drake Hotel, where the dirty deal was being brokered. Norris angrily denounced Hart as an "ingrate," and vowed to sue *Sports Illustrated*. He never did. Why? He was worth anywhere from $50-200 million, and certainly could have afforded the lawyers.

* * *

Max Schmeling would be tarred by the American media as a bad guy for being a prominent German citizen in the time of Hilter. In truth, Schmeling was always one of the good guys. At a time when vicious anti-semitism infected every aspect of German life, the *New York Times* reported that, "The refusal of Max Schmeling and Walter Neusel, after years of warning, to discharge their Jewish managers 'in the interest of Germanhood' has angered the Nazi newspaper, the *Frankenkische Tageszeitung*." With Hitler screaming for a "Jew-free" Germany, this propaganda sheet was incensed that Jacobs had given the Nazi salute with a stubby cigar protruding from his hand. The *Tageszeitung* demanded action on these "shameful conditions in the German sports world."

Schmeling continued to ignore public policy. He posed in a French newspaper with prominent Jews, and was ordered to come to Joseph Goebbels' office, where he was dressed down by the arrogant Minister of Propaganda. Hitler even tried to get Max to fire Jacobs, but Max artfully refused.

As Jews were stripped of their citzenship and property rights, Schmeling quietly used his stature to spare lives. Sculptor Franz Torak, who fashioned an impressive bronze of Max, had a Jewish wife who was scheduled for deportation. Torak frantically asked Max for help. Schmeling went straight to Goebbels. Goebbels was outraged, but Torak's wife was spared.

"What separated Schmeling from a lot of stars in a similar position was that he took risks and tested the limits of what he could do," claims David Rathrick, a historian with America's Cornell University. "He made arguments for protecting Jews and others who were in political trouble. He went directly to authorities. He had a direct line to Hitler, through Hitler's private photographer Heinrich Hoffman. He could call Hoffman directly and say, 'I've got to speak to Hitler.'"

Rinzie Van der Meer, a Dutch boxing writer/broadcaster, and friend of Schmeling, agrees. "Max saved lives. He was never a Nazi. His wife had a movie production company in Czechoslovakia, and half her employees were Jews. There was another German heavyweight, whose wife was a Jew, and he pleaded, 'Max, help me.' Max saved her life as well."

Through the propaganda of the American and German media, Schmeling came to symbolize the Third Reich, but Max was actually so repulsed by Hitler, he turned down two public ceremonies with him – though you didn't dare turn down the mad little corporal a third time. He did, however, refuse the Dagger of Honor from the Stormtroopers, again risking his life.

Because of the importance of the heavyweight championship, Schmeling was robbed of his chance to fight Jimmy Braddock for the title. The politics of the time demanded that the championship couldn't go back to Germany. Louis annihilated Braddock instead.

Though Schmeling tried to deflect the political issue, he still met with his Jewish friends, but was ordered to appear in Goebbels' office again. This time, Goebbels, an insidious hatemonger, tried to be more polite. "Herr Schmeling. You want us to help you with your friends, but still you publicly cavort with these Jews. I must warn you. *You are being watched*." Schmeling could have ended up in a concentration camp, or been quietly murdered.

In March 1938, Hitler marched into Austria. On 22 June 1938, Schmeling faced Louis in their historic rematch in New York City. This wasn't sport; this was an awesome international symbol. It was democracy versus tyranny. No sporting event in history has ever had such significance. President Roosevelt had even asked Louis to the White House and told him, "We're going to need muscles like yours to defeat Nazi Germany."

As Schmeling "the Nazi" made for the ring, he was pelted with fruit and spat upon.

In just 2:04 of the first round, Louis annihilated his German challenger and, symbolically, Hitler's theory of the "Master Race." One right hand was so hard, Schmeling actually let out a scream as he turned away and caught the shot on his kidneys. The radio feed to Germany was abruptly cut. The next day the German ambassador visited Max in the hospital and tried to get him to say he was fouled, but Schmeling refused, despite the overwhelming Nazi pressure. Schmeling spent two weeks in the hospital, and rumours were that Max would be killed when he came back home.

On 9 November 1938, *Krystallnacht* erupted. Men, women and children were murdered as Nazi-inspired crowds looted Jewish businesses and torched over 200 synagogues. "My father asked Max Schmeling to take me in his house," recalled Henri Lewin, now a prominent Las Vegas businessman. "He took us [Henri and brother Werner] for three days. Max Schmeling helped my father. My father was not a rich man anymore. Everything was taken away from him. There was nothing this man could gain. He brought us back to our family in his car. There were two cars like this in Berlin. Everybody knew this was Max Schmeling. If this wouldn't have happened, I wouldn't be here."

In September 1939, Germany invaded Poland, and Schmeling was drafted into the German army. He was thirty-four, too old for military service, but was made a paratrooper anyway. He injured his back during a drop into Crete. Yet after the War, Schmeling returned to the ring. He was broke. He won three of five bouts before losing to someone called Richard Vogt in October 1948.

By 1953, James J. Farley, one of Roosevelt's "New Dealers" and one-time head of the New York State Athletic Commission, was president of Coca-Cola International. He helped Schmeling get a franchise in Hamburg. It was a success, and Schmeling became wealthy again.

In 1967, he met with Louis, his broken-down old rival and tearfully told him, "I'm sorry about all the hate our second fight brought on. I never felt that way."

"We were both crying," recalled Schmeling. "I was crying, he was crying." History's fiercest rivals became wonderful friends.

Poor Joe Louis, the fabled Brown Bomber, eventually became a drug addict, before he was committed by his son to a mental institution. He died a "celebrity doorman" at a Las Vegas hotel on 12 April 1981, still owing the government more than $1 million in back taxes.

After Joe took his final count, a shaken Schmeling called Henri Lewin from Hamburg. "Henri, Joe Louis died. His coffin is displayed in the ballroom at Caesars Palace." Max cabled Lewin a "large amount of money," and Lewin put it in an envelope and gave it to Joe's wife.

"I went over there," remembered Lewin, his voice beginning to break. "I was sitting next to Mrs Louis on a chair, and I said slowly, 'Here's an envelope from Max Schmeling.'"

"Oh Henry," she said, shocked by the envelope full of money, "Max Schmeling – our true friend."

Max Schmeling recently celebrated his ninety-seventh birthday. In a world where crybabies like Mike Tyson routinely spend $700,000 on a Rolex watch, a man like Schmeling set up the Max Schmeling Foundation, where his $5 million estate will quietly go to help the youth of Germany.

★ ★ ★

In 1942 and '43 Jimmy Bivins was the number one contender for the heavyweight crown. World War Two was raging. London had survived the Blitz, bebop was in, and Joe Louis was a sergeant in the United States Army. Titles were "frozen" for the duration of the war, but Jimmy Bivins was named "interim" champ.

Bivins was just 5-9, pitifully short for a heavyweight, but he was also the number one contender for the light-heavyweight crown. The stocky youngster from Cleveland, with the gentle, perennial smile, did a brief stint in the Army in 1944, and was honorably discharged, but inside the ring, he was virtually unbeaten from 1942 to 1945, and whipped greats like Archie Moore, Ezzard Charles, Joey Maxim and Lloyd Marshall, before finally losing to Jersey Joe Walcott.

Bivins never got the title shot against Louis that he deserved. Walcott became the first black man to challenge Louis for the heavyweight title, but Bivins did fight Louis in August 1951, when both were just apparitions. Louis, just months before he was finally demolished by Rocky Marciano, won his bout against Jimmy, one of the first fights in America to be on closed-circuit television. Yet, with the Mafia controlling the fight game, it's hard to believe Jimmy saw much of his $40,000 purse.

After Bivins hung up his gloves in 1955, he got a job as a driver for the Laub Bakery Company. He was a proud, quiet man, who did his job well, but stayed close to the sweat and blood by training amateur boxers at Kilbane's Old Angle Gym. Neighborhood punks drifted in and out, but those who stayed became well-schooled under Jimmy's tutelage, particularly Gary Horvath, who won four Golden Gloves titles.

Bivins was a firm, dedicated teacher as he showed kids how to "pop a jab," or "fire a right from your shoulder," but by the 1970s, Cleveland was best known as the lair of Don King, the predator/promoter. Bivins had been swallowed by obscurity. In 1988, the fifty-nine-year-old Jimmy trained three Cleveland cops for the National Police Olympics. Years after James Davidson belted his way to the light-heavyweight championship, he remembered, "He is my mentor. The guy is an inspiration. He could recite poetry. He had wit."

In 1995, Bivins's wife died, and he never got over it. Bivins was also having a lot of trouble with his daughter, and was slowly withdrawing from the world. Still, a fight fan sent Jimmy some rare video of his old fights, and Bivins was suddenly "young again" against Moore and Charles. The 72-year-old began to unconsciously roll his shoulders as he slipped the punches that came his way fifty years earlier.

By now, Jimmy was so ancient, youngsters found it hard to believe that this gray-haired, grandfather had ever boxed, but they respectfully patted him on the back, once they saw what he had done. Bivins was still hurting inside, but helped served the homeless from a kitchen near St. Malachi's Church, adjacent to the gym. In 1997, he finally sold his home on East 137th Street, and moved in with his only daughter Josette, and her family.

Davidson visited Jimmy, and the old fighter told him, "I'm quite content." But when his old friend of forty-five years, the Reverend Emory Kirk, who'd been searching for him, finally found the old "interim champ," he claimed, "They let me talk to him at the door, but would not let me come in. He sounded pretty good and looked in good shape … I thought it was a family thing." Other people, however, got the phone slammed down. Bivins's two elderly sisters had been looking for him for eighteen months.

On 4 April 1998, Cleveland police finally found Jimmy Bivins. Instead of the robe he once proudly wore, cops discovered him under a excretment-covered blanket, in a cold, dark attic, and they recoiled from the stench. He weighed just 110 pounds.

Bivins, who was once Joe Louis's top contender, was too weak to even cry out in pain. He was near death, but Bivins' "loved ones" had given him a can of pork and beans. As Jimmy groped about in the dark, frantically trying to tear the can open with his bare hands, he'd horribly cut his right hand and gangrene had set in. The old man was in great pain, and kept whimpering. He had been gashed to the bone. The middle finger of his right hand had to be amputated. Doctors also treated a bad infection on his left shoulder, and numerous bed sores. Jimmy's right, the one that had creased the brow of Louis, Charles, Moore and Walcott, is just a crooked claw now.

For months, he was terribly disoriented. His mind seemed gone. Hospital visitors cried when they saw him, but Bivins would gasp, in a bare whisper, "My daughter was just tryin' to take care of me, that's all."

CHAPTER TWO

The Notorious Mister Gray

IN 1939, HARRY Markson, a young publicity director for the New York Hippodrome, wrote the following words in a boxing yearbook:

> Honest boxing!
>
> Those two words, furnish, perhaps the best explanation of the lofty position which Michael Strauss Jacobs occupies in the world of fisticuffs ...
>
> Honest boxing!
>
> Mike Jacobs has made a genuine effort to reduce to zero the influence of gamblers in boxing and has taken strong measures to prevent them from operating at the Garden ... Jacobs permits no known gambler to loiter in or around his clubs.
>
> Jacobs will not tolerate 'monkey business' by any of the men who perform on his programs – or by their managers.
>
> Boxing today is immensely more honest that in was fifteen or twenty years ago.

Mike Jacobs was then the biggest name in boxing, the promoter who controlled Joe Louis, the world heavyweight champion, and Madison Square Garden, the sport's spiritual home. Yet eight years later, the *New York Times* openly asserted that Jacobs himself was controlled: by a gangster called Frank Carbo.

Far from being honest, boxing had entered its most corrupt phase, and Jacobs was part of it. The sport had always attracted gangsters. It's a rough, tough business, and the money has generally dwarfed anything that could be made in other sports. In the late 1920s, Babe Ruth was the highest-paid player in baseball, making $85,000 a year, yet Gene Tunney made $1 million for his rematch with Jack Dempsey. In 1920, baseball fans were shocked to learn the 1919 World Series had been fixed. A former federal judge was named Commissioner of Baseball and integrity was restored to the game.

But in boxing, it wasn't that easy. Boxing was a far-flung sport with thousands of fighters in America alone. Even with boxing commissions in most states, the fight game was impossible to supervise without strong federal racketeering enforcement.

By 1940, Owney Madden, who had run much of American boxing behind the scenes, was harassed into abdication. Vincent "Mad Dag" Coll, who had been involved with Madden in the exploitation of Primo Carnera, was a baby-faced twenty-three-year-old crazy even by Mob standards. He had been an enforcer for Dutch Schultz, once the top racket man in New York, before brazenly trying to take over the Dutchman's $20 million empire. Between hijacking Schultz's beer trucks by the dozen and killing his drivers, he not only murdered the mobster's loyal lieutenant, Vincent Barelli, but blew away Barelli's girlfriend too. Coll looked like a choirboy but even had the chutzpah to kidnap Madden's chief enforcer, "Big Frenchy" Demange – who was also in on the Carnera scam – and hold him captive till he got a $35,000 ransom.

After Coll had strong-armed a way into Schultz's policy (illegal gambling) racket, the Dutchman furiously put a $50,000 bounty on his head. Coll's brother was kidnapped, then riddled with bullets on a Harlem street. With Coll swearing revenge, Schultz sent out a hit team to scour New York for him. As Schultz's top enforcer, Joey Rao, stalked Coll with his two best gunmen in July 1932, their prey found them first. Coll spotted Rao and his henchmen walking down East 107th Street. It was hot, with children happily splashing in front of the fire hydrants that had been opened in the neighbourhood streets. Coll roared past in a speeding auto, spraying machine gun fire. The gangsters ducked. Amid hysterical screams, five children were left writhing on the bloody pavement, and one died. They ranged from two to four years old.

With Coll now an outlaw even by Mob standards, the tabloids started bellowing that this Mad Dog had to be taken off the street. But Coll got one of the best mouthpieces in New York, Samuel Leibowitz, and incredibly was acquitted. He had raised his $30,000 "defence fund" by kidnapping another Madden underling. He flaunted his infamy by marrying chorus girl Lottie Kreisberger. But if Schultz couldn't get Coll, Madden didn't forget. One day Coll was threatening Madden from a drug store phone kiosk on West 23rd Street. A man quietly walked into the store, pulled out a submachine gun and cut the Mad Dog to pieces.

In October 1935, Schultz was gunned down with three of his henchman at the Palace Chophouse in Newark, New Jersey. Schultz had insisted that New York special prosecutor Thomas E. Dewey, a dedicated gangbuster, be killed, but the "board" of the newly-organized national crime syndicate said no. When Schultz vowed to do it anyway, he was rubbed out. Dewey nearly became president of the United States in 1948. By then Madden was retired in Hot Springs, where gangsters went to relax. Gangsterism had become "Organized Crime," and a ruthless punk like Frankie Carbo was on his way to running the fight game.

Carbo was twenty-nine years old when he got into boxing in 1933. His real name was Paolo Corbo, not Carbo, but he had at least ten aliases, among them, Paul L. Carbo, P.J. Carbo, Frank Fortunati, Frank Marlow and "Jimmy the Wop," and even had two different versions of "Mr. Gray." He was born on 10 August 1904, on Second Avenue in New York City. His father, Angelo Corbo, was a twenty-seven-year-old laborer, who would die of tuberculosis in 1931. His mother, Clementinia Petrono, was also twenty-seven and a native Italian. Though records are sketchy, Carbo later said he had two younger brothers and two younger sisters. After his father's death he supported his mother till she passed away in 1942, but it was obvious, even when Carbo was a young punk, that he was a gangster. He drove cabs and trucks for a time, but often showed up at his mother's house in a chauffeur-driven limousine. He was also in and out of taxis.

Carbo's long rap sheet began when he was eleven, and he was sent to the Truant School in New York in 1915. By adulthood he was working as a hack driver. He stood 5-8 and weighed 170 and, because of his hair colour, would acquire the slightly sinister nickname Mr Gray. Nobody's sure how many times he was arrested – many files more than twenty years old simply disappeared in corrupt New York City – but his huge FBI dossier runs to perhaps half a million pages. Carbo was still getting picked up in the 1950s for petty things, like being a "suspicious character," under assumed names in Philadelphia and Miami.

One thing not in doubt is that young Frankie Carbo was a killer. He began to put the muscle on taxi drivers in New York, demanding they pay tribute. One driver refused to pay. Carbo refused to let him work. The cabbie returned to see Carbo with a friend, Albert Weber, described in an FBI file as "a husky butcher". Husky or not, Weber was shot dead.

In December 1928, Carbo was taken into custody in New York for Weber's murder. The charge was dropped to manslaughter and Carbo began a two- to four-year sentence at Sing Sing Prison in February 1930. Men routinely went to the electric chair for less, but Carbo was out on parole within eighteen months and was arrested by New York City Police Department in September 1931 on another murder rap. According to his FBI file:

> At this time he was charged with the murder of Michael J. Duffy, a South New Jersey and Philadelphia, Pennsylvania, beer baron and racketeer who had been slain a few days previously in Atlantic City … At the time of this arrest

Carbo stated he was a bus inspector, earning $50 weekly … Carbo offered the alibi that he was in New York City undergoing treatment at an ear clinic not long after Duffy was killed. However, a special policeman … stated that he saw Carbo loitering in Atlantic City at this time … A confidential informant advised that Carbo AND Hyman Stromberg, alias 'Nig Rosen,' another racketeer, killed Duffy.

Carbo was not convicted of Duffy's murder. He told the cops he didn't work regular hours in his alleged bus inspector's post. In fact his real job was hired killer.

Carbo "made his bones" with Murder Incorporated, the most notorious hit squad in American history. Headed by leading gangster Louis "Lepke" Buchalter, it was one corporation that never made the New York Stock Exchange. Murder Incorporated was the muscle of organized crime. In the early 1930s, New York mob barons Charles "Lucky" Luciano, Vito Genovese, Abner "Longy" Zwillman, Frank Costello, Meyer Lansky and Buchalter divided up their city and inaugurated a new era of racketeering in the United States. To protect their rackets from outsiders, they made their gunmen available to associated mobs throughout the country.

It was a business, and anybody could get "hit." Initially, Jewish mobster Benjamin "Bugsy" Siegel was in charge of Murder Inc. Bugsy hated his nickname, earned for his uncontrollable rages, and would kill anyone who called him that to his face. "Pittsburgh Phil" was another maniac, who begged to go on "hits." His real name was Harry Strauss. He loved flashy threads and would break into a torrent of profanity if some "bum's blood" got on his clothes. Like most of the killers, Pittsburgh Phil didn't carry weapons unless it was absolutely necessary. He once stalked a victim into a movie theatre, grabbed a fire axe out of glass case, then descended on the victim as he was enjoying the film. Phil slammed down his axe, blood and brains spilling out, then ran with the rest of the screaming crowd toward the exits, dropping his weapon along the way.

In 1932, mobster Abe Wagner was in St. Paul, Minnesota, after fleeing New York. He was trying to survive by pushing a fruitcart, and went by the name of Loeb, but two of Bugsy's guys fired seven bullets into him, and Wagner quickly expired from a bad case of "lead poisoning." In 1937, Walter Sage, who handled the Murder Inc. slot-machines, was caught skimming money. Taken for a ride, he bawled and begged, but Jack Drucker drove an ice pick into his chest thirty-two times, then tied Sage's body to a pinball machine, and cops found him floating in the East River. A lot of guys ended up in the New Jersey swamps. If a swamp or warehouse couldn't be found, Murder Inc. even had its own undertakers.

As Carbo hustled his way into the fight game, some of the thugs he knew on the way up were Vito "Socko" Gurino, Angelo "Julie" Catalona, Dasher Abbandando and Abe "Kid Twist" Reles. They were all deadly members of Murder Incorporated.

Carbo was a dapper man who liked showgirls and had a remarkable ability for staying out of prison. In April 1933, with Prohibition still the law, Max Hessell and Max Greenberg, partners of bootlegger Waxie Gordon, were blown away at a hotel in New Jersey. Two brave bystanders fingered Carbo. According to FBI files:

> Greenberg and Hassell operated a brewery in New Jersey. Other New Jersey racketeers desired to gain control of this brewery, and they hired Carbo as a killer. Carbo was associated with Benjamin "Bugs" Siegel, outstanding West Coast racketeer, at that time. There were two witnesses to these murders, both from Philadelphia.

Carbo was arrested in 1936. The police picked him up at Madison Square Garden, where he was becoming a familiar, but shadowy, figure. He was released on $10,000 bond and the case never came to trial.

From 1927 into 1940, Murder Inc. operated with virtual impunity. Then, in the spring of 1940, the flat-nosed Abe Reles began squealing to cops. Reles had been implicated in the 1933 murder of a teenager called Red Albert. The cops made him squirm, and for the first time in Syndicate history a hoodlum sang for immunity. Reles warbled for two long years. A $50,000 contract was put on his head as he implicated Mob heavies like Joe Adonis (who movie tough guy George Raft based himself on), Albert Anastasia and Lucky Luciano.

Reles claimed that 1,000 people had been "rubbed out." He alone killed seven when Louis Lepke put out a contract on witnesses who could have testified against him. Reles did business with a smile. Muddy Kasoff was told to walk 100 yards. As he turned around, his head was blown off by a shotgun. "We left the bum under a billboard that says Drive Safely," Reles laughed to investigators. Reles had been Bugsy Seigel's bodyguard, and matter-of-factly admitted killing dozens of people.

In November 1941, after testifying in court, Reles somehow went out of the sixth floor window at the Half Moon Hotel in Coney Island. There were six cops in Reles's room at the time. The "canary" couldn't fly, and expired on the sidewalk.

Bill O' Dwyer, the "rackets busting" DA from Brooklyn, had refused to produce Reles for a trail involving Siegel in Los Angeles. Reles then went out the window while guarded by an O'Dwyer intimate, Frank Bals, a New York police captain. After O'Dwyer became Mayor of New York City, it was eventually revealed that Bals, who was made Deputy Police Commissioner, was the bagman for corrupt cops and politicians. The take was $250,000 a week. O'Dwyer had to resign just one year into his second term. Mafia boss Frank Costello, who Carbo worked for, was involved with O'Dwyer and controlled all the important judicial and political appointments through the rancid Democratic party machine at Tammany Hall. How could you possibly clean up boxing, when New York was a city in chains?

Reles's testimony had, however, already sent Mendy Weiss, Louis Capone, Happy Malon, Abbandando, and Pittsburgh Phil to the electric chair. Reles also fingered Frankie Carbo, Allie Tannenbaum, Whitey Krakower, and Siegel in the 1939 Thanksgiving murder of Harry "Big Greenie" Greenberg, a hitman who had "gone bad." Carbo reportedly fired the bullets, on a residential Los Angeles street. Siegel drove the getaway car. "Tick Tock" Tannenbaum swore too that Carbo blasted Greenberg. But with Reles not surviving for long enough to testify, Carbo beat this rap in 1942. The jury deliberated fifty-three hours.

It is hard to know how many murders Carbo committed, but some said he was one of the "top torpedos" of the time. He was arrested a total of seventeen times, five of them for murder.

* * *

Frankie Carbo was twenty-nine years old when he got into boxing in 1933. Gabe Genovese, cousin of the New York mob lord Vito Genovese, was managing Babe Risko, who became middleweight champion in 1935. Carbo got a piece of Risko through Vito. That alone makes you wonder if some of Risko's later fights weren't "in the bag."

From 1932 till February 1937, when Risko lost his final chance to regain the NBA-New York version of the middleweight title, the tough, light-hitting boxer had only been stopped twice in fifty-four fights. Then, with Risko out of contention but still a "name," he was suddenly halted in eight of his last eleven bouts. Had Carbo and his cronies laid some bets?

Mr Gray's influence spread swiftly – and right to the top. On 1 March 1940, the extraordinary "Hammerin'" Henry Armstrong should have became the first man to win world championships at four different weights, but gangsters scared referee George Blake so badly that he called Armstrong's fight with middleweight champ Ceferino Garcia a ten-round draw, then practically ran out of the ring. Carbo was in Los Angeles at the time.

Bugsy Siegel was on the West Coast too. He had moved to Hollywood, and would eventually control most of the racketeering in Southern California. Movie legends like Clark Gable and Ramon Navarro fawned over the handsome killer, and the Countess Dorothy di Frasso loved having the deceptively charming gangster to her star-studded lawn parties. Actresses Wendy Barrie and Marie "the Body" McDonald were a few of Siegel's lovely conquests. Bugsy however, was a rapist as well. Back in New York, goons warned one girl who had been raped by Siegel, "You finger Bugsy, we'll put your face in acid."

Though Siegel had charmed his way into Hollywood, movie mogul Jack Warner, a miserable sonofabitch in his own right, was never fooled. He was petrified of Siegel, the *de facto* ambassador for organized crime. The Mob controlled the projectionists' union, and Siegel threatened to close down theatres nationwide. Since the average American hit the movies three times a week, that would've beeen catastrophic. The million-dollar payoff seemed almost cheap.

Siegel would eventually make it to celluloid himself, in a roundabout way. Years after his death, Warren Beatty played him in the movie *Bugsy*, a somewhat sanitized version of the life of a man who, in April, 1931, had gone with Joe Adonis and Albert Anastasia to murder Joe "The Boss" Masseria and so displace him at the top of New York's underworld. According to the authoritative *Encyclopedia of Crime*, "Siegel was also involved in a half dozen murders of rival gangsters in the war between New York bootleggers Waxie Gordon and Charles 'Chink' Sherman. In 1934, one of Gordon's henchmen, Francis Anthony Fabrizzio, gently lowered a bomb into the Bug and Meyer gang's headquarters on Grand Street in Manhattan [Bug and Meyer were Bugsy Siegel and Meyer Lansky]. As the bomb blew up, Siegel was injured. His buddies survived, but Bugsy swore he'd kill Fabrizzio, and hunted him down, before he finally got him in Brooklyn."

On September 30, 1935, Siegel, and his then-bodyguard, Abe Reles, (who hadn't yet tried to defy the laws of gravity) gunned down rivals Joey Amberg and Louis "Pretty" Amberg, who wasn't quite so pretty when they got done with him. Siegel not only killed Abe Weinberg, he stabbed him in the stomach so his body wouldn't float in the East River.

By the late 1930s, Siegel's pal Frankie Carbo was too hot to stay in New York, and relocated for a time in Los Angeles, and Seattle, Washington, on the West Coast. Conflicting reports were that Carbo was involved in horse racing in Seattle. During July and August, 1938, while residing at the Roosevel Hotel, he stayed in steady contact with Siegel.

Harry Greenberg, known as "Big Greenie" was a member of the Buchalter-Lepke mob. When Greenberg, Buchalter and others were indicted, Greenberg lit out for Montreal, Canada, and wrote to a friend, intimating that he was going to talk if "hush money" wasn't forthcoming. He had to go.

An attempt to lure him to Detroit failed, so finally Bugsy Siegel was sent to Montreal. He discovered from a snitch that Greenberg had de-camped to Los Angeles, and trailed him there with a faithful lieutenant – Frankie Carbo. Another mob came out from New York with two untraceable guns and cartridges. Siegel was in charge of the hit. On 22 November 1939, at around 11:00 on a sunny morning at Yucca and Vista del Mar streets in Hollywood, Greenberg was sitting in his car when he was cut down by a hail of bullets. According to testimony before a Los Angeles grand jury, Siegel "drove the murder car," while "Carbo was the trigger man and did the killing."

After cooling off for a couple of days, Carbo left Los Angeles, and went to Cleveland, Ohio. In August 1940, he was charged with flight to avoid prosecution for murder. In August 1941, he surrendered to the DA's office in LA. He was tried in Los Angeles during January and February of 1942. Peggy Schwartz, a researcher at a movie studio, identified Carbo as the man she saw running down the street in Hollywood moments after Greenberg was gunned down. Walter Rheinschild, an attorney, said Siegel and Carbo were the men he had seen slowly driving by Greenberg's house. It was damning testimony, but after fifty-three hours of deliberation, an amazing amount of time considering the evidence, the jury was discharged, unable to render a verdict.

In March 1942, the murder charge against Carbo was suddenly dismissed, after William O'Dwyer, then District Attorney of Brooklyn and later Mayor of New York, ruled that an important witness wouldn't be allowed to re-testify in Los Angeles. Once again, strong circumstantial evidence suggests that the fix was in.

The Manhattan District Attorney's office tried, unsuccessfully, to tie Carbo to the fight game. Meanwhile, in February 1946, US Attorney General Tom Clark (the top law enforcement official in the country) asked the Secretary of the Treasury to supply copies of Carbo's income tax returns for 1939–43. The FBI was conducting an "official investigation" on behalf of the Justice Department.

In June 1946, FBI agent August J. Micek summarized what he had learned. He asserted that Carbo had been arrested for three murders after his spell in Sing Sing but had not been convicted, although information indicated Carbo had done all three in connection with his racketeering activities:

Carbo was trigger man for Bugs-Meyer and Buckhalter-Schapiro mobs. About fifteen years ago he became connected with the boxing game, first backing Babe Risko through instructions of Vito Genovese, outstanding New York racketeer. Has since controlled Sammy Angott, Johnny Greco, Chalky Wright and Marty Servo, and is also interested in Freddie Steele,

Popeye Woods, Tony Janiro and Tami Mauriello. Carbo said to control entire boxing game in New York City, even controlling Mike Jacobs, the promoter. He cannot be a manager of record because of criminal background, but uses front men as name managers. Said to manipulate odds by causing desired results in fights, and to cash in heavily on fixed fights.

Most of the fighters named were champions. In a little over a decade, a vicious strong-arm man and killer had taken over the entire sport. How?

★ ★ ★

The Feds knew that Carbo liked showgirls, had fallen in love with a twenty-year-old redhead in 1931, had a case of gonorrhoea in 1940, and was a "criminal psychopath" unfit for military service, even in time of war.

They also had information that Carbo owned a piece of middleweight Freddie Steele's contract. Steele hailed from nearby Tacoma, Washington. He was cut up "very badly" after Carbo took control from his manager Dave Miller. In March 1936, Steele defeated Carbo's middleweight, Babe Risko, over ten rounds in Seattle, and on July 11 won the NBA–New York version of the middleweight title when he decisioned Risko in fifteen. After five defences, Steele defended his title against Al Hostak, who also boxed around Seattle.

"Carbo wagered large sums of money that Hostak would defeat Steele during their championship fight," claimed an FBI informant. On 28 July 1938, Hostak shockingly vanquished the champion in the first round. The murderous-punching Steele had come out with his hands down and was floored four times. It was all over in just 1:43 as referee Jack Dempsey counted Steele out, only the third time he had been halted in 138 fights. Hostak was a terrific banger but there were strong rumours around Seattle that the fight was fixed.

The match, the first championship fight ever staged in the North-west, grossed $85,000, and drew 30,102 fans, but Hostak, a local kid, got just $800 as challenger. The disenchanted Steele became a stunt double for movie star Errol Flynn (and old heavyweight champion Jack Johnson begged him for work as an extra).

Carbo was too hot for New York, so he was keeping the middleweight championship in Seattle. On November 1, Solly Krieger, who was managed by convicted fight-fixer Hymie Caplan, decisioned Hostak in Seattle. He was a 7-1 underdog. On 27 June 1939, Hostak stunnningly halted Krieger in the fourth round in Seattle to regain the championship, and Carbo ended up with him.

In the modern era (contended the FBI's 1946 report), the first fighter Carbo is known to have been connected with was Sammy Angott, former light-weight champion. Angott's manager, Charlie Jones, was from outside New York City, and needed some connection in New York City, in order to secure fights at Madison Square Garden ... An arrangement was made whereby Carbo secured an interest in Angott's contract.

In 1940, Angott decisioned challenger Davey Day in Louisville, Kentucky. Hymie "the Mink" Wallman was Day's front manager. Carbo had both fighters. In May 1942, Angott made his third defence in Madison Square Garden, decisioning New York's Allie Stolz in fifteen. "He ruined my dream," Stolz moaned, decades later, of Carbo. The verdict was supposedly fixed, because Stolz "wouldn't go with him."

In connection with Angott's later retirement, which resulted in the vacancy in the lightweight championship, there was a general report in the boxing game at that time that there was a "deal" behind the scenes. If Carbo arranged this "deal," it is said that he did not do so for himself alone, as Mike Jacobs, the promoter, benefited by the title being vacated.

Angott, a light puncher but incredibly tough, announced his retirement in November. By January 1943, he had decided on a comeback, and eventually won the NBA version of the championship. On March 19, he became the first man to whip young phenom Willie Pep, after Pep's sixty-two straight wins. Pep wouldn't lose for another seventy-six bouts, till Sandy Saddler finally halted him in 1948 for the featherweight championship.

Another boxer whom Carbo is said to control is Johnny Greco. Greco is from Canada, and he was originally brought to New York City by some Canadians, who tried to manage him exclusively. However, since they were not on the "inside", they had no success in New York City, Greco became disgusted and returned to Canada.

A gangster front for Carbo named Jimmy Doyle, who was actually an "Italian parolee," got Greco's contract. Doyle was associated with leading New York mobster Tony Bender.

Greco recently fought the last of a series of three fights with Tony Janiro, (a) young boxer from Youngstown, Ohio. Greco won the first match, Janiro was the victor in the second fight, and Greco decisively defeated Janiro in the third match. After Janiro won the second match from Greco, the odds were greatly in his favour for the third engagement.

Insiders told the FBI that Carbo caused "Greco to lose the second fight with Janiro, and that Janiro was no match for Greco in their third fight." Though handsome Janiro was one of the biggest draws at the Garden, and destined for greatness, the beating he suffered at the fists of Greco ruined him. The FBI heard "that a big killing was made in the betting on the third Janiro-Greco match. Carbo controls Janiro, as well as Greco, but … Janiro did not know anything about the deal in this series,"

Janiro, a poor, fatherless kid, came to New York from Youngstown, Ohio, to earn enough money to buy his scrub-woman mother a house. He finally bought the house but ended up a penniless alcoholic. Booze killed him in 1985. Carbo also "caused" Greco to throw his fight with Bobby Ruffin, the FBI learned.

* * *

In 1937, a struggling black fighter who had been working in a Los Angeles car wash descended on Freddie Steele in a Tacoma gym and asked to borrow $75.

"Why do you want it?" Steele asked.

"So I can become featherweight champion of the world," Chalky Wright told him.

On 11 September 1941, Wright won the title, stopping Joey Archibald in the eleventh round in Washington. Archibald was Al Weill's fighter. Weill had been Carbo's partner since 1934.

On 20 November 1942, Wright lost his title to the brilliant young Willie Pep after two defences. Eddie Walker, who was Wright's manager, sold his contract to Jack Bluman. Bluman and his partner were new to the fight game, but they went to Carbo after they couldn't get fights in New York City.

By 1945, Bluman was wise to how Frankie Carbo ran boxing. In October 1945, Bluman and two other middle-aged gents from Brooklyn, Frank "B.O." Tummillo, a mortician known for his pungent smell, and Louis Schiaro, another beefy fight manager, were arrested in Toledo, Ohio, along with Carbo. They were charged with "suspicion," after an informant had called and warned Toledo police that they'd come to Toledo to "fix fights." A top Toledo racketeer named Leonard Benson, known on the streets as "Chalky Red," was their local man. Chalky *Wright* had boxed Bobby Ruffin in nearby Detroit the night before. Although Ruffin was the favourite, Wright won. "It was the opinion of the Toledo Police Department that this fight had been fixed by Carbo, Bluman, Tummillio, and Schiarro," the FBI recorded.

In March 1946, the *Detroit Tribune*, a black newspaper, claimed that

Wright "had not done his best in a fight against Enrique Bolanos, at the Olympic Auditorium in Los Angeles, California." Wright lost the decision to the hot young Mexican contender after beating him on points six months earlier in LA. Then there was the "mysterious" knockout against Henry Armstrong in 1938.

In 1957, Wright officially "drowned" in his own bathtub. *Confidential* magazine, a notorious rag out of Hollywood, claimed he'd been murdered.

An informant told the Feds that Carbo not only fixed fights but had "scouts" who sized up a fighter's ability, then Carbo swooped in for the kill. Carbo had his hands in everyone's pocket, and "reportedly controlled about 300" fighters. The fight guys at Stillman's, the famed New York gym, weren't naive but were "overawed" or scared because of "Carbo's gangster reputation," or "possible political influence."

★ ★ ★

On 19 June 1946, Joe Louis knocked out Billy Conn in the eighth round in the first defence of his heavyweight crown after the War. Fans had been clamouring for this clash since their epic first fight in 1941. The rematch grossed $1,925,564, with Louis getting forty per cent of the net and Conn twenty. It was a hugely symbolic event, signalling an end to World War Two austerity.

In 1945, after the bout had been announced, Carbo brazenly approached Johnny Ray, Conn's manager. "I'm in for fifty per cent of Conn's purse, or else," he growled, sounding like he'd seen too many Jimmy Cagney movies.

Ray, a tough bastard, told Carbo, "I've got good contacts in the FBI. If you come around again, I'll get the FBI after you."

Surprisingly, Carbo "left and has never returned," a member of the New York Boxing Commission told the FBI, but Conn knew, even before getting demolished by Louis, that his career was over. At twenty-eight, he announced his retirement. He briefly came back but never boxed in New York again.

The fight was so disappointing that congressman Donald O'Toole, a Democrat from New York, called, J. Edgar Hoover the next afternoon. The FBI boss and his assistant. Clyde Tolson, were unavailable. "I'm sending a wire to the boxing commission," O'Toole then told Special Agent Nichols, who took the call. "There's got to be an investigation. People were swindled last night. Both fighters' purses should be held up. There should be an investigation of Jacobs. It's the duty of the boxing commission to clean up boxing. Another fiasco like that will ruin the sport forever."

Months earlier, in February 1946, Freddie "Red" Cochrane had been slated to defend his welterweight championship against Marty Servo in

New York. Cochrane had been a scrappy clubfighter until he somehow pulled off a 10-1 upset to win the title on points from Fritzie Zivic. He had then joined the Navy and had never defended his title. Young middleweight Rocky Graziano annihilated him twice in non-title bouts in 1945.

According to FBI reports, there were rumours even before the Cochrane-Servo championship fight that it was fixed. According to FBI info, Carbo was actually the manager of Servo, though Al Weill was manager of record. "The fix was to be that Cochrane would receive $50,000 over and above his share of the fight proceeds to give up the title to Servo," read the FBI's confidential file.

On February 1, 1946, Servo halted Cochrane out in the fourth round. It would be Cochrane's last fight. "According to the informant, Cochrane was in no shape to fight Servo on the night he lost his title ... although he had trained for six weeks, he could not get into condition."

Though the bets were laid down, and Servo ended up with the welterweight championship, he didn't get a dime. The gate was only $42,000. Apparently, Carbo and Weill paid Cochrane his promised $50,000 out of the gate money. Servo, controlled by Carbo, never defended his ill-gotten championship. He was blasted out by Graziano in March 1946, and his badly busted nose hastened a premature retirement.

* * *

By the mid 1940s, Bugsy Siegel was throwing lavish parties in his sumptuous Beverly Hills abode. He went at least twice a week to the race track and routinely dropped $10,000. Despite a wife and family in New York, he became romanticaly entangled with Virginia Hill, a beautiful brunette prostitute, extortionist, and Mob mule, who used to transport huge amounts of cash to various "families" around the country. Hill, who lived in a Beverly Hills palace, also blackmailed Hollywood stars.

Siegel, by now, was smuggling millions of dollars of heroin across the border from Mexico; Hill had made the initial contacts. Siegel was also dreaming of starting a legal gambling mecca, out in the middle of nowhere, in a little Nevada desert town called Las Vegas. People scoffed, and Bugsy's blood pressure rose as he screamed, "Don't you mugs have any god damn vision?" Eventually Lucky Luciano and Meyer Lansky, the Mob's financial genius, bankrolled him for several millions dollars. Siegel put up $1 million of his own money.

Suddenly a man possessed, Siegel built the Flamingo Hotel and Casino out of sheer sand. Flamingo was his nickname for Virginia Hill. With Bugsy obsessed with creating a gambling paradise, his dope-dealing began going to hell in Los Angeles. Gangster Mickey Cohen, a kill-crazy, publicity-happy punk, had let business slide. But construction on the Flamingo was also way behind. Siegel got real nervous.

One day Del Webb, the construction mogul who later owned the New York Yankees baseball team, heard Bugsy excitedly screaming into the phone, "Hit 'em! Fix 'em! Take care of it!"

As Webb turned pale, Siegel turned to him and cracked, "Don't worry Del, we only kill each other."

The Flamingo finally opened, but turned into a terrible bust. Las Vegas was practically a ghost town and Siegel had a neon monstrosity financed with Mob money he couldn't pay back. Chilling ultimatums came from New York. "We want our money," said Luciano. "Go to hell," replied Siegel, who now saw himself as a Mob titan in his own right.

Luciano then got ahold of Lansky, Siegel's old partner in the Bug-Meyer Gang. "Ben's gonna get hit, and there ain't gonna be no argument," growled the Italian.

On 20 June 1947 Siegel was sitting comfortably in Hill's Beverly Hills mansion with Allen Smiley, an aquaintance. Hill was in Europe. As Bugsy reclined in the corner of a plush couch, three bullets from a 30-30 rifle rocketed into his head, blowing his left eye out of its socket. He slumped in the chair, blood and brains splattered everywhere.

Las Vegas eventually turned into the best investment organized crime ever made, yielding billions in prostitution and legalized gambling, but not even Virginia Hill went to Bugsy's funeral. Movie tough guy George Raft had "asthma" that day.

It would be forty-five years before protected Mob stoolie Jimmy "The Weasel" Frattiano fingered Carbo for the killing. And three months after the hit, the *New York Times* was claiming that the mysterious Carbo controlled Mike Jacobs, the biggest promoter in boxing.

* * *

In January 1947, Willie Ritchie, the former lightweight champion of the world, wrote J. Edgar Hoover a letter requesting Carbo's criminal record. Ritchie was living in Beverly Hills, among the movie stars, but was the chief boxing inspector for the Southern District of California commission.

"P.S.," added the former lightweight king, "Hope my great sport, boxing, can be saved before it's too late. Incidentally, is it possible to use the return addressed stamped envelope? Afraid my wife may worry if you use your official envelope. My battle for clean boxing (began) here a couple years ago … (but) with phone calls after midnight, waking the entire house, when I was cursed … makes her very nervous."

In 1945, Los Angeles Police raided Mickey Cohen's gambling joint in

Hollywood. Cops confiscated a slew of phone numbers. There were two for Carbo. Carbo also knew Babe McCoy, the corrupt Los Angeles match-maker. Carbo, Cohen and McCoy obviously conspired in the fixing of fights, and Adolph Alexander, a Deputy District Attorney in LA, quietly told the FBI in April 1947 that an "unidentified prize fighter" gave "damaging" information to the DA, admitting that he was paid for "taking a dive" in San Antonio, Texas, "at the direction of one Frank Carbo, New York hoodlum."

"The fighter got paid when he returned," Alexander told the Feds, "Carbo's got the reputation as the king fight-fixer in the States."

Back in New York, the boxing commission was conducting another cosmetic investigation. But in July, 1947, when they discovered that Carbo owned Bernard Docusen, a fine welterweight out of New Orleans, who later went the distance with a peak Sugar Ray Robinson, "ownership of this boxer allegedly changed hands." Gangster "Frank Costello's check paid for the contract when it was transferred."

By the 1950s, the FBI learned that Hymie Wallman was "designated as the manager of Cesar Brion, Davey Day, Johnny Bratton, Luther Rawlings, and Orlando Zulueta, all current headline prize fighters."

"It's common knowledge," a source told the FBI, "that Al Weill gave Carbo a piece of Rocky Marciano so he could get the right fights when he came to New York." Feds learned that it was Nig Rosen, another Carbo murder-mate, who was the "mob control" behind Marciano, who was then heavyweight champion. As for Jersey Joe Walcott, Clarence Henry, and Coley Wallace, then top contenders? "There is a prevalent rumour that they obtained these fighters by going to their former managers, sticking a gun in their bellies, and asking what the selling price was."

★ ★ ★

On 14 November 1947, Billy Fox stopped Jake La Motta in the fourth round at Madison Square Garden. Fox had once scored forty-three consecutive knockouts, but the stench was so bad after La Motta was rescued by the referee that angry reporters began charging the fight had been fixed. The New York State Athletic Commission was forced to with-hold both fighters' purses, and chairman Eddie Eagan promised an investigation.

LaMotta, Carbo, Fox and Fox's manager, Frank "Blinky" Palermo, were summoned to the District Attorney's office six days later. LaMotta showed up at 10:30 AM with his father Joseph and younger brother Joey.

As Jake sauntered in, a scowl on his round face, a horde of fedora-clad reporters began to shout, "Jake, did you throw the fight?"

"I have nothing to say. All I know is I fought the best I know and I was in fine shape."

But LaMotta, cockily chewing a toothpick, had been seen three days before the fight talking to Carbo and Palermo at the Park Arena, a fight club LaMotta had a secret interest in. This was where the final planning allegedly took place.

"It's a dirty rotten lie," snarled LaMotta.

But gangsters had been trying to get to the Bronx middleweight for years, and they had finally succeeded. In 1962, the embattled LaMotta finally admitted in a magazine article, "Honest Fighters Finish Last", that "my brother Joey came to me and said I could have a fight with Tony Janiro, a very good boy, under certain conditions. I would have to put up $15,000 as a guarantee that I would make 155 pounds ... and I would have to agree to lose. For losing I would get $100,000.

"I told Joey to forget about it, and that I was only interested in a title fight. He went away and came back to report that they couldn't do anything about a title fight but they were willing to fight me if I put up the $15,000 guarantee and made 155 pounds ... It took me ten rounds to beat Janiro and I still don't know how I managed it because there was no strength in me."

What LaMotta didn't admit was how much he enjoyed smashing in Janiro's pretty face. Vikki LaMotta, Jake's stunning blonde wife, had jokingly told Jake, "I think Janiro's cute," and LaMotta, who was insanely jealous, replied darkly, "He won't be pretty when I get done with him."

For years, LaMotta had been regarded as the uncrowned king of the middleweights, but he wouldn't play ball with the gangsters who controlled the fight game. So he had a lot of trouble getting big fights.

LaMotta admitted "carrying" Cecil Hudson in Chicago, on September 3, but "outsmarted myself" because Hudson got the split decision. "After the Hudson fight, Joey came to me again, with another $100,000 bribe offer, this time to lose to Billy Fox. Fox was a Negro who had run up a string of 43 consecutive knockouts, a world record, under the guidance of Blinky Palermo, his manager. The record was strictly fake. Fox could not fight a lick."

Fox had actually gotten a light-heavyweight title shot, losing in the tenth to Gus Lesnevich. Now LaMotta was supposed to be the fall guy so Fox could get a rematch. "I'm not interested in the money," Jake insisted to his brother. All he wanted was his title shot. "We signed for the fight without a deal but they kept after me to agree to a dive. I refused."

LaMotta said that he had injured his spleen in training, and it hurt terribly when he got hit there. "Finally, a day or two before the fight, Joey brought me word that I had the guarantee of a title fight if I should lose to

Fox." Jake started a 3-1 favourite, but a lot of money suddenly started coming in on Fox from Philadelphia, where Palermo was the numbers king. Soon, bookmakers wouldn't touch the fight.

"When I came into the ring, I kept my eyes down ... I didn't want to look at the crowd. I don't even remember hearing the referee's instructions. All I was thinking was that I had to make it look good. Against a fighter like Fox, I couldn't even do that," admitted LaMotta, who was a savage, but a purist in his own way. "In the first round, when I threw a few punches, I realized that I didn't dare throw any more for fear of knocking him out with even a light punch ... He couldn't take anything at all. He couldn't punch either. There was just no way to make him look good."

Though LaMotta had agreed to dump the fight, the "Bronx Bull" took enormous pride that he had never been knocked off his feet. As he lay on the ropes, and allowed Fox to whale away, he staggered and fell back, but wasn't convincing. Finally, referee Frank Fullam jumped in, to the crowd's howls.

With columnists like Dan Parker demanding an investigation, the New York State Athletic Commission finally fined Jake $1,000, and suspended him indefinitely, but under the threat of a lawsuit, LaMotta got his license back after seven months, because the crusading DA, Frank Hogan couldn't prove that he'd thrown the fight.

It wasn't until June 1960 that LaMotta publicly revealed that Carbo, Palermo and "Honest" Billy Daly had fixed the Fox match. But Jake still might not have gone through with it, had Thomas Milo, the underworld "money man," not agreed that Jake would get his long-sought shot at the middleweight crown. "My chance at the middleweight title did not come until a year and a half after the Fox fight. I sweated it out..."

By then, Rocky Graziano and Tony Zale had completed their barbaric trilogy. Zale, boxing's "Man of Steel," ended up on the scrapheap in Jersey City, after France's Marcel Cerdan stopped him in the twelfth round in September 1948.

Finally, on 16 June 1949, after nearly a decade and eighty-nine pro fights, LaMotta got his chance in Detroit. But he had to pay $20,000 to Lew Burston and Sam Richman, Cerdan's American representatives. LaMotta's purse was $19,000. Burston later denied under oath that he got anything when subpoenaed before a Senate subcommittee, but he was known for his double-dealing. (Jack Solomons, the London promoter, had wined and dined him in his home shortly after the war, when Burston asked to use his phone to make a very expensive call to America. He called Mike Jacobs, and the very fight Solomons was trying to make ended up with Jacobs, because Burston shamelessly worked both ends.)

LaMotta won the middleweight championship when Cerdan injured his shoulder and couldn't come out for the tenth round. LaMotta had walloped the hell out of wounded French-Algerian, but to make money, Jake actually had to bet $10,000 on himself, as an 8-5 underdog, and came away with $16,000. Years later, despite everything he suffered, he still says, "The price was cheap. I was *champ*."

A rematch with Cerdan was scheduled for September in New York's Polo Grounds but LaMotta abruptly pulled out. The fight was re-scheduled indoors for Madison Square Garden on December 2, but on October 27, 1949, Cerdan and his manager Jo Longman were killed when their commercial aircraft slammed into a mountain in the Azores as they flew to the States.

La Motta was haunted by Cerdan's death because he had pulled out of the second fight. Like Dostoevski's wretched protagonist in *Crime and Punishment*, LaMotta almost went out of his way to punish himself. He was a vicious wife-beater who drove away gorgeous blonde Vikki. In Miami, he went to jail for taking money off a fourteen-year-old whore. After being thrown in solitary confinement, Jake started screaming and smashed his fists over and over into the cement wall. In an act of brutal symbolism, LaMotta was trying to destroy the very things that made him – his fists – but by the early 1960s, he had gotten his self-destructiveness and his frightening rage under some control. "I'm not trying to whitewash myself," he admitted sadly. "I was a thief. I threw a fight. I did two terms in jail and I'm lucky I wasn't a murderer. But those rats who run boxing made me look like Little Lord Fauntleroy."

Sportswriter W.C. Heinz, who has nothing bad to say about anybody, recalled LaMotta as "a miserable human being." In June 1960, when LaMotta testified before a Senate investigation into boxing corruption in Washington, it was a shock. He knew the code of silence that prevailed on the mean streets. "Jake, you're a fucking moron! You're gonna get us killed!" his brother Joey screamed at him before he went to testify.

As newsreel cameras whirred away, LaMotta was asked by Senate probers: "Have you or your family ever been threatened Mr LaMotta."

Jake fidgeted in his seat. He sweated heavily and tore at bits of paper. Finally he said softly, "I'm not afraid for myself … "

Then the old Bronx Bull blew up. His beefy face got red as he bellowed, " … and I'm not afraid of none of them rats!"

But LaMotta was afraid, and his memory got very selective. He refused to publicly name Palermo or Daly as the scum who had actualy made the Fox pay-off. He had done so in a sworn deposition but word quickly got back that if he didn't stop talking, he was gonna get "hit in the head."

Joey LaMotta refused to answer any questions. He took the Fifth Ammendment against self-incrimination. As for Billy Fox, he got his return bout with Lesnevich, and was blasted out in the first round. Thirteen years later, he was just another patient at the Kings Park State Mental Hospital in suburban Long Island.

★ ★ ★

His name was Frank Palermo, but fight guys simply called him "Blinky." He was also known as "George Tobias" or "Mr. Bodine." He was supposedly born in Philadelphia on 26 January 1905, though not even the FBI could be sure. "File review in the Philadelphia Division reflects Palermo's first wife of record to be Mrs. Josephine Byrnes (nee Guiro). Mrs Byrnes divorced Palermo in the year 1940," say the records. Other FBI files claim she "absconded with a Negro." FBI records also contend "Frank Palermo married one Clair Cori on April 29, 1955 in Arlington County, VA," and, "On Ocotber 12, 1961 the Philadelphia Police department file on Palermo indicates that he was married by proxy to Margaret Dougherty by the Justice of the Peace D.M. Yerkes at Melbourne, PA."

Palermo was married so often he practically needed a wash-and-wear tuxedo. He was apparently even married to Dougherty before, hints the FBI, but under an assumed name. The FBI got hold of marriage "license 107776 of the year 1944, which reflects that one Frank Palermo, 1925 North 61st Street, Philadelphia, PA., born December 11, 1909…and Margaret K. Dougher of 1925 North 61st Street, born January 15, 1917…were united in marriage on April 30, 1944."

Palermo was a short, stocky sparkplug of a man, 5-4½ and 169 pounds, who had dark brown hair combed back and a flat, rather nondescript face. When he was young, he was a crazy bastard. In April 1928, he was arrested in Philadelphia after he worked someone over with brass knuckles and was charged with aggravated assault. That September he stood trial. He was ordered to pay $200 to the victim and sentenced to six months. Incredibly, the sentence was "reconsidered" to no time and a $500 fine. One month before, in August, Palermo had been arrested and charged with stealing the complainant's rented car. Palermo was found not guilty.

Cops not in the rackets busted Palermo for petty things like being a "suspicious character." In October 1933, he was arrested in Philadelphia for threatening to kill someone, and he was held on $2,900 bond. Proving the fix was in, which was common with mobbed-up guys, FBI records show there was "no further disposition." In January 1934, he was busted for running an "illegal lottery" and got six months. In July the "sentence was reconsidered" and Palermo got sixty days. In March 1935, Palermo was charged with hit-and-run after the car he was driving ran down sixty-year-old Aaron McIllvane. Palermo had failed to stop though the elderly man was unconscious and sprawled out on the trolley tracks. McIllvane suffered a possible fractured skull and was in serious condition. Yet the case was quickly "discharged by Magistrate T. Connor."

In January 1948, this fine, upstanding citizen was actually pardoned by the State Board, but on 15 August 1950 he was arrested again and charged with intent to kill after he apparently shot some crooked "pick-up men" who were turning in fake wins to the illegal lottery he was running. He walked again, and the Pennsylvania State Athletic Comission gave him "a clean bill of health" and reinstated his boxing manager's license. Palermo even had top cops showing up to vouch for him.

Palermo had quit school at thirteen to go to work for his family, and the FBI claims his IQ was only ninety-seven, which made him dumb. Yet he kept walking from all these criminal beefs. His second wife, Clair Cori, told the FBI "he was a wonderful family man" and blamed other people who were always saying mean things about him. In October 1962, he was charged with statutory rape. Though the common wisdom was that "fifteen can get you twenty," once again, there was "no disposition in this case." Amazingly, his appeal bond wasn't even revoked, though he had been convicted of racketeering and extortion and was appealing the case.

★ ★ ★

In December 1946, a tough New York racketbuster named Frank Hogan had burst into the headlines by trying to clean up sports. Hogan was inspired by Thomas Dewey, the nemesis of organized crime, and had got some startling wiretaps that revealed that two members of the New York Giants football team had been approached to throw the 1946 NFL championship game with the Chicago Bears. Phonetaps also revealed that boxer Charlie Fusari's long winning streak wouldn't be jeopardised because his fight with veteran contender Chuck Taylor had been fixed.

Rocky Graziano made even bigger news when bettors suddenly began placing huge wads on his opponent, underdog Ruben Shank. Three days before their fight, Graziano suddenly pulled out, claiming a back injury. Hogan subpoeaned Graziano to testify in front of the grand jury and Rocky was forced to admit that he'd been offered $100,000 to lose to Shank, but pulled out because he didn't want to go in the tank. Graziano knew better than to try to double-cross anyone who thought the fix was in. For Graziano, the "Dead End Kid," who had been redeemed by boxing, this wasn't the first approach. Ray Arcel, the gentlemanly trainer, claimed that Stillman's Gym where Rocky trained, "had more criminals than Sing Sing."

In May 1945, Graziano KO'd Al "Bummy" Davis in the fourth round. Davis was eventually murdered resisting a candy store hold-up. Graziano had been offered a bribe in this fight, and there had been two different offers to lose to Shank. Though Graziano was under oath, and faced jailed for contempt for not coming clean, he refused to identify who made the bribe offers. It didn't take much imagination to grasp that it was Frank Carbo.

In February 1947, Graziano's boxing license was suspended in New York. At the time he was one of the hottest properties in boxing. Though Carbo testified in front of the New York State Athletic Commission that he did everything for promoter Mike Jacobs but sign commission contracts, he wasn't charged with anything. All Jacobs got was a pitiful $2,500 fine.

In August 1951, fans were eagerly awaiting the third fight between Billy Graham and Kid Gavilan for the welterweight title. A few days before the August 29 Madison Square Garden fight, Carbo summoned Irving Cohen, who managed Billy. They met at the old Forrest Hotel on 49th Street, a block from the Garden.

"You want your boy should be champ?" Carbo asked.

"Sure, sure," said Cohen, who was very nervous.

"Give me twenty percent – and the title's yours."

Cohen, who looked like an aging cherub, and blushed easily, protested: there wasn't enough for everyone. Jack Reilly had brought him Graham, and he deserved his piece.

"Talk to the fighter," Carbo ordered. "Let him decide."

Soft-spoken Irving spoke to Graham, but Graham, who was one of the finest stylists of his generation and would never hit the canvas in 126 fights, refused to go for it.

"Sure, I wanna be champ," said Billy, "but if I got to turn on Reilly, then the hell with the title."

Cohen reluctantly got back to Carbo. Carbo gave him a cold stare. "Does the kid realize he ain't gonna win?

"Yeah, he knows," said Cohen sadly.

Millions watching on television were treated to a superb contest, and Graham, who hailed from New York, looked like he'd outboxed and outfought the popular "Keed." When ring announcer Johnny Addie announced a split decision in favor of Gavilan, howls echoed throughout the Garden. Referee Mark Conn had it all even at 7-7, but under New York supplemental rules, 10-7 Gavilan. Frank Forbes also had it 7-7, but went for Graham, 11-10 on supplemental points. When Artie Schwartz called it nine rounds to six for Gavilan, irate fans began storming the ring. Graham stood crestfallen, was robbed of his supreme moment, and he'd never be the same fighter again. Years later, as Schwartz lay dying in hospital, he begged Cohen to come to see him. "When I voted for Gavilan, I had to do it," he said. "It's bothered me all these years. The boys ordered me."

★ ★ ★

By 1951, Sugar Ray Robinson was unquestionably the greatest fighter in the world. Only LaMotta had beaten him, and he'd whipped Jake four subsequent times. In 124 fights, only that loss and draws with Henry Brimm and Jose Basora marred his magnificent record. But he admitted carrying opponents, like Charley Fusari. "I never considered it morally wrong," he said.

Robinson was a shrewd businessman, who virtually managed himself. But he could be a soft touch, recalled matchmaker Teddy Brenner. Robinson gave a lot of money to the Damon Rumyon Cancer Fund, and Brenner, the then new in the game, came to him to do a benefit for the Sports Lodge at the B'nai Brith. In September 1950, Robinson fought Billy Brown for just $1,000 and $750 radio rights. Initially Ray protested, "I got $57,000 when I fought Gavilan," but Brenner promised him an "easy fight." It turned into ten rounds of hell. Brown lasted the distance.

Robinson was scheduled to face Jake on 14 February 1951 at the Chicago Stadium, with the middleweight championship of the world on the line. One day, while training in Pompton Lakes, New Jersey, Ray got a call to meet "Mr Gray." Robinson, who owned a block of Harlem and tooled around in his own pink Cadillac, was a regal being, but when Mr Gray called, Robinson remembered, it was a "command performance."

"Ray, you win the first fight. Jake, the second, and the third one's on the level."

Robinson coolly looked at him, and said, "Mr Carbo, that's not the way I do business."

After butchering the Bronx Bull in a savage match later dubbed the "St Valentine's Day Massacre," Robinson faced Rocky Graziano in Chicago in April 1952. Graziano, the legendary tough guy who ended up in Leavenworth Prison and was dishonorably discharged after flattening an army officer, was so scared of Robinson that he nearly left town two days before their fight. Graziano was forced into the fight by his *real* manager, Eddie Coco, an East Side gangster who had a long criminal record going back to 1931. Coco was charged with murder and needed money for lawyers.

A couple of days before the fight, Ray was summoned by the top gangster in Chicago, who he refused to identify, but was probably Tony Accardo.

"Look, we'll give you a million dollars. Graziano wins the first fight. You win the second, and the third one's all square."

"No," said the Sugar Man.

The fight was sensational while it lasted. It packed the Chicago Stadium, and broke box office records for a middleweight championship. Graziano even managed to drop Ray in the third, before the incomparable Robinson knocked him out later in the same round.

Rocky's manager of record, Irving Cohen, was a kind, genial man who set up an annuity for Graziano. Coco was another matter. In 1951, Coco had been in Miami Beach getting his car washed.

Suddenly Coco, a psychopath, pulled out pistol and shot the man dead. Coco was granted bond. Jim Norris who had by then become the biggest promoter in boxing, later claimed, "A lot of pressure was put on me to write a letter, which I considered innocuous, on the behalf of Eddie Coco. I regret it now … I never knew Coco very well. Certainly, we were never intimate friends. But I learned after being in the boxing business … a lot of strange things existed. One was that Graziano would not fight without Coco's consent."

In June 1951, Norris wrote on behalf of a man he claimed he barely knew: "I have known Eddie Coco for a period of about 10 years. In my association with him I have always found him to be a man of his word, well liked and highly respected by many of his friends."

Al Weill also wrote a letter to the judge, after Coco reportedly became the first white man ever convicted in Florida for a killing a black. "I've known Eddie Coco for twenty-five years and I've always found him to be a straight shooter."

The judge didn't think Weill's play on words was funny. Coco got life.

★ ★ ★

Teddy Brenner was a brash kid from Brooklyn who sold papers during the Depression and eventually became one of the great matchmakers. He was a protégé of manager Irving Cohen and followed him slavishly around to fights. Brenner once did 156 straight shows at the old Eastern Parkway Arena in the Fifties, and quickly lost his naivete about the fight game. In May 1938, young Teddy was with Cohen in Garfield, New Jersey. Cohen's boy Edie Alzek was fighting future welterweight champ Freddie Cochrane. The joint was practically empty. The referee came over to Cochrane's corner before the fight, and asked, "What's in it for me?"

"Take a walk," snapped his manager, Willie Gilzenburg. Then the ref walked over Alzek's corner and asked the same thing.

"Geez," protested the ever-polite Cohen, "we're barely making expenses."

The two fighters fought a war for eight rounds. Alzek deserved the nod, but since the crooked ref didn't get paid off, he declared it a draw. "God, what a rotten game this is," moaned Cohen, as he drove home with Brenner.

In September 1948, Bruce Woodcock, Britain's best heavyweight since Tommy Farr, halted Lee Oma at Harringay. Peter Wilson, then Britain's top boxing writer, blasted the contest, and the headline over his story in the *Daily Mirror* was, "Oma! Coma! Aroma!" Brenner agreed it was a "water job" (euphemism for a fix – also known as a "tank job").

In August 1946, heavyweight contender Lee Savold was stopped in two by Elmer "Violent" Ray outdoors at Ebetts Field in Brooklyn. The "ring was very wet though not a drop of rain had fallen," wrote Brenner of this splashdown. Savold would eventually gain British recognition as heavyweight champion of the world after halting Woodcock, but Brenner claims that Savold's reputation was so bad after the Ray fiasco, New York boxing commissioner Eddie Eagan refused to let him fight in Madison Square Garden. Brenner, then assistant matchmaker, pleaded, and bet his license that Savold would perform. In February 1948, the blond heavyweight unleashed a monstrous left hook on Italy's Gino Buonvino and it was all over in fifty-seven seconds. Poor Gino got hit so hard, he crapped his pants. As Garden janitors cleaned up the mess, Savold's manager, Honest Bill Daly, hooted, "We'll fight the sonofabitch again, but next time he's got to wear a diaper."

By 1949 Brenner was the real matchmaker at Madison Square Garden, though Al Weill still held the title. Weill, who was heavily beholden to Carbo, was sick of being harangued by mobsters to put on their fighters. Weill, a "boxing politican" in Brennner's opinion, had all kinds of undercover pieces of pugs. In February 1950, Charley Norkus, a rugged young heavyweight, lost every round to Curt Kennedy, a former national amateur champ from Wichita, Kansas. For some strange reason, Weill kept insisting on a rematch.

"What? Are you crazy!" argued Brenner, who was a purist.

"Look, Jim Norris wants this," insisted Weill.

Finally, Brenner agreed. Irving Brown, a gambler and trainer Freddie Brown's brother, told Brenner that he heard the rematch was fixed. Everybody in the balcony was betting heavily on Norkus. Brenner went to Dan Dowd of the New York commission, and said, "I hear Kennedy's in the water," but he was given assurances that all was well. On 5 April 1950, Norkus lumbered out and threw two left jabs that missed. A third one landed, and Kennedy went down, to thunderous boos.

The next day Weill came to the Garden. The furious Brenner lunged and began choking the life out of him. Weill gagged as his head slammed against the wall, until Harry Markson, the Director of Boxing, heard the commotion and pulled Brenner off. Weill had turned blue. "You set me up!" screamed Brenner, as Weill limply fell to his feet. "I won't work for that fuckin' Weill. If Norris wants me to work here, Weill's got to go!"

Next day, Brenner walked into Jim Norris' office to explain. Norris brushed him off with an aristocratic wave of his well-manicured hand. "The punch looked fine to me." Brenner quit on the spot. He refused to work for Norris again.

Was Norris, a degenerate gambler, in on a betting coup? Kennedy was Blinky Palermo's fighter.

In January 1952, Ernie "the Rock" Durando battered Rocky Castellani into submission in the seventh round. After referee Ray Miller rescued the groggy middleweight, Castellani's manager Tommy Eboli, AKA Tommy Ryan, jumpd into ring and attacked Miller. After security got everything quieted down, Weill wandered into Castellani's dressing room. Eboli, a notorious gangster, jumped Weill and knocked off his glasses as he threw him to the floor. Eboli was finaly pulled off the cowering Weill, and next day strutted into Markson's office to apologize.

Markson, who Brenner likened to "an English professor," took one look at the volatile gangster and told him calmly, "You have just sixty seconds to leave, before I call the police." Eboli tried to protest, but Markson said, "Now, you've got thirty."

Eboli never managed another fighter. One night he went out to see his girlfriend in Brooklyn. Cops found his body in the trunk of a car.

CHAPTER THREE

Octopus Incorporated

"JIM NORRIS WAS a nice guy, but he just had a thing about gangsters," figured Bill Cayton, who then ran his own New York advertising agency, and was worth a million dollars by the time he was thirty.

James Dougan Norris was born on 6 November 1906, and lived at 1420 Lake Shore Drive, on Chicago's posh Gold Coast. As a scion to an enormous fortune, Jim had to get a good education, but he relished getting kicked out of his high-priced prep schools. At nineteen, he bought a stable of race horses. Instead of broadening his mind with literature, Norris buried his aristocratic nose in the *Daily Racing Form*. As he strutted around the stables at Hawthorne, or Washington Park, in suburban Chicago, he was greeted like the prodigal son, inevitably followed by, "Hey Jim, could you lend me a sawbuck?"

Norris was an easy touch who would peel out a hundred, and seldom got it back. In many ways the closest to everyday life that Norris came, even as the Depression ravaged America, was the horseshit he'd always get on his gleaming shoes.

In 1930 the handsome young Norris, looking like something out of *The Great Gatsby*, was enjoying another routine afternoon at a Chicago racetrack. Norris, an indolent twenty-four-year-old, who went to the track a couple of times a week, barely noticed the thousands standing in soup lines.

After driving back to his swank North Side home, he was getting out of his car when three men appeared.

"Give us your money."

Norris, fumbling for a moment in shock, sputtered, "I don't have any money."

"Kill him!"

"No!" one of thugs shouted, and instead they began rifling Norris's pockets.

His expensive clothes were ripped and a pistol was pressed to his head. His heart raced, but he still wouldn't give up his cash. The thugs even checked his socks but couldn't find a dime.

Then one of them noticed Norris's golf bag on the back seat. They dumped out his clubs and found a wad of cash, about $1,000, a fortune in those days for a street crime. They were about to take off with the cash and the golf bag when Norris, who should have been thankful to be alive, pleaded, "Don't take that club. It's very special to me. I won it in a tournament."

Norris was so persuasive, so likeable, one of the robbers asked, "Are you broke?" He gave Norris back $10.

Norris reported the hold-up but couldn't identify the perpetrators. The next day at the track, a spindly, bespectacled man approached him. He looked like an accountant, or a teacher.

"How much they get you for, kid?"

"About eleven hundred," stammered the surprised Norris, who wondered how the man knew.

A couple of days later, Norris was shocked when this nondescript stranger sidled up, and slapped $1100 in Norris's beefy hand. "Golfbag" Sam Hunt was one of the most notorious killers in the Capone mob. He got his nickname not for stealing golfbags but because he often carried his machine gun in one, hidden among the clubs. The joke was that he hollered, "Fore!" as he opened fire.

Norris was the junior partner to his father James and Arthur M. Wirtz, a Chicago real estate tycoon. They "controlled and held sporting interests," recorded the FBI, in the Chicago Stadium, the Detroit Olympia, the St Louis Arena, and later Madison Square Garden, along with the Detroit Redwings and Chicago Blackhawks, two out of the six teams in the National Hockey League.

The FBI noted that Jim Norris, "his father and Wirtz also promoted as far back as 1947 … boxing matches in Chicago and New York."

> The financial interests or Norris are many and varied. In 1947 he was Vice President and Treasurer of the Norris Grain Company with offices at the Produce Exchange Building Chicago, Illinois, and in New York City … In 1947, he was President in the firm of Norris and Kenly, which is a member of the New York Stock Exchange. In 1947 he owned the Springfield Farm, a breeding and racehorse stable, located in Paris, Kentucky.

Though Norris had been involved in the Max Schmeling-Harry Thomas fix in the 1930s, he first came to the FBI's attention in 1947. His confidential FBI file, which runs to approximately 100 pages, does not record a single arrest, but cumbersomely contends that Norris "contributed $10,000 by personal check in (1943) to bail bond money for … one of the Capone mobsters. We are currently investigating allegations of fraud and bribery in granting of … parole August 13, 1947."

He was summoned for an FBI interview. Norris was pleasant and readily volunteered that he'd served as a Lieutenant Commander in the US Navy from 1942 to December 1945. But once the flag-waving was done, the Feds wanted to know, "Why did you post $10,000 of the Norris Grain Company's funds to bail out a Capone mobster?"

"Look, some people came to me, trying to raise the guy's bond," replied Norris.

"What people?"

"I dunno … It's been four years … "

"You don't remember *any* of these people's names?"

"Nope."

The agent persisted. It came out that "a notorious Chicago bookie," Morris Schmertzer, AKA Max Courtney, had told Norris, "Jim, we need your help. We've got to raise a hundred grand to help one of the boys. I'm puttin' you down for ten gees."

Norris arranged through his attorney, J. Arthur Friedland, to come up with the $10,000. They were obviously trying to launder it and bury the expense, so they wouldn't have put it through the Norris Grain Company.

"Did you get the money back?"

"I don't recall," answered Norris, obviously lying.

"How did you know Capone's guy?"

"Look, I've been involved in horse breeding for about fifteen years. He's one of those guys that just hangs around race tracks. He used to come up to me all the time and ask me about my horses. Y'know, he wanted inside stuff, tips."

Norris was a heavy bettor. For fifteen years he had been placing bets with a notorious Mob bookie. Either he was degenerate gambler, or a fool. Perhaps both. By 1949, Jim Norris was forty-three years old yet still hadn't escaped the shadow of his intimidating father. He had his mother's good looks, but she'd been dead since he was a boy. Norris's life was a quiet rebellion against his old man.

His opportunity came when, in January 1948, a dying Mike Jacobs publicly announced he was quitting boxing. Jacobs's meal ticket, Joe Louis, was also on the way out, after scraping a scandalous decision over Jersey Joe Walcott, who had been fired as Louis's sparring partner. Walcott had Joe on the deck twice, but the decision went to the champ. Amid a storm of boos, Louis went to his opponent and said, "I'm sorry, Joe." At sixty-seven, Jacobs dreamed of Florida, lying in the sun and raising his adopted daughter, who was just four. But neither Jacobs nor Louis would bow out till the rematch with Walcott in June 1948.

Louis harnessed the last ounce of his dying youth and knocked out the shifty Walcott in the eleventh round at Yankee Stadium. In his dressing room afterwards, Louis, who was always more nervous of speaking in public than of his opponent's fists, said simply, "I've been around long enough, and I think it's about time I quit." After a record twenty-five defences, despite missing four years because of the War, the Brown Bomber was hanging up his gloves at thirty-four.

But Louis had huge money problems. The man sportswriter Jimmy Cannon called "a credit to his race – the human race" had shamefully been hit by the IRS for tax on two purses he had given to the Army and Navy Relief Funds. Sol Strauss, Mike Jacobs's lawyer-cousin, had also screwed up Louis's divorce to Marva, and the IRS gouged him on that settlement too. Though Louis was prohibited from fighting during the war, the IRS interest kept snowballing because he had no income. Though he had earned around $4 millon in his career, Louis owed approximately $600,000, with no way to pay it back.

Harry Mendel, a roly-poly press agent, came up with a brilliant idea. He conceived Joe Louis Enterprises, which would sign the four leading heavyweight contenders to determine Louis's successor. Like a medieval alchemist, Mendel had conjured something out of nothing. After a Florida hotel owner decided against bankrolling the plan, Mendell suggested Jim Norris. Louis, Mendel and Truman Gibson, a pale, strikingly handsome black lawyer, met with Norris on a golf course in Florida. Though both Louis and Norris loved golf, Norris's eyes had become mournful and pouchy, and he was hung over after another bout of drinking.

"It sounds good," Norris said, after hearing Gibson and Mendel outline their plan. "But I want to run it by my partner first."

Arthur Wirtz, a University of Michigan graduate, negotiated long and hard with the increasingly desperate Louis. And so the International Boxing Club was born. Though the IBC became the "Rosemary's Baby" of the sport, Louis got $150,000 in cash, $100,000 less than he wanted, and a twenty per cent stake in the IBC. But Wirtz, who was adept at creating dummy corprorations, kept funnelling their profits elsewhere, and would make sure the IBC's boxing revenue actually made five or six pitstops before it trickled down to Louis.

Proving that a smart accountant can steal a lot better than John Dillinger or Bonnie and Clyde, the IBC's books actually showed a loss, or a couple of hundred dollars profit, before Louis resigned in 1953. Louis's financial problems should have been resolved but he was forced to make a disastrous comeback. He got trounced by new champ Ezzard Charles in 1950 and hadn't even had time to fully train for the outdoor bout, held quickly at Yankeee Stadium before cold weather set in. By October 1951, Louis, fighting from memory, couldn't fire his right hand anymore, and got blasted out of the ring by young, undefeated Rocky Marciano, who Nat Fleischer said would've lasted just a couple of rounds when Louis was in his prime.

By 1956, Louis ended up a pro wrestler. If being part of sweaty burlesque wasn't bad enough, he actually showed up on a TV quiz show with his new wife, where it was announced, "Trying to pay his back taxes ... here's former heavyweight champion, Joe Louis!" As he slowly spiralled into drug addiction and eventual madness, he was admitted to a mental hospital. He told his third wife, Martha, "I'm on a Mafia hit list," and would arrange his bed so he could see anyone coming. He'd huddle under the blankets like it was a tent, and peer out furtively. He got so bad he smeared mayonnaise on cracks in the walls so "they won't hear me talking."

The IBC however, prospered mightily. In June 1949, Ezzard Charles outboxed Walcott for the NBA title, and the IBC began a period of promotional domination. It would eventually be dubbed "Octopus Incorporated." With Norris's immense wealth, and Wirtz also worth a good $50-75 million, they had financial muscle that nobody in boxing history has ever matched. Television had also arrived and boxing sold millions of "magic boxes."

As TV boxing boomed, the Managers' Guild in New York demanded its piece. In April 1949, it struck for the then "outrageous" TV fee of $1,000 for every pug who appeared in a main event on a major televised show. The fee had previously been $212.80. In 1950, the Guild went on strike again. There was no boxing for two months at the Garden, except for the middleweight title clash between Jake La Motta and Italy's Tiberio Mitri. As problems with the Guild increased, both Norris and Wirtz kept worrying, "We're going to blow our TV contract."

Jack Kearns and "Honest" Bill Daly were two of the leaders of the Guild. Kearns was so concerned about fighters' rights that he actually signed a *blank* contract with London promoter Jack Solomons when his fighter Joey Maxim knocked out champion Freddie Mills in 1950. "Kearns spent all his money, and most of mine," recalled Maxim, who had 115 professional fights, seven of them for world championships, but ended up a cab driver and bellhop.

Daly was a notorious front for Frankie Carbo. But Carbo, playing both sides, reached out to Norris, promising "labour peace." Norris, now firmly in bed with the devil, made payoffs to Kearns and "Tex" Pelte, $135,000 over the next three years. Carbo, who got a big piece, greedily wanted more. So the IBC, through one of Wirtz's front companies, the Neville Advertising Agency, paid Miss Viola Masters $40,000 a year. This was about fifteen times what the average working woman would make, but Viola Masters was Frankie Carbo's girlfriend.

By 1951, the IBC had three televised shows a week. There was a minor show on Monday from the St Nicholas Arena in New York. On Wednesday, Pabst Blue Ribbon brought fights from Chicago, and on Friday, there were matches from Madison Square Garden.

* * *

In 1951, Ike Williams was the lightweight champion of the world, a brilliant boxer-puncher from Trenton, New Jersey. "I'm not being conceited," he said, decades later, as he prepared for induction into Boxing's Hall of Fame, "but on my best night, I think I could've whipped any lightweight that ever lived."

In the 1930s, when Ike was growing up, a sporty black youngster's dreams were limited. You couldn't play major league baseball, there was no pro basketball, and pro football was still a fledgling enterprise. "One night in 1933, I was reading the *Trenton Evening Times* newspaper, and I saw a picture of this old-time boxer who'd just died. His name was Jim Corbett. When I saw that picture of him, that's when I became a fighter. I was just nine years old."

Williams turned pro in March 1940 at sixteen. He boxed mostly around Trenton and other soot-blackened cities in New Jersey, but by 1943, he was fighting all over the Eastern Seaboard and was *Ring's* sixth best lightweight for the year. In January 1944, he tangled with the "Bobcat," Bob Montgomery. "He was truly one of the all-time great lightweights. We'd been very good friends," recalled Ike, who spoke very precisely, with an amazing accuracy for dates. "But in 1943, I fought his friend Johnny Hutchinson. I knocked Johnny out. Bob was sittin' at ringside and that ended our friendship. He and I fought January 24, 1944, and Bob gave me a vicious beating, knocking me out in the twelfth round. We had a return match three or four years later [4 August 1947 for the unified world title], and I returned the favour. We were never really good friends after that."

On 18 April 1945, Williams won the NBA version of the lightweight championship, knocking out Juan Zurita at the *Circo de Toros* bullring in Mexico City. "It was right around the time President Roosevelt died. I knocked Zurita out in the second round, and the Mexicans resented it. On my way to the dressing rooom, two Mexicans came up and said, 'Gimme the belt.'

"My manager Connie McCarthy said, 'I don't have any belt.'

"I told my manager, 'Give the man the damn belt!' They was gonna kill us."

In September 1946, Williams faced British champ Ronnie James at Ninian Park in Cardiff, Wales. Britain's biggest promoter, Jack Solomons, staged the outdoor match as war-weary Britain struggled to get back on her feet. Solomons, a homely, round-faced man who Mickey Duff claimed was "ruthless" but "did business with a smile," felt Ike was a difficult, spoiled character, "used to getting what he wanted." Despite years of war-time austerity, Williams kept demanding fruit juices during training. Solomons finally told him, "Bloody God, Ike, we haven't even seen an orange since the war!"

"I want some juice!" Ike shouted angrily, and Solomons was forced to go to the US Embassy in London to get the champ his nutritious drinks.

Though Williams was champion, racism was a big problem and Ike had trouble even finding decent lodging. He also fought constantly with his manager, Connie McCarthy. It was obvious to Solomons that they hated each other. McCarthy was a drunk. "That bloody sod never leaves my liquor cabinet," claimed Solomons.

Days before the fight, torrential downpours seemed certain to cause a cancellation, but hours before the match was to begin, the sun broke through and workmen were happily getting double time as they laid down planks of wood, while spectators gingerly made their way to their seats. Williams boxed with regal diffidence. As he rose from his stool before the seventh round, Solomons heard him say, "Time to go to work." He knocked James out with a wicked left hook to the liver.

"When we came back to LaGuardia Airfield (in New York)," Williams recalled, "I told the newspapermen, 'Gentlemen, from now on either I'm doin' my own business or I'm gettin' a new manager.

"McCarthy was a good manager," Ike remembered, "but he put whiskey before me. It started when I was in Mexico City and fought Zurita for the championship. McCarthy was drunk every day. When I fought Ronnie James, he was drunk every day. He signed me to fight James, but I told him, 'I'm not signing another contract.'

"Connie McCarthy then took it to the Manager's Guild. They blackballed me, I couldn't get any fights. They said, 'If any promoters give Ike Williams a fight, we're not going to let our fighters fight for him. If any fighter fights him, he's blackballed too.'"

Williams didn't box again until January 1947 in Chicago, when he faced clever Gene Burton, and surprisingly lost a non-title ten. In the interim, Frank "Blinky" Palermo came along.

"He was my real downfall," Williams said, shaking his sadly, as he stopped to reflect. "Palermo said, 'You can't get any fights. Sign a contract with me, and I'll straighten it out with the Guild.' I couldn't get any fights," insisted Ike, "so I signed a contract with him. He paid me some money … but that's the worst man I ever seen in my life."

Williams, a surprisingly well-preserved old man then in his seventies, shook his grey-flecked head, and gave an involuntary whistle. "Boxing was controlled by crime. I'd say fifty to seventy per cent of it was. They just stole money. That's all they wanted. I made almost a million dollars, but two (championship) fights that I had, I never saw a penny."

On 25 May 1948, Ike defended his lightweight title against Enrique Bolanos before a big outdoor crowd at Los Angeles' Wrigley Field. It was supposed to be one of "my largest purses," but Ike didn't get paid.

Six weeks later in Philadelphia, against Beau Jack, "The only thing I got out of it, I had a perfect set of teeth and he knocked one of 'em out."

Though Ike vehemently complained to Palermo, the Philadelphia gangster barked, "Shut up. I owe people. Ya tryin' to get both of us killed." Williams even had to pay income tax on the $65,000 he never saw.

Williams claimed in 1960, before the Kefauver Committee, that he turned down four offers to throw fights that totalled a then staggering $230,000. Ike said that he turned down $100,000 to dive against Kid Gavilan in 1949, though he lost him to twice anyway, and KO'd Juste Fontaine in Philadelphia in 1947, instead of laying down.

He also refused to go into the tank against Freddie Dawson. But while Ike was in his dressing room before the bout at Convention Hall in Philadelphia, word suddenly came down that his crown was going to be stolen by dishonest officials. Williams, who was a smart guy, sent a fast message to sportswriters Red Smith, Jack Sarnes and John Webster: "After I fight tonight, come back. I'll have a story for you." The judges got word of what happened, so there was no bum decision. Williams gave Dawson a bad beating, and got the unanimous verdict, but Leo Raines, who was chairman of the Pennsylvania State Athletic Commission, fined Ike $500 for casting doubt on the integrity of the officials. Raines was a good friend of Palermo's. Blinky had even paid his way to California to see an earlier Williams fight.

Though Ike had defended his title often, he ended up broke. He went nearly a year and a half before he put his championship on the line again. In a big upset, he was knocked out in the fourteenth round in Madison Square Garden, by Jimmy Carter, on 25 May 1951. Beforehand, Williams turned down another bribe offer. The fight drew just 3,594 fans into the TV-ravaged Garden.

Carter was handled by a Mob-connected manager named Willie Ketchum. His real name was Willie Friedlander; he got the name "Ketchum" because mobsters looking for good fighters used to send him out with the instructions, "You catch 'em, Willie." Carter was a good fighter, but strangely won and lost the lightweight title three times. When he challenged Williams, his purse was just $3,627. Without TV, it would've been an even more pathetic $1,377. Carter had 120 fights, and was stopped only three times, but ended up working twenty years at an animal shelter in Hollywood before his death in the late 1990s. There wasn't enough money even to bury him back home in Aiken, South Carolina. "I love animals," Carter said a few years before his passing. "They're kind, they're not like people."

Freddie Dawson was more expansive. "Man, they 'd cut your manager down to ten per cent," Dawson remembered in 1977, sitting in the old Windy City Gym where he once sweated and dreamed in the days when it was Coulon's Gym. "You could not fight in a big arena like the Garden, or Chicago Stadium, without having a connected manager. Now, you could fight in these little clubs like Marigold. Sure, you could do that all you wanted, but to make any money, you had to fight in the big places, like the Stadium or the Garden and on television. Man, they had that all tied up."

Finally, Dawson got tired of his purses being carved up and went to Australia. He had twenty-one fights. "It was wonderful. Oh man, the women," Freddie said, suddenly lost in the past. "I was treated like a king. I made money. The fans loved me."

Aussie sportswriters called him the "greatest fighter ever to fight Down Under," high praise, considering Jack Johnson stopped Tommy Burns for the heavyweight title there in 1908, and Archie Moore, the Ancient Mariner of the prize ring, had campaigned there. Freddie was so big, one boxing magazine advertised a mail order course that shouted,, "Learn How to Box like Freddie Dawson!" But after nearly killing Aussie hero Vic Patrick in a fight, Dawson got a detached retina and lost an eye.

He spent the next twenty years kicking around Chicago's bleak South Side. Finally, Dawson was either drunk and fell, or was thrown from an elevated train platform, and crashed heavily to the pavement a good thirty feet down. The *Chicago Sun-Times* reported his death. "He didn't die," insisted Owen Putnam, an amateur boxer who was briefly trained by Dawson. "But when I went to see him in the hospital, he'd been in a coma and didn't know who I was."

★ ★ ★

Heavyweight Coley Wallace agreed that Carbo controlled boxing but you had to go through Palermo to get to him. Twice, that he knows of, Palermo beat him out of his purse money. "He ruined boxing for me," Wallace said. He got just $3,000 of the $20,000 he was promised for fighting Ezzard Charles, and didn't get paid at all after beating Bill Gilliam at the Eastern Parkway Arena.

Wallace bore a striking facial resemblance to Joe Louis, and portrayed the great champion in the low-budget film *The Joe Louis Story.* He was a good boxer, who easily beat Rocky Marciano as an amateur in the 1948 Eastern Olympic Trials, but could never get a shot at Rocky's title as a pro.

"I wanna fight Marciano," he told Palermo.

"Ya do? Well, ya gotta take a dive."

"Forget it," said Wallace, "I got my pride."

Beau Jack earned $1.3 million and was Madison Square Garden's biggest draw during World War Two. In February 1947, he broke his leg against Tony Janiro but kept hobbling forward, like a fighting cock with a broken wing, trying to throw punches. "Were it a good fight?" he asked between sobs, after it was stopped in the fourth.

Beau couldn't read or write and was fleeced out of his money. The "Georgia Shoeshine Boy" ended up back shining shoes. One day in 1961, fight manager Cus D'Amato was shocked to see him at the posh Fountainbleau Hotel in Miami.

"Shine, sir," said the ever-polite Beau, but D'Amato, then one of the most powerful men in boxing as heavyweight champ Floyd Patterson's manager, refused to get into his chair.

"No," insisted D'Amato, as he dropped in front of Jack. "I'll shine your shoes. *You* were the lightweight champion of the world."

In February 1953, Kid Gavilan, one of the best fighters in the sport, badly battered Chuck Davey into defeat in the tenth round in defense of his welterweight championship. The one-sided match, held at the Chicago Stadium, broke box office records for the division. Poor Davey almost did a cartwheel as he was sent to the canvas. Davey, who was really the first "TV glamour boy," had been so popular, one poll named him the "second favorite athlete on television."

Yet fight guys didn't think Davey could fight. The slender strawberry blond had a fast, pecking southpaw style and could move like hell for ten rounds, but his biggest plus was that he was a clean-cut college boy who had graduated from Michigan State. Rocky Graziano lost his last fight to Davey, and later joked, "I didn't realize I was an actor till I fought Chuck Davey."

Journalist Jack Newfield says that Davey's win over Ike Williams was fixed, though there's no evidence to support that. Tom King, who was involved in Davey's management, said in 1980, just before he chaired Senator Edward Kennedy's Illinois bid to unseat President Jimmy Carter, "Williams was through. That's why we took the fight."

Davey was finished as a contender after Gavilan. He became a million-aire insurance mogul, but broke his neck in a body surfing accident just a few years ago, and is paralysed from the neck down. In a tragic case of *déjà vu,* the pretty young nurse who tended to him in the hospital after the Gavilan slaughter, married him, and looks after him today.

In August 1953, six months after the Davey-Gavilan match, the FBI interviewed Jim Norris again. According to the files, Norris "volunteered" that a certain gentleman "occasionally gets in touch with him" and "asks of Norris the favour of finding a spot in a Madison Square Garden bout for some manager friend. Norris said he often did this favour and as a result has an understanding that in the event (deleted) receives information regarding an attempted or actual 'fix' of a fight (deleted) will advise Norris." Of course, Norris was just bullshitting the FBI. This fine gentleman was Frankie Carbo, and Norris had been seen with him.

* * *

In September 1953, Carmen Basilio, a craggy, battle-scarred ex-onion farmer from Canastota, New York, became only the second man who would ever knock down Kid Gavilan in 143 fights. But he lost a fifteen-round decision to "the Keed" in Syracuse, New York. "I thought I won," recalled Basilio, "but the judges gave it to Gavilan. The decision caused quite a stink. A lot of TV fans thought I won."

A year later, Gavilan faced Johnny Saxton in Philadelphia. "Johnny Saxton may be an orphan, but no one can say he lacks for cousins in Philadelphia," bristled Budd Schulberg, then writing a hard-hitting weekly boxing column for *Sports Illustrated.* "Referee Pete Pantaleo and judges Jim Mina and Nat Lopinson … gave the defending champion, Kid Gavilan, the treatment a GOP candidate expects in Mississippi. They voted the straight Saxton-Palermo ticket." Schulberg contended that Pantaleo's scoring was so biased that he awarded Saxton "even those rounds in which he failed to throw a single punch." Gavilan protested bitterly in his dressing room, then went to see Carbo, who was at the fight.

"My managers say I have to talk to you about a rematch," said the normally fun-loving Keed.

There would be no return.

Saxton lost the title to bomb-throwing Tony DeMarco in Boston in 1955. Basilio then knocked out DeMarco in a Cro-Magnon contest to finally win the title. After the bout ended, he dropped to his knees, said a prayer and cried in the ring. The brawl drew a hefty $119,794, and Basilio's manager, John DeJohn, later admitted that he had to give Carbo $10,000 right off the top or there'd be no fight.

"He knew within a thouand dollars what a fight would draw," claimed boxing manager Bernie Glickman.

Basilio had been getting the brush-off for years because he wouldn't "do business with the boys." In March 1956, Saxton got another crack at the welterweight title, and won a shocking fifteen-rounder over Basilio in the

Chicago Stadium. "I just can't get a decision in Chicago," Basilio moaned to his managers, Joe Netro and DeJohn. Carmen subsequently knocked Saxton out in nine, and then in two, to cement his hold on the championship. Though Basilio would be lauded for failing to knuckle under to Carbo, in 1961 it was revealed that the vicious, white-haired gangster had actually extorted nearly $80,000 of his purses.

In March 1959, just eighteen months after he was destroyed by Basilio, Johnny Saxton was charged with burglary. Though Saxton had reputedly grossed $250,000 during his stint as a fighter, all he got was $5.20 out of the crime.

"Johnny, where did all your money go?" asked an incredulous judge.

"I didn't get much of it," Saxton replied, sheepishly.

The man once called the "new Sugar Ray" was committed to the Ancora State Hospital in New Jersey. He was just twenty-nine. "No one ever gave me more than a couple of hundred dollars at a time," Saxton later sobbed to a reporter who came to visit him. "Now, I'm here in the hospital. That's what boxing did for me."

Saxton was eventually released, but in the 1990s, long after Norris and Carbo were gone, the former welterweight champion of the world was homeless in Florida.

★ ★ ★

On 16 May 1955, Rocky Marciano hammered brave Don Cockell into submission in nine brutal, foul-filled rounds in San Francisco. Half of Britain stayed up into the early hours of the morning to listen to Cockell's hopeless challenge. Radio commentator Eamon Andrews, who got splattered with Cockell's blood, finally bristled, "Marciano is one of the toughest champions who ever rubbed a foot in resin, but he has never read the rule books. He played a different sport from the one Cockell was taught. He butted unmercifully, he hit with the elbows, he hit low. A British referee would have sent him to his corner after three rounds."

Teddy Waltham, who eventually headed the Board of Control, agreed. "Oh, Rocky, you were so dirty! I'd have disqualified you," he told Marciano in 1965. Rocky believed in winning at all costs, even against a roly-poly punching bag like Cockell, who was only fighting at heavyweight, because he had a glandular condition that caused him to gain weight.

After the appalling match, Marciano told listeners, "England can be proud of Don Cockell. I hit this guy something awful."

Cockell, who later lost his voice to throat cancer, was surprisingly charitable, considering what he'd been through: "He didn't foul deliberately: it was the way he fought. Mind you, he was a bit deaf when it came to hearing the bell."

Marciano behaved like he was in a back alley. He kidney-punched Cockell in the first. In the third, he belted the podgy Brit after the bell. In the fourth, Rocky's head opened a gash on Cockell's forehead, and Don was again hit low in the fifth and sixth. He was also slugged *three times* after the bell. In round seven, Marciano butted and whacked him downstairs again. In the ninth, Cockell was even bashed while he was on the floor. Yet, referee Frank Brown saw nothing. He never even issued a warning.

Marciano's purse was $130,124. Brown, who got $1,000 to "officiate" the fight, received the highest fee ever paid to a California official. There was no way Carbo was going to let the challenger win.

A couple of days earlier, Marciano had been in his hotel room when another gangster said excitedly to him, "Hey Rocky, why don't you throw the fight? We could get some bets down. Think of all the money we'd make."

Marciano absolutely recoiled at the suggestion. "You disgust me," he spat out. "Don't ever come around me again."

Marciano was a very popular champion. Italian-Americans worshipped him. Gangsters revelled in his presence, and even the Mob didn't want him sullied. But that didn't mean that Carbo and his manager Al Weill weren't going to steal off him.

A week before the Cockell clash, Truman Gibson of the IBC wrote Jimmy Murray, the show's local promoter, that "my understanding of the deal with you on the fight is – $10,000 off the top of the promoter's percentage ·which will be charged to you for services." In California Governor Goodwin Knight's investigation on boxing, Knight's special consultant, James E. Cox, claimed that this ten grand went straight into Weill's pocket, without Marciano knowing about it.

Would Weill have stolen off Carbo? Probably, but he risked getting killed. More likely, this was Carbo's payoff so the fight could proceed. Ten grand was the usual figure Carbo demanded before he'd give his blessing to a big fight.

During the California investigation, Murray refused to admit who this ten grand was for. He told at least three different stories, all of which were disproved. Sweating under oath, Murray lied, equivocated, and even claimed he gambled it away. He never honoured the subpoena for the check, while the person who cashed it, conveniently forgot who it was made payable to. Since the $10,000 cheque didn't go through a clearinghouse in San Francisco, it wasn't microfilmed.

In April 1956, Marciano surprised everyone by announcing his retirement. He had knocked out Archie Moore the previous September in a war that officially drew $948,117, the biggest gate in decades, but Rocky was furious about Weill's theft of the ten grand. "I believe Al's an honest guy," Marciano told a press conference after the story broke, but deep down, he knew differently.

Rocky Marciano was an American hero but was so pathologically cheap that he once gave Willie Pep hell for picking up a dinner tab, claiming, "You're making me look bad." As host of a 1961 TV show, *The Main Event*, he'd show up at the studio in old ratty clothes every week, forcing producers to spring for a new suit just so he could go on, swore scriptwriter Jimmy Breslin. At the end of his life, Rocky was crazily stuffing bags of money in water pipes to hide his loan sharking cash, and was nearly indicted by the IRS. In some bizarre way, Ricky was still a poor shoemaker's son from Brockton, Massachusetts, and this was one sick aspect to how Carbo and Weill stole off him.

"That guy's taken enough money off me," Rocky bitterly once said of Carbo, whom he feared but wouldn't confront. Rocky may have retired the only undefeated heavyweight champion in history, but the podgy Weill routinely used to slap his face, and Rocky actually ended up fronting a New York restaurant for Carbo, claims Lou Duva, who was Rocky's good friend. Marciano absolutely loathed Weill.

It all ended when Rocky was decapitated in a tragic 1969 plane crash. Or did it? Marciano behaved erratically in the last years of his life, and told friends he couldn't take cash because Weill was still getting half of everything. It wasn't Weill, or Carbo: it was the Mob. Before his death, Rocky used to coo to his cute, "mod" teenage daughter, Mary Ann, "One day little girl, you're going to be very, very rich." But he was so secretive, nobody could find even his insurance policies after his death. By her forties, Mary Ann Marciano was slinging hamburgers at a Burger King, and got so hooked on drugs, she was even implicated in an armed robbery. By the 1990s, she was a sad, obese, cement-block of a woman.

* * *

On 25 April 1956, the International Boxing Club went on trial in New York City for anti-trust (monopoly). It was a beautiful Wednesday morning, redolent with spring, and the handsome, well-dressed Jim Norris seemed unconcerned as he sat with Arthur Wirtz. General Reed Kirkpatrick of Madison Square Garden was there, and so were Ned Irish, Truman Gibson and Harry Markson.

Most people in boxing had thought this glorious day would never come. Since 1952, the Department of Justice had been kicking the case around but some at "Justice" even wondered whether professional boxing fell within the scope of interstate commerce. Since *professional* athletes crossed state lines, and paid income tax on the earnings, that should've answered the question in 1952, but it took four long years before the federal government, (the Republican, pro-business, Eisenhower administration, no less) finally challenged Norris's ruthless abuse of power, and overcame a Norris appeal to do so.

In 1955, Norris and a manager, Hymie "The Mink" Wallman, testified in front of the New York State Athletic Commission that they had only a "social relationship" with Carbo. Norris absurdly claimed that he didn't even know Carbo had a criminal record, but if Norris was ridiculously naive, figured Julius Helfand, head of the New York commission, and never bothered to ask what Carbo did for a living in the twenty years he admittedly knew him, the FBI knew.

"Frankie Carbo, born as Paolo Corbo, 8/10/04, NY, NY, FBI #187-972, resides at 2637 Taft Street, Hollywood, Florida [read a confidential 1957 FBI report that originated in Miami]. Prior to 1941, he reportedly had been a business associate of Robert Walsh, Seattle, Washington, who ran food concessions at race tracks on West Coast." In 1955, it was reported that Carbo was in New Orleans with Frank Costello and was involved in the running of race track that ultimately went bankrupt. Costello, dubbed the "Prime Minister" of the Underworld, was one of the founders of the national crime syndicate in the United States, Through payoffs and political influence, mostly in New York City, his multi-million dollar rackets were protected from prosecution. Costello had a cool head, and still served on the national crime commission, which mediated disputes, but had wisely gone to prison in August 1952 for refusing to answer Senator Estes Kefauver's probing questions on organized crime.

"Frank Costello, currently under investigation in New York division as top hoodlum. Carbo was reportedly one of his top killers in 1946, and stayed with him at the same New Orleans hotel in 1955," contended one FBI file.

"Carbo reportedly a member of the crime syndicate in New York City, and (said) to control the boxing racket," read another. "He reportedly fixes fights for gambling benefit and had been reported to control various crap games and bookmaking. In 1953, it was reported his New York mob was taking over prostitution, 'junk' traffic, gambling, and bookmaking in Miami, Florida.

"Caution: Because of his past record of homicides by gun and reported association with other top hoodlums, subject should be considered dangerous … He reportedly always has a bodyguard with him."

By the 1950s, Carbo, was a short, dusky, round-faced gent, who favoured fedoras and black glasses. He was immaculately attired, but his big brown eyes were dead. According to the FBI, "The records (name deleted) show on May 24, 1942, the subject claimed to have been self-employed as a booking agent for prizefighters since 1934, giving his business addresse c/o Al Weill, Strand Building, 1585 Broadway,"

Carbo claimed he was "best suited" to be a chauffeur, but when he was arrested for vagrancy in June 1944, he said he was in the dress business. In October 1955, the New York gangster was "listed as a public relations chief of Lincoln Beach, a negro amusement park." It must have been a tough daily commute. The park was in New Orleans.

Though nobody in boxing ever saw Carbo holding a job, he stayed at the finest hotels in New York and ate in the best restaurants, Somehow, Paul J. Carbo owed the Internal Revenue a staggering $741,022 by April 1955. This was just for the years 1944, 1945, 1946, 1951, and 1952. Carbo had been finally served "for unpaid federal income taxes" in January 1954 at the luxurious Hotel Lexington in New York City, yet wasn't indicted for income tax evasion. Frank Costello's political influence certainly helped. Joe Louis, a legend and inspiration to millions, was going mad trying to pay his back taxes. Yet, Carbo, a career criminal and hitman for the Mob, deemed unsuitable for Army service in 1942 because he had a "psychopathic personality and a perforated eardrum," kept getting a free pass.

Carbo also stiffed the states of Florida and New York on $10,000 more in various taxes, yet the closest the Feds came to actually indicting him for his brazen tax evasion came in November 1957, when the United States Attorney in Miami requested collection, and a judgement was finally filed against Carbo in New York City for $23,803. It was never paid, yet Carbo was still on the street. It was incredible.

On 22 November 1947, Carbo and two companions, fight managers Jimmy Doyle and Frank Marino, were arrested for breaking up the bar in the Hotel Markwell, and for refusing to leave after closing time. Charges were quickly dropped after the hotel declined to prosecute. Carbo was running an illegal gambling book out of the bar.

Waterfront gangster Johnny Dio, under close scrutiny by the FBI, was "described as a syndicate associate of Carbo in 1953. Tommy Dio, "fight manager, (was) reportedly fronting for Carbo in 1946."

"Vito Genovese … reportedly head of the New York crime syndicate (was) over Carbo in 1953," asserted the FBI.

In March 1953, one FBI informant who had "furnished reliable information in the past, advised that Frankie Carbo is an accepted member of the crime-controlling 'Mafia,' or 'Syndicate,' which is allegedly controlled by Vito Genovese or Thomas 'Three Fingers Brown' Luchese. He described Carbo as a fight promoter and manager of various fighters owned entirely by the Syndicate. He added that Carbo controls all betting and gambling in midtown New York City sports activities."

Carbo was far more influential than anyone realized. Charles "Lucky" Luciano, who turned organized crime into a huge business in America, and who was at Bugsy Siegel's New York hotel room with Carbo in 1934, "has been reported as going to meet with Carbo in Havana, Cuba, soon."

Snitches also told the FBI that "George Raft, movie actor, who helped show friends of Carbo around town on his visit to Los Angeles in approximately 1937 … was reported in December 1957, to be going to a meeting with Lucky Luciano in Havana, Cuba," where Carbo "would also be present."

During his half-century in boxing, fight film mogul, manager and TV producer Bill Cayton met a lot of gangsters, including Luciano. "I could do business with anybody because I was honest," he recalled. "They looked down on Carbo."

But in June 1946, an FBI snitch reported that "Carbo, whom he described as one of the principal killers for Siegel, Costello and (Joe) Adonis, is considered reliable and fearless by them."

Federal Judge Sylvester J. Ryan presided over the IBC's antitrust case in the spring of 1956. The FBI had plenty of damning information in its files in 1952 and 1953, but this info wouldn't make its way into the antitrust trial. It had come from a "private agency concerned with crime conditions," and was also given by a "confidential source" who had been around the fight game for "many years." This source told the FBI:

> Mobsters managed all the fighters, and assigned exclusive promotion rights to the International Boxing Club. Monday night Dumont (network) telecasts and Saturday night ABC television programs, are also from mob controlled arenas, where none but mob owned fighters are featured. The only way you can get top notch boxers to perform for you is to cut in the mob and IBC.

The source listed the following mob promotions:

Rocky Marciano, heavyweight champion through (deleted) Al Weill.
Jersey Joe" Walcott, ex-heavyweight champion through (deleted) Felix
 Bochchiccio.
Joe Louis.
Archie Moore, light heavyweight champion through (deleted) Jack Kearns
 and Charley Johnston.
Joey Maxim, light heavyweight through (deleted) Kearns.
Carl 'Bobo' Olson, middleweight through Carbo.
'Kid' Gavilan, controlled by Carbo.
Johnny Bratton, welterweight through (deleted) Hymie 'the Mink' Wallman.
Gil Turner, welterweight (deleted) George Katz.

Billy Graham, welterweight, (deleted) fronting for Carbo.
Jimmy Carter, lightweight champion, through (deleted) Willie Ketchum,
    fronting for Carbo.
'Sandy' Saddler, featherweight champion, deleted (through Charley Johnston)
Willie Pep and Danny Nardico ... (deleted) Lou Viscusi for Carbo.
Jake LaMotta, middleweight controlled by Carbo.

The overwhelming majority would end up broke.

> Carbo also had Solly Krieger ... who won the middleweight title from Al
> Hostak (in 1938), and that for years Carbo's main sphere was the
> middleweight championship, which he kept bottled up in Seattle with cham-
> pions Freddie Steele and Al Hostak.

In September and October 1953, this intriguing source claimed "that Carbo
owns outright, enough fighters and managers to arrange boxing matches to
his own liking. He controls the fight manager's Guild and managers have to
cater to him to get fights for their boxers."

Middleweight Ray Robinson was the only important fighter of the
post-war era who was able to remain free of hoodlum control and the
mMob did everything it could to get him licked.

In New York City, the evidence of the IBC's cancerous monopoly was
mounting up. As Jim Norris sat in the courtroom, gazing sternly, William J.
Elkins, a deceptively frail-looking man, hammered away for the
Government. He proved that Norris and Wirtz had promoted eighty per
cent of all the world championship fights from June 1949 through May
1953. The other twenty percent didn't mean much: American television
wasn't interested in bantams or flyweights. With just $165,000 in seed
money, Norris had signed the top heavyweights to exclusive contracts, and
held a stranglehold on the sport. Records showed that Norris and Wirtz
were generating millions with their far-flung empire. With no access to TV,
other promoters found it impossible to compete.

As the trial proceeded, Norris knew the IBC's control of major arenas
like Madison Square Garden, the Chicago Stadium, the Detroit Olympia,
and the St Louis Arena would harm his case. Luckily much-respected trainer
Ray Arcel didn't testify, like he might have in a criminal case. Arcel's skull
was crushed with metal pipes in a Boston street after he tried to buck the
system. Much of the Feds' case was presented in cold, clinical documenta-
tion, and the lack of a human factor hurt the Government.

Samuel Becker was a good, effective witness for the Government. He was
an ageing Cincinatti clothing manufacturer who had promoted many of
Ezzard Charles's early fights but found himself in Siberia after Charles beat

Joey Maxim in 1949. Becker wanted to promote Charles against Jersey Joe Walcott, but Becker testified that Norris told him, "If you want to promote Walcott and Charles … you have to give me $150,000. Then I can turn the fight over to you."

"Why all the money?" sputtered Becker, who was flabbergasted. "I've promoted Charles since he was fourteen years old."

"Well, Charles and Walcott belong to me," replied Norris.

When Charles finally defeated Walcott in Chicago in June 1949, the live gate, in the second largest city in the country, was only $246,546. Radio and TV increased it to $281,000. Had Becker, or anyone, paid Norris $150,000 just for the rights to stage the fight, he'd have drowned in red ink.

Judge Ryan was obviously touched by Becker's testimony. At one point, the elderly promoter said, "I just celebrated my fifty-first year in the clothing business."

Ryan, a rather scholarly, bespectacled Irish-American with a gentle sense of humor, cracked, "Mazel tov," and the courtroom erupted in laughter. Norris sat there, as stiff as the sphinx.

Doug Michaels, a promoter from Buffalo, New York, took it on the chin when he presented Charles against Freddie Beshore in August 1950. Michaels contended that he had to cough up five per cent of "all money received." Harry Markson of the IBC, and Sol Strauss, had Michaels come to New York City. Al Weill, who managed Marciano, was also there. Though it didn't come out in court, and would have been devastating for Norris if it had, Weill was obviously there as Carbo's envoy. Charles's reputed managers, Jake Mintz and Tom Tannas, weren't even there. Michaels reluctantly agreed to pay the five per cent off the top, less the applicable state and federal taxes. Suddenly, there had to be a postponement: Charles was diagnosed with a heart condition, and Michaels incurred a lot of additional expenses. Though Charles trounced Beshore, it was Weill, Carbo's bagman, who came to pick up the five per cent – not anyone formally affiliated with the IBC.

When Weill showed up and gruffly asked for the dough, Michaels angrily told him, "I'm not going to pay you. You didn't deliver the god damn fighter when you promised."

"You won't get any more fights," Weill said, staring a hole through him.

Michaels ignored him. But when he tried to make Charles against Lee Oma, he couldn't do the fight. Charles would eventually beat Oma in 1951 in New York.

Though the Government presented just eight witnesses, its pile of documents was impressive. An even bigger factor against Norris was the way he was hammered in the newspapers. Though judges aren't supposed to be swayed by anything unless it's admissable evidence, they are human beings, and couldn't help being influenced by Dan Parker, or Jimmy Cannon, who really kept teeing off on Norris, Carbo and the Octopus-like IBC. By the last nine days of testimony, the normally pleasant Judge Ryan was snapping at Norris's attorneys as he continually batted down their arguments.

On 2 July 1957, Judge Ryan found the International Boxing Club of New York and Illinois, and the Madison Square Garden Corp, guilty of violating the Sherman Antitrust Act. In a draconian measure, Ryan ordered Norris and Wirtz to divest themselves of their monopoly, giving them five years to sell their Garden stock. Ryan dissolved the IBC in New York and Chicago, and enjoined it from presenting more than two world championships annually.

It was a devastating ruling. The flat-nosed, scar-tissued denizens of Stillman's Gym couldn't stop talking about it. The *Wednesday Night Fights* of Chicago generated $18,500 in TV money a week, while the *Gillette Calvalcade of Sports* on Friday at the Garden did $25,000. Thought the IBC's books claimed $3,500,000 in gross revenue for 1956, with just a $100,000 profit, that's ridiculously misleading. Wirtz had so many subsidiary companies that were directly related to the weekly boxing that even Norris often told him, "Art, you've got me confused." When it came to the bottom line, Wirtz and Norris wouldn't have stayed in a business where you had to play ball with gangsters just for a meagre three per cent return. In figures far closer to the truth, in just seven and a half years Norris and Wirtz had more than doubled the value of their investment: $1,723. 580 had become $3,948,300.

After Ryan slammed down his gavel, Norris and Wirtz vowed an appeal. Kenneth Royal, their chief attorney, claimed in court, "What we have done is the acceptable practice in boxing."

Trying to re-litigate what had earlier been decided, Royal also added, "It has been our belief that sport does not come under the scope of antitrust (monopoly) laws. We have no idea of wrong-doing."

* * *

In July, 1957, with the IBC down but not out, a boyishly handsome thirty-four-year-old named John Bonomi was transferred by Manhattan District Attorney Frank Hogan to the Rackets Bureau. Bonomi, with his round earnest face and short dark hair, won the Columbia College welterweight championship in 1943, but was hardly Ivy League. Though he was not even old enough to legally buy a drink, Jack, as he was called by his friends, flew aboard B-24s during World War Two and won six battle stars as a member of the 492nd Bomber Group. Bonomi was *en route* to Okinawa when the atomic bomb was dropped on Japan.

After hitchhiking around Europe, Bonomi decided to study law at Cornell College and got his degree. He ended up at the Reconstruction Finance Corporation, where he dug in with both hands, ferreting out corruption. In August 1953, he married pretty Pat Undergraff, a young secretary who had been working for California senator Richard Nixon, now vice-president. In November 1953, Bonomi joined Hogan's office in New York City. Starting in the Complaints Bureau, the well-built, six-foot, 175-pounder handled fraud, larceny and extortion cases.

"It was an excellent way to develop investigative skills," he later told Walter Wager, who wrote a lavish piece on him in 1962 for *True* magazine's *Boxing Yearbook*. "It was a first-class school. We got results too. Nobody could 'fix' a case in Hogan's office. We were all proud of that."

Though anyone who knew New York politics finds that impossible to believe, in July 1957, he was promoted to the Rackets Bureau, which was Hogan's feeble weapon against organized crime. In Bonomi's first case, he convicted Johnny Dio, the notorious labour racketeer. As Bonomi painstakingly went over wiretaps, he noted that Dio was in constant phone contact with Anthony Corrallo and James Plumieri. Corrallo was known as "Tony Ducks," while Plumieri was dubbed "Jimmy Doyle." All three thugs were involved in all sorts of illicit activities; the FBI already knew that they were fronts for Frankie Carbo in boxing.

As columnist Dan Parker continued his crusade to clean up boxing, he predicted that the IBC would stay in business under a new name. Judge Ryan's decree had too many loopholes. Parker, a diligent, courageous journalist at a time when so many like Red Smith, the finest stylist of his generation, were on the take, unearthed a seldom-used statute in New York. Undercover promoters, managers, or matchmakers could be prosecuted.

"Look, that's a bullshit law. It doesn't carry enough time," Hogan told Bonomi.

"Hey, they got Al Capone on income tax evasion," Bonomi replied.

Bonomi got just a month to find something, but got court orders to re-tap the phones of Ducks and Doyle. A small squad of detectives began "sitting" on the wires. Since Bonomi knew there was terrible corruption in the police department, he personally selected his men. Only honest gumshoes, fluent in Italian, got a chance to monitor taps.

Later, Walter Wages claimed that Bonomi told Senator Estes Kefauver, who had a passion for going after organized crime, "The taps showed that this was a coast-to-coast operation. The combine was busy in every major city where important fights took place. That was unusual. Ordinarily, a hood runs a racket in his home town ... Here I could smell that somebody was bossing shady fight operations all over the country.

He told important underworld figures what to do, and nobody argued. He had to be a top guy."

Bonomi got more court orders to wiretap Jimmy White, a Colorado matchmaker, and Hymie Wallman, the hefty, world-weary Manhattan furrier known as "the Mink." As Bonomi went through the wire transcripts, there was constant reference to a big man in charge, but they never refered by name; it was always "the Uncle," "the Ambassador," "the Superintendent," or even "She."

Initially, Bonomi figured it might be Frank Costello, who was nicknamed "the Uncle," but Costello, who had virtually run New York City, had lost a lot of power in the Mafia, and had been shot by Vito Genovese's chauffeur, Vincent "the Chin" Gigante.

Gigante was another with boxing connections. Once upon a time, in the world of fedoras, fast money and "wise guys," Gigante had dreamed of being a fighter. But the Chin had no "chin," and never got further than prelims. Once the final bell rang for Gigante, the glass-jawed thug worked as a bodyguard for New York mob boss Genovese. The brother of a priest, he specialized in throwing people off roofs. He was arrested seven times in eight years for crimes ranging from receiving stolen goods to posession of an unregistered handgun and gambling. Since he was "mobbed up," the longest he ever did was sixty days.

In 1957, he tried to shoot Costello on Genovese's orders, but only grazed his head. Heeding the Mafia code of the streets, Costello clammed up at Gigante's trial, and the ex-fighter actually said, "Thanks Frank," on his way out after beating the rap. Costello, who was Frankie Carbo's boss, quickly went into retirement, and the murderous Genovese took over the most lucrative crime family in the world.

In 1959, Gigante and Genovese were nailed for heroin trafficking. Gigante hit the bricks again after five years. The career criminal tried to murder Mob Godfather John Gotti in the 1980s. He also found a novel way around taking responsibility for his crimes. It was a combination of Chaplin and Freud: Gigante feigned mental incompetence.

By now, the Chin was underboss of the Genovese crime family, but was often observed wandering near his South Greenwich Village head-quarters wearing pyjamas or a bathrobe, garbed in slippers. If Gigante felt he was being watched, "he'd just pull out his pecker in broad daylight and pee like a dog," laughed one New York cop. The FBI tried to subpoena him at the home of his mother, but found Gigante standing naked in a shower holding an umbrella. Every six months, claimed one agent, Gigante checked himself into Westchester Mental Hospital for a "tune up."

"Mentally incompetent," is what Gigante's high-priced mouthpiece

Barry Slotnick claimed, but Feds wondered how someone mentally incompetent could direct the Genovese family's $100 million criminal schemes. Eventually, "Da Chin" was take off the streets for the final time, and now resides in the Springfield Medical Facility for federal prisoners.

So if Frank Costello wasn't the Mr Big of boxing, who was – and what was to be done about him?

CHAPTER FOUR

The Big Clean-Up

AT 10:15 ON THE morning of 25 October 1957, Albert Anastasia was getting his customary shave at his favourite barber shop in the swank Park Sheraton Hotel, in the heart of New York City. Gunmen swiftly entered the room, and shot the towel-swathed figure dead in his chair. As screams rang out, and the gunmen fled, Anastasia, "the Lord High Executioner of Organized Crime" lay sprawled on the floor in a huge pool of blood.

Anastasia, fifty-four, a frightening man, was the real-life model for Luca Brazzi in Mario Puzo's classic *The Godfather*. He had reportedly killed more than fifty people himself, and was responsible for hundreds more deaths, according to the *Encylopedia of Crime*. He was so feared, so volatile, that even other mobsters were petrified of him. He once ordered a "do-gooder" named Arnold Schuster murdered after he saw Schuster on TV proudly proclaiming that he had turned in a bank robber.

Anastasia controlled gambling, prostitution and drugs and was one of the five crime barons who carved up New York City. The FBI soon knew that Vito Genovese, "the boss of bosses", had him killed. Genovese and Anastasia "controlled" the Eastern Parkway Arena in Brooklyn, according to the FBI, though the front was clothier Emil Lence. Genovese, a vicious thug who killed his second's wife husband so he could marry her fourteen days later, was visited by Rocky Marciano on his deathbed.

After Anastasia's murder, his wife Else tearfully told a writer, "I never heard him say a bad word in front of me or the children. He used to go with me to church every Sunday. He gave generously to the church. Now, he's not even buried in consecrated ground."

"Carbo, Top Boxing Racketeer, Sought for Questioning in Anastasia Slaying," proclaimed the *New York Post*. For more than ten years, despite Bonomi's professed naivety, Frankie Carbo had been publicly rumoured to be running boxing. *Life* magazine, one of the largest weeklies in America, said so way back in 1946. Maybe Bonomi didn't have the absolute proof he was looking for, but it's simply not true for him to say that he didn't *know* who he was looking for. (The FBI definitely knew, but J. Edgar Hoover's boys were notorious for not sharing files with other agencies. Incredibly, as the Mob ravaged America, adding an estimated eleven cents on the dollar to all goods and services, Hoover had just four Feds working organized crime in New York City).

On one phone tap, Hymie Wallman complained, "They want to talk to the Uncle." Now Bonomi positively *knew* he had his man.

On 6 February 1958, a confidential informant advised the Feds that "Carbo may have been (Genovese's) undercover representative on boxing and that explained his power." Another chart prepared for the FBI figured the hierarchy was: Carbo reported to Anastasia, who paid tribute to Genovese.

Before Genovese took over as top boss in New York, Carbo had been protected by Costello. Costello went into retirement after Genovese's bid to kill him and, without Costello's ability to fix things, a state grand jury was convening in New York. Carbo was nowhere to be seen, but he was certainly feeling the heat. Though the FBI's info on Carbo was far ahead of Bonomi's, what the FBI didn't realise until June 1958 was that Carbo had been a patient at St. Claire's Hospital in New York from January 17 till January 20. His heart condition was worsening. His diabetes was acting up. This was a typical Mafia ailment. Stress kills. Carbo officially had a "cystoscopy" and paid the $218 bill in cash. An additional $43 bill sent to Carbo care of his brother Anthony in Brooklyn was never paid.

The FBI was quietly looking for Carbo. On 11 February 1958, Special Agent George Walker went to the Miami Beach Auditorium trying to find him. Walker also went to the Community Barber Shops on the 11th, 14th and 18th, and the FBI staked out addresses, on Collins Avenue. One source in the fight game told the FBI on March 14, "I don't know where he's at, but I don't want to get mixed up with him because of his reputation. Look, all I know is that he comes to Miami Beach on and off during the tourist season, but he won't stay in one place very long."

Carbo complained bitterly, "I got these Fed bastards on my ass, day and night. Then it's the local cops every time I turn around." He had a penchant for jumping in and out of cabs, checking out of hotels on a whim, and having a flunky pick up his luggage days later. He was very hard to tail, and always looking around.

Throughout March, surveillance was conducted on-and-off at the Community Barber Shops, but no Carbo. On March 26, a detective with the Miami Beach Police told the FBI, "I saw Carbo getting a shoeshine at Tony's Barber Shop at 69th and Collins."

Mob-controlled Primo Carnera, possibly the most exploited athlete in history. His career became a byword for boxing corruption and inspired the novel and movie *The Harder They Fall*.

Top: Frankie Carbo, as a young Mafia "torpedo", arrested in New York City in January 1936. He was already on his way to taking over boxing.

Middle: Frank Costello was the most powerful gangster in America in the 1940s. Carbo was very close to him and Costello even paid $7000 for the contract of one boxer Carbo handled.

Right: Jack Sharkey, the man who whisperers claimed "threw" the heavyweight title to Primo Carnera. The embittered and reclusive Sharkey always denied it, though he did admit rejecting a bribe offer to lose another title fight.

New York's Mike Jacobs, the former ticket scalper who became one of the greatest of all promoters. The public believed he ran boxing in the 1930s and 1940s, but FBI informants insisted Frankie Carbo "totally controlled Jacobs."

Bugsy Siegel shot dead in his Beverly Hills apartment in June 1947. It would be 30 years before a Mob turncoat revealed that Frankie Carbo was the triggerman. In his younger days (inset) Siegel had been not only a ruthless killer but also one of the founders of the gambling mecca of Las Vegas.

Abe "Kid Twist" Reles, centre, with US attorneys in 1941. Reles exposed the workings of the killing machine known as Murder Incorporated. He later fell to his death from a sixth-floor window while being guarded by six New York policemen.

German Max Schmeling and Harry Thomas clash in Madison Square Garden in the 1930s. Thomas allegedly took a dive. Schmeling, one of the sport's good guys, later saved Jews in Nazi Germany.

Joe Louis and his good friend Sugar Ray Robinson, two of the greatest of all, in the late 1940s. Louis was promoted by Mike Jacobs, while Robinson resisted overtures from Carbo to throw a fight. Both legends ended their lives suffering severe mental disabilities.

Marty Servo's hand is raised after his knockout of Red Cochrane in February 1946 for the world welterweight title. According to FBI informants, the fight was fixed, at a time when Mob control of the sport was almost total.

Young contender Tony Janiro. According to FBI informants, his victory over Canada's Johnny Greco was a betting coup. When they fought for real, Janiro took a beating.

Jimmy Bivins was dubbed the "Duration Champ" while heavyweight king Joe Louis was in the army. Fifty years later, he was living in appalling conditions, horribly mistreated by his own daughter.

Coley Wallace, who beat Rocky Marciano as an amateur. "I never enjoyed boxing after I got hooked up with Frank Palermo," claimed Wallace, who wanted a title fight but was told he would have to dive

Ike Williams, the all-time great lightweight who was robbed of two of his championship purses by mobster/manager Blinky Palermo. He ended up broke and raking leaves for his hometown council.

FBI men John Bassett (left) and William Roemer flank an arrested Milwaukee Phil Alderesio, the notorious Chicago killer. Alderesio reportedly had a "Murder Mobile" for doing hits.

Bernie Glickman, a Carbo front manager, after receiving some "love taps" from Alderesio. Glickman fell out with the Mob over a proposed Muhammad Ali-Ernie Terrell fight.

Jack Bonomi, the assistant Manhattan District Attorney who chased Carbo. The FBI knew "Mr Gray" ran boxing by 1946, but didn't share its information with the crusading Bonomi.

"When was that?" asked the Fed excitedly.

"The twenty-first or twenty-second," replied the Miami cop.

"Where does this guy live?"

"I dunno," shrugged the Miami detective, squinting into the hot sun, "But I think this guy uses aliases, and when he stays at the big hotels on the beach, the management protects his identity."

Also on March 26, a sharpie at the Gulfstream Racetrack in Hallendale, Florida, told the FBI, "I ain't seen him. Nobody's seen the guy. He was down here all the time last year."

Meanwhile in New York, Virgil Akins came from behind to halt Issac Logart in the sixth round in a welterweight championship eliminator at Madison Square Garden. Carbo controlled both fighters. Bonomi knew it, and twenty-five plainclothes detectives from Bonomi's office descended on the Garden and handed out fifteen subpoenas to testify in front of the grand jury. Akins was in his dressing room, being congratulated by Julius Helfand, the chairman of the New York State Athletic Commission, when he got his. Helfand looked stunned.

Bernie Glickman and Eddie Yawitz, Akins's managers, had given Carbo $10,000 earlier. They couldn't explain why. Jim Norris had also paid Carbo between $10,000 and $15,000 so the fight could take place. Bonomi had become so skeptical of the NYSAC, Helfand was intentionally not told of the raid.

Helfand, the former "rackets busting" King's County Assistant DA, had been specifically appointed in 1955 by New York Governor Averril Harriman to clean up boxing. In the beginning, Helfand came out fighting. In December 1955, after a seven-month investigation, he called the New York Boxing (Manager's) Guild "a continuing menace to the integrity of boxing in the state," and contended that out-of-state managers had "cut in" a Guild manager to get a fight in New York. The Guild ultimately collapsed after Norris suddenly sided with the New York State Athletic Commission.

"Are you on the side of law and order?" Helfand asked the sweating Norris between a break in testimony. Norris nodded grimly. Helfand then spoke to him the way his father did when he was a small boy. "Well, what I expect you to do ... is make an announcement that you will not recognize the Manager's Guild anymore."

Norris did as instructed, but knew that meant defying Carbo. Still, the former New York State Athletic Commission chairman, Robert Christenberry, publicly blasted Helfand and demanded a list of the gangsters he had actually run out of boxing.

In February 1958, Joe Brown KO'd Orlando Echeverria in the first foreign fight ever broadcast live back to the States. Records proved that Norris had paid Helfand's way to Cuba.

★ ★ ★

Carbo had gone into hiding. Only two of the fifteen witnesses had come clean in front of the New York Grand Jury. In Miami, however, the FBI was able to develop a lot of contacts. Another source said, "Look, Carbo's big interests are boxing and gambling. He's got to be in a place that gives him that kinda action, and it ain't Hollywood, Florida. Now, Carbo visits Hollywood, but he don't live here. Nobody knews where the hell he lives, or how to get in touch with him. I think you guys should be looking in Miami Beach, or maybe New York, but he's hard to track because he's constantly on the move. Nobody knows when he's coming or going."

Carbo however, was definitely in the area. A snitch told the FBI that he was driving a white 1957 or '58 Cadillac convertible, but nobody had the license plate.

The FBI began asking questions about Harry Curley, an emaciated, sixty-something fight manager with grey hair who hung out at Miami's Fifth Street Gym and had fallen on hard times. He was a "good friend" of Carbo's, and whenever the gangster saw Curley at the fights, he gave him a handout. Curley's real name was Harry Curley Bonderfsky. He didn't drink, gamble or smoke, but he trained Carbo's fighters whenever they had a match in Miami Beach. He also rented flashy cars for fight promoters when they hit town.

The authorities kept "beating the street." Another source "spoke freely regarding his activities, until he was asked about Frankie Carbo." Then he growled, "Carbo is not in Miami. I don't even think he's in the fight game anymore." The source was almost certainly Chris Dundee, the grizzled Miami Beach promoter who actually was a front for Carbo, despite his latter election into boxing's Hall of Fame.

In Washington, D.C., the FBI was able to record a conversation in Goldy Ahearn's restaurant. Ahearn promoted in an arena secretly owned by Carbo. Those in attendance were Carbo, Wallman, Tony Ferrante, who managed Joey Giardello, and a young Angelo Dundee, who was making a name as a manager/trainer but was still mostly a gofer for his brother Chris. According to an informant, Willie Pastrano, the artful light-heavy ostensibly managed by Angelo, was really controlled by Carbo. An FBI snitch also claimed that a nationally televised fight out of Washington in January 1958 was actually declared a draw because Carbo hadn't notified judges which fighter to vote for.

In New York City, Assistant DA Alfred Scotti was publicly calling Hymie Wallman a front for Carbo, and flat-out dubbed the elusive gangster, "the underworld czar of boxing."

"I've never been a front man for anyone," protested Wallman. "The fighters in my stable are my own, and no one else's." In truth, he'd been Carbo's man since at least 1942.

Scotti demanded that Wallman's records be turned over to the grand jury. Wallman had a good stable. Some of top fighters he managed were Argentine heavyweight contender Alex Mitef, middleweight Charley Cotton, lightweight Orlando Zulueta, and Ike Chestnut, a top feather-weight. "I've know Carbo for thirty-six years," the Mink finally admitted, "but I've never done business with him. I don't even know where he lives."

In Houston, Texas, Special Agent Hollis Q. Boone was conducting his own investigation, on behalf of the FBI. "You've got to keep my name confidential," one boxing insider told him nervously. "I don't know Carbo, and have never seen him, but from what people tell me, he's a hoodlum who makes his living off the fight game. He lives anywhere he hangs his hat.

"Now, you'll never prove it. Carbo's too smart to have anything on paper, but Lou Viscusi is a front for Carbo, and he manages this colored fighter Cleveland Williams. I don't know when Carbo was actually in Houston, but the word is about a year ago."

According to Boone's report

> ... it was his opinion from hearing various talk around Houston that the Boxing Promoters were building up Roy Harris, a high-ranking contender in the Heavyweight Fight Division, for a 'kill.' ... It was his belief that some of the racketeers of the fight promotion were going to build up Harris and get a lot of the 'big (oil) money' in Texas to back him, and then Harris would get beat badly and the managers, of course, would have a big score ... It was his opinion, as well as others who were well schooled in the boxing game, that Harris was no fighter at all.

On 18 August 1958, Floyd Patterson battered Harris into submission in the twelfth round in defence of his heavyweight championship. Harris had actually dropped Patterson but was outclassed. The soft-hearted champion refused to aim for Harris's badly-cut eye, and afterwards admitted he didn't want to hit him. Texas authorities hadn't allowed the fight to take place in Houston, where it would've drawn big. The mismatch was held outdoors in Wrigley Field in Los Angeles. The promoter of record was Al Weill. Harris's manager was Lou Viscusi. Both were fronts for Carbo.

A police officer from the East Haven, Connecticut, Police Department, told the FBI in January 1958 that Carbo was now handling the comeback of a former champion. This fighter was observed in the cocktail lounge in the Hotel Bond in Hartford, Connecticut, with Carbo. This cop heard that he "threw a fight about a week ago somewhere around Boston."

Special Agent Ronald Weaver of the FBI conducted a further investigation into boxing around Boston, Massachusetts. He talked to Sam Silverman and Rip Valenti, though their names were blacked out. Though neither were "considered in Boston to be racketeers," both had to do business with gangsters in the crime-laden North End. Valenti had a ticket agency less than block from Boston Garden. An investigation a year earlier revealed that the "Sharkey Athletic Association," with the blessings of the International Boxing Club, was promoting the high-grade fights in Boston.

The Sharkey Athletic Association was named for Jack Sharkey, but it was run by Jerry and Johnny Buckley, the brothers who trained and respectively managed the old heavyweight champion. Raymond Patriarca, later called the "Godfather" of New England crime, also had a piece of the fight game in Boston "through Frank Carbo."

In 1958, a young middleweight from Boston named Paul Pender angrily declared, "Boxing is corrupt. They should ban the sport, then start all over again." Pender was one of the few fighters ever to speak out, but he was publicly criticized by the Massachusetts Boxing Commission, and threatened with revocation with his license. He was managed by Johnny Buckley, who'd once been controlled by gangster Owney Madden.

Though the FBI couldn't track dawn Carbo, his sinister presence was being felt all over the country. In February 1958, the Baltimore office of the FBI "advised that during the summer of 1954, a group of racketeers on orders from Frank Carbo . . . called at the shore property of (deleted) in Anne Arundel County, Maryland, where they proceeded to break up a large number of slot machines, which were in operation in that place at that time ... Some of the other slot machine operators had refused to agree to pay off this group for protection."

Carbo "and his group" reportedly owned "a quarter" of all the slot machines in Anne Arundel County. They held their meetings at a joint called Big Tom's Tavern. The FBI learned that Carbo allegedly "had an interest in the Trocadero" nightclub, and conducted his fight business downstairs. Carbo had gotten angry, picked up a bar stool and threw it through the bar mirror. As people scattered, Carbo bellowed, "It's nobody's goddam business. I paid for it anyway."

Carbo and his flunkies, such as Baltimore promoter Benny Trotta, were trying to establish a TV base in Baltimore, but the corrupt Trotta's boxing license had been revoked in 1956, and Governor McEldin of Maryland was adamantly opposed to granting a new one. Incredibly, a political hack, Charlie Rosenbaum, who headed the Maryland State Athletic Commission, had publicly declared, "We would welcome Trotta, or any substantial citizen who applies for a license to promote here."

The United States Immigration and Naturalization Service was also trying to subpoena Carbo. It wanted Carbo to furnish information on Hyman Stromberg, *aka* Nig Rosen, whom it was trying to deport. Stromberg was allegedly the boss of the Philadelphia rackets and controlled prize-fighting in the city through promoter Herman Taylor (another one now enshrined in the Boxing Hall of Fame. Taylor went to the funeral of Boo Boo Hoff in 1941.)

By 1958, Stromberg had just been convicted of drug trafficking, and the FBI's info was that he "was the mastermind and big financier of an international dope ring" allegedly worth a staggering $100 million. The judge who sentenced Stromberg, Carbo's old Murder Incorporated and book-making buddy, characterized him as "engaged in organized crime for three decades." This was all true. So why did this vicious thug get just five years in prison and a $10,000 fine? He could have been deported.

★ ★ ★

In April 1958, Truman Gibson, of the newly-configured IBC held his first press conference in New York, as Jim Norris's stooge. He piously proclaimed, "I have never associated with Frankie Carbo and won't start now. And I don't have to tell you [that] Harry [Markson, managing director of the surgically-enhanced IBC, now called National Boxing Enterprises] never asssociated with Carbo either." Though Gibson was the front man, Norris still exercised all fiscal control.

Meanwhile, boxing insiders were privately telling the FBI that whenever they tried to make a fight, it always took at least two hours to get an approval. Carbo still had to give his blessing. A memorandum to J. Edgar Hoover from the Miami office was by now asking for a wider investigation into Mr Gray, to include Toronto, Canada, "to determine Carbo's international connections with the boxing racket."

In New York, Carbo had used Jack Dempsey's restaurant as a mail drop, and did business with impunity. Finally, with Carbo so hot, Dempsey had politely asked him to stop coming in.

"Aren't you afraid? asked the FBI.

"I'm not afraid of anybody," growled the former champ.

At the Broward County Courthouse, the FBI again scoured the federal tax liens against this man who had no assets, no income, no job, and no social security number, but somehow owned a Broadway ticket agency, a Washington fight arena, and a Baltimore night club. Why didn't federal prosecutors simply charge Carbo with income tax evasion? How do you run up $741,000 in tax liens with "no visible means of support"?

On 12 January 1959, the United States Supreme Court finally laid the IBC out for the count.

It appears that appellants (Norris, Wirtz, the IBC), had continued exercising their unlawful contract long after they well knew that this activity was within the coverage of the Sherman Act. Their conduct violated the Sherman Act … which is so important to our free enterprise system. Still they continued their illegal activity. In fact from all appearances, it is continuing today.

The IBC was broken up and the monopoly was at an end.

★ ★ ★

In October 1958, Jackie Leonard and Don Nesseth, who handled a Los Angeles contender named Don Jordan, had been summoned to promoter George Parnassus's office regarding a fight with Virgil Akins. Akins had floored Vince Martinez ten times in St. Louis and given him a terrible beating to win the welterweight championship of the world. (Martinez was one of the few fighters in the Fifties to escape with his money. Martinez, who hailed from New Jersey, had been getting robbed by his manager "Honest" Bill Daly until his father and his brother grabbed Daly, held the screaming manager out of a third floor window, and threatened to drop him if it ever happened again. For a while Martinez couldn't get fights, after he was boycotted by the Managers' Guild.)

Truman Gibson was also in Parnassus's office and made a phone call. He was checking with Blinky Palermo at the Bismark Hotel in Chicago. Palermo spoke more forcefully now for Carbo, who was on the lam.

After speaking with the stocky Palermo, the suave Gibson then handed the phone to Leonard.

"Do you know we're in for half?" Palermo rasped.

"Half of what?"

"We're in for half of the fighter, or there won't be a fight."

Somehow, Gibson had neglected to tell Leonard. Finally, the pasty-faced lawyer, who had almost an embalmed look, told Leonard, "You know how Carbo and Blinky are. They want everything before you can get a title fight. Just go along with it. I'll straighten everything out."

Leonard was still wary. But Gibson waved one of his soft, well-manicured hands. "Look, this is the way the lightweight and welterweight title has worked since Carbo and Blinky got involved," he insisted.

On December 5, Don Jordan pulled off a big upset, battering Akins over fifteen rounds to win the championship. Jordan was a tough, fast-handed Dominican, who fought out of Los Angeles, and Akins was his ninth win in a row. The mocha-coloured part-Indian had seemed like just one more kid on the road to nowhere after losing to Britain's Dave Charnley, but his manager, Don Nesseth, hooked up with Leonard, the shrewd matchmaker of the Hollywood Legion Stadium, who would be "Promoter of the Year" for 1958. Leonard then buttonholed Truman Gibson, who suddenly got him TV fights. Wins over contenders Issac Logart and Gasper Ortega propelled him into his exciting TV title fight over Akins. Jordan got just $13, 500 for the win, but big money was in the future. Even his cold, distant father burst into ring afterward and said proudly, "You are my son."

Leonard flew to Miami on 5 January 1959. Palermo met him there, along with Abe Sands, who was Carbo's bagman. Sands had picked up the $10,000 Bernie Glickman had to pay before the Akins-Logart eliminator. On January 7, at the Charleton Resort Motel, in strutted Carbo, who had been laying low since his indictment in New York, in July 1958, for undercover matchmaking.

Though thirty years later Leonard claimed that he had no agreement with Carbo, and he'd said to them, "You're in for nothing!" after Palermo had demanded half, there obviously was some sort of understanding, or the Akins fight wouldn't have taken place.

On January 7, Carbo again asked him, "What about your partner? Can you control the sonofabitch or not?"

"Yeah," nodded Leonard. But Palermo was demanding that Jordan defend against Garnett "Sugar" Hart, who he'd just taken over.

"Nesseth don't wanna fight Hart," protested Leonard. "He's too tough. There's easier fights out there than him."

"He's gotta fight Hart!" screamed Palermo. "I got him by telling his manager I'd get the title shot.

"What's the difference," Blinky finally said, exasperated, "If Hart wins, Nesseth gets fifteen per cent of him."

Carbo was strangely silent. His heart was acting up again. Suddenly, Chris Dundee, the Miami Beach promoter, came in with Gabe Genovese, nephew of crime boss Vito and Carbo's first partner in boxing.

"I'm glad you've joined the family," Genovese said, warmly extending his hand to Leonard. "Frank's a great guy. With him helping you, you'll get a lot of TV fights. He'll just tell Gibson."

Before Leonard was driven back to the Greater Miami Airport, Carbo shot him a baleful look, and growled: "You got everything straight? Can you handle it?"

"I'll try."

"God dammit. DON'T TRY. You're responsible."

Leonard grew very scared.

Jordan was due to fight Mexico's hard-hitting Alvaro Guttierrez in Los Angeles in a non-title fight. Jordan's purse was $12,500, plus expenses. Carbo was expecting a piece of it.

"Just tell him everything's all right," Gibson supposedly told Leonard.

A couple of days before the fight, Palermo called and told Leonard to send the money to Clare Cori in Philadelphia. Cori was Palermo's second wife.

Jordan stopped his opponent. A few days later, Leonard, Nesseth, and Babe McCoy, a notorious matchmaker, met with Gibson in the posh Ambassador Hotel in downtown LA. Leonard and Nesseth eventually left, but once they got to Leonard's home in suburban LA, they got a message to call Palermo from a phone booth. At 3:23 Eastern time, Palermo got the call. He had not received the payoff, and was furious.

"You bastard. You double-crosser."

Leonard meekly tried to explain that it was Gibson who was supposed to pay. Gibson had conned them. Anyway, they weren't going to kick back a piece of Jordan's purses. Gibson had lied to them just so Jordan would fight Akins on TV.

Suddenly Carbo snatched the phone away from Palermo, and hissed, "You sonofabitch double-crosser. You're no good. Your fuckin' word is no good. Just because you're two thousand miles away, don't think I can't have you taken care of. I've got plenty of friends. They know how to take care of punks like you. *The money had better be in.*"

By now, Leonard was practically pissing his pants. Carbo was still making dire threats when the operator broke in, demanding more quarters for the pay phone.

Leonard got hold of Gibson the next day. Gibson promised to send $1,800 to Leonard so he could pay Carbo. But the smooth-talking "front" for Jim Norris's crumbling empire didn't send a dime. Finally, after repeated calls from Palermo, Gibson wrote an $1,800 cheque from the Chicago Stadium corporate account. It was made payable to Leonard, but it was logged as an "advance, promoter's share of April fight."

Despite what Gibson may have told him before the Akins-Jordan fight, Leonard was going to have to take care of the gangsters. In April 1959, two weeks before a Jordan-Akins rematch in St Louis, Palermo demanded that Leonard come see him. Palermo screamed that things had to be settled, and Jordan had to fight Hart.

"What are you doing, taking over complete control of Jordan?" Leonard asked.

"In a way, yes."

Palermo met with Leonard's partner Nesseth in St Louis. Nesseth, who was in the used car business, told him, "I don't care if Truman Gibson gives you $10,000 every time we fight. I'm not giving you a dime."

Palermo called Leonard. *Did Nesseth want to die?*

"Nesseth is his own master," Leonard nervously told him, but that wasn't good enough. Palermo again threatened Leonard.

Days later, Gibson called Leonard in his office at the Hollywood Legion Stadium, and promised to take care of "these people" from Jordan's purse. But an enraged Carbo had also rung, and snarled, "If I was out there, I'd gouge your eyes out." Leonard, a former pro fighter, raced for the ladies' room and threw up.

On 1 May 1959, Palermo held a "meet" with Leonard in Puccini's Restaurant in Beverly Hills. He brought some "Mob muscle" with him: Louis Tom Dragna and Joe Sica, both top LA hoods. Leonard figured he wouldn't get killed in a posh eatery, with so many witnesses. But as he tried to blame Nesseth and Gibson for the trouble they'd caused, Palermo shrieked, "Shut up! Leave Truman out of this."

Finally, Sica told the frightened Leonard, "Jackie, you made a choice. It's either you or Don Nesseth who is going to get hurt."

Palermo was also jittery. "You'd better fix it. I'm in a helluva jam with the Gray," meaning Carbo.

Nesseth called Gibson, and told him his life was being threatened, but the unflappable black lawyer simply said, "Do everyone a favour and simply fight Hart."

Though Carbo hadn't killed him yet, Leonard suddenly got a notice that his lease on the Hollywood Legion Stadium would be terminated in five days. Then Palermo and Sica called Leonard at home and ordered another "sit down" with them and George Raft, the old Hollywood actor.

This time Leonard didn't go. He knew he wouldn't come back. Instead, he contacted the Los Angeles Police Department. He should have called the FBI. The LAPD was one of the most corrupt big city forces in the country, but Sgt Conwell Keeler took the trembling promoter back to his home in Northridge and hooked up a tape recorder to his phone. As Leonard's hands shook, he called Palermo and told him that Nesseth still wouldn't accept Hart, but that Jordan would fight Del Flanagan, a classy vet from St Paul, Minnesota, who'd beaten Akins in a non-title fight, and was managed by Glickman, who was used to paying Carbo.

"That's good," cooed Palermo. "That gets both of us off the hook."

But next morning, despite the glowering presence of Sica, Palermo and Babe McCoy in Leonard's cluttered office at the Hollywood Legion Stadium, Nesseth refused to fight for Carbo or Palermo. Nesseth had balls the size of coconuts, and protested, "I worked hard to get Jordan where he's at."

"Do you think you got the Akins fight alone?" Palermo asked.

"Yes."

There was derisive laughter. Sica just shook his head.

"Jack, you got yourself in a helluva spot. It's terrible. How could you let people double-cross other people?"

Before the confab broke up, the hulking gangster whispered darkly in Leonard's ear, "Jackie, you're it."

On 20 May 1959, Leonard swore under oath before the California State Athletic Commission that Carbo and Palermo were muscling in or Jordan. Gibson too, was called, but tried to come off as the conciliator, not as the man who supposedly conned Leonard into the Akins fight by promising to pay Carbo under the table.

Traditionally, boxing commissions have no guts, but with Governor Pat Brown demanding the sport clean up or be banned in California, Captain James Hamilton of the LAPD police intelligence unit was ordered to investigate Carbo, Palermo, Sica, Dragna and Gibson. Hamilton turned over all evidence to the FBI and to US Attorney Frances Whelan.

On 3 June 1959, Leonard drove into his garage at home. As soon as he pulled down the door, he felt a crushing blow on the back of his head. He fell to his knees and was kicked and battered. He heard two men's angry voices. Leonard suffered a concusssion and couldn't identify the men.

When the story hit the papers, Chief William Parker described it as an assault by mobsters. Two weeks later, Parker incredibly reversed himself and ludicrously claimed that, "Mr. Leonard suffered some acute physical incapacitation of a stunning nature that produced the likeness of an assault."

Meanwhile, after a long, convoluted trail that led from New York City, to Miami Beach, Palm Springs, California, Reno, Nevada, Philadelphia, Pennsylvania, and even Mexico, Carbo was finally captured on 31 May 1959. He had been hiding out in Haddon Township, New Jersey, at the home of Willie Ripka, an ex-bootlegger. Carbo had been watching a late-night movie on television when, shortly after midnight, Detective Frank Marrone rang the doorbell. Blinky Palermo's son-in-law opened the portall and recognized cops as the white-haired fugitive was scurrying out of a bedroom window. He hit the ground and was preparing to run when a voice bellowed, "Stop or I'll shoot."

Carbo was relieved. He had figured it was the Mob trying to kill him.

At 3:30 that morning, Carbo met Jack Bonomi, who had got up early and driven across the Hudson River just to see him.

"You're the guy from Columbia," shrugged the aging gangster, who didn't look well. Carbo then eyed his two captors. "Bonomi, Marrone, the *paisoas* ganging up on me?"

"Yeah, it's the Mafia," somebody snapped.

Carbo tried to make small talk about baseball. The fugitive who had no income had over $2,700 in cash on him. Bonomi was furious when cops actually wanted to take Carbo out and buy him breakfast.

* * *

In September 1959, Gibson was arrested in his Chicago home as he watched the Chicago White Sox try to capture their first baseball pennant in forty years. As Gibson was thrown into handcuffs, the dapper lawyer huffily said, "You'd think I was John Dillinger or something."

In Los Angeles, Siga and Dragna were also grabbed. Palermo was pinched in Philadelphia. Carbo, who made bail in Bonomi's case, was re-arrested at Baltimore's John Hopklns Hospital, a mere six-minutes from Gibson. Normally, organized crime had moles all over, but earlier in the day, in a brilliantly-conceived sting, the Federal Grand Jury in Los Angeles had quietly returned a ten-count indictment charging the five men with conspiracy to violate federal anti-racketeering laws, as well as extortion and conspiracy. Honest Bill Daly, the mobbed-up fight manager, was also named a co-conspirator, but he was never indicted. Obviously Daly, later called "everybody's friend," had been giving the Feds inside information.

Carbo went on trial in the Court of General Sessions, New York, on 27 October 1959. It was amazingly quick, considering New York's monstrous backlog of cases, but the man presiding, John Mueller, was known as a prosecution's judge. Three days after the jury was chosen, Carbo wisely pleaded guilty. On November 30, he shuffled into court to hear his sentence. Though Carbo had ruled boxing with an iron hand, the old gunman's hair was now snow white, his heart was bad and he was diabetic. His kidneys were also failing, and nobody thought he'd live long. He was fifty-five but looked a good twenty years older as Manhattan Assistant DA Alfred Scotti sternly said, "The name Frank Carbo today symbolizes the degeneration of professional boxing into a racket."

"You enriched yourself to a degree I can't contemplate," said Judge Mueller. Yet after theatricaly lecturing the old killer – who still owed $750,000 in unpaid taxes – Mueller gave Carbo just two years. As Carbo was led away, he smiled and said, "Thank you, Judge."

In 1960, Carbo was brought before the Kefauver Committee that was investigating boxing. Not only did he enjoy his brief foray out of prison, he cockily took the Fifth Amendment twenty-five times, and cheekily said to the Tennessee senator, "There's only one thing I want to say. I congratulate you on your re-election."

It was a grave injustice that Jim Norris and Wirtz weren't indicted. They had profited with Carbo, but if "rich man's justice" was more of a rule than an exception, in Los Angeles, the Feds were finally weighing in. In February 1961, Carbo went on trial with Palermo, Sica, Dragna and Gibson. All but Gibson were denied bail.

In the interim, Los Angeles mobster Micky Cohen was giving the evil
eye to Don Jordan, the welterweight champion, who was at the centre of
the case. "I was like a slave to them," Jordan remembered years later. "When
they disowned me, I said, 'You're no friends. You're dogs. Now you're my
enemies.'

"They said, 'Talk and you die.'"

Leonard and Nesseth showed real guts in testifying but, aside from the
wiretaps, the most damning evidence was Carbo's threat on Leonard's life
in January 1959. In April of that year, Carbo had again threatened to have
the two fight figures killed. Leonard's home was set on fire.

When Jordan testified, he was obviously cowed. Though he had been the
one extorted, and it was his sweat and blood that others were profiting from,
he actually told the prosecutor on the witness stand to "kiss my ass" in
Spanish.

"The choice which this big business made," said Special Prosecutor
Alvin H. Goldstein, "was to use the underworld in order to obtain a monopoly in professional boxing and make millions of dollars at the expense of the
poor fighters and public."

On May 30, the jury of ten women and two men agreed. On June 11,
Judge Ernest Tolin suddenly died. That created chaos, but Judge George
Boldt took over, and on 2 December 1961, he threw the book at the
defendants: Carbo got twenty-five years and a $10,000 fine; Palermo, fifteen
years and a $10,000 fine; Gibson, five years, suspended, and a $10,000 fine;
Sica, twenty years and a $10,000 fine; and Dragna, five years.

All vowed appeals, but according to Carbo's FBI files, he was claiming
to be flat broke. In February 1963, Dragna's conviction was overturned, but
Carbo, Palermo, and Gibson's sentences were re-affirmed. After leading a
charmed criminal life, the now-shackled Paul John Carbo was moved from
Alcatraz. After it closed, he went to McNeil Island in Washington State.
Palermo, who didn't begin his sentence till June 1964, ended up at
Leavenworth, where he became the manager of the prison baseball team –
but not before a congressman from Philadelphia tried to protest Palermo's
treatment, and told the Department of Justice, "Frank's a nice guy." Palermo's
appeal bond was even revoked, though he'd been charged with statutory
rape.

The American press could have aided greatly in the clean up, but
Bonomi discovered that many of the top sportswriters in the country were
on the take. W.C. Heinz says the beat writers used to line up outside
Madison Square Garden to get their envelope. Once Jake La Motta tried to
hand him money, but Heinz bristled, "Jake, first, I'm insulted that you tried
to bribe me. Second, I'm insulted that you're trying to bribe with just
twenty dollars."

Usually, Bonomi found, if it wasn't money it was free hookers or bar tabs at Toots Shor's restaurant. Red Smith, the finest sportswriter of his generation, not only lambasted Kefauver's call for federal control of the sport, in print he called Carbo "the benevolent despot" of boxing.

★ ★ ★

In 1964, Blinky Palermo finally went to prison, at the age of fifty-nine. Even then, a US congressman had asked for special treatment for him, claiming "he was a nice guy." Palermo also got married "by proxy" (for what would've been at least the fourth time). In 1971, he was paroled. FBI files show he went right back into the rackets. In 1978, in Philadelphia, he tried to regain his manager's license in connection with heavyweight contender Jimmy Young, but was finally rebuffed after a public outcry. He still operated in the shadows of the fight game. He ended up with the regional closed-circuit TV rights to the Ali-Larry Holmes and Holmes-Gerry Cooney fights. As a member of "Crazy" Nicky Scarfo's notorious Atlantic City gang, "Uncle Frank" also once sent word to heavyweight Tim Witherspoon that he had better settle a lawsuit with Don King, or else. Witherspoon was forced to carry a gun. In May 1996, Palermo quietly died in a Philadelphia hospital. He was ninety-one.

Carbo had gone twenty years earlier, at St Francis Hospital in Miami, of "acute heart failure." That was a surprise. Nobody ever thought Carbo had a heart. He was seventy-two and unrepentant to the last.

A decade earlier, the FBI went to see Carbo in the federal penitentiary in Atlanta. They were hoping to turn him into a snitch. As the frail old gunman, milk-white from a lack of sun, was led into the room with shackles, guards at his sides, he refused to be seated, till they identified themselves

"Whatcha want?" Carbo asked.

"We're FBI, Frank."

Carbo literally turned around and ran from the room. In his best New Yawk-ese, he bellowed, "I got nothing to say to youse!"

CHAPTER FIVE

The Tragedy of Sonny Liston

IN OCTOBER 1958, Charles "Sonny" Liston, a hulking black heavy-weight from St Louis, battered Bert Whitehurst through the ropes in the final seconds of their nationally televised ten-rounder. Luckily for Whitehurst, the bell rang. It was the first time a US TV audience had glimpsed Liston, though gym rats had been buzzing about him for years.

"That was the most terriblest heavyweight who ever lived," recalled Freddie Mack, an American journeyman, who once knocked out British light-heavyweight champ Chic Calderwood, and routinely sparred with top British dreadnoughts like Henry Cooper, Brian London and Billy Walker. "I sparred with Liston once – for about fifteen seconds. I ran out the ring. Freddie Mack was not going to be a punching bag for anybody."

As Liston, with his menacing scowl and wrecking ball fists, slammed his way into contention, he became the most feared heavyweight since young Joe Louis.

"Why do you always look so angry?" asked Germany's Albert Westphal, prior to their December 1961 fight.

"Tonight you'll find out," muttered Sonny, before laying out Westphal in the first round.

"We don't want to meet this geezer Liston walking down the street," cracked Henry Cooper's manager, Jim Wicks.

In the late 1950s and early 1960s, Sonny Liston personified the term *bad nigger*. He was portrayed by sportswriters almost as a beast. He was seemingly inhuman, devoid of compassion and didn't feel pain. In a time of growing black emancipation, Liston simply scared the hell out of people, black and white.

On October 30, 1952 Liston came out of the Missouri State Penitentiary at Jeffersonville, and won the 1953 national AAU heavyweight title, beating Junius Griffin. But the awesome myth of Sonny Liston nearly died before it was born. "He was gonna be kicked off the team because of a rape," a former St. Louis policeman, William Rice, told writer Nick Tosches, who wrote the recent Liston biography *Night Train*.

Liston's long, painful odyssey began when he arrived in St Louis, the twenty-fourth of twenty-five children sired by an aged Arkansas sharecropper, Tobe Liston. Sharecropping was just a couple of notches above slavery, and "Sonny Boy" didn't even have shoes. He didn't know when he'd been born. He had huge welts on his back, and once said bitterly, "The only thing my old man ever gave me was a beatin'."

"He hitchiked up here from down South," remembered Sonny's wife Geraldine, though some say he sold a big bag of peanuts for bus fare. "His mother came up here first and he had a sister. I think he was twelve years old. He didn't really even know where his mother was." Liston tried school, but he was so much bigger than the other kids, they laughed at him. He couldn't write his own name.

Early arrest records in St Louis list a Charles "Sonny" Liston as being born in 1927 or 1928, making him a good five years older than his "ring age." It was inevitable that Liston ended up with a long rap sheet. He was arrested nineteen times, mostly for strong-arming people, and in June 1950 ended up in the Missouri State Penitentiary, a nineteenth century fortress that serves a monument to man's inhumanity to man. Liston was sentenced to five years. The "Silent System" prevailed at Jeffersonville, and inmates weren't allowed to speak.

"I didn't mind prison," Liston later said, "it was the first time I ever got three meals a day."

Liston was a strong, sullen young man. Old mug shots show his eyes looking so weary, like he had seen more than anyone should. The prison chaplain, Father Alois Stevens, introduced him boxing and soon nobody would venture into the ring with him. The burly fighter was rather crude and lunging when he beat Griffin for the national AAU title in 1953, but his power was remarkable. Shortly after his release, there was a riot at Jeffersonville, and a couple of inmates died.

Frank Mitchell, who published a black newspaper in St Louis, ended up with Liston's contract. Mitchell was a schizoid character, with connections to the underworld, and Liston quickly ended up the property of John Vitale, a notorious labour racketeer. Liston did some construction work, but mostly he was a labour goon for Vitale. On September 28, 1957, he was arrested for "strong arming."

"They said that he was hooked up with the Mob ... but to me, if he was hooked up with the Mob, we sure were poor," said Geraldine Liston.

Sonny met Geraldine shortly after he was released from prison. It had rained, and Liston, showing a rare smile, called out, "What's a pretty girl like you doing out in weather like this." Then he spread his coat over a mud puddle, so she could walk on it.

"Geraldine was the only person who could do anything with Liston," recalled Ben Bentley, who later served as his publicity man. They ended up living together, till Geraldine's mother finally suggested they get married. "He treated me real good," she remembers.

By March 1956, the menacing young heavyweight had won all but one of fifteen professional matches, losing only to Marty Marshal, who busted his jaw in September 1954. Liston had led a terribly hard life, and had often been hitched to a plow in the sweltering Arkansas fields, but one of his saddest memories was riding back to St Louis alone with his broken jaw throbbing.

In May 1956, Liston he got into a helluva brawl with a white policeman. St Louis was a very segregated, Jim Crow city, far closer to the Deep South racially than the Midwest. Blacks suffered, and Liston ended up being charged with "assault to kill." This cop ended up with a broken knee, as Liston angrily took his cap and gun. "Him and the cop got into it, and the cop called him a black-assed nigger. He pushed the cop, then he took the cop's gun and got seven months for it," recalled Geraldine.

Liston dumped another officer head-first into a garbage can. Finally, a surly black cop named James Reddick took him aside "and talked his language." As they slammed billy clubs atop Liston's head, Liston kept getting up and punching. That was supposed to teach him the majesty of the law. In case it didn't, Reddick told Liston he could get killed next time.

FBI records show he was also arrested in St Louis in October 1956 for stealing. Liston got nine months in the City Workouse after pleading guilty in January 1957. And he was finally run out of St Louis. Cops hate nothing more than someone who goes after one of their own, but things weren't much better for him in Philadelphia, the "City of Brotherly Love." The cops had Liston's picture on their car visors.

Sonny got back into the ring in January 1958, knocking out Billy Hunter in two rounds on an Irv Schoenwald show in Chicago. Ben Bentley, who was Schoenwald's buddy, remembers Liston asking him for ten bucks at the weigh-in, since he had no money to eat. Though Bentley, an old hand in the fight game, claimed that "Schoenwald had Liston," somehow kindly Irv got aced out of the picture. Mobster Blinky Palermo moved in once Sonny moved to Philadelphia. Vitale still had his piece too.

Trainer Johnny Tacco, who first knew Liston in St Louis, claims he was so devastating that he had trouble finding sparring partners. Sonny had a massive eighty-four-inch reach and fifteen-inch hands that required specially-made gloves. "His jab's a bitch," moaned sparmate Sammy Smith.

"It's just like other guys' right hands." Liston hit so hard he broke swivels on punching bags and knocked the padding out of headgear. In 1958, Wayne Bethea lost seven teeth in a brutal fight that lasted less than a round. Top contenders like Mike De John, Cleveland Williams, Nino Valdes and Willie Besmanoff were annihilated in 1959.

Liston was arrested for gambling while in St Louis in August 1959, but Jim Norris and the Mob realized that Liston was the man they needed to wrest the heavyweight championship back from manager Cus D'Amato, who had sworn that incumbent Floyd Patterson would never again fight for the IBC. Patterson had won the vacant title after Rocky Marciano's retirement by knocking out Archie Moore on 30 November 1956.

D'Amato wanted nothing to do with Liston. "He's got to rid himself of the unsavoury elements he has around him," D'Amato self-righteously proclaimed. Of course, D'Amato said nothing when "Fat Tony" Salerno, one of the most notorious gangsters in New York, put up dough for the first Patterson-Ingemar Johannson fight after a young promoter, Bill Rosensohn, was muscled out. Johannson publicly complained that the Mob was trying to cut up his purse. Johannson surprisingly won their first fight, flooring Floyd seven times before it was stopped in the third. Patterson then became the first man to regain the title, leaving Johannson unconscious in the fifth round with a pulverizing left hook, and got off the deck twice in the first to knock out Ingo in their final rubber match in March 1961.

Finally, because of growing criticism in the press, Patterson broke with D'Amato, and said of Liston, "I think he's proved himself the number one contender. I think he has every right to fight for the championship, despite his unfortunate background."

In the spring of 1962, there was a story in a Washington newspaper headlined, "D.C. Officials Favor License for Liston." FBI Director J. Edgar Hoover saw the report and commented angrily in the margin, "Just how blind can these three mice, the boxing commission, be!"

★ ★ ★

In the midst of the Civil Rights movement, the NAACP (the National Association for the Advancement of Colored People) was aghast at the way Liston represented blacks. President Kennedy even summoned Patterson to the White House, and urged him to beat Liston. Yet Sonny was a man badly scarred by life, a victim. "Sonny wouldn't shower with his back to the door," said Ben Bentley, who had served as his publicity man. "He was afraid somebody was going to come up and hit him over the head when he had soap in his eyes."

Liston blasted out Patterson in just 2:06 of the first round to win the heavyweight championship. Then he told radio broadcaster Jack Drees, "If the public would let bygones be bygones, I would be a good champ."

"After Sonny won the title in Chicago," recalled Philadelphia newspaperman Jack McKinney, who flew back home with him, "he was going through some of the things he was going to say at the reception at the airport, and he said, 'I know a lot of my own people were against me. I want to prove to them that I'm not going to embarrass them. I'll make them proud.

"So when we finally landed in Philadelphia, he took a step outside and stood there for a moment, just looking. I could see him looking both ways. *Nothing.* Nobody was there. I could almost see the air go out of him. The big broad shoulders in front of me just seemed to sag."

* * *

In 1963, Liston was sued by his bodyguard, a former Chicago cop, after Sonny allegedly raped his wife. The case was hushed up, claimed writer Nick Tosches. Liston was living in a posh house on Chicago's Southside, and the Mob tried to tidy up his image. Bentley got him made guest of honour at a "Big Brothers of America" dinner in Washington. Columnist Drew Pearson, the toughest muckraker in Washington, wrote glowingly about Sonny's ideas to combat juvenile delinquency. Sonny had a good sense of humor, and told Pearson, "I used to find things before they were lost." But J. Edgar Hoover, the head of the FBI, was monitoring Liston closely, and he cryptically scrawled on the article after he read it: "It is nauseating the way Pearson presents Liston as a 'clean person.'"

Sonny could always revert to type. While in Washington, he met vice-president Lyndon Johnson in his office. As Johnson began to talk compulsively and show him around, the sullen Liston looked at Bentley and whispered in his ear, "Whaddya say we blow this bum off." Four months later, Johnson was president of the United States after John F. Kennedy's assassination.

In July 1963 Liston destroyed Patterson again in just a round, this time in Las Vegas. A month later, Sandy Smith of the *Chicago Sun-Times* broke the real story of Liston's arrangement with the Mob. It was so accurate that it ended up in Liston's FBI file. "HOW MOB 'CUT UP' LISTON," screamed the story's headline. Then in smaller case, it added, "'Commission' Edict Settled War Among Gangsters."

> Gangland's all-powerful 'Commission' settled a squable between mobsters over the control of Charles (Sony) Liston, before he won the world's heavyweight championship, Justice Department officials said Tuesday.
>
> … an edict from the Commission, the supreme council of organized crime, ended a 1961 quarrel between Chicago and Eastern gangsters over

shares of Liston's earnings ...The burgeoning federal inquiry into the Commission and its secret society, La Cosa Nostra, revealed how the twelve gangsters on the crime council acted in 1961 as boxing commission of the underworld.

Eastern mobsters were given the right to muscle in on purses of West Coast fighters, but the 1961 fracas over Liston, claimed Feds, brought Chicago crime boss Sam Giancana into conflict with three other Eastern bosses in the Commission: Angelo Bruno of Philadelphia, Tommy "Three Finger Brown" Lucchese, and Carlo Gambino. Four lesser gangland figures were also involved in the bickering: Frank Carbo, Blinky Palermo, John Vitale, aged fifty-four, "a St. Louis gang boss," and "Bernard Glickman, a Chicago boxing manager ... and a pal of crime syndicate gangsters." The FBI concluded that all four "held secret shares" in Liston from 1958 to 1961.

Vitale started Liston's pro career, but Glickman came in for twenty-five per cent after Liston went twenty-one months without a fight and Vitale needed a professional manager to move him. In 1958, Liston's contract went to Joseph "Pep" Barone, with Glickman retaining his interest. Glickman was able to keep his piece but had to make payoffs of $10,000 and $35,000 to Carbo and Palermo. In 1960 the US Senate subcommittee investigating boxing heard testimony that Liston was cut up this way: Carbo, fifty-two per cent, Palermo, twelve, Vitale, twelve, and two persons not identified, twelve. In 1961, before he became champ, Liston had his first real big money fight, the closed-circuit massacre of Albert Westphal. FBI records showed the purse was slightly over $65,000. After everybody got done stealing, Liston was left with just $14,975.

Having been pushed away from the trough, Glickman complained to the psychotic Chicago Mob boss Sam Giancana. But Giancana, who actually was sharing a girlfriend (Judith Campbell) with the then-president of the United States, John F. Kennedy, was rebuffed by Bruno, Lucchese and Gambino. Bruno, the mob boss of Philadelphia, and Giancana would eventually be murdered.

* * *

"Sonny Liston was a nice guy. He was a gentleman," recalled Cleveland Williams's beautiful wife, Irene, who danced with him before he knocked out her husband a second time in 1960. "I really think he was looking for his place in society."

According to his FBI file, Liston was spotted in a Black Muslim mosque in San Antonio, Texas. He went to Britain for a series of exhibitions, and the FBI followed his trail very closely, though he'd broken no laws. After getting a rousing welcome, and with Liston suddenly all smiles, he abruptly came home early.

"I'm ashamed to be an American," he spat at newsmen, after he deplaned in New York City. Liston was angry because racists in Birmingham, Alabama, had blown up a black church, and four little girls were killed.

"Look who's ashamed to be an American," crowed columnist Dan Parker who, like so many, held Liston responsible for being hostage to the Mob.

"Even after Liston became champion the Philadelphia police went right on harassing him," claimed writer Pat Putnam. "Petty things. Picking him up for standing on a street corner, or talking to someone. For Sonny, the last straw was when they picked him up in the park for driving too slow."

Liston finally left Philly, uttering the memorable quote, "I'd rather be a lamp post in Denver than the mayor of Philadelphia."

By 1963, Liston was going to church regularly, and actually became good friends with a priest in Denver named Father Murphy. "He hoped that would be the end of the police harrassment," said McKinney. Murphy taught Liston how to read and write, and "was one of the one or two people in the world that he ever trusted," according to Ray Collins, a Colorado newspaper editor. "He was childlike around Father Murphy."

But even Murphy felt that Sonny was doomed: "We've got to pray for the poor bastard."

Nat Fleischer called Liston "the greatest I've ever seen" after his second one-round demolition of Patterson. Yet "the Denver police harrassed Sonny," claimed one of his few white sparring partners, Ray Schoeniger. "I thought they treated him very bad. If he'd step one foot on the golf course where he (and I) ran, they were there with a ticket."

Finally, Liston moved to Las Vegas, the neon wasteland.

"He was like a big teddy bear," remembered the daughter of Ash Resnick, one of Liston's cronies. She was about ten at the time. Everyone agrees that Liston loved kids, but sadly he just couldn't seem to sire one of his own. The Listons adopted a beautiful little boy. "Sonny just loved Davey," remembers Geraldine. Liston probably felt his most relaxed around children. He would shadow box with them. Resnick's daughter would peck him on the cheek and he'd just beam.

There was, however, a man-child on the horizon who infuriated Sonny. His name was Cassius Clay.

★ ★ ★

Clay, the beautiful boy-poet from Louisville, Kentucky, had won nineteen fights in a row, and often predicted the round. He would prove to be the most colourful fighter ever, but in June 1963, he barely escaped beheading as Henry Copper landed one of his famed left hooks and floored him. 'Enery was bloodily slashed to defeat at Wembley before 55,000 in the very next round.

On 25 February 1964 Liston defended his heavyweight championship against Clay in Miami Beach. Clay was a huge 7-1 underdog. No-one believed that the man Henry Cooper decked could survive against Sonny. Robert Lypsyte, who covered the bout for the *New York Times*, was ordered by editors to find the nearest hospital beforehand, because they figured Clay might get beaten to death once he entered the ring.

Before the bout, Clay had brutally ridiculed the deadpan champion. It go so bad that when Clay ventured up to Liston while he was gambling in a Las Vegas casino, Sonny turned and angrily slapped him in the face.

"What's that for?" yelped Clay.

"'Cuz you're too fuckin' fresh."

Clay shrieked hysterically at the weigh-in, and fight groupies figured he was scared to death. His pulse raced to 120 from a normal 54. He was fined $5,000 by the local commission for his antics. Many opined they should call off the fight. Sonny darkly flashed two fingers, meaning the mismatch would end in the second round.

Credible rumours had been circulating that Clay had been seen with Malcolm X, the most controversial man in America. Malcolm, a minister in the Black Muslim movement, had outraged white America by publicly crowing, "The chickens have come home to roost," after President John F. Kennedy's shocking assassination in November. He'd reportedly been "silenced" by Elijah Muhammad, the leader of the cult, but in truth, Muhammad had told Malcolm not to get visibly involved with Clay. It would look bad for the Muslins, once Liston annihilated him.

Promoter Bill McDonald had threatened to cancel the fight because of Clay's rumoured Muslim involvement, and ticket sales were poor. The truth is, McDonald was just a front, and "the boys" were promoting that fight, remembered Bill Cayton. "The boys" was a euphemism for the Mob. Chris Dundee, Carbo's old stooge, was also involved.

Liston came out winging big left hooks, but Clay didn't crumple. He calmly jabbed, and actually rocked the "Big Ugly Bear." As Clay's jabs flashed out, Liston's dour mug began to bleed from a circular cut high on the left cheekbone. As the crowd of 8,297 rose, not believing what they were seeing, Liston was like "a bull hurt and maddened by the picadors' lances," wrote Lipsyte. Sonny kept hurling his massive 218 pounds forward, trying to finish his tormentor. He staggered Clay with a long left in the third. There wasn't much action in the fourth, but Clay was wincing badly.

Between rounds, Clay had screamed to Angelo Dundee, "Cut off my gloves, I can't see!" But Dundee simply pushed him out, and yelled, "Stay away!"

Something was in Clay's eyes, blinding him. He somehow avoided most of Liston's ponderous blows but took a beating to the body. At the end of the sixth, an exhausted, demoralized Liston simply quit on his stool. It was incredible. Clay went running over to the press section, bellowing, "Eat your words! Eat your words!"

The next day at the 11:00 AM press conference, the brash new champion announced, "I don't have to be what you want me to be. I'm free to be who I want."

"Are you a card-carrying Black Muslim?" a reporter asked.

"Card-carrying, what's that mean?" retorted the twenty-two-year-old champion angrily.

The soon-to-be Muhammad Ali then began to speak with religious fervour about the group's separatist doctrine. He bashed civil rights and calls for open housing. "In the jungle, lions are with lions and tigers with tigers. Redbirds stay with redbirds, bluebirds with bluebirds. That's human nature, to be with your own kind. I don't wanna go nowhere I ain't wanted."

Ali's rant was so shocking that people didn't realize he was ushering in a new age. Sonny Liston, the most reviled heavyweight champ since Jack Johnson, was suddenly the "hero" in the rematch. Years later, his cornerman Joe Polino publicly confessed to putting a burning substance of Liston's gloves so he could finish Clay in their first fight.

A 1995 HBO documentary called *Sonny Liston, the Mysterious Life and Death of a Champion* showed FBI documents, dated 8 May 1964, in which informants told the Bureau that the return match was going to be fixed. Johnny Tocco, who was running a gym in Las Vegas by then, heard things too.

"John Vitale was livin' at that time (and) he said, 'Don't pay attention to what you hear (good) about the next fight. You might as well not go with him."

"Why is that?" Rocco claims he asked.

"The fight's gonna be a one-round fight," Vitale supposedly said.

★ ★ ★

The rematch had been scheduled for November 1964, in Boston, Massachusetts, but Ali came down with hernia, which cancelled the fight. With rumours abounding, suddenly, nobody wanted to host the heavyweight championship of the world. Finally, on 25 May 1965, it ended up in a quaint little hockey arena in Lewiston, Maine, in front of 4,280 spectators.

Before the fight, Teddy Brenner, the Garden matchmaker, and Joe Louis walked into Liston's dressing room.

"Good luck, Sonny."

"Joe, I don't feel so good," grumbled Liston.

"Whaddya mean?" asked Louis.

Liston's head was on his massive chest, before he finally looked up and mumbled to Louis, "Just ain't right, Joe."

Brenner finally realized that "Liston was trying to tell Louis something in the dressing room."

In the first round, Ali danced with hands down before suddenly flashing a right lead. Liston hit the deck from a punch few ringsiders even saw. Films proved there was a right, which Ali twisted as he threw, but as Liston rolled on the deck in outrageous fashion, his awesome muscles didn't even tense as he supposedly tried to get up.

As cries erupted of "Fix! Fix!" and "Give us out money back," referee Jersey Joe Walcott didn't even count Liston out. He had lost complete control of the fight and was unable to get the furious Ali to a corner. Nat Fleischer, the feisty gnome who still edited *The Ring*, was actually tolling the count from ringside, and yelled to Walacot that Liston had been down more than ten seconds.

"I was standing right behind Fleischer," recalled Al Braverman, who had been brought in to handle Liston. "Fleischer was waving his arms back and forth, counting, like he was official or something. He yelled to Walcott and Walcott just panicked. You can't tell me a guy can get counted out when there ain't no count."

Though Fleischer was merely covering the fight as a reporter, and Liston finally had got up to resume, the match was halted. It was one of the worst boxing scandals in history.

"I took the mouthpiece out of Ali's mouth," claimed Abdul Rahman, who seconded him, "and he told me, 'He laid down.'"

Rahman replied, "No, you hit him."

Viewing the video of the 1965 fight, after Ali stands over the flopping Liston, screaming, "Get up!" you can see Ali in his corner with a quizzical look on his face, saying to his brother, "I hit him," like he can't quite believe it.

Liston's FBI file proves that there was an investigation of "sports bribery" but the Feds could get no hard evidence. According to William Roemer, a Chicago FBI agent who admitted to "black bag" jobs – illegal burglaries – on behalf of the Bureau, "We learned that there had definitely been a fix in that fight. Another guy who was very close to the Mob in Chicago, a guy by the name of Bernie Glickman, was very, very close to Liston. While he was conversing with Liston before the fight, and with Geraldine, Geraldine said to Liston that as long as he had to dump the fight, 'Don't take the chance of getting hurt. As long as you're going to go down anyhow, go down early.' Of course, he went down in the first round." Geraldine Liston subsequently denied this. But what's a loyal wife going to say?

At the weigh-in, Sam Margolis had been spotted, sweating heavily. Margolis was Blinky Palermo's old restaurant partner. Though Carbo and Palermo were in prison, "I thought Blinky was a great guy," said Braverman. "He got me the job with Liston."

Braverman claims he told Liston weeks before the fight, "If you give me any God damn trouble, I going to hit you over the head with a broken bottle." After the farce, "Sonny didn't wanna face anybody," recalled Braverman in 1991. "He wanted to go out the back door. I grabbed him and said, 'Come on. You're going out the front.'"

Paul Venti, a New Jersey boxing judge and referee, later claimed that Carbo and Palermo were actually making matches out of prison. Palermo supposedly had a phone. That sounds hard to believe – but Braverman always insisted that Palermo got him the job with Liston.

Why would Liston dive? Since Ali was the underdog, a betting coup? Nobody could've predicted a first-round KO, but what critics don't understand: while the Mob may have controlled Liston, Ali wasn't going to be so easy. He definitely had protection. The Muslims killed Malcolm X. There's no question that Black Muslim leader Elijah Muhammad was behind that. Only a fool believes that Muhammad wouldn't have dispatched some of the "Fruit of Islam" to take care of people in the Mob if they got greedy. As Black Muslims converged on Lewiston, rumours were that even Liston grew afraid.

Muhammad Ali was a money machine. "God *needs* your money," Herbert Muhammad always told him. Herbert, Elijah's son, eventually became Ali's manager. He knew so little about the boxing business that Chris Dundee was actually negotiating the contracts. In a fabled career, Ali continued to fight way too long, until he suffered so badly from Parkinson's, he has terrible tremors and can barely speak. Once upon a time, he "floated like a butterfly and stung like a bee." Now his wife Lonnie has to wipe the food that spills from his mouth.

* * *

Liston's outrageous flop destroyed his reputation. He became such a pariah in the States that he couldn't get a license. Maybe Jim Norris, Carbo and Palermo were gone, but the Mafia was still in the fight game.

Intercontinental Promotions was now official promoter of heavyweight championship contests. Bob Nilon, the supposed head of Intercontinental, was Jack Nilon's brother. Nobody in boxing had ever heard of Bob before, but Jack was the Mob's "front" manager of Liston. Bob was the front promoter. The Kefauver Committee proved that in 1960, when Intercontinental was formed, Liston was voluntarily giving up seventy-five per cent of his stock in the so-called promotional company, which they deemed excessive. Sonny actually paid George Katz, another Mob front, $75,000 to purchase his managerial contract back. Since Liston couldn't read or write, he didn't know what he was signing. He just got bled, in and out of the ring.

Geraldine Liston swears that Sonny got no money for throwing the fight to Ali. According to Liston's 1965 income tax return, he had a taxable income of just $100,000. The IRS claimed Liston's taxable income was actually $199,000. Still, that was only about a quarter of what his purse should have been. There's no question that Liston got robbed blind.

Intercontinental couldn't do business in New York or Pennsylvania, but Las Vegas was blatantly run by the Mob in the 1960s. On 22 November 1965, Intercontinental promoted Ali's first defence, against former champ Floyd Patterson. It was so one-sided that Lipsyte likened it to a "little boy pulling off the wings of a butterfly." Patterson had foolishly turned the fight into a religious war between Islam and Catholicism, and promised to "bring the title back to America." But as Mob-friendly stars like Frank Sinatra and Dean Martin sat ringside, Patterson was taunted and humiliated by the magnificent young champion, before his back gave out and he had to be rescued at 2:18 of the twelfth round.

Twenty-one days earlier, however, there had been another "heavyweight championship" fight. The World Boxing Association had stripped Ali of the title for his religious beliefs and in Toronto, Canada, gangling Ernie Terrell defended his lightly-regarded WBA title against rock-jawed Canadian George Chuvalo. Though Terrell would bitterly say after his career, "I never had a manager," Bernie Glickman, Carbo's old front, was now "managing" Terrell. "Bernie Glickman came up there and he scared everybody to death," recalled Chuvalo thirty years later. "He said, 'If you throw punches, you're going to end up in Lake Erie.'"

For six rounds, the Terrell-Chuvalo fight was fairly competitive, but in the last half of the fight, the video shows that the normally free-swinging Chuvalo barely punched at all. Terrell won a decision. According to Bill Roemer, the Chicago FBI man, Glickman then tried to match Ali with Terrell in Chicago, but Glickman was warned by New York heavy Frank "Funzi" Tierri, who became a member of the ruling commission of La Cosa Nostra, "that the fight had better take place in New York or you'll get your legs broken." According to Roemer, the New York mob had "accommodations" with the Garden's matchmaker Teddy Brenner. Brenner had been the promoter at the old Eastern Parkway in Brooklyn when it was controlled by Albert Anastasia and Vito Genovese.

Glickman was good friends with Tony Accardo, the *de facto* boss of the Chicago mob, and ate breakfast with Accardo every Sunday. Normally, when the bald, spindly Glickman, who looked twenty years older than he was, brought up the sport, the dapper Accardo, who looked more like a middle-aged fruit vendor than a former contract killer for Al Capone, waved him off, saying, "Don't bring me your boxing business."

But this time Glickman had big problems. "Tieri told me they had a piece of Terrell. I think they're trying to steal the fighter," he said, furrowing, his homely brow. Accardo finally agreed to send "Milwaukee Phil" Alderesio to New York with Glickman.

On the way back, Alderesio suddenly turned on Glickman. For reasons that Roemer couldn't understand, Alderesio began pounding the hell out of the frail man. The beating left Glickman in fear of his life, but these were "love taps." Alderesio was the top killer in Chicago. He even had a special "murder mobile" to do hits. The FBI calculated he'd done about fourteen.

For some reason, Alderesio sided with New York on Terrell. Accardo didn't know, but Alderesio suspected, that Glickman was an FBI snitch. Maybe Glickman scared Chuvalo and his people in Toronto, but this frail, grandfatherly aluminium siding manufacturer had been apprising Roemer of fight fixes for some time. He had been "turned" years earlier by Johnny Bassett, a former pro light-heavy who became an FBI man. Bassett had been Roemer's partner for ten years. Since Roemer had also been a Marine Corps, and four-time Notre Dame University boxing champ, it was a perfect scenario for Glickman to roll over.

Though Carbo and Palermo were behind bars, Jim Norris and Kefauver were dead, and Bonomi was history, the FBI was conducting an investigation "about the Mob's involvement in the fight game all over the country, a heavy involvement at the time," contended Roemer. Glickman feared Alderesio was going to kill him, but Roemer told him he would get a pass as long as he testified in front of a secret grand jury. Glickman was caught between the Mob and the FBI. He'd have to testify under oath against Alderesio and Tieri, but Glickman absolutely refused to implicate his friend Accardo, whose Mob nickname was "Joe Batters" because he used a baseball bat on people – unless it required a gun. A couple of years earlier, when Accardo was indicted for tax evasion, Glickman had flagrantly lied under oath for him.

Before Glickman agreed to testify against Tieri and Alderesio, Roemer and Bassett filled out an FD-209 informant report; then an FD-302, which was an investigative memo. They finally took him to Ed Hanrahan, the volatile US Attorney for the Northern District of Illinois, in downtown Chicago. They intentionally left out all references to Accardo. Hanrahan nodded his head. He understood.

As Hanrahan paraded Glickman through the secret grand jury, Bernie proved to be a fine witness. Then Hanrahan asked about Accardo. Glickman looked stricken. He'd been double-crossed. As Hanrahan furiously pounded away about Accardo's involvement in organized crime, Glickman sputtered badly and repeatedly lied under oath. He absolved Accardo, but in doing so had perjured himself so badly that he blew away the rest of the Feds' cases. None of his testimony was any good.

Hanrahan was so furious, he hissed at Roemer and Bassett, "Take him out of here. The case is down the drain. Finished. Kaput. Put him on the street. We're finished with him."

Roemer protested. "He'll be dead before he gets to State and Madison."

Hanrahan didn't care. (In 1969, at the height of the protest movement, Hanrahan would be allegedly responsible for the Chicago Police Department firing ninety-nine unanswered rounds into an apartment that housed Black Panther Party leaders Fred Hampton and Mark Clark, killing them at four in the morning. In 1983, the slain leaders relatives were awarded millions in damages in federal court.)

Roemer and Bassett felt betrayed, but responsible for Glickman. They didn't want his blood on their hands. Before he had testified, they hid him out at nearby Camp Sheridan, an army base, under the ruse of him being a colonel. Though Glickman should have stayed quiet, the fool contacted a Chicago reporter, Sandy Smith, wanting to write a book. Art Petaque, Smith's rival at another Chicago daily, heard about it. Suddenly, Glickman's "secret" grand testimony was in two different papers.

"Kill him," Accardo growled to Alederesio. "He's got to go before he hits the stand."

Mob crews combed the streets. Roemer and Bassett pleaded with their boss, but Marlin Johnson, who headed the Chicago office, got another call from the unstable Hanrahan. "Throw him out on the street!"

Bernie was a dead man. Roemer called in a favour and got Bill Duffy, a commander in the Chicago Police Department, to put the hyper-ventilating "song bird" under his protection for the night at the Pick-Congress Hotel. But Roemer had to act fast. A lot of Chicago cops were on the Mob's payroll.

Roemer got hold of Ralph Pierce, the Southside Mob boss who'd been around since the days of Frank Nitti, Al Capone's successor. Though FBI men are normally white collar, button-down, don't-make-waves types, Roemer told Pierce, "I need to see Accardo. It's a matter of life and death."

Pierce was sceptical. He didn't want Accardo coming after him if it was a trick, and he definitely didn't trust Roemer or the FBI. Pierce finally called Roemer three hours later. He had gone out to see Accardo at his River Forest home. Pierce muttered "Sears parking lot, North and Harlem at midnight," then hung up the phone.

It was desolate and dark as Roemer arrived. It was great place to get killed, but Roemer, who was alone, had a good reputation with wiseguys. He'd never tried to frame them. He always "got them square." Pierce appeared out of a shrouded building. He had been watching Roemer and checking for tails. Roemer was worried, too. He had thrown out the FBI manual as he tried to save Glickman's life. Roemer was instructed to walk three blocks to nearby Elmwood Park, a notorious Mob neighbourhood. Then Accardo appeared.

Roemer, suddenly worried that Accardo might be setting him up, politely said, "Joe, I've got to search you." He wanted to ensure there was no recording device so Accardo could blackmail him.

As soon as the burly FBI man reached for Accardo, out jumped six mobsters, including Jackie "the Lackey" Cerrone, who would later run America's "Second City." Roemer already had him on an illegal wiretap bragging about a slew of killings.

Finally, after small talk and nervous banalities, Roemer got down to business. He explained Glickman's deal with the FBI. As Accardo's bushy eyebrows flared, Roemer told him that Bernie was only supposed to testify about Alederesio and Tieri "but not about you." Roemer insisted that the deal was Glickman would never discuss Accardo, even though Hanrahan and the Department of Justice desperately wanted him to. Finally, Roemer told the grizzled crime boss, "He lied to protect you."

Accardo knew that the legal case was finished. He asked, "What do you want from me?"

"Call off the contract."

Accardo gave a cynical laugh: "Do you believe everything you read in the papers?"

Roemer pleaded that Glickman was a mess. His health was terrible. He was out of his mind with fear.

Finally, Accardo looked at the rugged FBI agent, and sneered, "Roemer, I thought *we* were supposed to be the bad guys."

"Bernie's your friend," Roemer insisted.

The next day FBI agents took Glickman out to Accardo's house. The petrified Glickman thought he was having a heart attack as he waited for Accardo. After looking at his broken-down "former friend," Accardo took the trembling fight manager to his personal physician, and he was put in St. Luke's Presbyterian Hospital. Accardo paid all the bills.

Ernie Terrell and Muhammad Ali did fight, on 6 February 1967 – in the Houston Astrodome, before 37,321, then an indoor record.

In 1986, Glickman died of old age in Palm Springs, California.

* * *

On 29 June 1966, Sonny Liston was back in the ring. Once a scowling, menacing wrecking ball of a man, he was now an object of ridicule and scorn. But he needed money, and stopped former German heavyweight champion Gerhard Zech in Stockholm, Sweden. On August 19, Liston knocked out Amos Johnson, who had upset Henry Cooper nine months earlier. In March 1967, Philadelphia trial horse Dave Bailey went out in the first. In April, former contender Elmer Rush was halted in the sixth. But Liston hadn't dare venture outside Sweden.

He desperately wanted to fight in the States again, so he reluctantly descended on Nat Fleischer, in his old, horribly cramped office at *The Ring* in New York. Sonny was practically begging for a second chance.

"I should be ranked," Liston began, uncomfortably.

"Where at?" snapped the prudish old man, who came up to about Liston's waist.

"Top of the heap."

Fleischer finally stopped glaring and gave a derisive laugh. He looked at Liston like he'd lost his mind. Then he lashed into him with fiery, Old Testament wrath.

"Your record as a fighter doesn't justify that," intoned Fleischer, his huge, saddlebag eyes now flashing. "Besides, what about your record as a man?"

"What's that got to do with it?" sighed Liston.

In June 1970, Liston stopped Chuck Wepner in ten of the bloodiest rounds ever seen in a Jersey City ring.

"Is Wepner the bravest guy you've ever seen?" asked *Newark Star-Ledger* sportswriter Jerry Izenberg."

"Nah, his manager is," deadpanned Liston.

Wepner ended up with sixty-seven stitches in his battered football of a mug. He later recalled, "Every time he hit me in the face, it felt like he broke something."

A local mobster had promised Liston $16,000 for the fight. Sonny was supposedly given just eight. Some say he ended up with nothing.

In early January 1971, Geraldine Liston worriedly flew home from St Louis, after a visit to her mother over Christmas. For some reason, she wasn't able to get Sonny on the phone. As she entered their tasteful Las Vegas home, she was hit by an odd smell, but thought that Sonny had burned something while cooking. As she walked into the bedroom, she suddenly recoiled: there was Sonny's decomposing body, sprawled in bed. Geraldine began to scream, then ordered their toddler stepson Davey to "get back."

Lore has it that Sonny was murdered. Las Vegas cops say drug paraphernalia was found at the scene. In all likelihood, this tragic, broken man died of a heroin overdose. He was officially thirty-eight.

Davey Pearl, the former Las Vegas referee, grew very close to Liston in his final years, and he laments that the public never knew the Liston he did. "He was such a nice guy, and it's a shame. Most people don't realize what a nice guy he was. Sonny was a very hard man to get to know. He was quiet. He was a loner. He was very rarely with anybody. He didn't trust people, and I don't blame him. People beat him out of millions of dollars. Phoney managers."

Schoeniger remembered Sonny drunk one night, and Liston said to him, almost pitifully: "You like me, don't you?"

"Sure I like you," the sparmate said. "Sonny always expected people were going to hurt him. Y'know, beat him with a stick."

"Sonny Liston died the day he was born." figured publicity man Harold Conrad, who believed that he was murdered.

* * *

J. Edgar Hoover attended big fights, so why didn't he do anything to drive out mobsters? The FBI's own records prove that Hoover had known the Mob was heavily involved in boxing since at least 1946. Why did Hoover, who ran the Bureau despotically for half a century, repeatedly say, "There's no such thing as organized crime," despite overwhelming evidence to the contrary?

According to Anthony Summers, who wrote the brilliant book *Official and Confidential, the Secret Life of J. Edgar Hoover*, this incorruptible bulldog, this icon who embodied all that was good about America, was horribly compromised. Summers devastatingly proved that Hoover was a closet homosexual and said the Mafia had pictures of Hoover giving Clyde Tolson, the number two man in the FBI, a blow job.

There's no question that Hoover and the handsome Tolson were lovers. Hoover had even been arrested in New Orleans in the 1920s on a homosexuality charge. He was also a transvestite, and the Mob had damning proof. On New Year's 1936, after dinner at New York's Stork Club, Hoover and Tolson were seen by two of gossip columnist Walter Winchell's friends holding hands. Jimmy Braddock, then heavyweight champ but controlled by gangster Owney Madden, dined with them that evening. Dozens of people knew about Hoover and Tolson but nobody dared speak out. Hoover was the most feared man in the country.

Hoover was routinely seen at racetracks fraternizing with gamblers. They reportedly fixed races, then passed on tips so he'd win. Mob associate Seymor Pollock, who was involved with Meyer Lansky, claims he saw Hoover and Tolson holding hands at one track in 1948, when Frank Bompensiero, a deadly West Coast gangster, actually began mocking Hoover to his face. After spying Hoover, Bompensierro suddenly bellowed loudly, so everyone could hear, "J. Edgar Hoover's a punk, he's a degenerate queer."

Later, in the men's room, Hoover, the most feared man in the United States, pleaded, "Frank, that's not a nice way to talk, especially when I have people with me."

In 1972, when President Richard Nixon got word that had Hoover died, he simply exclaimed, "Why, that old cocksucker!" Teams began arriving at Hoover's Washington home to frantically destroy his secret files.

Six years later, Ethel Merman, a Broadway star, and closet lesbian, came out against Anita Bryant's gay-bashing campaign and proclaimed, "Some of my best friends are homosexual. Everybody knew about J. Edgar Hoover, but he was the best chief the FBI had."

Hoover should have resigned, long before the possibility existed of blackmail. Instead he compiled thousands of confidential files on senators, congressman, and presidents, and simply blackmailed them to stay on. For years, the liberal media demanded that Hoover be fired, but a frightened President Lyndon B. Johnson gave him a lifetime appointment in 1965 because "I'd rather have that sonofabitch pissing outside the tent than pissing in."

Hoover was one of the most dangerous man in American history, but by the 1960s, even FBI agents were privately referring to him as "J. Edna" and his sidekick as "Mother Tolson."

In the late 1950s, Susan Rosenstiel, wife of mobster Lefty Rosenstiel, knew Hoover well and socialized with him, along with her husband. According to her, in 1958 Hoover helped her corrupt, liquor baron husband to bribe a number of politicians, including Lyndon Johnson, so a protective piece of liquor taxation was passed. Johnson supposedly got $500,000. She also claimed that she caught her husband having sex with rabidly anti-communist lawyer Roy Cohn, who'd helped spread the demagogic Senator Joseph McCarthy's virulent message, and made it virtually impossible to have an intelligent discussion on communism, which ultimately resulted in the millions being killed in the Vietnam War. Cohn was finally disbarred. The avidly anti-homosexual mouthpiece died of AIDS in 1986.

Susan Rosenstiel claims she was with Hoover, Cohn and her husband at another party, where Hoover was in drag, looking like the world's ugliest 1920s flapper, garbed in a black wig. Cohn laughed as he told her to call the feared Director of the FBI, "Mary." Young men were then brought in for Hoover's pleasure.

In 1969, the Los Angeles police were investigating a child pornography and teen prostitution ring. Cops heard from kids they talked to that Hoover and Tolson, on another of their endless "inspection tours," picked up boys in an FBI limo. One fifteen-year-old was supposedly given a stern lecture by Hoover, about his long hair, before he had sex with the old man.

"The homosexual thing was Hoover's Achilles heel," claimed Pollock. "Meyer (Lansky) found it, and it was like he pulled strings with Hoover. He never bothered any of Meyer's people." Pollock claims Hoover knew who killed Bugsy Siegel in 1946, but nothing was done. Time proved it was Frankie Carbo, the Underworld Czar of Boxing.

Even frightened insiders in the Bureau wondered why Lansky, and Frank Costello (who was Carbo's protection) were untouchable. In 1971, a year before Hoover's death, Ash Resnick, Sonny Liston's old buddy, told writer Pete Hamill that Lansky was the guy who really put organized crime together. He was the one who "nailed J. Edgar Hoover."

"Lansky was the guy who controlled the pictures, and he had made his deal with Hoover to lay off," Hamill was told.

Though organized crime was given a fifty-year head start to prey upon America, and drugs and prostitution are a fact of life, few suffered as badly as the forgotten prize-fighters who sweat, bled, and occasionally died in the ring.

Sonny Liston ended up broke. Tommy "Hurricane" Jackson shined shoes. Nino Valdes, Marciano's top contender, washed dishes. God-fearing Ezzard Charles went bankrupt, and was evicted from his modest Chicago home. He died in 1975 of amyotropic lateral sclerosis, which made him unable to speak or move anything but his eyelids.

The corruption that made all this possible didn't end with Hoover. According to John Miller, a correspondent with ABC News, "There was a time in Forties, and the Fifties in particular, when you did not become a judge, or anybody of any significance in New York City politics, without getting Frank Costello's OK."

According to Joe Coffey, a former New York State investigator, "Prohibition gave the mob its financial base. It brought so much money into them, they were able to branch out into other areas." Dirty money bought cops, politicians, judges and district attorneys. According to writer Ernest Volkman, who wrote *Gangbusters*, "Costello established the trinity, for making politics, business and crime all co-exist together."

Leonard Katz, who wrote the Costello biography *Uncle Frank*, agreed: "He was a corruptor. When judges are bought, when police chiefs are bought, when people in government are bought, it changes our system of government. It's much more dangerous than Vito Genovese, who merely kills."

In 1961, the Attorney General for the United States, Bobby Kennedy, allowed Jackie Leonard to go into the Witness Protection Program. The former fight promoter ended up working for the Government in the Army Corps of Engineers. Jackie commanded projects in Hawaii, the Marshall Islands, in Saudi Arabia, and built hospitals, schools and roads all over the world. He was in charge of a de-salinization project near the Red Sea, where he was "resident engineer." But he couldn't come home. There was a $50,000 contract on his life.

When Leonard testified against Carbo, there was a machine gun on the front lawn of the North Hollywood motel where he and his wife stayed. Carbo died in 1976, while the released Palermo got out of prison in 1971 and actually tried to get back his license to manage fighters, but Jackie was still on the lam. Finally, in 1990, a good thirty years after he testified, he showed up in Florida and got himself a dumpy old gym. One day Chris Dundee saw him and groused, "If the boys were here, they'd know how to take care of ya."

In 1961, when Carbo and Palermo were convicted, Bobby Kennedy publicly called it a victory over oranized crime. But when Bobby, who was virtually "co-president," was asked to push Estes Kefauver's bill for federal control, he turned his fellow Democrat down. Why? Was it because he didn't want to embarrass his brother, John, who was president, with a bill that wouldn't pass? Or was it because Owney Madden, who ran the fight game in the 1930s, and Frank Costello had once been bootlegging partners with Bobby and Jack's crooked father, Joe?

CHAPTER SIX

Send in the Clowns: the WBA

PROFESSIONAL BOXING ALWAYS has been a rogue sport. In 1921, it wasn't unknown for fighters like "knockout artist" Young Stribling to travel the backwoods flattening their sparring partners, who boxed under aliases. In that same year, the National Boxing Association was formed in Rhode Island. It promised to bring order out of the chaos of boxing administration. In reality, it was a loose coalition of state commissions who would invariably ignore edicts from above. In the early days, the NBA meant well but had no legal power to stop states going their own way, especially if it meant stealing a lucrative fight from fellow members.

Wall Street was the financial centre of the universe and New York City was the Holy Land of boxing. During the "Roaring Twenties," a greedy, conniving ticker scalper like Mike Jacobs could end up with his own bank vault, fronting money to Tex Rickard, the biggest promoter in the world. Rickard regularly filled Madison Square Garden and ballparks like Yankee Stadium and the Polo Grounds, which could hold 75,000 screaming people for a big fight. The Garden accommodated 20,000 for boxing but could pack in 23,000 if the fire marshal looked the other way.

On 18 June 1923, at the cavernous Polo Grounds, Welshman Jimmy Wilde lost his world flyweight title to Pancho Villa. Around 40,000 showed up, paying a record $127,000. Wilde had drawn just $27,500 in London when beating Young Zulu Kid for the title in 1911. "You just couldn't believe the publicity boxing got in the old days," recalled Bill Cayton, later to co-manage Mike Tyson and others. "In New York, there were huge pictures and stories all over the papers." Baseball and boxing were the only major professional sports in America, and while baseball deity Babe Ruth struggled to reach $85,000 a year, Gene Tunney made a cool million for his rematch with Jack Dempsey. "You're not a champion till you fight in the Garden," was the sport's credo.

Yet when the NBA came along, with more of a whimper than a bang, it was located in *New Jersey*. Maybe New Jersey was just a short Model T ride away, but it might as well have been another galaxy. The political hacks who ran the New York State Athletic Commission, the most powerful in the world, wanted nothing to do with the NBA.

In 1923, Ireland's Mike McTigue defeated Battling Siki for the light-heavyweight title in Dublin on St Patrick's Day. The gate was equivalent to $17,500. When Paul Berlenbach whipped McTigue two years later in New York City, they drew $58,500. In July 1926, Jack Delaney dethroned Berlenbach in Brooklyn, a borough of New York City. This time the take was a staggering $461,768.

There's an old saying: Everybody wants New York, but New York's gotta want *you*. While the NBA decided on its own world champions, the rival New York champs were much more widely recognised. On 30 August 1927, Jimmy Slattery outboxed Maxie Rosenbloom to win the NBA light-heavyweight championship. Despite Rickard's prediction that Slattery "was the next Jack Dempsey," they fought in the backwater of Hartford, Connecticut. Five weeks later in New York City, Tommy Loughran outpointed McTigue for the true title and drew $72,502. In September 1927, squat Benny Bass, dubbed "the smallest heavyweight in the world," outslugged Red Chapman in Philadelphia to win the vacant NBA featherweight title. A month later, brilliant young Tony Canzoneri whipped ex-champ Johnny Dundee for the *real* title in the Big Apple.

In London, the National Sporting Club had once decreed that a British championship couldn't be won unless it was fought under their auspices. For years, New York's dollar signs had been saying the same thing. On July 10, 1939, Len Harvey defeated Jock McAvoy, to win Britain's version of the world light-heavyweight championship. Just three days later, in New York City, Billy Conn outboxed Melio Bettina for *the* world crown.

Even by 1940, there was little interest in NBA titles. After twenty years, it had sanctioned few "championship" fights. In December 1933, Andy Callahan took on Vince Dundee, who had just won both the New York and NBA versions of the middleweight championship. The match was in Boston, Massachusetts. The Great Depression was on. Paul Berlenbach, who'd earned $500,000 when he was a champ, was openly pleading for a job in newspaper ads. On the eve of the bout, W.A. Hamilton, who covered the contest for the *Boston Herald*, wrote, "Should Callahan win the title, he will hold the distinction of being the smallest man ever to win a middleweight crown." But on December 8, the very day of the fight, reporters were barred from the official weigh-in "for the first time in the history of the sport."

Dundee won a bitterly-contested match on points. As fans streamed out of the Boston Garden, Johnny Buckley, Callahan's manager, started bellowing.

"They really gave it to me tonight!" Turning towards anyone who'd listen, Buckley screeched, "Andy weighed 141 pounds, which was why reporters weren't allowed to watch Andy and Vince on the scales." Dundee, a strong middleweight, had just defended his title against a junior-welter, in violation of state law.

Years later Billy Ames, who had been the Boston Garden matchmaker, confessed what had been done: Buckley had taken a 100-pound weight that belonged to the official Fairbanks scales and "had it drilled out and padded with mercury or some other substance, so instead of being a 100-pound weight, it really made it 115. My job was to distract Mitch Hambro (of the Boxing Commission) a nice fellow, while Buckley made the switch. I managed to do it, and I'll never forget Mitch's eyes when Andy got on the scales and it showed him weighing 151 pounds."

The fight ruined Callahan. He didn't get paid. His girlfriend had promised to marry him – but only if he won – and the colourful youngster became a drunk. He lived with his parents until he joined the U.S. Army in 1941, and was killed in combat two years later in Italy. Jack Sharkey "loved Callahan like a brother," and went to Monte Cassini when Andy had fallen, trying to find his grave. Callahan wouldn't be brought back to Lawrence, Massachusetts till 1949. His body was accorded a hero's welcome.

The Dundee-Callahan fight had promised the near-bankrupt Boston Garden some badly-needed revenue. Yet the gate receipts were ridiculously low for an 18,000-seat arena that was almost packed. Ames claimed that the fight drew enormous local interest and they had "$22,000 worth of advance seats sold," but two sets of final figures were officially given, one of $15, 276, while the Associated Press claimed $14,200. Somebody had dipped into the till. Buckley was both promoter and Callahan's manager. According to John Bonomi, who later served on the Kefauver investigation of boxing in 1960, Buckley was a business partner with the notorious Owney Madden, who ran the fight game. The Boston Garden was only two blocks away from Boston's North End, the local headquarters for organized crime.

The Massachusetts commission and the holier-than-thou NBA were involved, though nobody alleged that they stole money. But why didn't Massachusetts State boxing chairman Daniel J. Kelley show up at the weigh-in? Why did Ed Foster, the president of the NBA, come in late? Was it because they both knew Callahan wasn't a middleweight and didn't want to be accountable under state law? When the scandal finally broke, Bobby Goldman, a Boston Garden official, swore he had banned the reporters at Kelley's request. Foster's absence at the weigh-in also points a finger at him and the NBA.

* * *

In October 1942, with World War Two raging, the NBA announced that its championships would be frozen for the duration of the conflict. "A man in the Service is entitled to complete protection of his championship under all circumstances until he's able to defend," said Abe J. Greene, who now headed the organization. The NBA also introduced an early version of the sanction fee. "From now on, two per cent of a fighter's purse, and a manager's cut, will be deducted. We want it said, that we were able to do our part," Greene said. "Greene was the best boxing commissioner ever," said Teddy Brenner, who spent fifty years in the game.

In November 1943, the NBA announced it would end "shotgun" championship return bouts – where a winning fighter automatically had to give his opponent a rematch – not "based on championship merit," and refused to sanction any fight unless it was first submitted to the NBA for approval. Greene claimed this was adopted to "avoid the see-saw game operating between [lightweights] Bob Montgomery and Beau Jack, in which first one, then the other, gets a return match." It was also a power play against the New York State Athletic Commission. Beau Jack fought out of Madison Square Garden and was the biggest draw during the War.

In 1946, with the War finally over, the NBA issued an edict for champions to defend against their top contenders. Unlike *Ring* magazine, the NBA didn't issue a Top Ten. It only sent out a list of logical contenders. However, the public wanted to see Joe Louis against Billy Conn again, not against the more deserving fellow black Jimmy Bivins, who had been the "interim" champ while Louis was in the army. Other great black fighters like Archie Moore, Holman Williams and Charley Burley would never get a shot at middleweight champ Tony Zale. "We don't use coal," a New York matchmaker told Irving Rudd, then a young publicist. "Coal" was a euphemism for black people.

Mike Jacobs, who had taken over the promotional reins in the mid-1930s, held that black fighters wouldn't draw. Moore fought seventeen years before he got his chance at a world crown, and made all of $800 for taking the light-heavyweight championship off Joey Maxim in 1952. "Charley Burley was the best fighter I ever saw. He could take your head off with one punch," recalled Moore forty years later, his voice still filled with awe. Eddie Futch, one of the best trainers in the history of sport, agreed. But Burley, good as he was, stayed a Pittsburgh garbage collector even though the powerless NBA decreed that he was the number one middleweight contender. Even Sugar Ray Robinson, who was the Mozart of the prize ring while other pugs were simply street corner musicians, had to trounce four ex-welterweight champs – Henry Armstrong, Fritzie Zivic,

Freddie Cochrane and Marty Servo – before finally winning the vacant title against Tommy Bell in 1946.

Ring editor Nat Fleischer, who was one of the most powerful voices in boxing, had long campaigned for equal opportunity, and Greene agreed. "There's got to be a way for champion to be compelled to fight his top contender," he said.

On 20 September 1946, Tony Zale and Rocky Graziano waged war in Yankee Stadium. Blow-by-blow announcer Don Dunphy's voice kept breaking as Zale came back from the abyss to flatten Grazano in the sixth. The first middleweight title fight in five years broke the box office record for the division at $342,497. Zale and Graziano were both tough, exciting, and white – and they could draw a crowd.

Never mind the no-return policy; there had to be a rematch. Then Graziano, who had been dishonourably discharged from the army for slugging an officer, was abruptly run out of New York for not reporting a dive offer against Reuben "Cowboy" Shank. Still his rematch with Zale went ahead, in Chicago. In July 1947, he blasted out the "Man of Steel" in another barbaric, breathtaking fight. This one drew $442,000, guaranteeing a *third* match. In September 1948, with the bright lights of Manhattan visible, Zale finished the brutal trilogy by laying Graziano out in the third round in Jersey City. This generated another $405,000.

Maybe matchmaker Teddy Brenner and George Kanter, the ancient booking agent, were probably right when they said, "[Charley] Burley and [Holman] Williams would've destroyed Graziano," but professional boxing is show business with blood, and Graziano was a star attraction.

On 22 June 1949, Ezzard Charles won a fifteen-round decision over Jersey Joe Walcott at Comiskey Park in Chicago for the NBA heavyweight championship. Charles, who had been the top-rated middleweight in 1941, was much better as a light-heavy and wasn't taken seriously as the new heavyweight champ until he vanquished the slow, bloated Joe Louis, on the Brown Bomber's sad comeback in September 1950. Meanwhile Lee Savold stopped Britain's Bruce Woodcock for the British version of the "world championship" – but the States was where the money was, and nobody took Savold's claim seriously.

By the late 1950s, boxing had become much more of an international sport, but glorious headlines like "Louis Stops Baer ... as 95,000 Look On" were long gone. Even New York was in terminal decline. Television had drastically changed cultural patterns. In America, "the magic box " practically killed boxing. In the 1950s, there were two, briefly three, nationally televised boxing shows every week, and it was too much. Fans stopped attending shows that they could watch on the box instead. The Garden virtually went down for the count when ABC cancelled the last remaining contract, the TV interest waned, and living rooms finally went dark on September 11, 1964.

★ ★ ★

The National Boxing Association was renamed the World Boxing Association. On 25 February 1964, a young, brash Cassius Clay heralded a new age when he stopped "the Big Ugly Bear," Sonny Liston, in Miami. The Mob-controlled Liston had been bad for the game, but with many screaming "Fix!" and Clay suddenly unveiling himself as Muhammad Ali, Black Muslim, the WBA stripped *him* "for conduct unbecoming a champion."

In May 1964, in Accra, Ghana, Sugar Ramos won a deplorable decision over Ghana's Floyd Robertson to retain the world featherweight championship. The crowd of 30,000 booed loudly and even Londoner Jack Solomons, who promoted the contest, kept sputtering, "Bloody incredible. This is an outrage! Robertson won." Robertson had even knocked down Ramos, a Mexican-based Cuban, in the thirteenth, but Ramos simply brought his own judges. Referee Jack Hart of Britain gave the verdict to Robertson, but Ramon Velasquez, who years later would be accused of sweaty palms which stuck to money, and Ed Lassman, of Miami Beach, who was WBA president as well as being one of the judges, voted for the champion. Ghana later reversed the result and made Robertson the winner, but the rest of the world accepted the original decision. Ohene Djan, Ghana's sports director, called for the reversal because of the "dramatic and irregular decision of the two American-based nominee judges of Sugar Ramos" (actually Velasquez was a Mexican). Months earlier, Lassman had called for the WBA to strip Ali, despite the champ's constitutional right to practise his religion. This was the second time in three months that one of his decisions had sparked international controversy. But as president of the WBA, Lassman was being asked to overturn his own decision.

In March 1965, Ernie Terrell was anointed as WBA heavyweight champion after an appalling match in Chicago against Eddie Machen. Five thousand fans continuously booed a dreadful maul that was so bad it stunk out the Chicago stockyards. There was so much hugging and grabbing that one wiseass in the cheap seats bellowed, "Cut the lights out. They wanna be alone."

With boxing off the tube, and everyone from the Pope to the *New York Times* calling for it to be banned following the high-profile ring deaths of Benny Paret and featherweight Davey Moore, the WBA wasn't very active. Sure, they had conventions, where *Ring* editor Nat Fleischer was shouted down for trying to plead Ali's case that "titles should be won and lost in the ring." The WBA's lack of clout was exemplified by Arch Hindman, an obscure Indiana guy who drew up the ratings. Hindman had to beg Teddy Brenner to even get a free ticket into the near-empty Garden.

The WBA was a haven for political hacks. From 1921 to 1973 it had all American presidents except for two Canadians. There were protests about this, but in 1964 Ed Lassman vowed, "If I get one more goddamn letter from overseas, I'm gonna wad it up without even openin' it."

Still, there were people in the organization who tried to do the right thing. "I was president of the WBA during Sonny Liston's reign," recalled Dr Charles Larson, a noted pathologist, "and we finally sent him to Father Edward Murphy in Denver, where he was taught to read and write some. When he was champion, we had a problem giving him a decent image. He was always in trouble, it seemed. He drank too much, he brawled too much, he hung out with punks too much. We were forced to assign detectives to trail him and keep him in line." Yet the World Boxing Association couldn't even find out who owned Liston's contract.

By 1968, the WBA was on the ropes. It had made a terrible blunder in stripping Ali of his title, something he regained by trouncing Ernie Terrell – sneering between salvoes, "What's my name, boy?" because Terrell insisted on calling him Clay. Yet in 1967 it had defrocked Ali again after he refused induction into the army.

ABC television sponsored an elimination tournament that Ali's sparring partner Jimmy Ellis won to become new "heavyweight champion" in April 1968. Since Ellis was Ali's old punching bag, that cheapened the WBA title even further. With Ali sentenced to five years in prison, and appealing his draft conviction for the next three years, he could not fight, but nobody took Ellis's claims seriously.

In September 1968, former champion Floyd Patterson was robbed against Ellis in Stockholm, Sweden. Though the thirty-three-old broke Ellis's nose and battered him throughout, the lone official, American referee Harold Valan, raised Ellis's hand. An obvious knockdown wasn't called, and even Angelo Dundee, Ellis's manager, made a Freudian slip and admitted his guy lost when interviewed.

By 1968, there was a squat new destroyer on the scene. New York called Joe Frazier the heavyweight champion of the world after he opened the "new" Garden on April 4 and deflated the blimp-like Buster Mathis. In August, during the Democratic national convention, there were riots in the streets of Chicago. Young anti-Vietnam War protesters were tear-gassed and beaten with billy clubs. After what was officially labelled a "police riot" was broadcast live, crowds chanted, "The whole world is watching. The whole world is watching." With black civil rights activist Martin Luther King, a Nobel Peace Prize winner, gunned down that April, and Bobby Kennedy murdered that June, America was being torn apart.

In Pittsburgh, Pennsylvania, even the WBA's annual convention was filled with strife. There was a revolt from the East. "Unless the WBA shows greater concern about its Oriental Boxing Federation members, they will resign and form their own version of a directional body," wrote Johnny Ort of *The Ring* magazine. Justiano Montano, who headed the Filipino delegation, pulled his country out of the WBA and proposed a new regulatory body called the World Boxing Federation. The Orient Boxing Federation also lodged a formal protest and charged the WBA with "discriminating against non-American members." It said, "There is no reason why Asiatic or other non-American members should not be on equal footing with any and all American members of the WBA, since we are in a WORLD organization and not in one such as the defunct, and unlamented National Boxing Association."

The OBF urged "an end to the unsavoury practice of WBA officials attending world championship fights at promoters' expense, often under the guise of being named officials of the world title fight, since such practices ... cheapen the WBA." The OBF even contended there was no uniformity in the WBA's interpretation of the rules, particularly when it came to title defences. "The WBA thus can stand accused of favouritism; of being lax and accommodating with certain champions, strict to the letter with others. In one unbelievable instance, the WBA *forgot* it no longer stood merely as a national organization, but as an international body, and in an outburst of 'patriotism' penalized and caused to be ostracized World Heavyweight Champion Cassius Clay, for the American Negro's refusal to be drafted into the US Armed Forces."

The dissidents weren't through. "The OBF deplores the limited composition of the WBA ratings committee ... which prevented foreign boxers from just inclusion. The OBF further recommends that the WBA ratings include explanations ... Thus the WBA can avoid embarrassing repercussions such as was caused by the Joe Frazier case [Frazier had refused to participate in the WBA elimination tourney, and was punished, and ludicrously rated seventh, when he was clearly the most dangerous contender in the world] which exposed the WBA ratings as being subject to whim." The OBF even insisted "on the restitution of rapport between the WBA and WBC [which was just five years old], and mutual respect for each other," for the good of boxing.

The WBA remained a good ol' boys' club for Americans, and reform was ignored. Emile Bruneau of Louisiana was elected president, and Abe J. Greene, still floundering around after thirty years, was given another title as "international commissioner." But their days were numbered.

In 1974 two Panamanians, Dr Elias Cordova and Rodrigo Sanchez, staged a coup. Under the WBA's noble-sounding constitution, any regulatory body that supervised boxing at any country, provincial or city level was eligible for membership. But to vote you had to be physically present at the convention. Not many Third World countries could afford to send representatives, which is how Americans had held control for so long.

Cordova and Sanchez, like so many South American dictators before them, began rigging the election. They imported delegations from countries like Panama (which had four registered commissions, hence four votes), Venezuela, (six), and tiny El Salvador (four more). The Virgin Islands somehow got three votes, though there wasn't a commission there.

Their plan worked. Cordova, a surgeon from Panama, was elected *El Presidente* and served from 1974-77. Then it was Fernando Mandry Galindez's turn. He was from Venezuela. He reigned for two years, before the Cordova-Sanchez tandem wrested back control. Sanchez held power until his death in 1982, when he was followed by Gilberto Mendoza, also from Panama. Mendoza has held on with an iron grip ever since. Gilberto Junior is next in line.

Though the old NBA and the American-dominated WBA had always been guilty of nickel and dime things, once the Latins grabbed power, *ay caramba!* That was when the incredible corruption began.

* * *

Ring magazine called itself the Bible of Boxing. "If *Ring* is the Bible of Boxing, then boxing needs a New Testament," Teddy Brenner would always say.

The glossy-covered *Ring* was the publication that stitched the American fight game together. Its founding editor, Nat Fleischer was a good, idealistic man. But he wasn't perfect. He was far too close to Mike Jacobs. Irving Rudd, the brilliant publicist, served a brief stint as a writer for *Ring* in the 1940s, and claimed "Fleischer could be gotten to."

By the mid-Seventies, even with Fleischer dead, *Ring* was still the real boxing authority in the United States. In early 1976, Don King conceived an idea for the so-called U.S. Boxing Championships, and sold the idea to ABC. They were receptive to the idea, as long as the magazine was on board. With the Montreal Olympics producing "boffo" prime-time ratings, and people falling in love with gold medallists like Sugar Ray Leonard, boxing was about to climb out of its tomb. In theatres all across the country, patrons were roaring as they thrilled to a low-budget movie called *Rocky*.

ABC committed more than $2 million and twenty-three hours of programming to the tournament. The linchpin of the deal was "the quality of fighters participating be the best possible, determined by the rankings established by *Ring* magazine." The once-proud mag had fallen on hard times and badly needed the $70,000 it would be paid. Johnny Ort, associate editor of the *Ring* and the *Ring Record Book*, was responsible for authenticating everything. Ort, a handsome, dark-haired, sharp-featured man in his late thirties, was known to ignore people standing in front of his desk for twenty minutes at a time while he concocted boxing deals on the phone.

On 11 December 1976, before the tourney began, Alex Wallau of ABC lambasted Ort's selection of fighters and expressed grave doubts about their ability. "Why isn't Marvin Hagler fighting?" Wallau kept asking his bosses. Hagler had been cutting a bloody swathe through the sport. Yet he was out, while fellow middleweights like Mike Colbert, who ran so fast he could have been the leg man on an Olympic relay team, were in. Colbert was also constantly getting puff pieces about him in *Ring*. The word was that Ort was his undercover co-manager.

There were worse embarrassments: Paddy Dolan and John Sullivan, two white clubfighters handled by the duo of Al Braverman and Paddy Flood, who operated out of Don King's Manhattan office. Inept Hilbert Stevenson gained entry through Chris Cline, another "business associate" of Ort's. Juan Cantres was a preliminary boy who had never gone more than six rounds. By December 21, Wallau had cranked out another frantic memo to his bosses, this one emphatically stating that only twenty-five of the fifty-six fighters should be competing. Fourteen were simply a disgrace. Still, the tourney began.

More controversy followed. The entrants had to sign contracts that gave Don King promotional rights on all winners. The matches were strangely held in places like the Marion Correctional Facility (a prison) and a navy aircraft carrier in front of thousands of non-paying seamen. State boxing commissions were virtually bypassed. Why?

Flash Gordon, who published a hilarious, hard-hitting New York newsletter about boxing, figured this was simply a way to make sure the decisions went the "right way." Scott Ledoux, a rugged Minnesota heavyweight, thumped Houston's Johnny Boudreaux, but when the favoured Boudreaux got an obscene decision, Le Doux was so incensed he publicly charged the verdict had been fixed and knocked off TV presenter Howard Cosell's toupee in the melee that followed. Years later, in a confidential recording made by FBI agent Joe Spinelli, Richie Giachetti, a King underling, claimed that the decision had indeed been "fixed."

Flash Gordon frothed like a madman about corruption and kickbacks, but nothing really happened until Gary Deeb, who wrote the toughest TV column in the country for the *Chicago Tribune*, blasted ABC in March in a column called, "King and ABC Give Boxing a Black Eye." This writer was his quoted, unnamed source. I was Chicago correspondent for *Ring* at the time. In ten succeeding columns, syndicated nationwide, Deeb revealed the rigged records of guys like Ike Fluellen and Jerry Kornelle, the kickbacks, and how records were phonied up at the *Ring* by Ort.

A furious Howard Cosell, who claimed to "tell it like it is," called Deeb and screamed over the phone, "What are you trying to do to me?" Roone Arledege, Cosell's producer, threatened to sue, but Deeb replied, "Go ahead." John Schulian, an award-winning writer for the *Chicago Daily News*, asked Cosell, "What's it like to swim in a sewer?" Cosell, who publicly postured for forty years about his integrity, tartly replied, "Young man, how much money do you make a year?"

Finally, on 16 April 1977, ABC put the $2 million tournament "on hold," where it has remained for last twenty-six years. But not before the network issued a cover-your-ass press release: "ABC has discovered that the very basis of the tournament has been severely compromised. As a result … ABC has suspended telecasts."

According to the Armstrong Report, which was later commissioned by ABC and written by Mike Armstrong, (former chief counsel for the Knapp Commission, which documented extensive police corruption in New York City in the early 1970s), not only were there rampant conflicts of interests and kickback schemes, there were also twenty-three fighters with "inaccurate" records in the *Ring Record Book*. Eight others had logs that were "unverifiable."

Biff Cline, Chris Cline's son, had five "undisputably phoney" (*sic*) first-round knockout wins. Pat Dolan had four bogus wins, Hilbert Stevenson five fraudulent victories in 1976, and Anthony House seven sham wins. Ort gave Ike Fluellen "honorable mention" in *Ring's* 1976 Progress of the Year awards; Fluellen admitted in a sworn affadavit that he did not have nay fights that year, and that two wins Ort credited to him in Mexico never happened. Fluellen also swore that he had been contacted by a would-be manager who said he could get into *Ring's* ratings if he agreed to kick back part of his purse. Harlan Hass, the long-time Texas correspondent, was fired. After a four-month investigation, Armstrong simply concluded, "*Ring* lacks the credibility necessary for it to carry out the assigned role in the tourney."

Though it was hard to believe that a street-savvy thug like Don King didn't know what was going on, according to Armstrong, "On the subject of active wrongdoing, we were unable to find any evidence that King himself was involved in kickbacks, false ratings or other similar irregularities. The most disturbing action by King for which we were able to acquire direct evidence of personal involvement was his clearly improper payment of $5,000 to John Ort … which seriously compromised the integrity of the selection process."

"John was paid for public relations work, which I allowed him to do," alibied Nat Loubet, the editor of the *Ring*, which ironically never got the $70,000 it was promised for authenticating the event. Surely "public relations work" had to compromise Ort's evaluations of fighters? But in 1975, before the Ali-Wepner fight in Cleveland, there was Loubet introducing King before the bell. As editor, Loubet was Ort's boss, and ultimately responsible for what happened, but he simply blamed managers for submitting false records. Apparently, it was all a big coincidence that Ort just happened to enter a slew of bogus wins into the *Ring Record Book* and these "wins" benefited his business associates and friends.

After decades in the fight game, Loubet wasn't naive. Why were there no press clippings of these fights before they were entered into the record book? Loubet, who was in his late fifties, was terribly cynical about the fight game even before the scandal. "He never liked boxing," said historian Herb Goldman, who got started as writer with *Ring*. "He married Nat Fliescher's daughter, and that's why he got involved."

In September 1971, about eight months before he died, the feisty, eighty-one-year-old Fleischer was still eager to talk boxing, and feverishly took notes when a young man told him that he'd not recorded a fight that belonged in a Mexican heavyweight's record. Fleischer died after fifty years at the helm of a publication known for its integrity. But by 1975, *Esquire* magazine was calling *Ring* the "worst-written mag in America." Ort was an absolutely talentless writer, a Shakespeare in reverse, and was arrogant as well. While he sat on his ass hatching deals in office, unedited copy and horribly blurry pictures went straight into the publication. Loubet didn't care.

By the fall of 1977, Ort was fired, and Loubet kept asking, "Do you think we'll survive?" The magazine did. Bert Sugar bought it in 1979 but, good as it became, the *Ring's* once pristine reputation was destroyed. Johnny Ort and Nat Loubet should be remembered as the hacks who gave birth to the "Alphabet Boys."

★ ★ ★

In 1977, while the *Ring* was going down, a Japanese promoter was trying to stage a title fight. Dr Elias Cordova, who suddenly realized that he had real power, told him that to get a WBA sanction there had to be seven round-trip plane tickets, plus first-class hotel accommodation. When the plane touched down, out stepped Cordova, Rodrigo Sanchez, the ratings chairman, their wives, Pepe Cordero, and two more flunkies.

The Japanese promoter greeted them politely, but privately complained. Next day, he had to take them shopping. The happy wives picked out pearls, jewellery and silk kimonos, while the seething promoter paid for everything.

"Why do you do it?" an American official asked.

"If I don't, I won't get the sanction," fretted the promoter, who resolved to get out of boxing.

In Colombia, a fight manager was desperate to get his pug rated. He had no money, but in Colombia at the time were a lot of cheap emeralds. The fighter got rated after one WBA official's daughter got her shimmering bauble.

The notorious Pepe Cordero was a close confidant of both Sanchez and Cordova. He was also a convicted thief. In 1964, Cordero was nailed on two counts of burglary and was given two-to-five years on one count, and five-to-ten on the next. After getting out of prison, he was somehow given a pardon in the early 1970s by then-governor Rafael Hernandez Colon. Cordero had sunk his talons into WBA champs Angel Espada and Sammy Serrano, who were the pride of Puerto Rico, and Ernesto Espana, who hailed from Venezuela but fought out of San Juan. "There's one bagman in the WBA," claimed Bob Arum in Ring in 1983, "and that's Pepe Cordero. Any time you want a fix in the WBA, you bribe Cordero and he takes care of it." Arum contended that Don King was paying off to the tune of hundreds of thousands a year.

In the early 1980s, Ray "Boom Boom" Mancini was an American TV darling. After he was stopped by WBC lightweight king Alexis Arguello in 1981, Arum was desperate to resurrect Mancini's ethnic, blue-collar marketability. Mancini's poignant story – he was trying to win a world title because his father, Lenny, a top contender in 1941, was denied his chance by World War Two – was classic melodrama.

In May 1982, Mancini destroyed Arturo Frias in one round to win the WBA lightweight title. Frias, who had won his title just five months earlier, should have been allowed at least one easy defence to make some money, but Cordero, who didn't even hold office in the WBA, said no. Arum admitted paying the still-thieving burglar $10,000, plus a $25,000 bonus every time Mancini defended his crown. This guaranteed easy defences for the colourful Youngstown, Ohio, native. In July 1982, Mancini annihilated Ernesto Espana in six. Not only was Espana Cordero's fighter, but Arum was forced to guarantee the washed-up challenger a staggering $250,000, one-third of which had to be kicked back to the greedy Cordero.

In November 1982, Mancini outslugged an unknown Korean, Duk Koo Kim, in a brutal fight. "I'll die before I lose," Kim had pledged, but the WBA's mandatory challenger was so lightly regarded even in South Korea that a year earlier, when Bert Sugar tried to get local authorities to send the top forty fighters' records for inclusion into the *Ring Record Book*, Kim's record wasn't submitted.

After a terrible battering in the fourteenth round, Kim slumped to the canvas, and later died. His fiancee became hysterical and vowed she would never touch another man. Kim's mother drank pesticide. Referee Richard Greene, considered one of the best in the business, would later commit suicide because he couldn't get Kim off his mind. Years later, Mancini, a sensitive sort who writes poetry, was still haunted by nightmares. "Hey Ray, what's it like to kill somebody?" strangers would say, sidling up to him.

Four years earlier, when a newly-elected Mandry Galindez became president of the WBA, he had toured the Orient. When he stopped off in South Korea, fight managers kept running up to him, placing money in the startled Galindez's hands and asking, "Are you the man we now have to pay for ratings?"

* * *

In July 1979, Mexican great Ruben Olivares was trying to win back his WBA featherweight title but was going up against the cruel, artful fists of Panama's Eusebio Pedroza. York Van Nixon, an American on the WBA's executive committee, was dispatched to Houston, Texas, to act as official supervisor. Just hours before the televised fight, Pedroza's manager, Santiago del Rio, demanded that the champion's $110,000 purse be paid in cash.

"That's impossible," said Van Nixon.

"Then we no fight," screamed del Rio. After a long, fierce argument, del Rio prevailed.

Van Nixon had a police escort from the box office back to the Ramada Inn, where Pedroza was staying, and arrived with the huge bundle of cash. The desk clerk refused to be responsible for it, but Rodrigo Sanchez requested that the money be placed in the hotel security box, with Van Nixon holding the key. Sanchez, who had no business being involved, hired a guard to stand watch.

Pedroza stopped the thirty-two-year-old Olivares in the twelfth round. The next morning, when Van Nixon returned to the hotel, Sanchez imperiously demanded the key.

"No, this money belongs to the fighter," insisted Van Nixon.

Still, Sanchez, who had no legal right, kept demanding the key. Finally, American Bob Busse, another longtime WBA official, fined del Rio $1,000 for threatening to scuttle the fight. Sanchez simply whipped out a wad of cash and paid his fine. Reluctantly, Van Nixon gave del Rio the key. Later, Van Nixon discovered that it was Dr Cordova and Sanchez who had wanted Pedroza paid in cash. It's questionable how much of the $110,000 Pedroza ever saw.

Shortly afterward, Cordero's fighter, Ernesto Espana, then WBA lightweight king, was in Washington, D.C., to defend against Colombia's

Leonardo Asprilla. Suddenly, there was a demand that Espana be paid cash before he entered the ring. "We want the money," insisted Pepe Cordero.

This time Van Nixon wouldn't yield. He was the head of the Washington commission. Van Nixon had learned that Sanchez and Dr Cordova were in Washington, but ducking him. He knew the same thing that had happened in Houston was going to happen here. Espana would fight, but Sanchez, Cordova and Cordero would grab the money. Finally, the bout was cancelled. Promoters lost a bundle, and nobody got paid. Espana was suspended by Van Nixon for refusing to enter the ring.

★ ★ ★

By April 1980, Sugar Ray Leonard was slated to fight Panamanian legend Robert Duran for the WBC welterweight title. This eagerly-awaited clash would gross a staggering $30 million, but initially the negotiations bogged down. Leonard's advisor, Mike Trainer, wearily said, "Forget Duran, we'll fight Pipino Cuevas." Cuevas was the WBA champ – and a Mexican.

On 10 April 1980, Cuevas's manager, Lupe Sanchez, took a disturbing phone call from a man who identified himself as Colonel Rueben Paredes, commander of the Panamanian National Guard. "There will be no Leonard–Cuevas fight," said Paredes adamantly. "If you fight him and win, it will mean nothing, because we will strip you of your WBA title." Lupe Sanchez was frightened by the call. He quickly announced that Cuevas had been cut in training.

Duran was an idol in Panama, a symbol of national might. Paredes, one of the strong men under Panamanian dictator Omar Torrejos, could have had Sanchez killed. What would it take to liquidate one little fight manager? Political dissidents disappeared all the time.

On June 20, 1980, Duran beat Leonard in a famous battle in Montreal. Less than five weeks later, in Detroit, Cuevas lost his version of the title when Thomas "Hit Man" Hearns transformed him into a swaying piece of rubble before Lupe Sanchez jumped into the ring and stopped the slaughter in round two. The Hearns fight had gone ahead only after promoter Harold Smith gave Cuevas $1 million in a suitcase in Mexico City. According to Dean Allison, who later prosecuted Smith (see Chapter Eight), there was also a $75,000 payoff to Cordero, *bagman emeritus* for the WBA.

In December 1981, Eusebio Pedroza defended his WBA featherweight title for the thirteenth time, knocking out top contender Bashew Sibaca in the fifth round. "Not even the most naive or patriotic South African fight follower ever really believed that Bashew deserved his number one ranking," observed local boxing writer Pete Moscardi. But then, alliances have always played a crucial role in professional boxing. Though South Africa was a leper on the international sporting scene because of apartheid, the sweaty palms at the WBA eagerly embraced it because of the money it could generate.

In the States, the Reverend Jesse Jackson led pickets when rugged South African heavyweight Kallie Knoetze had his first fight there. Advertisers feared a black boycott, so American TV networks didn't want to put any South Africans on the tube, but in South Africa, which was angrily chafing under international sanctions, Sigma Motor Company put up 750,000 Rand to bankroll Robbie Williams against Ossie "Jaws" Ocasio for the newly-created WBA "junior-heavyweight" championship. In the chief support, Gerrie Coetzee would face America's Franco Thomas in an eliminator for the WBA heavyweight crown held by Mike Weaver. The *Sunday Express* ridiculously crowed, "It will be the fight extravaganza of the year." Moscardi was more realistic, calling the card "the latest insane edict proclaimed by the WBA from their distant bastion in Panama City."

Williams, a bronzed Durban beach boy, was just a handsome kid who had lost to former WBA heavyweight champ John Tate's sparring partner, Dwain Bonds. He had also been vanquished by a Weaver punching bag, Rahim Muhammad. Maybe Williams had stopped the totally washed-up Knoetze, but when the WBA announced its new division, and the men who'd joust for the belt, Bert Blewett, editor of *South African Boxing World*, lambasted it in a major South African newspaper: "There is nothing logical about the (WBA) ratings. The hocus-pocus begins right at the top and extends all the way down to the junior-flyweights."

Ocasio was also an odd choice, but hailed from Puerto Rico, which was Cordero country. In his previous fight, at Wembley, London, he had put up such an atrocious performance against Britain's John L. Gardner that *Boxing News* called it a "Splashdown." Coetzee, possessor of a so-called "bionic right" that was actually PR man Irving Rudd's invention, was being set up for a third time to fight for the WBA heavyweight title. "Thomas, from Fairmount, West Virginia is a tough, two-fisted battler, a throwback to the days of Carnival Booths that spawned world cruiserweight champion Freddie Mills," wrote Norman Canale of the *Sunday Express*. Franco had been rated 9th by the WBA.

Surprisingly, the British Board of Control was trying to join up with the WBA, but Moscardi figured, "the WBA is personally engaged in extramarital affairs with willing partners such as South Africa and Korea. There is no room for Britain."

★ ★ ★

While mediocrities like Sibaca and Williams could get title shots, top-notchers like Ayub Kalule, a classy Ugandan southpaw who fought out of Denmark, couldn't get championship shots they had earned.

In 1974, Kalule won the British Commonwealth, All-Africa, and All-World amateur titles and was named African Athlete of the Year. In 1976, after touring with the Ugandan amateur team, he decided to stay in Denmark to pursue a professional career. Within twenty months of turning pro, Kalule, who fought at 154 pounds, had whipped three former WBA champions, stopping two. In May 1978, he won the Commonwealth middleweight title. On November 9, he beat Sugar Ray Seales, the globe-trotting American middleweight contender. Former British middleweight champ Kevin Finnegan was beaten a month later. By November 1977, after just thirteen fights, Kalule was the mandatory contender – but for the next two years, the WBA would lead him and his Danish manager/promoter, Mogens Palle, a terribly frustrating chase.

"Those people at the WBA are criminals and liars," Palle complained to Harry Mullan, then editor of *Boxing News*. "They've told me, 'Be patient, your turn is coming,' but I have been patient, and what has it got me? I sent these bastards all kinds of letters, and they claimed they didn't get them. I've called. I've cabled, and I've even travelled to conventions. I've spent a good fifteen thousand pounds, but they do whatever they want."

According to the WBA's own rules, Nicaragua's Eddie Gazo had to defend against Kalule within six months. But Cordova didn't want the title in Palle's hands, and let the slow, flailing Gazo make his first four defences in the Orient, where they just don't produce good fighters beyond 130 pounds. In June 1977, Koichi Wajima, who was thirty-four and hadn't won since February 1976, was stopped by Gazo and never fought again. Another Japanese, Kenji Shibata, was next and he lost a fifteen-round decision. He'd been rated sixth. In December 1977, Korea's Chae-Keun Lim got his shot, and Gazo escaped with a split-decision, though the Korean was ranked only eighth. Gazo got $80,000, a big purse for an obscure division.

By now, Manny Galindez, Cordova's hand-picked replacement, was the new titular head of the WBA. Galindez, an accountant with the Venezuelan Ministry of Transport, showed an occasional rebellious streak, but he too ignored Kalule. In August 1978, a game but limited Japanese, Masashi Kudo, ended Gazo's reign with a split-decision ten months after Kalule was supposed to have had his mandatory challenge.

When the furious Palle fired off protests, it backfired; Kalule was suddenly demoted to number two while Gert Steyn, a fair South African, was rocketed up to the top spot. Spang Thomsen, the general secretary of the Danish Boxing Commission, wrote Galindez, "We find no justice and sporting spirit among WBA officers." Galindez claimed that it all had been a mistake and Kalule regained his top spot in January 1979. Mike Mortimer of South Africa, who headed the championship committee after Cordova's resignation, tried to challenge Galindez for the WBA presidency but failed. Mortimer had promised to enforce Kalule's rights, but the way the WBA was run, with Pepe Cordero controlling things, rules meant nothing. There hadn't been a mandatory defence for eighteen months.

Like a bloodhound trying to pick up the scent, Palle finally cabled Japanese promoter Saburo Arashida and offered Kalule to fight the winner of Kudo's defence against Joo Ho fight in Osaka. Arashida cabled back that Kudo was already contracted to fight Argentina's Manuel Gonzalez, who was ranked only at number five. Palle was livid. Kudo beat Gonzalez in March in Tokyo, but the fight was closer than expected and American official Bill Miller said that there should be a rematch. So there was, which Kudo won again.

In the interim, Galindez had met with Palle in New York and promised there would be no more fights with Gonzalez. Mike Mortimer, who was the WBA's attorney, now tried to justify the rematch legally, even though a mandatory defence against Kalule was twenty-two months overdue under the WBA's own rules. In April 1979, after Kudo had won his first decision over Gonzalez, Ron Cayton, who headed up the Canadian federation, and chaired the WBA's grievance committee, threatened to pull Canada out of the WBA if it didn't do the right thing and give Kalule his chance. Galindez ignored him.

Instead, Galindez listened to his promoter/friend Ramon Machado, who hailed from Colombia and handled a boxer called Emiliano Villa. He approved a Tokyo fight between Kudo and Villa. When Palle was told, he got so hot he stormed right into the 1979 convention in Miami Beach, and started swearing.

By now, Cordova and Sanchez were losing power, and wanted Galindez out. Cordova decreed that Sanchez run against Galindez for the presidency. Richard Farrah, a minor promoter who represented tiny Trinidad and Tobago, likened it to choosing between a shark and a school of piranhas. The vote went to the WBA executive committee. In a palace coup, Sanchez regained the presidency by a mere four votes. That same day, 24 October 1979, Kalule chased Kudo down and won the WBA championship in Japan. This classy southpaw would make several defences before losing his title to the even better Sugar Ray Leonard in 1981. Leonard would give up the belt to win the more prestigious welterweight title against Thomas Hearns in a massive promotion that generated $30 million and launched Lou Duva, the volatile patriarch of Main Events, from being a New Jersey club show promoter to the Big Time. Duva got the closed-circuit TV rights, despite having just $138 to his name.

The title vacated by Leonard was won by yet another Japanese, Tadashi Mihara. Soon Harry Mullan was publicly charging that the WBA had breached it own rules again, when America's Davey Moore was allowed to challenge for the title within thirty days of his first rating. Moore battered Mihara into submission in six rounds, even though he was very inexperienced. What roused Mullan's ire was the WBA's approval of "an arrangement whereby Mihara would earn more for *losing* to Moore than for beating him … If this report is true, it's astonishing that the WBA blessed such an extraordinarily unethical arrangement." Moore was next set to fight South Africa's Charley Weir in the synthetic state of Bophuthatwana and, wrote Mullan, "according to reports, the budget for Moore's Sun City defence against Weir includes a R750,000 bonus payment for Mihara."

Bob Arum was the promoter, but with Pepe Cordero pulling strings, who knows where the money really went?

* * *

On 10 December 1982, Mike Weaver lost his WBA heavyweight title on an incredible first-round TKO to Michael Dokes, who was "managed" by Carl King and promoted by his step-father, Don. The fight went sixty-three seconds. With the crowd outraged at referee Joey Curtis's ludicrously premature stoppage, they started chanting on national TV, "Don King sucks, Don King sucks." Weaver publicly accused Don King and Curtis of "fixing it."

"What was I supposed to get if it was a fix?" bristled Curtis, a long-time Nevada referee. "I'm a millionaire." Maybe he was. Yet Mob turncoat and hitman Sammy "the Bull" Gravano testified in front of Senate subcommittte that Curtis had been willing to pass on bribes to get a fighter ranked by the WBC, and would drop into the Ravenite Social Club – gang boss John Gotti's headquarters – in New York City to discuss such a plan.

Dokes in turn lost the title to South African Gerrie Coetzee. On 1 December 1984, Greg Page beat Coetzee. Page's win was a shock even by the WBA's standards: Coetzee was counted out fifty seconds *after* the round should have ended. At the close of round six, Coetzee was dropped by a couple of powerful punches after the bell had rung. Instead of penalizing Page, or giving Coetzee an additional five minutes to recover, referee Isidro Rodriquez claimed, "Coetzee was acting. He wasn't hurt." By the eighth, both fighters were exhausted, but as the round approached the three-minute mark, the stiff, lumbering Coetzee actually began to outbox Page. When the round again extended way beyond three minutes, Janks Morton, Page's cornerman began to scream, "Ring the bell! Ring the bell!"

Boxing people have a clock in their heads. They deal with three-minute intervals virtually every day of their lives. Morton stopped bellowing, however, when, at about 3:25, Page suddenly mounted a fierce counter-attack. The South African fell to the canvas and referee Rodriquez incredibly counted him out – when he should've been sitting on his stool resting. The TV tape proved that Coetzee had lost at 3:50 of the eighth round. To cover everyone's ass, the time was officially recorded as 3:03. The twenty-nine-year-old Coetzee protested to the WBA but Dr Elias Cordova, then chairman of the championship committee, decreed that the result stood. Page was a Don King fighter.

Yet the WBA had acted on appeals – when the circumstances were right. It had mandated a rematch between Dokes and Weaver which ended in a controversial draw. And in June 1982, it had acted when a badly-cut Samuel Serrano lost his junior lightweight title on an eleventh round TKO to Benedicto Villablanco in Santiago, Chile. Though the Chilean crowd went wild saluting their new champion, three weeks later, the WBA declared the result null and void, citing "irregularities." Serrano was still champion even though he had been stopped. Villablanco threatened legal action, so the WBA quickly reversed itself again and declared the bout a technical draw. The important thing was: Serrano still held on to his belt. Serrano was Pepe Cordero's fighter.

* * *

For years, Americans who have worked WBA title fights have quietly claimed that they wouldn't work if they didn't vote the organization's way. Some claim that Sanchez even came up to them in South America and said, "Look, we want the title to stay down here." Yet in Nevada, where most of the world's most lucrative fights happen, Dr Elias Ghanem, who headed up the state-supported commission, gutlessly allowed these *banditos* to appoint officials. By now the American media was screaming that both the WBA and its main rival, the WBC, were corrupt. So why were they allowed to befoul boxing in the United States?

In 1989, Jesus Salud won the WBA 122-pound title in a bloody, foul-filled fight against Mexico's Juan "Dinamita" Estrada, who was disqualified in the ninth in Inglewood, California. Salud should have been allowed to pick an optional first defence, but the WBA demanded that he come down to Colombia and defend, even though the US State Department had issued a strong advisory against Americans going into the country due to its violent civil unrest. Even Colombian presidential candidates were being assassinated by drug lords. Salud offered to defend in Inglewood, against anyone the WBA decreed, but they simply stripped him of his title.

On 17 December 1993, in Tucuman, Argentina, the WBA pulled off its most incredible rip-off, in a fight that couldn't be believed – except it was live, in living colour, on Argentine television. Argentine hero Juan Martin Coggi squared off with challenger Eder Gonzalez for the WBA junior welterweight title. The site was the *Estadio Villa Lujan*.

The contest started slowly. About forty seconds into round two, the pale, swarthy Coggi suddenly tore in and floored Gonzalez along the ropes. As the crowd erupted, the badly-hurt Colombian stumbled up at four. Coggi hurtled in to finish him. Both fired wildly, and less than ten seconds later, a whizzing right hook exploded on Coggi's chin and put him flat on his back.

Coggi was so "out" he was practically limp, and TV replays proved that, after he had somehow staggered to his feet, he had been down for more than ten seconds. With the round only half over, and Coggi barely able to stand, he fell into a corner to remain upright.

Venezuelan referee Eusebio Rodriquez did one of the worst jobs in boxing history. Not only did he give Coggi a slow count, he wouldn't stop the fight, though the champion could barely stand. As Coggi wobbled back and forth, barely conscious, Rodriquez pulled hard on his gloves to shake him awake.

After twenty agonizing seconds, Gonzalez was finally allowed to run in. Coggi was blasted with eight brutal shots before a last, crunching right put him almost in a sitting position on the middle ropes. Four or five more terrible blows thudded home. Rodriquez was trying to protect Coggi's championship, but was risking getting him beaten to death. Still, this so-called referee would not stop the horrific spectacle.

With a minute to go and with Coggi still barely off the ropes, the champion was defenceless. Rodriquez pushed Gonzalez away and wouldn't allow him to hit Coggi any more. Coggi, however, was so groggy that he collapsed to the nearest ropes, where it finally looked like the fight would be stopped. But no – though Coggi had crashed down almost sideways in a corner, the referee pulled him up!

Coggi now couldn't even stand without help, but Rodriquez still would not stop the fight. Nor would he allow Gonzalez to finish it. Another twenty seconds went by with the WBA champ barely able to stand. The arena was in uproar; everyone was on his feet. A Coggi cornerman jumped on the ring apron – which normally calls for a fight to be stopped – and, in another unbelievable scene, was actually allowed to snap the waistband of his blue and white trunks, trying to shock him awake.

Like something out of the most ghastly fight movie, Coggi was slumped along the ropes and barely conscious as Gonzalez bolted in and hurled an overhand right like a javelin. The punch thudded home with frightening impact, flush in the face. As Coggi started to go down, his cornerman on the apron grabbed him and held him up by his waist. As the challenger continued punching, trying to end it, Coggi's cornerman was stiff-arming him away.

Finally the timekeeper rang the bell – sixteen seconds early. A Gonzalez cornerman jumped in the ring to protest but, with one incredible outrage after the other, where did he start?

Coggi was still barely conscious at the start of round three. As Gonzalez tried to pound him down, giving him a terrible two-fisted beating, the referee kept jumping in and pushing him away. With the battered champion in terrible trouble, the timekeeper came to his rescue again, this time twenty-seven seconds early.

In the fourth, Coggi was "protected" yet again when the bell rang fourteen seconds early. In the fifth Gonzalez floored him with a resounding right that knocked him back a good six feet, but Rodriquez refused to count. By the seventh, the pace had slowed, though the insane crowd, which had seen more barbarity in twenty minutes than most see in twenty years, was clapping for action.

Somehow, despite the savage beating he had taken, Coggi came back from being staggered yet again to open up in the seventh and send his dispirited challenger to the deck. As programs rained down like confetti, and fans screamed themselves hoarse, there was Coggi's cornerman again, standing on the apron, calmly giving instructions and holding his man's arms before he could finish it. As poor Gonzalez had trouble getting his mouthpiece in, Coggi roared ahead and blasted him with a torrid barrage of six punches. This time, having seen their man fight everybody but the ticket takers, Gonzalez's corner rescued him. The crowd went berserk. One of the most dishonest spectacles in the history of sport ended at 2:26 of round seven.

Maybe anything goes in Argentina. Death squads and military coups are routine, but this televised fight was so outrageous, even the Argentine newspapers denounced the WBA. The nicest thing they called it was "corrupt." There was such a scandal, the WBA was kicked out of the country for six months. Referee Rodriquez, the timekeeper, and the so-called supervisor, Dr Carlos Sanchez, were banned for life.

Though this disgrace should have been called "no contest," the best the WBA would do was order a rematch. Gonzalez, whose heart was perhaps no longer in it, got halted in the States after a weak effort.

★ ★ ★

Howard Cosell, who called boxing on US television for thirty-five years, didn't see the first Coggi-Gonzalez fight, but in 1985 he made it abundantly clear what he thought of both the WBA and WBC. "While each is supposed to be an independent regulator of boxing, both are in reality conspirators in rigging ratings. These organizations are basically instruments of extortion – playing by their rules, creating their own champions – easily manipulated by the gifts and favours or promoters and managers." Cosell contended that they existed because of the shoddy journalism in America, and "the financial support of … television networks, which continue to telecast phoney title fights."

Jose Sulaiman, chief poobah of the WBC, sued Cosell for libel – and lost. Cosell, who was also an attorney, made great amends for being part of Don King's U.S. Boxing Championships scandal. He insisted that if American TV stopped recognizing these bastards, you'd greatly clean up the sport.

A sixty-one-year-old lawyer from Philadelphia disagrees. James J. Binns, *magna cum laude* graduate of LaSalle University and Villanova Law School, chaired the Organized Crime Task Force in Philadelphia and once headed the Pennsylvania State Athletic Commission. "I am a strong proponent of the rules," he claims, though he has been the WBA's mouthpiece since 1981.

On July 29, 1992 Arum gave a deposition before the Permanent Subcommittee on Investigations, and claimed that Mike McCallum was stripped of his championship because Arum wouldn't heed the WBA mandate that he pay Binns' $100,000 legal fees. Arum claimed, referring to the WBA, "They rip off money like you canot believe." Arum also blasted both the WBA and WBC and called them "Terrorists. They will rape, and loot and pillage and smile about it, saying they are doing it for the best interests of boxing."

In the early 1990s, Bob Arum contended that he had seen the WBA's books, and eighty per cent of the sanction fees were used to pay Binns. That's not true. According to the WBA's income statements, it had "total revenue" in 1989 of $679, 863; and "total expenses" of $574, 829. The "net assets or fund balances at the end of the year" were $284,491. The WBA's single biggest expense was $185, 959 for travel in 1989. $15,000 a month seems high, considering that promoters pay for fight officials to and from championship fights.

"Professional" fees were $126,639, the second highest expense of 1989. The WBA doesn't pay its officers and directors, and there's nothing listed for legal fees. For "conferences, conventions and meetings," there was $95,538 spent. $12,500 was paid for championship belts and cases.

According to the extensive 990 form that non-profit organizations have to file with the IRS, the WBA had "total revenue" of $874, 876 for 1990. The "total expenses" came to $956,075. The WBA had a deficit of $81,199.

The "net assets or fund balances at (the) beginning of the year were $284,491. The "net assets or fund balances at (the) end of the year were $203,292.

According to the "Statement of Functional Expenses," the WBA listed $8,400 for salaries; $7,685 for supplies; $111 for postage and shipping; $65,149 for printing and publications; $147,279 for travel; $101,443 for conferences, conventions or meetings; $2,193 for property depletion; $1,982 for advertising; $106,291 for office expenses; $4,900 for insurance; $29,767 for miscellaneous; and $44,613 for "other."

The biggest expense, taken out of all this blood money, was a whopping $436,262 for "professional fees," which is a nice euphemism for Jimmy Binns. Somehow, "professional fees" increased 350 per cent, from $126,639 from the year before. If that seems disgustingly high, office expenses were $106,291, an incredible 1,600 per cent increase from 1989.

Though the WBA is theoretically in South America, its mailing address for tax purposes was Philadelphia, Pennsylvania, right in the good ol' USA. And though Mendoza takes the heat, the real power seemed to be James Binns, known as "Jimmy Pinstripes" in the fight game. He looks every bit like the powerful lawyer that he is. Tall and suave, in a grandfatherly way, slender, with swept-back white hair, and gold wire-rim glasses, he's impeccably tailored and looks like he was born into a world of fox hunts and lawn parties. On $436,262, he was definitely not eating peanut butter and jelly sandwiches.

On the WBA's 2000 income tax form, the last one available, it listed "total revenue" of $1,837.568. It claimed "total expenses" of $1,603,213. There was an excess of $234,355. The WBA claims in its mission statement, which it has to have to be tax exempt, that it "provides a competitive framework for the sanctioning of professional boxing bouts independently and the continued support to a world wide campaign against use of drugs by our world society."

It's so independent, Jimmy Binns is listed as the WBA "Legal Advisor to the President." He also has served as a lawyer for Don King. In the August 2002 ratings, "the big winners," according to Internet fight scribe Scott Shaffer "were (heavyweights) Larry Donald, Hasim Rahman and Fres Oquendo, who are all promoted by Don King. All have been inactive and all were moved ahead of fighters who they lost to. The big losers were David Tua, Kirk Johnson and (Britain's) Danny Williams, none of whom are currently promoted by King."

"It's sickening," said Dino Duva, who filed two protests, that weren't answered, despite the requirements of the Ali Act, which governs boxing in the United States. Steve Farhood, now a Showtime commentator, said, "There's no way to justify these movements."

The WBA was finally forced to call a press conference and retract these absurd ratings, after the Association of Boxing Commissions in the United States demanded that they be prohibited from collecting any more sanction fees. After $10,000 was withheld, following an October 2002 Eric Morel flyweight title fight, the WBA complied, but the money they have generated is just not going back into boxing. According to the 2000 IRS form, $487,216 was spent to run the "central office." Another "$50,276" as spent for "office communication" and $171,465 was spent on the president's "operating fees." What exactly does Mendoza do with this money? The ratings committee only spent $16, 078, and that's supposd to be the WBA's primary function. Between the Awards Dinner, $81,378; publicity, $89,520; the annual convention, $290,856; the $487,216 for operating the central office, and the other $171,465 for President Mendoza's operating expenses, that's the WBA's expenditures right there. Add on an antidrug campaign, which may be politically correct, but undoubtedly ineffective, since it has no expertise in combating drugs, you have another $212,421 going someplace, other than to help fighters who need desperately a pension. The Mendozas, father and son Gilberto Sr and Jr, are taking damn good care of themselves though. While other salaries at the WBA vary from $5-10,000, the Mendozas are making $80,000 and $40,000 a year respectively, though it's listed under the IRS form as "expense account."

Binns claims to have "successfully defended" the WBA in twenty-four cases. When you look at the list – (Claude) Noel vs World Boxing Association; Equal Opportunity Commission vs World Boxing Association, 1984, Witherspoon vs World Boxing Association, 1987 – it gives you only a hint of how many dreams died. Binns, as an officer of the court, is sworn to uphold the law. So why is it that so many fighters not connected to Don King are stripped of their titles with impunity?

"The WBA just introduced this nonsense called 'super champions'. It's just another excuse for a sanction fee. It's hard to follow who's even the champion. The WBA is a disgrace," said *Boxing News* editor Claude Abrams.

"They shouldn't be allowed to do business in the United States," agreed Bob Papa, who calls fights on America's ESPN 2.

On the IRS 990 form, question seventy-six asks, "Did you engage in activity not previously reported to the Internal Revenue Service." Binns answered no. Yet he represents the WBA at the same time he has been Arum's lawyer, and latterly Don King's. Of the 200,000 lawyers in the United States, why would you hire Binns unless you were trying to gain some sort of competitive advantage with the non-profit, tax-exempt WBA? Binns's dual representation is an egregious conflict of interest. How is it possibly legal under the IRS's stringent codes?

How did Evander Holyfield end up fighting John Ruiz three times for the WBA heavyweight championship when the WBA was supposed to be against rematches? Was it because both were promoted by Don King?

Why is it that Binns never speaks about the 1994 Nevada lawsuit in which John Davimos, who managed Michael Moorer, swore under oath in front of a judge that Binns tried to shake him down to gain the WBA's support for the George Foreman-Michael Moorer title fight?

With fighters sweating, bleeding and ending up with brain damage, how in God's name does the WBA even hold on to its tax exemption? Why hasn't there been a criminal investigation?

CHAPTER SEVEN

The Lunatic Fringe

"DIGNITY, DEMOCRACY, HONESTY." These noble words are inscribed on the World Boxing Organization's globe-like logo. But if there was really "truth in advertising," the WBO's symbol would be more like a hungry pig, feverishly sticking its snout in a trough full of money.

The Puerto Rican-based WBO started in the late 1980s as a mutant offshoot of the World Boxing Association, based in Venezuela. The late Pepe Cordero, the convicted Puerto Rican burglar, had lost out in a power struggle to the WBA's long-reigning poobah Gilberto Mendoza. Though Cordero is now in that great Madison Square Garden in the sky, no doubt trying to figure out a way to carve up Jack Dempsey or Joe Louis's purses, another great humanitarian, Bob Arum, gave a fitting testimonial way back in 1983 as he recognized Cordero's rare talents: "There's one bagman in the WBA and that's Pepe Cordero. Anytime you want a fix in the WBA, you bribe Cordero and he takes care of it.

"I have nothing," protested the ever-whining Harvard-educated promoter/attorney to *Ring* magazine. "I don't control the WBA. I'm friendly with a lot of guys, but when I want anything done, I also have to bribe Cordero. You have to give him money. Anything you want done in the WBA, you have to pay Cordero. To get (Ray "Boom Boom") Mancini a title shot, we had to pay Pepe Cordero hundreds of thousands of dollars. We paid by cheque to his promotional company, Salinas Productions of Puerto Rico."

Nick Kerasiotis was the WBO's long-serving treasurer. Kerasiotis briefly played guard for the Chicago Bears NFL team in the early 1940s, but he earned his spurs in boxing by presiding in Chicago over one of the worst commissions in the country in the 1970s and '80s. George Morstardini, of Chicago, was a great white hope. He was so bad they had to bring in unlicensed bums from Memphis, wearing dirty sneakers and faded gym trunks, who routinely fell without being hit, while the fools at the Aragon Ballroom chanted, "George, George." Kerasiotis looked the other way.

In 1990, Arum promoted six WBO "world title" fights, but by 1992, he wouldn't touch them. By then it was obvious that the WBO was little more than a motley crew that conferred "world championships" on fringe contenders and second-raters, mostly campaigning out of Great Britain. Mario Martinez Rivero, a former sportswriter who became the WBO's PR man, candidly admitted, "Thank God for Britain." Without the deep pockets of British television, the WBO would barely be in business.

HBO television's Larry Merchant acerbically calls the WBO, "one of those off-brand 'world' championships." Yet in 1992, a big player like the late Dan Duva of Main Events was one of the major American packagers who promoted WBO title shows. So was Don King, and Cedric Kushner, though years later Kushner angrily swore to one of his trusted subordinates, "Never fuckin' again. That bastard Cordero told me he wanted $50,000 or he was gonna pull the sanction. He tried it right before the TV show."

In 1991 and '92, British promoter Mickey Duff did seven WBO shows. Barry Hearn, the one-time snooker king, staged ten, while the emerging power of British boxing, Frank Warren, did four. Danish promoter Mogens Palle was also a steady source of income, staging three title fights a year from 1990 to 1992.

In theory, the WBO derives its revenue from the sanction fees it places on promoters and fighters. According to a well-researched study, conducted nearly a decade ago by British boxing writers Bob Mee and Steve Holdsworth (who is also a TV commentator for Eurosport), the WBO charged $1,500 for a "license fee" and $3,000 for the "promoter's sanction," along with two per cent of the champion's purse, to a maximum of $100,000, plus two per cent of the challenger's purse, with a minimum of $750. The WBO magnanimously pays for the championship belt, but the promoter pays hefty expenses flying in, feeding, and housing the WBO-appointed officials.

"Man, you've got to watch those foreign officials and get a receipt for everything," sighed one source who has had to deal with them. "Otherwise, they just nickel and dime you to death. You end up paying for all kinds of things that have absolutely nothing to with the show. Hell, you don't even need 'em. It would be a lot cheaper to use local officials, but you're stuck with their judges, or no sanction." Yet the WBO's percentages were actually less than the WBA and WBC's fees – the promoter's sanction fee alone in the WBC could then reach a massive $150,000.

If the WBO was really sanctioning world championship boxing, why couldn't Manning Galloway, who hailed from Columbus, Ohio, get any fights on American TV, even though he was the WBO welterweight champion? Because he was a glorified clubfighter. Yet after he predictably lost his title in Denmark to popular Dane Gert Bo Jacobson, Galloway moaned bitterly, "I needed a knockout to win."

Jose Torres, the former light-heavyweight champion, author, and one-time columnist for the *New York Post*, was annointed president of the WBO and proclaimed, "The sport of boxing cannot tolerate any official whose reputation is not beyond reproach."

If that's the case, how did Torres get the job? In 1987, he was fired as head of the New York State Athletic Commission, six months after he disgracefully allowed Carl King – who wasn't even a licensed manager in the state of New York – to officially "manage" two contestants in the same bout in a WBC heavyweight championship. The card was promoted by Don King, Carl's stepfather. Tim Witherspoon, who had trained to fight someone else, was suddenly given James "Bonecrusher" Smith as an opponent, because Smith, who is a college graduate, and had a lawyer for a wife, had filed an antitrust monopoly lawsuit against the Kings after being forced to take on Carl as his so-called manager. To get him to drop his lawsuit, Don King gave Bonecrusher a title shot against Witherspoon.

In his massive civil lawsuit against Don King, Smith contended that Carl King forged his signature to their contract when Witherspoon didn't want to face him. When Witherspoon, who has a year of college, protested, he says Torres irritably told him, "If you don't go through with the fight, I'll ban you in New York and you won't be able to fight anywhere." Witherspoon got annihilated in the first round.

Though the British Board of Control has slipped badly, it's still the finest regulatory body in the world. But the WBO gets away with steady junkets for its annointed referees and judges in the UK, rewards for its loyal hacks. Referee Ismael Wiso Fernandez has done so many gigs in Britain, he's practically eligible for dual citizenship. How was the sport of boxing possibly served when Fernandez publicly criticized a fellow Puerto Rican official for not scoring on behalf of countryman Jose Ruiz when he lost his IBF title fight to Mexican-American Robert Quiroga? Though Fernandez is paid to be impartial, he actually told the *San Juan Star* that under such circumstances, he'd always score for his countryman.

WBO officials have repeatedly turned in scores that baffle long-time observers. For years it seemed that Chris Eubank, who generated huge sanction fees for the WBO, had to be knocked out to lose. Prince Naseem Hamed, who was a huge money earner for the WBO, was allowed to duck his mandatory challenger, Juan Manuel Marquez. Though Home Box Office (HBO) television, which pays the biggest money in the sport, graciously allowed the Prince to renegotiate his American contract, they finally put their foot down and refused to pay Hamed his usual exorbitant purse for facing Istvan Kovacs, a clever boxer from Hungary who meant absolutely nothing in the States.

The WBO however, which purports to act in the interest of boxing, found a unique way to protect its revenue. Hamed's title would reluctantly be declared vacant, but the eventual winner would have to make the first defence against ... Hamed. In September 2000, the Prince abdicated. "I regret to announce that I have voluntarily relinquished the WBO world featherweight championship crown," he said in a statement. "This decision stems from my desire to fight the world's top fighters, battle-tested world champions, rather than the manufactured contenders of boxing's governing bodies ... the titles claimed by Derek Gainer, Paul Ingle and Guty Espadas are political gifts, and each wears a paper crown until they face the true champion, Prince Naseem."

In February 2000, in the States, Mexico's Marco Antonio Barrera lost a questionable verdict to his countryman Erik Morales in a war. Though the fight was a WBC/WBO unification contest, it would generally be easier to get Iran and Iraq together. After the WBO champ Barerra lost, the organization's president, Francisco Valcarcel, a lawyer, autocratically decreed that Barrera was still WBO champion. Though the WBO is supposed to be impartial, Valcarcel said, "*My kid* was screwed. (Judge) Shirley had Barrera ahead after a few rounds, then his scores mysteriously become all in favour of Erik. They were very unfair. I have requested a full investigation from (the) Department of Justice in the State of Nevada."

Though his actions were appalling, and Valcarcel as an attorney is supposed to be held to a higher standard, he bristled, "We've made our decision. Barrera will be our champion." Translated: Barrera would still pay big sanction fees.

★ ★ ★

British sportsmanship was once hailed around the world. A visiting journeyman like Amos Johnson could become a contender by getting a controversial decision over national hero Henry Cooper, who was being primed for a lucrative rematch with Muhammad Ali. Almost nowhere else in the world would the visitor have been given such a close call. Welshman Howard Winstone would lose a similarly close verdict to Vincente Saldivar for the featherweight crown. The fairness of British officials was unmatched.

But by the 1990s, the once-proud Board was a doormat to renegade outfits like the WBO. According to Steve Holdsworth, the Eurosport commentator, "The Board is so damn scared of being sued, it won't do anything."

In April, 1998, Herbie Hide, of Norwich, the WBO's heavyweight champ, blew out a glorified American preliminary boy, Damon Reed, in just a round. *Boxing News* editor Claude Abrams calls it "the worst heavyweight championship fight ever."

The WBO had become such a farce, there were eventually two different factions legally fighting over its name. That didn't stop either of them from sanctioning WBO "world" championships that were actually in conflict in the same division.

The WBO's real concern is money, but it was Denmark, tiny Denmark, that told the WBO: take your cheap plastic belt and shove it. On 19 August 1994, the Danish Professional Boxing Federation "unanimously agreed (1) to ban, with immediate effect, any further WBO championship contest from taking place in the Kingdom of Denmark; (2) to withdraw all boxers licenses by the DPBF from any and all WBO ratings list; (3) to withdraw permission from all DPBF license-holders to act as judges or referee in WBO championship contests.

"This drastic action has been taken after long and mature consideration, in what the DPBF considers to be the best interests of the sport. It has been prompted by the desire to avoid future scandals of the kind which have marred our relationship with the WBO, including the manipulating of boxers and the exploitations of managers and promoters who are obliged to agree to outrageous option terms."

How a sanctioning group could possibly demand options like a promoter defies belief. As long as Pepe Cordero was involved, nobody could ever discount the appearance of such conduct. If Danish law couldn't penalise the WBO for it, American law certainly could. The WBO, a "for profit" corporation, does business out of Puerto Rico, and was reportedly incorporated in the state of Illinois. Yet nothing was done.

"Dignity, Democracy and Honesty the WBO's motto, are noble words and intentions," the scathing DPBF announcement said, "but are misapplied to an organization whose officials repeatedly abuse their supposedly unpaid positions by using it as an excuse to travel first class, often accompanied by wives or girlfriends, at the expense of local promoters." Though the Danish Professional Boxing Federation claims that it regretted "the necessity to take this step," it contended it had "been done in full consultation with the boxers involved, including WBO super-flyweight champion Johnny Bredahl, who has relinquished his title today."

Going for the jugular, the DPBF invited "its fellow-members of the EBU (European Boxing Union) to reconsider their affiliation to the WBO, an organization which no longer acts for the benefit of the sport it was ostensibly created to serve."

Though Denmark was the hardly the Mecca of international boxing, by the time the WBO was ousted, Gert Bo Jacobson had won the WBO's *papier mache* crown. Brothers Jimmy and Johnny Bredahl had become champs at super-feather and super-flyweight. Danish promoter Mogens Palle – who really was Danish boxing – bitterly complained that Jacobson and Norway's Magne Havvna were intimidated into giving up their titles. Palle got downright red in the face as he cursed Cordero.

"The WBO revolves around Cordero," Palle charged, "and he can make or break champions. When Johnny won the title, I had to sign away four options to Cordero at $25,000 each," yet within a couple of weeks of his fourth and last title fight, the WBO started threatening to strip him, "presumably so that they could get a new set of options by matching two other fighters for the vacant title."

In the 1950s, Frankie Carbo and Blinky Palermo enforced discipline with a lead pipe over the head. The WBO's skulduggery was all done with a nice little contract. Obviously, no sanctioning group, under American law, has the legal right to mandate who the *real* promoter or TV packager will be, but that's where the money is, not sanction fees. "The WBO has no class, no credibility," Palle bitterly told boxing journalist Harry Mullan.

This wasn't the first time Cordero's crew was kicked out of Europe. On 17 February 1990, Seattle slickster John David Jackson floored France's Martina Camara five times in defence of his WBO light-middleweight championship. Suddenly, in the eleventh round, the battered Camara flattened Jackson. As the American stumbled up, looking out on his feet, the ref called the fighters together, then stopped the bout.

Camara had pulled off a miracle finish – or had he? Camara and his corner thought Jackson had been counted out. Jackson was even placed on a stool, but as the MC announced the fight was over, the referee claimed the round had ended earlier. In the midst of this bedlam, it was forty minutes before a decision was given. Incredibly, the WBO called it "no contest," which saved the unbeaten Jackson's title. Camara was outraged. He'd made one the great comebacks in boxing history only to be robbed of the win and the lucrative title that went with it. The French Federation swore never again, and kicked the WBO out of France.

The WBO ultimately wormed its way back into both Denmark and France, but Cordero was constantly doing things that tore at the WBO's threadbare credibility. Spain's Jose Ramon Eriche was dropkicked into the WBO ratings simply because his promoter was a business associate of Cordero's. *Boxing News* broke the story, and Eriche suddenly plummeted through a trap door.

On 30 August 1993, the WBO outdid itself. Blond Tommy Morrison was the latest in the line of Great White Hopes. He was the WBO heavy-weight champ, and one of its highest earners. The WBO didn't do much business in the States, but Morris was slated to defend his championship in Kansas City, Missouri, and a near-capacity crowd of 12,000 turned out, paying more than $500,000 and making packager Bob Arum very happy. There was another $200,000 from ESPN-TV.

Suddenly, challenger Mike Williams, who had already been "knocked out" by Morrison in the film *Rocky V*, refused to take a pre-fight drug test. According to Williams's manager, Bob Jordan, "Drugs had nothing to do with it. He just turned yellow." Arum was beside himself. "I have to offer everybody a goddam refund," he screamed at matchmaker Bruce Trampler. "My God, we're talking close to a million dollars."

With just an hour till fight time, and Arum pacing the floor frantically, he suddenly saw a vision of loveliness. It was like Romeo first spying Juliet, King Arthur gazing upon Guinevere. There sat a portly, baby-faced, tank-town pug, Tim Tomashek. Faster than you can "sanction fee," Tubby Tim was hauled from his ringside seat. He was about to live a Walter Mitty dream, and fight for the *heavyweight championship of the world*. Well, the WBO's world.

Tomashek couldn't box – he was barely a six-round clubfighter – but the flabby 207-pounder, who looked like he trained on hot fudge sundaes, bopped and slapped the sculpted Morrison, who even allowed him to do a bit of showboating. When Tomashek had the gall to "dutch rub" Morrison and make an ass out of him in front of diehard fans, Tommy, who reportedly once smashed a topless dancer in the face with a beer bottle, got mad. He unleashed a hard left-right-left that sent Tomashek down on all fours late in the fourth round. Though a blood-thirsty roar erupted, Morrison, obviously holding back, would not go in and finish it. But the doctor wisely stopped the fight that never should've started between rounds.

Minutes later, the moon-faced punching bag was beaming. "The guys at work don't even know about this," laughed the podgy dockworker, a big grin on his round, battered face. "Jeepers creepers, they're going to be surprised if they watched on TV."

Bill Cayton, who was the brilliant svengali behind Morrison, was boiling with restrained fury. "He trains for Williams and he gets *Tomashek*," said Cayton, pronouncing the no-hoper's name like a vile epithet.

"WBO – What a Bloody Outrage," screamed the cover of *Boxing News*. The WBO suddenly announced it was giving back the sanction fee.

* * *

The British-based *Boxing News* has been a consistent critic of the Alphabet Boys, and no organisation has copped for it more than the WBO. "Boxing is a mess. But it took the World Boxing Organization only a week into the New Year to remind us how much worse it would be if they were in sole control," railed the magazine on 14 January 1994.

> New WBO strawweight champion Alex Sanchez of Puerto Rico, 16 days after winning the title vacated by (Britain's) Paul Weir, made a ridiculous first defense against an inept Texan named Arturo Garcia Mayen.
>
> Some of the details are obscure, and some of the unconfirmed reports concerning his state of health are horrifying if true. What is known is that Mayen claimed to have had only three professional fights, none of which can be substantiated. The wire sevices put Mayen down as a Mexican, but other sources say he is a Texan. Record compiler Phill Marder from Fight Fax Inc. says he's never heard of Mayen.
>
> Sanchez won after about 90 seconds of the first round when Mayen turned and ran to his corner. The Puerto Rican followed him and struck him in the back … . immediate reports suggest that the WBO have ordered a rematch on March 4.

By 1996, the WBO was up to more sleight of hand. At the Great Western Forum, in suburban Los Angeles, an obscure Mexican, Oscar Maldonado, faced Jorge Julio in a bout billed for the vacant WBO bantamweight championship. John Jackson, who handled boxing at the Forum, had signed documents proving that Francisco Valcarcel, the WBO president, had approved the match, and all sanction fees were paid. But only days after the nationally-televised fight aired, it was suddenly called a worthless "interim title" after the WBO had blown town. Why? Britain's Robbie Regan was still marketable for UK television, though he had not fought in a year. On Great Britain's side of the Atlantic, despite what American fans thought they saw on TV, Robbie Regan was still the WBO bantamweight champion of the world.

★ ★ ★

"People have been turned off by non-competitive fights. There have been too many over the years and that's why boxing is in the desperate shape its in today. You can't fool the public forever. My guys have to be tough because we're interested in promoting good fights, not their careers."

To prove that Bob Arum is truly a man of his word, on 13 April 1996 he put on a championship match in Boston, Massachusetts, featuring his baby-faced Jewish banger, Dana Rosenblatt, and Howard Davis, who was so old, vultures practically hover overhead whenever he does roadwork. The bout was for the vacant World Boxing Union middleweight championship. The WBU, which is based in Britain, had tried to cash in on British boxing the way the WBO had, but when Frank Warren announced he wouldn't work with them, 500-pound Jon Robinson, who created the so-called World Boxing Union, was forced to bring his bogus titles to the States.

Forget that a couple hundred men have died in the prize ring, and Davis was just one more to trod the mine-strewn comeback trail: Rosenblatt was young enough to be Davis's son, and he was a full-fledged middleweight, who strained to make 160. Davis was just a beefed up light-weight. "We're talking about a 40-year-old whose most important title – the 1976 Olympic gold medal – was more than 20 years and 28 pounds ago and who, last month, was not even among the WBO's list of top 30 middleweights," wrote *Boston Herald* boxing columnist George Kimball, damning the fight.

Davis, touted as a better prospect than Sugar Ray Leonard after coming out of the Montreal Olympics, had earned a reported $2 million in his first incarnation as a prize-fighter, but after failing in three shots at major "world titles" and squandering his dough, he was now going through a mid-life crisis. "This time I'm boxin' for me," he claimed.

Just a couple of months before this scandalous fight was made, Jon Robinson had a brutally loud phone call with this writer, emanating from Britain, where he accused everyone of trying to sabotage him. "Who is paying you? Who is paying you?" he brayed. He did finally admit, without much prompting, "I don't want to use Davis. He's too old. What if he gets hurt? I certainly wouldn't want him as our middleweight champion, but if he's broke, let someone throw a benefit for him."

Bob Arum will stoop awfully low to pick up a blood-stained dollar. ESPN bought the sham, but just ninety seconds in, a booming cross from the left-handed Rosenblatt had Davis on the deck. Davis, who once had a rapier jab and magnificent reflexes, was able to paw just eight so-called punches in the first round, before Rosenblatt exploded with a thunderous right hook in the second, which sent him crashing on to his side. As Davis groped drunkenly, fell again, and seemed positively stricken, it looked like a scene out of the *The Harder They Fall*.

"I just hope he's okay," said a worried Al Bernstein, ESPN's "color man," who had known how it was going to end before the bell but didn't have the guts to tell viewers because Arum had once got his sidekick, Randy Gordon, sacked fifteen years earlier.

"I hope he doesn't fight again," shuddered Bob Papa, ESPN's blow-by-blow announcer.

Ron Katz, who must have apprenticed under Attila the Hun, made the match. It wasn't the first time the WBU befouled Boston. Just before Christmas 1995, Angel Manfredy won the vacant WBU junior-light-weight title at the Roxy nightclub in front of a vast crowd of thirty-nine people. That's right, *thirty-nine* people, who donated a Christmas present for a needy kid to get in; TV packager Cedric Kushner wasn't able to get away with charging admission. Harold Petty, who had been a good fighter ten years earlier at a much lower weight, wasn't just the human sacrifice: he was the "fifth or sixth opponent of the week," recalled Jack Cowen, the matchmaker who exhumed him. Cowen was also handling Manfredy!

Neither Petty nor Manfredy was from the East Coast. The only reason this so-called world championship even happened was because Univision, the largest Spanish-language network in the States, was stupid enough to buy it. Manfredy pulverized Petty to earn his biggest purse of $17,000. Cowen claims, "He blew all his money inside of a week."

Though the WBU isn't even a minor blip on the radar screen in the States any more, TV championships have replaced world championships. While television is a huge factor in other professional sports, nowhere has the meaning of "world champion" been destroyed like it has in professional boxing. The WBA, WBC, IBF, and WBO are the major sanctioning organizations, and with the addition of the lunatic fringe like the World Boxing Federation (WBF), the International Boxing Organization (IBO), the Intercontinental Boxing Council (IBC), the International Boxing Association (IBA), and a few more too insignificant to name, the credibility of professional boxing has plunged to an all-time low. Championship belts used to mean something. Now all they're good for is holding up your pants. In the 1950s, there were approximately 5,000 fighters worldwide. There were generally eight weight divisions, with one champion in each. That breaks down to one champ every 625 boxers. Today, with just the major sanctioning bodies and not counting the whackos, you have about one "world champion" for every sixty-nine pros. It's ridiculous.

"The biggest change in boxing is that it's so much easier to become a 'world champion' from when I started," said Roberto Duran, who began at fifteen and won the so-called NBA middleweight belt on his forty-ninth birthday.

Don't think the WBO doesn't take its ratings seriously. There's money to be made. Darren Morris, an American from Detroit, Michigan, mysteriously cracked the WBO's rankings in July 2000. One year earlier, he'd whomped an old punching bag named Dave McCloskey, who'd lost sixty of his eighty pro contests. Though Morris hadn't fought since, he began a remarkable rise at super-middleweight that defied even Lourdes. Though Morris had no business being rated at all, he moved up to sixth in December, and then fifth.

He was obviously being groomed for a "mandatory" shot against Joe Calzaghe, the WBO super-middleweight king.

But Morris had a big problem. He'd been dead for four months. Ron Borges of the *Boston Globe* cracked, "If he'd died a little sooner, he might be a champion."

CHAPTER EIGHT

The Man Who Bought Boxing

IN 1911, A SPINDLY, craggy-faced teenager named Gershon Mendeloff signed a contract with London promoter Harry Jacobs. As Ted "Kid" Lewis, Mendeloff would fight an incredible forty-eight times that year, earning the princely sum of $1,980.

In June 1916 a two-fisted young slugger from Utah named Jack Dempsey made his New York City debut and got all of $16 for going ten hard rounds with big Andre Anderson.

By July 1921, promoter Tex Rickard had not only built his own rickety, outdoor arena, he had shocked the world by drawing 80,183 people to Jersey City, New Jersey, to pay $1,789,238 to see Dempsey destroy French war hero Georges Carpentier. "Start the fight early," Rickard said worriedly, as he looked on to a vast sea of people. "If we put anymore people in the seats, I'm afraid the God damn place will fall down."

By the 1920s, the age of ballyhoo had arrived. Rickard, a one-time Alaskan saloon-keeper and gambler, drew a staggering $2,658,660 for the legendary Dempsey-Gene Tunney "Long Count" rematch on 22 September 1927. Despite inflation, there wouldn't been a bigger live gate for the next fifty years, though a bald, homely ticket scalper with clacking false teeth named Mike Jacobs drew $1,925,564 for the Joe Louis-Billy Conn rematch in June 1946. It was the first great sporting event following World War Two and came with the unheard-of ticket price of $100 for a ringside seat.

On 8 March 1971, in the age of television and closed-circuit, Joe Frazier kept impaling his left like a meat hook as he trounced the unbeaten Muhammad Ali in what many still call the greatest sporting event of all time. Jerry Perenchio, a Hollywood talent agent promoting his first card, guaranteed each combatant $2.5 million. And on 15 September 1978, over 63,000 people streamed into the New Orleans Superdome to see the aging Ali find one last burst of youth and win the heavyweight championship for the third time by defeating Leon Spinks. Promoter Bob Arum's live gate was $4,806,675.

By 1996, pay-per-view television was accounting for receipts that no one could have dreamed of. The top ten grosses on Amerian pay-per-view have all been boxing, and Mike Tyson, a one-time purse snatcher from Brooklyn, drew nearly $100 million for his infamous return with Evander Holyfield in the "Bite of the Century." Promoter Don King, the flamboyant ex-con from Cleveland who took over boxing after leaving a prison cell, has been stoking the promotional fires for four decades. But after 100 years of big-time pugilism, historians still argue, who was the greatest promoter of all-time?

Now the worst promoter, that's easy. In 1979, Harold Smith was a stocky thirty-year-old with an aging athlete's body. At 6-2, he was tall, black and broad-shouldered, a pleasantly handsome man with a moderate Afro, moustache and beard. His strange voice was as high as a pre-teenr's but he spoke very precisely, and would have came across as a "professional," had it not been for the dark sunglasses he always wore, presumably to ward off the bright Hollywood sun. People wondered, *Just who is it behind those dark glasses? Why was it you never got a chance to really look into his eyes?* Smith also favoured rough workshirts and faded denim jeans, though he was no man of the people. His glittering designed jewelry reeked of "ghetto chic." Smith's trademark, though, was a white cowboy hat.

Harold was likeable, if mysterious, and lived in a fancy pad high above Hollywood's glamorous Sunset Strip. Visitors would marvel at his huge sunken hot-tub, or the well-tended pool. His interior decorator spent so much, it would've been cheaper to hire Michelangelo or DaVinci. There were always Cadillacs or Mercedes in the driveway. Harold would laugh and say, "Shit, man, beats takin' the bus." Despite his zest for the good life, Smith loathed having his picture taken. Whenever anyone brought a camera, he recoiled. Yet he loved to party. James Brown, Barry White, Diana Ross, would all blare from his fabulous stereo.

Harold also routinely strutted around with gym bags stuffed with cash. "Motherfucker's got to be a drug dealer," people said, but not even that could have explained the yacht, the racehorses or sleek Lear jet.

Though a lot of stars lived in the Hollywood Hills, nobody had ever heard of Harold. Who the hell was he?

★ ★ ★

Harold Smith was an enigma, a mystery man, who could drop $25,000 with one roll of the dice, but rejoice like hell on the rare occasions that he hit. Hundred-dollar bills would rain like confetti. "Harold had a heart of gold," remembered his secretary Terry Key.

One day in 1976, as Americans debated the kidnapping of heiress Patty Hearst, or the up-coming presidential election between Jimmy Carter and Gerald Ford, Smith happened to be leafing through the sports section of a newspaper and read about an amazing high school sprinter named Houston McTear. McTear was burning up the track but living in abject poverty. Smith, who had been anchor on the four-man relay team at American University and had been considered a long shot to make the 1964 Olympic team, impulsively called McTear's in Florida. Smith, who studied psychology in college, then made a lot more phone calls. Finally he was able to talk to Muhammad Ali.

"Champ," pleaded Smith in his impossibly childish voice, "we got a young brother, name of Houston McTear, that's just got greatness stamped all over him. He's a young Jesse Owens, but he's barely survivin' in a tarpaper shack."

"I'll take care of that," replied Ali, a very soft touch outside the ring. "I'll buy that boy a house."

Smith, excited and on a roll, impulsively asked if he could use Ali's name for an amateur track club that he was starting. Ali, who agreed to all sorts of things without his advisers around, hesitated for a second, but Smith began to wheedle. "Champ, it's for the young brothers." Years later, Ali remembered, "My impression was that he was a clean young man, striving to do business. Honest, I thought, and I liked him enough to let him use my name."

Smith promoted a few track meets in 1976-77. He also had some of his young, impressionable athletes shuttle him around in limousines. He became something of a Pied Piper in the Santa Monica black community, and sometimes there'd be fifty or sixty gladhanders around him, eager to soak up the good times. But track couldn't get out of the blocks when it came to network television, and Harold's creditors seldom got paid.

★ ★ ★

Ben Lewis was a short, dapper, black man of forty-eight years with a balding pate and horn-rimmed glasses. He had worked for Wells Fargo, the nation's eleventh largest bank and a household name, for twelve years when he first met Harold Smith. Lewis smiled readily when he met the good-looking ex-athlete; not many "brothers" came in to do business. Smith, for his part, sensed that Lewis was frustrated in his role as just another smiling black face in a white-moneyed establishment.

Smith had to have a steady bank to continue his business. He had already been given a Pele-like boot out of the posh Beverly Hills branch after his cheques had bounced like the finest Brazilian rubbber. "God damn," said Lewis, who worked at the Beverley Drive branch. "Your cheques are no good."

"Ben," Harold replied slowly, "I'm doin' it for the kids."

At first reluctantly, Lewis began to hold up the bank's collections.

"This will give you a couple days to get some money in the account, so the cheque will clear," Lewis said. It was supposed to be a one-off – but it just kept happening. Finally, Lewis, who realised he was getting in deep, decided to wash his hands of Smith. But Harold knew exactly how to play people, and was shameless. One day, in Lewis' office, he theatrically broke down and began to cry. "What will happen to all the young brothers and sisters without my program?"

Every instinct screamed that he should stay away from Smith, but Lewis had a good job, making $1,750 a month, and felt guilty. Smith had also introduced him to Muhammad Ali, whom Lewis idolized, and had allowed Lewis to glimpse a glamorous world, one he could only dream of while slaving anonymously at the bank.

"You've got to make these cheques good," Lewis insisted.

"I will, I will," promised Smith.

Lewis got on the phone to his buddy, Sammy Marshall, another rare black employee, at the Miracle Mile branch of the bank. Marshall was a mean-spirited fifty-year-old whom few liked, but Lewis convinced him to keep carrying Harold. If he didn't, Lewis would blow his job, because Smith by now owed Wells Fargo $14,000.

Wells Fargo was a huge institution, dealing with thousands of transactions a day. "Every bank that has branches in different places has to have some kind of system for allowing customers to take out money, to walk into a branch that's not theirs and draw money on the account," said former federal prosecutor Dean Allison. "Obviously, the bank has to have a way to keep track of the money that a customer takes out of Branch B, when the customer's account is in Branch A. At Wells Fargo, that system was called the branch settlement system, and it was basically a computerized system."

The system relied on two halves of one ticket that was generated on every transaction. They had to come together to explain debits and credits, but if two bank officials in different branches knew the right code, and were so inclined, a bad cheque could keep bouncing almost indefinitely.

As weeks went by, Smith kept saying to both men, "Brothers, do you know how much money can be made in sports? We could make millions"

"Just pay the $14,000 back," Lewis snapped.

Smith finally got rid of his sprinters and turned to boxing. He began scouting top amateurs, but Harold was still doing his sleight of hand. Lewis and Marshall were his special guests at the historic Ali-Spinks rematch in New Orleans in September 1978. Lewis was thrilled when Ali actually came to his hotel room, but days later back at his desk in California, he was furious when Smith's $19,000 cheque that paid for the trip, bounced.

"What happened," demanded Lewis, glaring at Smith as he slunk into his office.

"Well, our boxing team was supposed to box Joe Frazier's team. The profits were supposed to come from that." Boxing people knew there was not a dime to be made from the amateurs.

Smith had his sights set on the pros. He got Ali's permission, and began calling his company Muhammad Ali Professional Sports. MAPS signed Tony Tubbs, a fat heavyweight who didn't like to train, and gave Tubbs's parents a $50,000 house as a signing bonus. As Lewis and Marshall continued their juggling act, Jeff McCracken, a former U.S. Marine, was inked, along with J.B. Williamson, who would eventually win the WBC light-heavyweight championship but couldn't draw flies. Chuck Bodak was brought in to train the amateurs, while former WBA heavyweight champ Jimmy Ellis refined their technique. Wells Fargo was in the boxing business, though it didn't know it.

Lewis and Marshall had to steal increasing amounts of money to pay for it. Then Smith came up with another brilliant idea to get out of the financial quicksand. "Look," he said excitedly to both gents one day, "we'll get Ali for a rematch with [Joe] Bugner."

Unfortunately it would have to be an exhibition – in Australia, where Bugner had become a favourite. Though the blond Brit had already lost twice to Ali – with their second fight so bad that TV broadcaster Don Dunphy had to stifle his urge to ask Bugner, "Do you expect to get paid after putting up this type of miserable performance?" – Smith lined up a huge outdoor stadium, seating 45,000, for the pointless exhibition. His "money men" were worried. Smith brushed them off. "With the TV and live gate, I guarantee we'll get back all the money you done took. I guar-an-tee it." Then he laughed.

But first Ali had to get paid: he demanded $200,000. Normally, funds that large are handled via wire transfer, but Smith insisted to Ali's lawyer, Michael Phenner, that he wanted to bring the certified cheque himself. "Boy, that's odd," Phenner commented to a partner. On the raucous plane trip to Australia, Harold graciously played host to over fifty people, including actress Cicely Tyson. History would prove he had the wrong Tyson on board.

There could not have been more than 4,000 lost souls in the cavernous stadium, watching Ali and Bugner lazily slap at each other. It began to rain. If that wasn't bad enough, Smith hadn't been able to sell the farce to TV.

With Lewis and Marshall bemoaning the bank's big losses, Harold was nonplussed. Suddenly, on the way back, as everyone was about to enter customs, Smith rushed over to Lewis, pulled out a big wad of bills, and whispered, "Hold this!" Lewis took it without thinking. If caught, he could have been charged with federal currency violations for not declaring more than $10,000.

A week later, back in his office, Lewis fretted about how to keep the embezzlement scheme going. "Look, at least there's some bread coming in from the Australian show," he told Marshall. But he hadn't heard from Smith.

Finally, he called him. "Harold, when's the Australian money going to come?"

Smith paused a moment, then said angrily, "Mutha-fuckin' promoter done run off with the all the money." One more lie.

"The first clear embezzlement occurs in about October 1978," said Dean Allison. "By late '79, almost a year later, the total stolen was only about $200,000. If you go a year later than that, you get to 1980. They were up to about $15 million."

In truth, Smith knew nothing about fighters. Behind his shades, cocaine and flashy jewelry, he was a chronically insecure man, who wouldn't go out and hire anybody who knew anything. Though heavyweights are the cash cows of this business, Smith stupidly signed Leo Randolph, who'd won a 1976 Olympic gold medal at just 112 pounds. Commercially, flyweights are not worth their weight in smelling salts, but Smith still matched Randolph with tough Oscar Muniz in 1979 at the Los Angeles Sports Arena and grossly overpaid the fighters, to the tune of $41,250. The entire show grossed just $9,656, which didn't even pay the rent.

With Muhammad Ali Professional Sports up to its chin in red ink, you would have thought that Smith would have finally gotten smart, but in November 1979, this turkey got plucked again when he paid Henry Lumpkin, a flabby Chicago sparring partner, and promising Marty Monroe, an LA heavyweight, another $41,250. The gate this time was $5,821.

Chicago booking agent Jack Cowen quickly sent another "opponent" as more dollar signs danced in his eyes. In January 1980, Grady Daniels, a Baptist deacon, got the holy hell beaten out of him by Monroe. Not only did both fighters' purses again exceed the pitiful gate but Smith, trying to impress Monroe, lavished more cheques and cash on him, blowing an extra $20,000.

"Boy," laughed Cowen, decades later. "I sure hated to see Smith go out of business."

Lewis and Marshall had grown frantic. "Harold, we're losin' all sorts of money," Lewis said, almost crying one day. "Sammy and I have to keep going through all these changes just to keep our asses out of jail."

"Brother, don't worry, we're going to get the money back."

"How? Goddamn it, how? You've been telling us that we're gonna make money, but the mother-fuckin' bank ain't seen a dime."

"Know what our problem's been," said Smith, slowly, coolly assessing the situation. "We're losin' money 'cause we ain't jumped into this shit Big Time! We got to get us some stars. Get me $250,000!"

Smith was planning his boldest move. Larry Holmes was the WBC heavyweight champion, and the best big man in boxing. Holmes had a love/hate relationship with promoter Don King. King once said he "couldn't draw flies to a garbage dump" but he was the recognised champ, and a valuable commodity.

On 30 November 1979, with the fight fraternity in Las Vegas to watch Sugar Ray Leonard halt Wilfred Benitez in the final seconds of their fifteen-rounder, Smith, Marshall, and Papa Joe Daskiewicz, who managed face-first heavy Scott LeDoux, made their way up to Holmes's hotel room. Smith furtively looked around. He had a gym bag stuffed with money.

Their path was blocked by a furious Don King. "What are you mutherfuckers doing?" shrieked King, reaching for a gun. "I'll walk you down." He was still a street thug who had never really left prison.

"I'll walk *you* down!" Smith replied, angrily staring back.

With hotel doors opening, and decent folk wondering what the commotion was about, King bellowed, "Y'all better get the fuck outta here."

Smith and King nearly came to blows again in the elevator. Yet Holmes later admitted, "I was tempted to take his offer."

Smith failed dismally when he also tried to sweet talk Sugar Ray Leonard. "Well," recalled Mike Trainer, the droll lawyer who handled Leonard, "when we got to the specifics, as to how they were going to sell different rights that are connected to a fight … y'know, you have site rights that you can sell to Caesars Palace, let them sell the tickets. let them assume the risk. You can do delayed broadcast for television. You can do foreign TV rights overseas … (but) they weren't really familiar with the amount of money or how they would derive the money, and that frightened me."

On 27 September 1980, MAPS's most promising heavyweight, Marty Monroe, stopped Eddie "Animal" Lopez. That blew another $200,000. Yet, Smith kept telling everybody, "Baby, we're making progress."

On November 7, 1980, the Ken Norton-Randy Cobb fight squandered another $200,000, even with network TV. By now, Harold had gone out and signed Earnie Shavers, though the ferocious puncher was just about finished. Shavers was in Las Vegas when Smith rang and told him to meet him at midnight. "I got a call from Harold Smith," recalled the high-pitched Shavers, beginning to titter. "He said, 'Earnie, make sure you got an extra brief case.' So my friend Luke and I, we went by his condominium in Las Vegas and we got to talking. He says, 'Earnie, I got something for ya, a gift.' He opened a big, thick briefcase full of money! He gave me the money, and I started counting it."

Smith barked at him, "What are you doing?"

"I'm just makin' sure the money's all here."

"I give you a hundred thousand and you still counting it?"

It took Shavers two hours to go through it. "I went real slow and easy," he laughed.

Smith's deep pockets were the talk of the fight game. London promoter Mickey Duff had also been instructed to meet him in Las Vegas. Smith arrived with Ben Lewis and another bulging briefcase containing payments to entice two British boxers to fight for Smith. "Best I remember, I think it was $300,000," said Duff, who had been in boxing forty years and thought he had seen everything. "As I remember, $250,000 was for Jim Watt (the WBC lightweight champ) and $50,000 was for John L. Gardner (the British heavyweight champion). Smith went to a briefcase and couldn't count the money. I thought I was dreaming. I just couldn't believe it."

As Harold handed the heavy bag to Duff, who was then Britain's top promoter, Duff said to him, "I've never had cash before."

"Well, I just won $5 million in Las Vegas," said Smith.

"Suppose you don't come up with the two opponents? You lose the lot."

"I know," said Smith.

"I never heard from him again," recalled Duff tartly. "He didn't fool me a minute. I thought he was either a crook or crazy."

Watt finally fought Alexis Arguello, while Gardner squared off in the States against Michael Dokes. But it was for Don King, not Smith.

By November 1979, Harold Smith, had promoted seven cards. All were huge losers. He could have lost money on the David-Goliath rematch. Smith was running amok, and Lewis and Marshall had no way to stop him. They were in too deep. When Smith needed a respite from the stress of losing Wells Fargo's money, he bought a jet, a luxury yacht and racehorses. Though MAPS hadn't seen a penny in profit, Harold's ringcard girls were flown in from Hawaii. Naturally, he paid for their apartments as well. MAPS was supposed to be in the boxing business, yet somehow ended up with an "airforce" and a "cavalry."

Smith signed Matthew Saad Muhammad, the WBC light-heavyweight champ, who wasn't a great draw but was a wildly exciting fighter and a TV favourite. He insanely gave Saad $300,000 for "training expenses," then popped up with another $35,000 cheque which was apparently chafing Smith as it stayed in his pocket. Saad, who had grown up on the mean streets of Philadelphia after being abandoned on a doorstep as a baby, whispered to his manager, "Somethin' ain't right."

On 28 November 1980, Muhammad KO'd Zambia's Lotte Mwale down on the West Coast. Why would anyone in his right mind put on a fight between someone from Philadelphia and Zambia in a dead fight town like San Diego? It defied belief. But Smith wasn't content to blow $216,000 there. One day later, he flushed another $328,000 of Wells Fargo's money down the toilet as New York's Eddie Mustapha Muhammad defended his WBA light-heavyweight title against Dutchman Rudy Koopmans.

Smith's fight sites were abominable, he seldom got TV and he wasn't even signing his fighters to option contracts, the ball and chain that keeps promoters from bankruptcy. By now, everybody, including Smith, knew they would never make a dime. Smith so wanted to be a big man that his friends were staying in first class hotel rooms, and he had even taken to showering his ringcard girls with cars and gifts. Life was good as long as nobody did an audit.

One day Smith began to complain about "the company plane." The Lodestar was quickly traded, and the frazzled Lewis came up with another $210,000 as Harold continued to play "Break the Bank." Lewis, realizing he was probably going to jail, figured he might as well grab a bit for himself. In for a penny, in for a pound. He bought a house for $145,000, blew another $10,000 for a Honda Civic for his son, and paid off $15,000 on his wife's Buick. In just three years, thanks to the fringe benefits of Wells Fargo Bank, Lewis was able to steal $320,000 for himself.

By now, even the once unflappable Smith was subject to long periods when he would sit alone and brood. Then suddenly he would pop up with a regal flourish and announce, "If anybody wants me, I'll be at the track." Naturally, he'd depart via shining limo.

Lewis was a bundle of nerves, Marshall was glum and Smith tried to hide his fears behind ghetto machismo. He did so many incredibly stupid things, each one fanning more rumours. In June 1980, he invited the Kronk Gym's Thomas Hearns and Emmanuel Steward out to his swank Santa Monica office. Hearns was a helluva fighter, the rising young star of the welterweight division, but had never made more than $85,000 for a fight. Smith opened up a suitcase stuffed with $500,000 in cash.

"It's all yours," he said, "if you fight Pipino Cuevas."

As Hearns stammered back, Smith quickly interrupted him: "I'll give you another $100,000 when you sign."

Later that day, Smith eagerly hopped onto the MAPS jet and streaked off for Mexico City. He took along a heavy gym bag filled with $1 million in cash to tempt Cuevas, the WBA welterweight champion. The fight though, wasn't a done deal. Pepe Cordero, the WBA's card-carrying bagman, demanded $75,000. On 2 August 1980, in Detroit, the sinewy, merciless Hearns transformed Cuevas into rubble in two rounds. On the undercard, Hearns's stablemate, Hilmer Kenty, battered South Korea's Young-Ho Oh into submission in nine in the first defence of his WBA lightweight championship. And in Cincinatti, Ohio, a couple of hundred miles away, human threshing machine Aaron Pryor halted long-time WBA light-welterweight champion Antonio Cervantes, making Smith the first promoter to have two different televised cards on the same afternoon.

Alarm bells were ringing all over the boxing terrain. Bob Arum, a former "Kennedy Raider" in the United States Department of Justice, kept inquiring about Smith. One day Arum, whose New York-accented voice is somewhere between a nasal rasp and a malignant wheeze, said, "Harold, people are wondering where you're getting your funding." Arum had gotten into boxing in the early 1960s when he was still working for the Government and had tied up the receipts of the first Liston-Patterson heavyweight championship fight. He knew there was no way Smith could suffer these kind of losses and be legitimate. Smith, who did things on impulse, and at times was a bundle of manic energy, kept dropping hints that he was being bankrolled by an Arab sheik.

With Arum trying to find out about Smith, and hoping he could put him out of business, the renegade promoter's purses were so huge that he was drastically altering the price structure of the sport. He even made another futile grab for Larry Holmes, waving two cheques totalling $900,000 in front of the surly champion's face. If that brought a rare smile, Holmes, who quit school at fourteen to wash cars, was still scared to leave Don King.

Muhammad Ali Professional Sports had a lot of people running around but didn't have an accountant. Most MAPS employees never really seemed to be doing anything. Smith, with his desire to be needed, to be a big man, collected human strays and paid them so they'd all worship at the altar of Harold Smith. Lewis and Marshall had gotten so anxious that their hearts raced everytime their phones rang. But they couldn't quit. They couldn't even take vacations. Without these two insiders to juggle the cash transaction tickets, the whole scheme would collapse.

"Look," Lewis implored Smith one day. "We've got to bail out. Somehow, we've got to the get the bank's money back."

"Yeah, yeah, I know."

"Harold, Goddamn it, I'm serious! I must've been crazy to get involved with this shit. Crazy! You got me and Ben involved, now you'd better get us out."

"Hold on, now brother," said Harold, who suddenly feared Lewis might make a phone call to the FBI. "Ain't no reason to get nervous. I got me an idea."

Knowing there was but one way to stay out of jail, Smith become a hopeless gambler, risking everything on one last roll of the dice. He ordered Lewis to get him more money. By now duffel bags of Wells Fargo's cash were being smuggled out the door. Smith, who could've tried to be inconspicuous, picked it up in a limo. He used the swag to sign Ken Norton to fight Gerry Cooney, boxing's latest White Hope and a genuine threat to win the heavyweight championship.

On the same card, Matthew Saad Muhammad would meet his fellow Muslim Eddie Mustapha Muhammad, in a WBC/WBA light-heavyweight title showdown. Hearns would defend against super-slick Wilfred Benitez, while Pryor would go after Saoul Mamby, a classy but colorless New Yorker. The card was billed as "This Is It" – but "The Jig Is Up" would've been more appropriate.

The card, slated for boxing's tarnished shrine, Madison Square Garden, would be one of the greatest promotions in history. Though ticket prices were steep and "Reaganomics" was on, ducats moved briskly. Behind the scenes, like something out of a Chaplin comedy. Smith was still sending limos to pick up the huge mounds of cash Lewis and Marshall sent to guarantee the fighters' purses.

"Brothers, this is going to be huge. I'm tellin' ya, I can see fifty, maybe $100 million in revenue," Smith chortled to his petrified underlings.

"That'll be fantastic, Harold," said Lewis. "But then we can put the money back?"

Marshall nodded vigorously.

Though $100 million was highly unlikely, $50 million seemed a possibility. This star-studded card caught the public's imagination. But Smith, despite three years in the boxing business, still didn't know what the hell he was doing. This card could have been their golden parachute but Smith guaranteed purses like he was dealing with Monopoly money. In a burst of madness, Eddie Mustapha Muhammad was guaranteed $1.5 million, when nobody was coming to see him. Cooney, who generated a lot of excitement, was getting $1.25 million; the washed-up Norton, who had always needed an opponent like Muhammad Ali to draw big, was pegged at $1.1 million. Hearns was slated for $1.5 million, which was crazy. Good as he was, "the Hitman" was an $85,000 fighter before he met Smith. Benitez was a Puerto Rican idol but was never worth $1 million. Smith, letting his emotions get the best of any lingering common sense, insanely promised Matthew Saad Muhammad $2.1 million, when he had fought on national television for one-tenth of that.

With Smith's "money men" frantically juggling debit chits, and with sacks of cash leaving Wells Fargo like garbage on New Year's Day, the plotters nervously counted the hours till the show took place. Then, on 23 January 1981, Lewis got a phone call.

★ ★ ★

"Ben, we've got a problem, I just can't find the other half of the chit," complained Judy MacLardie, of the Miracle Mile branch of the Wells Fargo Bank.

"Ah, it's nothing," said Lewis, his heart pounding as hard as a conga drum. "It'll turn up."

As MacLardie continued to question Lewis, she detected his nervousness. Something was wrong. Lewis actually began to shake when he was called into his boss Brian Feeley's office.

"Ben, we've got a discrepancy here. What's the problem?"

Finally, with Feeley continuing to harangue him, and no way out, Lewis blurted, "I advanced Harold Smith some money." Feeley quickly called the bank's auditor, an ex-cop.

Just ten days before the fights were to take place, Lewis called Smith in tears. The game was up. "Look, why don't you just ask the bank to loan you $10 million?" Lewis suddenly said, sounding like a small child who still believed in Santa Claus. Smith gave a bitter laugh.

The FBI was called in and all twelve of Smith's bank accounts were frozen. A platoon of cops descended on MAPS's Santa Monica headquarters demanding the books. With employees in shock, and women sobbing "Harold had been so good to everyone," nobody could believe it was true.

On January 31, in Philadelphia, Jeff Chandler retained his WBA bantamweight title with a decision over Panama's Jorge Lujan. Smith was supposed to have been the promoter, but at the last minute CBS-TV arranged for Russell Peltz in Philadelphia to do the show, because federal agents had announced they'd uncovered "the biggest bank fraud in American history." In Los Angeles, Muhammad Ali called a press conference to announce he had nothing to do with the scam. The story was making front-page headlines and the lead on national TV newscasts. At one point at the press conference, a phone rang in front of Ali and he answered, "City Morgue." Meanwhile, Smith had disappeared.

On February 7, from parts unknown, Smith called a local radio station and, in his kid's voice, relayed this communiqué to the world: "I appeal to the media to go to the Wells Fargo Miracle Mile branch. It is there you will find the beginning of what I guarantee is the biggest case of fraud, embezzlement and illegal loan kickbacks, including numerous branches and personnel in the Wells Fargo system. I am not afraid and I am not alone because I know God is with me." The Almighty, however, wasn't about to accept any of Harold's cheques.

Wells Fargo's auditors worked long hours to unravel the theft and finally came up with a figure. It stunned everyone. They said $21,305,000 was missing.

"I'm innocent," Smith protested. "I had a line of credit." On the lam and still trying to con his way out of an impossible situation, he blamed a man called Gene Kawakami, who worked at Wells Fargo. Smith was such a liar that he even claimed that a Wells Fargo security force was out to murder him, his four-year-old son, and wife Lee. The Japanese Yakuza (organized crime) was also supposed to be involved. Prosecutor Dean Allison would debunk all of this.

The fight game howled in delight. Bob Arum suddenly realized where he knew Smith from. In 1972, Smith had run off with the closed-circuit proceeds in North Carolina for the second Ali-Jerry Quarry fight. Harold Smith turned out to be Ross Eugene Fields, who was already wanted along with his wife Lee, for a string of bad cheques. Lee was really Alice Vicky Darrow.

As the Feds prepared indictments, Lewis agreed to testify against Smith and to throw himself on the mercy of the court. Smith though, showing incredible chutzpah, filed a $274 million defamation suit against Wells Fargo, because "my good name has been tarnished." But it was all over for Smith. He intended to leave the country but, with the Feds out looking for him, he was caught in April 1981.

Somehow it took a sympathetic jury eight days to find him guilty. At his sentencing, the bumbling conman tried another trick. "You're a beautiful black woman. I love you," he told District Court Judge Consuela Marshall. He also tried to set up Don King for the Feds. Smith was lucky he was sentenced to only ten years. Ben Lewis got five on his plea bargain, Sammy Marshall, three, and Gene Kawakami, a minor Wells Fargo employee, two months.

In March 1987, Smith called from prison to give Tony Tubbs advice on how to fight Mike Tyson. Tubbs was demolished in two. Harold managed to leave Danbury federal prison after just five years and three months, on Hallowe'en, 1988.

Lewis and Marshall's lives were ruined. Even Feeley, who was Lewis's boss, couldn't get another job in banking. Harold Smith however, still claims, "I was framed." Nobody believed him, but the fight game is full of so many tramps and thieves, he still kicked around on the lunatic fringes of sport. In the mid-1990s. Smith was even mentioned as a co-promoter for a mooted Larry Holmes-George Foreman bout, disparagingly called "Two Geezers at Caesars," though it was mooted for the Houston Astrodome. It never happened, but somehow Holmes and Foreman got "upfront money."

In 1996, Harold promoted the first professional card in China. Chairman Mao must have been rolling in his grave. By the end of 2002, Harold Smith, the man who would be (Don) King, was simply sleeping on a friend's couch.

CHAPTER NINE

Tankers

TRUMAN GIBSON, THE former lawyer for the Mob-run International Boxing Club, claimed that in all the time he was in boxing, he knew of just three fixed fights. If you believe Gibson, who nearly went to jail for his role in the IBC, the Rocky Marciano-Archie Moore war was fixed. While that's preposterous – Moore looked like a man who'd been beaten with a baseball bat at the finish – fixed fights do happen, though not as often as lore suggests.

"We've got what I call 'legal' fixes," admits Larry Hazzard, the former referee and fighter, who currently heads the New Jersey Boxing Commission. "It happens when one fighter is so badly overmatched, he has no chance to win."

Out-and-out dives are rare, but they happen. On 12 December 1990, at the Royal Albert Hall in London, James Holly, a legendary stiff from Ashtabula, Ohio, went out in just sixty-eight seconds against promising Michael Bentt, a muscular American who was on fistic rehab in Britain. The flabby Holly, who claimed to be thirty-six but was actually forty, got grazed by a jab, yelled, "OOOOOH!" and hurled himself into the ropes before collapsing in a heap.

For the bout, which was somehow sanctioned by the Board of Control, Holly came into the ring with a stellar record of three wins and twenty defeats, nineteen by clean knockout. Holly had one no-contest, while his other loss came on a third round stoppage. In 1987, the *Philadelphia Daily News* did a feature on the worst fighters in boxing, and there was Holly's smiling face, although most people wouldn't have recognized him standing up. At the time, Holly was 1-12. After somehow winning his pro debut against Victor Salle in 1983, Holly realized the error of his ways and lost his next twelve by knockout.

Most people would have grasped that boxing was not for them. Over the next seven years Holly's license was suspended numerous times, and he was finally retired in states like New Jersey. In August 1990, less than four months before the Bentt farce, Holly was actually denied a boxing license to box in Ohio. "I'm absolutely amazed that Holly was allowed to box in Britain," a commission spokesperson told *Boxing News*.

The late Harry Mullan, then editor of *Boxing News*, figured, "The Board of Control must bear the ultimate responsibility for allowing into the country a man whose record is probably the worst of any professional fighter to appear in a British ring."

Bentt went on to win the WBO heavyweight title, destroying Tommy Morrison in a round, but was forced to quit after being badly hurt in a British ring. Holly, however, was still falling down in the States a decade later. Though Holly has been in the tank so many times his publicity photos should have him decked out in scuba gear, this cheeky bastard actually got his license back in Ohio – though after paying a fine with a bum cheque, he promptly lost it again.

In 1998, he fought under an assumed name in Boston. "How does it feel to be a tanker? To throw fights for a living?" he was asked.

"Hey, I legit," Holly said.

His record was four wins and fifty-four losses. He'd been stopped fifty times.

Since Holly was also fifty years old, it was time to pass the torch, and at the time of writing he was handling approximately forty-five so-called boxers who were virtually guaranteed to fall down on cue. They were poor black kids who were fed to white ticket-sellers in tank towns. By August of 2000, the collective record of Holly's "Ashtabula Acrobats" was twenty-five wins and 435 losses (427 inside the distance). Greg Sirb, who heads the Association of Boxing Commissions, has tried to stop Holly, but in Cincinatti, Ohio, one promoter has made his living for more than thirty years with his motley crew.

* * *

Mark Gastineau was a lantern-jawed, six-foot six-inch giant, who wore a dark, swept back pompadour with a long shag in back and scaled a massive 280 pounds. Gastineau was a defensive end for the New York Jets gridiron team. His "sack dance" became a Sunday ritual on national TV; he would smash a hapless ball carrier to the ground, then emote wildly in front of the cameras. Gastineau became both a fearsome presence on the football field and a cultural icon off it. But by 1988, after nine years in the National Football League, he was finished at thirty-three.

Gastineau had a massive ego, though, and couldn't give up the game, so he played briefly in the Canadian Football League before he was cut. With his celebrity, he could have earned a good living as a football announcer, but Gastineau couldn't give up the cheers. He decided to become a pro fighter.

Gastineau, however, had a couple of problems. He could not fight, and he had a glass jaw. Despite a year in the gym, he was still so dreadful that he practically got knocked out shadow boxing. That, however, could be "overcome" – or so Rob Russen told the award-winning American TV magazine *60 Minutes*. Russen was a flunky of Rick "Elvis" Parker, a chubby, bearded man who specialized in washed-up heavyweights and also promoted rock concerts and religious revivals. The revivals didn't stop Parker from snorting long lines of cocaine. Even when he wasn't high, he came across like a manic, demented elf. Under the best of circumstances Parker had a nasal, abrasive voice, and babbled compulsively. Septuagenarian matchmaker Jack Cowen, who has met a lot of scumbags in the fight game, remembers him as a "no good sonofabitch."

In 1993, Parker descended on heavyweight Bert Cooper with a restraining order, right on pay-per-view TV, just as Cooper was about to try and win a "winner-take-all" tourney. Somehow, Parker grabbed fifty per cent of Cooper's purse and took off without bothering to see him fight.

Russen claims that Parker buttonholed George Foreman's business advisors (Ron Weathers and brother Roy Foreman) and got a gentleman's agreement that if Parker could somehow get Gastineau to 12-0, Foreman would fight him. Of course, signed contracts don't mean much in boxing, let alone gentleman's agreements, but Parker was dreaming of a multi-million dollar purse. He ordered Russen, "Find me someone who'll take a dive."

In June 1991, in the Virginia hinterlands, the thirty-six-year-old Gastineau squared off with Derrick "Starfire" Dokes. Dokes claimed a few pro fights, but actually made his living as a fall guy in professional wrestling. "The guy wasn't allowed to throw a punch. He was told to get out of there at the first opportunity," Russen said.

Dokes says he met with Parker and Gastineau beforehand, and agreed to take the dive for $600. In an amateur video shot of the match, Gastineau is seen charging across the ring like he's about to manhandle a quarterback. Dokes leaps into the air and lands on his back, though clearly none of Gastineau's punches land. The abomination lasted eighteen seconds. According to Dokes, who readily admitted his role on *60 Minutes*, "(It was) totally fixed, a totally fixed fight." Dokes said how easy it was to jump off his feet, making believe he'd been hit. It's a standard wrasslin' move.

There was a brief, national stink, but in February 1992, Gastineau tangled with Kevin Barch in Carthage, Missouri. Barch was the brother of Sonny

Barch, who also worked for Parker. Kevin Barch, a simple, round-faced, good ol' boy who talks like he came straight out of the hills, was offered $1,000 to find a soft spot on the canvas. He'd done all his fighting in bars. "Like a dumbass, I said, 'Yeah.' A thousand dollars in my pocket, go in there and get hit, take a fall. Sounded like some easy money to me." Barch told the then-gullible Missouri commission he was 7-3. Apparently, they never asked how many he'd won with broken beer bottles.

In 1992, Gastineau made his nationally-televised debut as a fighter on the undercard of a USA Network show. His match just didn't make sense. Though Gastineau had a tentative two-fight deal with USA, he first had to beat Tim "Doc" Anderson, who was 25-11, had lasted two rounds with Foreman and had beaten a washed-up Jimmy Young (once robbed against Muhammad Ali for the heavyweight championship, in 1976). Insiders wondered how the useless Gastineau could win. "It's gotta be in the bag," the sharpies figured.

Once upon a time, the blond Anderson had been a straight-up technician, but the now burly thirty-four-year-old came right out winging, and damn near took off Gastineau's head. As the crowd roared, and Gastineau lurched around like the Frankenstein monster, Mark somehow lasted the full five rounds, but it was so one-sided, Anderson was actually dropping his hands like Ali, as he began playing with him.

The next day, the *New York Post* brutally ridiculed Gastineau with a big cartoon. By now, it was obvious to everyone that he couldn't fight a lick and his disgraceful boxing career should have been at an end. But Parker kept yammering, "He's got a name, and I put too goddamn much time and money in."

Meanwhile, Don Hazleton, head of the Florida commission, demanded an investigation by the Florida Attorney General's office. "When he (Parker) shows up, it's World Wide Wrestling, it's Barnum and Bailey. He's a con man," Hazleton said.

Though there would eventually be five people who contended on national television that Gastineau's fights were fixed, Parker angrily denounced them. "These people who are making allegations about fight-fixin' are low-life, scumball, pieces of crap. Liars, drug addicts ... They want to harm me, (and) destroy me for their own selfish reasons."

Somehow, Gastineau managed to KO Anderson in six rounds in Oklahoma City in December 1992. That rematch brought Gastineau's record to 13-1, with all thirteen wins inside the distance, but this fight had a terrible odor about it. Anderson told friends, "Parker drugged me." He also began to claim, "I'm dying."

"Anderson was a strange kid," remembered Cowen, who'd booked many of his early pro fights, around Chicago, and in the Calumet region near

Hammond, Indiana. Anderson's nickname was "Doc" because he ran a medical supply service. He didn't have to fight, but was a fairly promising light-heavyweight in the early 1980s, and won ten out of his first twelve. With his preppy hair and tight, clipped mustache, he looked more like a young insurance salesman that a fighter, but by 1986, he'd put on weight and was stopped by Angelo Musone in Italy. Realizing, he was never going to be more than an opponent, Anderson's dreams began to die, and in 1991, he was blasted out in one round by comebacking Larry Holmes.

However he lost the Gastineau rematch, Anderson now blamed Parker for everything, including his liver and kidney damage, which probably came because of his boxing. He kept insisting he'd been drugged.

On Friday, 28 April 1995, the burly heavyweight angrily confronted Parker in a Florida hotel room. There was loud argument, and suddenly Parker began to scream, "No! No! No!" Anderson pulled out his .38 caliber pistol and started firing, emptying the entire clip even as Parker lay dying.

With the burning scent of gun powder still in the air, and Parker's podgy body growing pale, Anderson calmly walked outside, and waited for the cops. He politely surrendered his gun. He faced the electric chair, but was finally sentenced to life in prison without the possibility of parole.

That definitely should've been the end of Gastineau's boxing career, but two years later, he was further humiliated in Japan by Alonzo Highsmith, another ex-NFL player who could actually fight. But the public hadn't heard the last of Gastineau.

On 29 August 1999, police arrested him for the second time in two months, for allegedly grinding out a cigarette on an unnamed girlfriend. Cops picked up the hulking giant and charged him with assault, at her pad in Queens, a suburb of New York City. This was the second time in a week, that Mark had pulled his lit cigarette trick.

A month earlier, Gastineau had also been busted for contempt after violating a court order and showing up at the home of his estranged second wife, Patricia Schoor. After bellowing outside and making a scene, Gastineau kept ringing the doorbell and refused to leave. Gastineau had been under legal restraint after pleading guilty a year earlier to slugging his wife and been given three months probation. He had also been arrested for slapping and punching his then-fiancee in a posh Manhattan eatery, for which he was charged with assault, menacing, and possession of a weapon, which was the glass cocktail table that he'd threatened to smash over Miss Schoor's head. But when Gastineau was finally hauled before the judge, Schoor refused to testify. According to Lisa Gastineau, Mark's first wife (who later dated Mafia godfather John Gotti), Gastineau had a long history of beating up women, including Brigitte Nielsen, the B-movie queen.

In September 1999, an exasperated Manhattan Court Judge told Gastineau, "I have given you beyond a second and third chance," and sentenced him to eighteen months behind bars in Rikers Island, which housed some of New York City's worst predators.

At forty-four, Gastineau was a badly broken man. "I did it. I did it all," he sobbed when visitors came to see him.

Physically, he was still a handsome, towering figure. Inside the walls he swore off drugs, began conducting prayer meetings and claims to have found Jesus. But Mark Gastineau, one-time terror of the NFL and heavyweight dreamer, had to be thrown into protective custody – because other inmates were going to kill him.

★ ★ ★

It was the Centennial Olympics in Atlanta, Georgia, on a stifling day in July 1996. As tourists excitedly milled out, after watching the boxing competiton, Evander Holyfield, the former heavyweight champion of the world, walked virtually unnoticed to his enormous, forty-foot gray stretch limo. A couple of Cuban giants, Felix Savon and Teofilio Stevenson, jabbered in Spanish. The biggest crowd, however, had gathered around a massive, shaven-skulled gent whose given name was Eric Esch but who fought professionally under the monicker "Butterbean."

Butterbean was just six-foot, but he weighed anywhere from 300 to 340 pounds. He smiled broadly as he signed autographs. In a sense, Butterbean is every couch potato's fantasy: a homely, pleasant guy who looks like he'd get out of breath mowing his lawn, yet who had run off a long string of knockout wins on cable TV. "Bean," as intimates call him, is a bulbous cartoon character all but created for TV. He came off the assembly line in a trailer factory, entered "Tough Man" contests and earned up to $60,000 a night. He eventually made more money than many "world" champions, and is far better known. He has been on David Letterman and Jay Leno's talk shows, a coup in a land where celebrities are deified.

Yet according to the Pulitzer-Prize winning *Miami Herald*, at least four of his fights have been tainted with fraud. In March 1999, in Long Beach, California, James Calvin Baker swooned in just eighteen seconds. "I knew when I stepped into that ring that I wasn't going to go more than one round," Baker told the *Herald*. "That was decided." Baker also went out in back-to-back matches against Gastineau. Unfortunately, for Baker though, the convicted bank robber didn't go quickly enough – his parole officer saw him on TV. After the eighteen-second match, Baker didn't get much chance to spend his purse, either. He had left the state illegally, and was thrown right into jail.

Bill Duncan, was "suspended indefinitely," after losing to Butterbean, the so-called "King of the Four-Rounders." In April 1996, Butterbean halted "Jack Ramsey" in one in Iowa. Ramsey turned out to be Darryl Becker, who had yet to win in twelve fights. An amateur video shows Becker going down from a grazing punch to the shoulder. The disgusted Missouri commissioner, Tim Luckenhoff, called it an obvious dive.

On April 30, Richard Davis folded up in one. "Another scared-to-death guy," sneered Sean Gibbons, who other boxers say fixed fights when he was an integral half of the so-called Indiana-Oklahoma Connection (see Chapter Ten).

James Baker got into boxing, or tumbling, at the behest of his half-brother Andre Smiley. Smiley himself claims that from 1990 to 1997, he fell down on cue, for money, but his careeer was put on hold after the gregarious stringbean ended up in the Missouri State Penitentary for possession of cocaine. According to Smiley, Sean Gibbons told him, during a match, "Fall right now. Fall right now, I'll give you $500 extra." Gibbons dismissed that as just jailhouse talk, but other fighters made similar claims.

Another Butterbean opponent crashed down three times after he had been outboxing Bean easily. TV colorman Teddy Atlas yelled, "The guy went down and didn't even get hit." Replays proved it. Gibbons was in the opponent's corner, even though to get a match with Butterbean you have to go through him. That farce finished Butterbean on ESPN 2. Their boxing honcho, Bob Yalen, said, "We have no more plans to use him. He's off the radar screen." Instead Bean headed for England, where fans stayed away in droves.

There was also a burgeoning scandal regarding Richie Melito, a muscle-bound heavyweight from New York. The brawny Melito, who is built like a bodybuilder not a fighter, was allegedly involved in a fixed fight against fast-stepping Thomas Williams, on the undercard of Evander Holyfield-John Ruiz on 12 August 2000. Melito, who can't fight a lick but was somehow rated by the WBA, stopped Williams, whom the FBI alleged took a dive, and Williams was indicted. It was not the first time there had been big questions surrounding Melito's fights. Rumours kept swirling before Melito faced washed-up "Smokin'" Bert Cooper that Cooper was in the tank. Cooper was even confronted by the New York State Athletic Commission in his dressing room, but promptly KO'd Melito in a round.

Shelby Gross, a woefully inept pug from South Carolina, claims he was offered $8,000 to lose to Melito. Gross, who tape recorded his conversation with manager/booking agent Bobby Mitchell, asked for $10,000, then made sure Mitchell repeated his demand that Gross lose. Gross allegedly got a $2,500 down payment, then used the tape to get out of his managerial contract with Mitchell. He also turned everything over to the FBI. Mitchell denied everything.

Months earlier, Bobby Goodman, the matchmaker for Don King Productions, had promised, "I'll put him [Melito] in with some serious guys. I won't line up ducks for anybody."

★ ★ ★

In 1963, a fight figure in Italy came to Teddy Brenner, wanting him to pitch Dick Tiger about throwing the middleweight championship. Brenner cussed him out. In 1970, Brenner was in Madrid, but wouldn't use the Spanish heavyweight sensation Jose Urtain because he thought Urtain's long KO streak was phoney. Still, out-and-out fixes are rare ... unless your name is Simmie Black. Black, who hails from Memphis, Tennessee, boxed from 1971 to 1996, and has probably thrown more fights than any man in history.

Black played tanktowns like Joplin, Missouri, Hattiesburgh, Mississippi, and anywhere they could pitch a ring. He won but thirty-three times out of 203 but fought under at least seven different names, and in 1994 admitted, matter-of-factly, "Lord, I must've had upwards of three hundred fights. I be fightin' since I was sixteen. Sometimes, I fight three times in one week. I'd be Spider Black, Sam Jackson, Thomas Tucker, Melvin Jenkins, David Tyne, Willie Johnson, L.C. Wright ... Now, dem's da names I use more than once. Dere's names I cain't recall."

Simmie, who has high, hollow cheekbones, and a tight, leathery brown face, was a heavily furrowed forty-one when this writer interviewed him for *Boxing News* in the mid-Nineties. The smooth-muscled lightweight was shy, and obviously wary of people. He spoke with a distinct stammer and, though his high, halting voice reeked of field-hand humility, there was a certain courtliness about him. There was also tragedy. "Takin' dem dives was my job," he says. Black was halted an incredible ninety-one times.

Like so many fighters, Simmie Black was a victim from birth. As a skinny, malnourished seven-year-old, he was forced into the sweltering Mississippi cotton fields, where his tiny hands bled as he plucked the soft white. "Everybody was tryin' to survive. It was just like slavery days. We was really poor. Dere was a whole house full of us. Fourteen, in two bedrooms."

For a moment, Black stopped, and struggled to continue. The memories hurt a lot more than any right hand. "I be workin' from six in de morning till six in de evening for three dollars a day. You be out in dat hot sun, but somebody else be gettin' all the money. I never did say nothin', but it was just like being a slave. I lived with my uncle, Percy Wright, and he be gettin' all de money. But on weekends, he'd give us kids fifty cents apiece, and we'd go into town."

Once Simmie and his cousins got into town, they naturally began to run and play. "Some of de kids be playin' fighting," he recalled with a sad, knowing smile. "You know how kids is. Next thing you know, people be payin' us to fight. Man, we'd be fightin' in parking lots, in de backs of houses, and dere'd be ten, fifteen people, drinking, laughing and carrying on." Soon Simmie and his cousin, Willie Johnson, were regularly going into town to fight other poor little black boys, who were eight to ten years old. "I got a dollar. I never got beat," Simmie said, his tired, rasping voice suddenly growing excited. "We didn't have no boxin' gloves, just bare fists."

Back at the plantation, Simmie claims he had to watch out for the rest of the kids, "cause the grown people liked to take off at night." Black was the second-oldest male. When he was eleven, there were twelve other kids, almost all girls, there with him and his cousin Willie in the house. "Me and my cousin had to take care of everything, but Willie kind of lazy, so that left me tryin' to survive for all fourteen people."

Black recalled where his "purses" went from his earliest street fights. "I'd buy some cookies and take them back to everybody dat be left at de house. Back in those times you could buy cookies two for a penny. I'd get fifty cents worth. *Oh man,* de kids be so happy, it be like somebody done give 'em a million dollars."

By June of 1964, after Sheriff "Bull" Connor had unleashed his dogs and firehoses on civil rights protesters, after racists blew up a church in Birmingham killing four little black girls, and after young "Freedom Riders" ended up in shallow graves in Mississippi for trying to give blacks the right to vote, young Simmie left the steamy Delta and began living with an aunt in Memphis, Tennessee.

"I stopped school in the seventh grade. I was gettin' suspended from school, but I couldn't go 'cause I had to work. I'd be out there in half-bare feet in de fields, and it'd be snowing. I had shoes, but I didn't have no socks, and my shoes was so tore up. Sometimes, my feet and toes was all out, and de kids would just laugh. On the days I would go to school, it was only because the weather was so bad I couldn't work de fields. But I liked to hide out," Simmie readily admitted, "because I didn't want the kids to laugh, 'His feet's out his shoes!'"

At fifteen, he was already one of life's throwaways. But he still had dreams. One day he spied a muscular young man wearing a beautiful satin Golden Gloves jacket. Simmie quickly entered the tournament, though he was underage. Black had all of three amateur fights at the Gaston Park Community Center, before he was "turned out," as pimps like to say, and began fighting professionally at sixteen. America's *Fight Fax,* the official record of the sport, has Black turning pro on 11 November 1971, when he was eighteen. Black however, says with acute politeness, "It might've been before that." He claims that he had three or four fights before his recorded debut against Tony Gardner, a 154-pounder who later challenged Elisha Obed for the WBC title. Black was blasted out in two.

Whatever the real date, some real flesh peddlers had gotten their hands on the shy teenager. "I was always fightin' guys out of my weight class. I'd fight a light-heavy, weighin' 130 pounds. Now, maybe dey'd try and hide his weight, and dey be listing him as 149, but I can tell when somebody weigh 165 or 170 pounds."

Black almost always boxed on short notice in the South, in states like Arkansas, Tennessee, and Missouri, where boxing commissions were pitiful. "In Oklahoma, Arkansas, and Alabama, dem places ain't even got no real commissions," said Black, his voice rising emphatically. "Promoter might get themselves a doctor, or notify a policeman, something like dat, so dey could check." Otherwise, a poor kid's life was in his hands whenever he got into the ring.

Today, a boxer can fight for a championship with just a handful of bouts, but Simmie had eighty-four official contests before he lost his first ten-rounder, to Chris Rizzo, in July 1979. "Only time I'd get a pretty good payday would be a ten-round fight. It'd have to be a pretty well-known fighter. If he wasn't up there pretty good, I wouldn't get nothin' but $150 for ten rounds."

In July 1972, Black won his fourth documented pro fight in Tennessee, against Willie Johnson. Black doesn't say so, but it probably was his cousin. Simmie had won two out of his first four recorded contests, but it was all downhill from there. He became a professional fall guy. "People'd say, 'I need a 135-pounder. I cain't pay him much money.'

"'Well, I know a guy,' somebody else would say, 'Simmie Black. Why fly him up? He'll drive and do the whole thing for $100.'

"During these times, I was doin' what I was s'posed to have did. Somebody'd say, 'I got this kid I'm tryin' to build up,' but I'd tell him I'm not in condition to go many rounds." The tanktown promoter would invariably say, "Come on down. Go a couple of rounds, then go down."

During that time, said Simmie, a slow agony creeping into his voice, "I didn't have no job. My icebox was empty. I might be fightin' three times a week, but nobody knew I'd been stopped 'cause I was fightin' under different names. The fights was mostly four and six-round fights. I wasn't going to be gettin' but fifty or seventy-five dollars. Any time I could get a fight, I would take it, but I'm not thinkin' what it would do to me as the years passed. I'm just thinking, *He gonna pay me and I don't have to go the rounds.*" Years later, Simmie's voice still rises, then gets raspy in disbelief. "Dog, that's some easy money."

He figured, "If I cover my face, don't get hit, and take a shot on my gloves,

I was gettin' another seventy-five dollars for going down, when I ain't gettin' but fifty to seventy-five dollars in de first place. I done *doubled* my money!"

Despite twenty-five years of performing, Black seldom saw a contract. "After I'd get done, my part would be fifty, fifty-five dollars. Lots of my fights, I never did know what I was gettin'. I done took what they give me." On the rare occasions when he did see contracts, "Now, I don't want to call out no names, but it's a true fact that dese fights was actually payin' $500, $800, a *thousand dollars.*" Simmie's voice rose incredulously, like that was all the money in the world.

"I fought in Jackson, Mississippi, about six months ago," he recalled in 1994. "I still got de cheque in my pocket. De cheque wasn't no good. I didn't get a penny. Plus, I made two trips to Jackson, tryin' to catch him at dis radio station, where he don't work no mo'. Stuff like dat hurt real bad."

Black's biggest purse after a quarter of a century in this dirty business was $1,000. He was sent down to Mexico to fight a world-ranked contender. He doesn't remember who – after twenty-five years, the names are just a blur – but Simmie predictably got stopped. It still turned out to be a wonderful thing. "I done kept all my money dat time," Black says, joy bubbling from him. "I put $500 down and got me a car. I got two of my daughters some clothes and shoes."

Though Black is reluctant to say who did him wrong, the record shows he was handled by Red Fortner in Memphis, and Tony Gardner. He even fought Gardner a couple of times, despite the fact that he was his manager. The late Pat O'Grady of Oklahoma City also (mis) handled him.

"O'Grady was a real double-crosser," recalled Ron Stander, the "Bluffs Butcher," who was himself butchered by Joe Frazier for the heavyweight championship in 1972. Stander claims that O'Grady brought his whole family to South Africa after he agreed to a ridiculously low purse for him to face Kallie Knoetze, one of the biggest punchers in boxing.

A year before Stander was annihilated by Knoetze, Simmie Black faced O'Grady's sixteen-year-old son Sean in Oklahoma City. "I think I got $100 for that, it couldn't have been no more than two. Pat didn't treat me too bad." He even got Black a job as a busboy at Denny's, a fast-food eatery. Simmie remembers how Pat O'Grady also paid him purses that consisted of "a handful of coins." Black not only fought Sean regularly, he was actually living in the gym and sparring with him every day. "I lived there at the same time I was fightin' him, but at the time I wanted to make somethin' out of myself."

The record shows that Sean O'Grady stopped Simmie Black in the fourth round. Further scrutiny of O'Grady ring log shows that he turned pro on in January 1975 against a "David Tymes," who he KO'd in one. In February, "Willie Johnson" also went out in the first. These were all names that Black admits to using in the ring.

It's pretty certain that Sean O'Grady fought Simmie Black at least five or six times under assumed names. Sean went on to win the WBA light-weight championship of the world, and has a career in television, while Simmie became one of the most infamous divers in boxing history. Does it bother him? "Sometimes, it do. But I was just doin' my job. Go a few rounds, then go down. When my peoples ask how me I did, I just say, 'I got robbed of de decision.'"

Black claims that he's never really been hurt in the ring, and admits that he's "a soft-hearted person that don't like violence." He didn't even spar. He would hit the bag a few days before a fight, if he got notice, but he stopped sparring because one time in Memphis he was working with a boy and his manager started yelling, "Take his head off. Take the motherfucker's head off!"

"Hey, man," recalled Black, stammering badly, "if I gonna get hit, I gonna be paid."

Growing more reflective, Black admitted, almost tenderly, "Sometimes before a fight, I get a chance to meet the person, and get to know him. I don't want to cut him, or hurt him, even though I know he be tryin' to do damage to me. I just try to box him."

But the fight game is a brutal, bloodthirsty racket, and for twenty-five years, Black was raw meat for the young lions. Though he claims he can "take a head shot," he readily admitted he has "bad ribs" and can't take it downstairs.

"One time," Simmie says, again stammering but becoming animated with stifled fury, "I was in wif a decent fighter, Dale Hernando [Dale Hernandez, whose brothers Art and Ferd actually drew with and beat a geri-atric Sugar Ray Robinson]. Guy who was managing me, guy who ah'm actually fighting for, he be yelling, 'Hit him in de ribs! Hit him in de ribs!' And dis be de guy ah'm makin' money for. They think I don't know, tryin' to make believe dey be tellin' me, but dey be yelling, 'Go to body. He got bad ribs.' A rib shot is the hardest punch anyone can give me." Black went out in the first round.

Fourteen years later, in 1992, the same thing happened when he faced Sergei Artemiev, an ill-fated Russian who was being built up by Bob Arum. Again, Black's own cornermen told the Russian that Simmie had bad ribs. "De was laughin' and frontin' it off, but I knew. He didn't do nothin' but go for my ribs." Ironically, Artemiev was nearly killed shortly thereafter in the ring, while Black continued his odyssey for another four years.

Black is something of a dandy outside boxing, and has ten children by nine women. He admits, "I real easy going. I don't like to argue wif nobody." He says he has enormous difficulty standing up for himself in the murky world of professional boxing. "I think that come from when I was a kid. I was always gettin' beat on. Told, 'Shut up. Don't talk back.' I been used to it, but now, I finally be able to talk back to dese boxing guys."

Beginning to stutter so badly that he sounded like an old Model T, Simmie said, "I told 'em, if you ain't wif me, den, you just get de hell away from me." Pausing after his tortured emotions finally broke through, he slowly added. "There was times I just never thought I was gonna make it." He began to weep.

CHAPTER TEN

The Thrill of Defeat

THE BIBLE TELLS us that Lazarus was resurrected from the dead after three days. In Oklahoma, that wouldn't have stopped him from getting a boxing license.

When it came to the fight game in Oklahoma City, Pat O'Grady was the Only Law West of the Pecos. A steely combination of Judge Roy Bean and Yellow Kid Weill, the fabled conman, he was a dreamer, a schemer, a tyrant and a crook. He would introduce himself with a hearty handshake and a business card that said he was in the oil exploration business, but the truth is, O'Grady had spent a lifetime hitting nothing but dry holes.

One of his last fighters was "Wimpy" Halstead, a fleshy white heavyweight who got his nickname because he'd cry when he got hit. Wimpy was billed as "the busiest heavyweight in the world." Of course, O'Grady didn't say he recycled his opponents under different names. Though Wimpy could not fight much, he had a flare for public relations. He was once asked by a reporter how he felt about blacks. "Hell, I like 'em. I think everybody ought to own one."

In the early 1970s, O'Grady had huge, blubbery Claude McBride, whom he called "Happy Humphrey" after the old character in the Joe Palooka comic strip. McBride was homelier than a mud fence, and built like an enormous mound of mashed potatoes. O'Grady outfitted him with garish, red, polka dot shorts and a dumb little matching cap like kids wore in the 1930s. He also got him about thirty straight wins, against guys who entered the ring in wrinkled boxing trunks and got starched by punches that nobody saw. McBride actually set the stage for a later flab monster called Butterbean, but there were still some standards in those days and, unlike Bean, there was no way O'Grady's mammoth creation would ever have made American TV. The closest McBride ever got to the big time was against Buster Mathis, another jumbo-sized heavy who, washed-up or not, stopped him. It was a lousy fight. Nobody cheered, but with a total of 550 pounds of beef, the ring certainly groaned.

O'Grady's partner in crime was Champ Thomas, a venal old carny who had a fighter who was blind in one eye. Thomas had a brilliant rationale for letting him fight. "Hell, he's got another eye, don't he?" Another pug actually wore a pacemaker. There were so many afflictions in the O'Grady/Thomas stable that faith healer Oral Roberts should have been carrying the spit bucket. O'Grady had a reputation for fixing fights. The house lights were known to go out if the hero mistakenly got flattened. In Oklahoma City, the *Daily Oklahoman* got so sick of his shenanigans that it refused to cover any more shows.

Surprisingly, O'Grady's baby-faced son Sean developed into a good fighter on his Holiday Inn cards. Pat turned him pro at just fifteen and young Sean ran off twenty-nine straight wins in his first year. One of his earliest opponents was an Iranian busboy named Muhammad Muffleh, who happened to walk into O'Grady's gym and innocently say, "We play box?"

Two weeks after his seventeenth birthday, Sean was thrown in with Danny "Little Red" Lopez in Los Angeles. Lopez was one of the gamest and hardest-hitting featherweights of all-time. It was practically child abuse. The kid had nothing to say about his affairs, being officially managed by his mother, Jean. He predictably got stopped in three.

Pat gave Sean all of six weeks before he had him back in the ring. He won another twenty-seven in a row, but his father was adamantly opposed to him venturing outside Oklahoma City again; there, nothing was allowed to go wrong. In June 1978, O'Grady fought his second TV bout. He bled so much after Shig Fukuyama broke a blood vessel over an eye that the babyfaced high school boy looked like one of the victims in a slasher flick. Viewers could not believe that the carnage was allowed to continue, but the ringside doctor didn't have the guts to stand up to O'Grady senior and halt the fight. In Oklahoma, there was no commission. Hell, Pat O'Grady was the commission.

A marketable white face was needed now that American television was getting back into the sport, and O'Grady would not give up control of Sean, the family's meal ticket. Bob Arum wanted the kid, but O'Grady refused to sign, and Sean went back to boxing virtually for nothing against clubfighters like Freddie Harris and Irish Beau Jaynes. "I want to be a doctor," he complained, but his mother told him, "Honey, you're doing it for the family."

"They treated him like a little boy," marvelled Sybil Arum, an Oriental beauty then married to Arum. "He had nothing to say."

Jean O'Grady was afraid of her husband. Few people stood up to him.

He had once been a ruggedly handsome lightweight who fought on club shows around Fort Worth, Texas, in the early 1950s. He fit right in with the gamblers and pimps. "I like Pat," Champ Thomas said, "but I just can't get along with the ornery sonofabitch." The entire O'Grady living room was covered with boxing posters.

By 1980, Sean's only wins of note in a ludicrously padded record were over a faded bantamweight champ, Romeo Anaya, and a couple of fringe contenders. Yet in the winter of 1980, he got a "world title" shot with Scotland's Jim Watt, who was WBC lightweight king and an impeccable southpaw. Pat took the entire brood to Scotland, where Sean trained: there was mother Pat, Jean, Sean, and a beautiful sister, who naturally was named Rosie O'Grady. Despite Sean's seventy-four previous "fights," he was a big underdog. Pat, being Pat, had to inject some phoney hype straight out of the 1920s. He claimed a bullet was fired at the clan as Sean trained. As proof, he cited a bullet hole. Coppers proved it had been made with a nail.

On 1 November 1980, in the chanting cauldron of Glasgow's Kelvin Hall, young Sean O'Grady was bloodied so terribly that his whole head looked like it had been doused with red paint. Henry Cooper had been slashed as badly both times against Muhammad Ali and the bouts had been stopped — but this went on. Finally, with the British Medical Association about to storm the ring, the grotesque affair was halted in the twelfth.

Five months later, Sean pulled off a miracle and pounded down Hilmer Kenty, who had left his legs in the famous Kronk Gym in Detroit, to win the WBA lightweight title. After thirty years in the fight game, Pat O'Grady had finally reached the top. He was immediately feuding with Arum over "Master Bob's" slave-like options. First O'Grady threatened and swore, then begged, "It's my turn at the trough." When that didn't work, he hauled Arum into federal court. On the surface, O'Grady had a winnable case: Arum's mandatory options to get a championship fight were clearly restraint of trade. But justice also has a lot to do with "venue shopping" and Arum, a lawyer who once worked in the Department of Justice, knew all about that.

Arum was then tight with Jimmy Binns, who was also in bed with the WBA. It was no surprise that the WBA hijacked Sean's title, less then six months after he had won it. With Arum a multi-millionaire and Sean the only marketable commodity in the O'Grady portfolio, Pat moaned to anyone who'd listen, "They just keep shufflin' paper on ya," while his legal meter continued to run. Sean was handsome and white, and could have become a big TV attraction. If his dad had been smart, he'd have worked with Arum and got Sean a couple of easy, lucrative fights, then sued. But Pat was very controlling and greedy, and the federal court ruled that Arum's options were legal. It was a devastating blow.

O'Grady's response was to form the laughable World Athletic

Association – with Thomas, naturally – and to proclaim Sean the WAA lightweight champion. In October 1981, Sean was annihilated in two rounds by rock-fisted Andy Ganigan.

Two months later, Pat was nervously awaiting a phone call in Chicago from Teddy Brenner, who was now working for Arum as a matchmaker. As baby-faced Sean snored loudly on the couch in their hotel room, Pat O'Grady looked down at his sleeping boy, and said with a contemptuous sneer, "What's going to happen with him? He might be finished."

Just eight months earlier, Pat had been cooing to Sean in his corner, as he was about to beat Kenty, "Son, can you do it for me?" Sean O'Grady had given up his youth for his dad. He had abandoned his dream of becoming a doctor, had risked punch-drunkenness. He had won a version of the world title at twenty-two, but now was finished. Years later, he would painfully admit, "Outside of boxing, I had no relationship with my father."

In the room while O'Grady was awaiting that call from Brenner was Monte Masters, a large man with tightly-coiled hair who was so good-looking, he should have gone straight to Hollywood and become an actor. He would eventually play a few bit parts. Masters became the heavyweight champion of Pat O'Grady's WAA. Almost all of his twenty-two wins had come in Oklahoma City, the first seventeen by knockout. His opponents gave bums a bad name. Carl Halliburton, an utter stiff from Memphis who used to enter the ring wearing purple gym shorts and ragged tennis shoes, was predictably dismissed in one, while "Razor Blade" Jackson apparently forgot his razor and went the same way.

Masters fought Ron Draper. Before the weigh-in, Draper grumbled to Pat O'Grady, who was manager, promoter, and "commissioner" in Oklahoma City, "Damn, I don't feel like fighting."

"Godammit, Ron," barked O'Grady. "You'd better not fold up on me, or you won't get a dime."

The veteran trial horse reluctantly hung around for the full ten rounds, became Masters' first opponent to go the distance. Jack Cowen, the veteran matchmaker, sneered, "Masters can't fight a lick."

"I know I can really fight," Masters was still insisting nine months later. There was even talk that he'd be next man for the comebacking Joe Frazier. Masters was managed by Pat O'Grady, who was not only his Svengali but also his father-in-law. Presumably, since they were family, that should have made the kid fairly comfortable, but Masters was so intimidated by Pat, he used to tiptoe around him like he was an Oriental houseboy.

Finally, Brenner's call came in. "Sir, the phone's for you," Masters muttered softly, as he crept up to Pat, afraid to meet his eyes. The heavyweight was dismissed without even a nod.

Eventually he could stand it no more. He abruptly left Rosie, who was Pat's daughter, and Pat furiously stripped him of his WAA heavyweight championship.

★ ★ ★

By 1996, Pat O'Grady was dead. His nephew, Sean Gibbons, and a partner, Pete Sussens, had taken over Oklahoma boxing. Sussens hailed from Indianapolis, Indiana, but after fifteen years there had been so many outrages that it resulted in a *Special Report to the Oklahoma Labor Commissioner*, subtitled "Allegations of Fraud and Other Corruption in Professional Boxing."

According to W.A. "Skip" Nicholson, a former Oklahoma state trooper and administrative assistant to the commissioner, Brenda Reneau, his extensive six-month investigation revealed:

> … a possible racketeering scheme that included tax evasion, Social Security fraud, harbouring of fugitives, transportation of fighters across state lines, fight fixing and forgery … the findings of the six-month investigation paint an unsavoury picture of a sport barely one step removed from the carnival atmosphere of professional wrestling. Boxing is a sport where the skill of the contestants is not always the determining factor in who wins or loses … It is a sport where some individuals compete using multiple names and fraudulent Social Security numbers, and it is a sport where unscrupulous promoters and matchmakers falsify fight records and buy and sell 'winners and losers.'
>
> This investigation revealed evidence of a scheme where 'club fighters' of little or no talent are hauled from state to state by promoters and matchmakers. The competitors often fight the same boxers over and over again, each time with a different name. A boxer might be known in Oklahoma as 'Jim Brown,' as 'Brownie James' in Missouri, and in other states by different names … This scheme allegedly enabled each fighter to compete more often than state and local regulators allow. In some cases (it) allows fighters to build fantastic records, while laying the groundwork for Social Security fraud, tax evasion and fight fixing.

For years, since Pat O'Grady, boxing in Oklahoma had been an insider's joke. In 1991, Phill Marder, a former schoolteacher, *Ring* magazine feature writer and owner of boxing records agency Fight Fax, simply refused to enter any more results on Oklahoma fighters. "I subscribed to the Oklahoma City newspaper," said Marder, "but they never published any results. But I kept getting calls from people calling in fights that people I trusted told me never happened."

   The Oklahoma Boxing Administrators office was created in 1994 to help dispel the sport's Wild West image. Two years later, Nicholson concluded that "young fighters are shamelessly exploited by those associated with the Indiana-Oklahoma Connection. According to the numerous fighters, promoters and regulatory officials who were interviewed ... young boxers are cheated out of their earnings and are forced to fight in mismatches ... where the risk of injury is significant. Additionally, they are forced to lose fights to help build the records of other fighters and – the final insult – many are robbed of their own fight records and their small place in boxing history." He said that events were referred to as "shows" and "that's exactly what boxing fans are getting – a show – complete with actors, directors, and in many cases, scripted endings."

   In March 1993, "King Arthur" Jimmerson KO'd Shane Mooney in the second round at Jefferson City, Missouri. Mooney didn't do too badly – considering he was dead. He was impersonated by a black cruiserweight named Mike Smith, even though the real Shane Mooney had been a white welter. Smith couldn't legally box under his real name as he had been stopped two weeks earlier in Kansas City, Missouri, by former heavyweight contender Tex Cobb and was under a mandatory thirty-day suspension. The purpose of such suspensions are to stop a boxer who has been knocked out from fighting again within a fixed time frame and to allow him to recover, otherwise there is a grave risk of secondary concussion, which can be fatal.

   Mike Smith is the brother of Buck "Tombstone" Smith, who claims to have had over 200 fights, with about thirty that can be verified as legitimate opponents. Four years after the fact, Smith confessed to his role in this sham and seemed genuinely shaken over assuming the role of a dead man. By then, he was serving ten years inside the walls at the Jess Dunn Correctional Facility, in Taft, Oklahoma. "I didn't have nothing to do with, you know, how they record fights," he said. "Basically, Sean (Gibbons) will call me and ask me, do I want to fight?" He admitted that, before his bouts, he didn't even know what name he was going to fight under. That was controlled by Sean Gibbons. "They never said nobody's real name that I recall," claimed Smith. "I knew it was wrong, but a lot of wrong things was happening in boxing. They used a lot of wrong names. Sometimes, they'd call me 'Ice Cube.' He'd [Gibbons] make things up, you know."

   Gibbons's partner, Pete Sussens, was a burly, slovenly man in his forties, who had a deceptively innocent face adorned by a filthy blond shag. He would log the "names" that they had used, so officially everybody knew who had been suspended after they'd been stopped. That name wouldn't be used again for at least thirty days. One month after Mike Smith posed as Mooney, Sussens cheekily faxed the result to record compiler Marder. Sussens didn't know that Jim Hall, the Missouri boxing commissioner –

who would later be fired for allegedly embezzling money – had also faxed
Marder the day after the fight, alerting him to the fact that Jimmerson had
stopped Smith, not Mooney, who had been killed in an automobile accident.

The fiasco had more plot twists than a Kurosawa movie. Randy Cross,
who promoted the card, insisted that everyone knew that Smith was
pretending to be Mooney. Hall "must have known," because as Director of
Boxing for the State of Missouri, he was ringside when Cobb had
dispatched Smith just two weeks earlier. Hall even reported that result to
Fight Fax.

Bogus names were the rule, not the exception on these cards. Buck
Smith outslugged "Tommy Bowles" of Houston. Bowles, another card-
carrying member of the Gibbons/Sussens theatrical troupe, was really
Verdell Smith, of Oklmulgee, Oklahoma. Buck Smith, who was a pretty fair
journeyman, boxed under numerous names. In Indiana, he was Tim Brooks,
while across the border in Illinois, he was Verdell Smith, and filled out
boxing licenses accordingly.

Once the fraudulent boxing applications of Buck's brother Mike were
tracked down, it turned out he listed his address as 3920 NW 23rd Street,
in Oklahoma City, which was the address of the late Pat O'Grady.

Indianapolis promoter Fred Berns had been in boxing since the late
1960s, and the former Chicago cop was a partner of Sussens till the heat got
too great. Berns figured it was Pat O'Grady who came up with the idea to
pad fighters' records with phoney names. Berns sneers at Sean O'Grady's
record, despite his nearly ninety fights. "I defy you to find twenty of them,"
said Berns, who knows the fight game. Many of Sean's opponents were
Hispanics."Yeah, "cracked Berns, "the same Mexican with twelve different
names. Old Pat, he'd bring in the illegals and then call immigration on them
so he didn't have to pay them."

Sean, still boyish in his early forties, won't have it: "My father? Not my
father. I don't know of any multiple name schemes."

Sean O'Grady told Nicholson that he wasn't very close to Gibbons, his
cousin, though both are in boxing and are separated by just ten years. But
when Sean was asked about Gibbons's practice of "running a stable of
fighters using multiple names and fake social security numbers," O'Grady
innocently replied, "That doesn't sound like him."

Boxing is a small world, and everybody knew what Sussens and Gibbons
were doing. Sean O'Grady and Buck Smith eventually had no choice but
to confirm that many of the battle-scarred thespians did live at the old
O'Grady homestead at times, or use it as a mail drop. While Gibbons and
Sussens were bounding around the country with a car full of boxers, mostly
playing the tanktowns in the Midwest or South, Buck Smith stripped away

the last vestige of romanticism when he admitted that when they weren't staying with Sussens in Indianapolis, or the O'Grady's old place, they were crashing at the Jesus House in Oklahoma City or other shelters for the homeless.

With Nicholson's investigation heating up, he got two more videotapes from the new Misssouri commissioner, Tim Luckenhoff. Both men were former cops and committed to rooting out the corruption. Gibbons and Sussens began to get worried.

In August 1992, a match between Buck Smith and "Tony Taylor" was recorded. Missouri officials positively identified Taylor as Kenny Kidd, another touring thespian. A second video, from March 1994, showed Buck Smith facing "Rodney Johnson." According to Luckenhoff, it was actually Rob Bleakley. Gibbons had worked both times in Smith's corner, though during the Bleakley bout he could actually be seen speaking to the tattooed opponent. After Smith won, Nicholson noted that Gibbons had another conversation with Bleakley.

According to Nicholson, "A picture is worth a thousand words," and on 2 April 1994, just three days later, in Kentucky, according to *Fight Fax*, Rob Bleakley took on Buck Smith again – this time under his true name. *Does it make any difference who won?*

In March 1993, in Jefferson City, Missouri, "Tim Bennett" had lost a decision to fast-moving Marty Jakubowski. Ringside photographs acquired from the *Jefferson City Tribune* revealed that Bennett was actually Craig Houck, a squat, balding light-welter who had won more than forty fights in a row. This time it had been Houck's turn to play the stooge. He admitted under oath in a 1996 civil deposition that he was "Gary Myers" as well.

Fred Berns claims he first became aware of Houck's "multiple personality disorder" in January 1994, when they were in Las Vegas's MGM Grand. They were walking to the ring, where Houck was to fight former Olympic gold medallist Meldrick Taylor. The fight, a prelim, was at 5 PM on one of Don King's impossibly long bills and there were just a couple of hundred diehards in the building.

Suddenly, a lone fan began to yell, "There's Tim Bennett! There's Tim Bennett!"

Houck got such a stunned look on his face that Berns asked, "What's the matter?"

"That's one of Pete's bogus names," Houck muttered.

"See you later," said Berns, turning around for the dressing room.

After Taylor stopped Houck, the confused fan marched into his dressing room "with a whole scrapbook of Tim Bennett." Berns claimed that when he finally got Houck alone, he asked him, "What the hell is this?"

"Well, Pete browbeat me into doing it," said Houck.

Boxing insiders knew for a long time what Gibbons and Sussens were doing. Sussens had not only gotten fighters for Fred's shows, he'd also worked for him as a rent collector in Indianapolis. Yet Berns contends he was in the dark. He confronted the burly Sussens and immediately severed all business connections with him and Gibbons. Houck later testified that his purse for the fight was $12,500 but after cashing his cheque at the MGM Grand Casino, he gave all but $285 of it to Gibbons.

Mike Smith maintained that Gibbons regularly fixed fights. An Indiana boxer named Keith Whitaker also claims that Sussens approached him to take dives. "They call it shamming," said Mike Smith. "You know I'm out there, not going full blast, just basically going through the motions. This guy (his opponent) come out like he's in a real fight, like he's really intending to hurt me. So I box him. Sean would say, 'They're not going to pay you if you win.' So I had to lose. They used to tell me to 'go out there, do your best, make it look good.' After two or three rounds, I already did what I'm supposed to do. Why go farther?"

But Smith also had some pride, and was upset by the role he had to play. "I did good and I would play to the crowd. Lots of people would say, 'What happened? You were fighting good.' I was ashamed to keep doing these things. I knew it was wrong. I wanted to win!"

On another occasion, back in Oklahoma, Smith claims his opponent, who had more artistic sensibilities than he did, actually wanted to rehearse the dive to make sure it looked good.

According to Keith Whitaker, Sussens was much more subtle when he tried to recruit him into his sweaty troupe. "He keeps talking about this one boxer, this Rod, Rod Brewer, I think that's his name."

"What do you think of the guy?" Sussens reportedly asked Brewer one day.

"Oh, legs like oak trees, stomach like a washboard, chin like granite, nose like a faucet," replied Whitaker, flippantly.

"I want you to make him look good," Sussens said.

"Yeah, I can make him look good," figured Whitaker, a longtime amateur, who didn't get the drift, "but it's going to take two or three months, 'cause this is what the guy needs to do to improve."

Sussens broke in, "Oh no, that's not what I want, I want you to make him look good."

"Pete, it's going to take some time."

"No, no, I want you to fight him."

Whitaker was surprised. "Well, I can beat that guy with one hand tied around my back."

"Yeah, I know," agreed Sussens impatiently, "but I got him under contract and I need a win."

"Well, what do you want from me?" snapped Whitaker.

"I want you to box him, and let him win."

"Fuck you, Pete! I live here. I'm not going to do that shit for you. Why would I want to do that?"

"Oh, for a hundred bucks, and so you can be one of the boys."

Sussens had a house full of fighters crashing at his dumpy pad in Indianapolis. When it came time to perform, they piled into his car and lit out for the tank towns along the way. Maybe Jefferson City, Missouri, or Owensboro, Kentucky, weren't the Big Time, but in many ways this was just like the old Orpheum vaudeville circuit.

"Yeah, but that goddamned Pete Sussens just ruined boxing in the Midwest," said one promoter angrily. "Him and that fucking Sean Gibbons. You try and go into a small town, where these guys have been, and newspapers won't give you an inch of publicity. They don't want anything to do with the sport because of them."

Sussens continued his seduction of Keith Whitaker. One day Keith foolishly got into a car with Pete and a mediocre white club fighter out of Minnesota named Danny Morgan. According to Whitaker, both guys harangued him about joining the show, and wanted him to take a dive against Rod Brewer.

"What are you so paranoid about? Why won't you do it?" Sussens asked.

"Fuck you," Whitaker said again. "I live here. Why would I want to throw a fight to that chump for, if I were going to fight for you?"

Sussens looked at him like he was stupid. "Yeah, you fight Marvin Johnson [the former light-heavyweight champion of the world] for free but you don't want to make a hundred bucks."

Whitaker was seething inside, but "they thought of it as a joke." Morgan later fought Michael Nunn for the WBA super-middleweight title in Mexico City. He got annihilated in one round. Sussens hid Morgan's $25,000 cheque inside his shoe, and when he took it out, it crumbled to pieces. Since this was professional boxing, he was lucky another cheque was cut.

★ ★ ★

If you had anything to do with boxing, you were bound to run into Sussens. In 1988, in Kentucky, Keith Whitaker swears he saw the burly backwoods huckster tell a fighter to go down. Whitaker had taken a boxer called "Indian" Billy Evans (*aka* Wayne Evans and Wayne Grant) for a match against Danny Morgan. Whitaker claims that Sussens, like a nervous stunt coordinator, went "from one corner to the other." He actually saw Sussens go over to Evans and say, "Time to go home. Take a knockdown in this round. I need a knockdown." Morgan needed a knockdown to sew it up convincingly for the judges, according to Whitaker.

Morgan got his shortlived title shot and a payday on the undercard of Julio Cesar Chavez-Greg Haugen, one of the biggest boxing shows in modern history. But the Sussens-Gibbons scheme was coming to an end.

On 29 July 1995, Julio Cesar Chavez, an all-time great, demolished Craig Houck in a scandalous match in Chicago's new United Center. Normally, basketball legend Michael Jordan held court here. The Chavez-Houck fight was such a mismatch, it would've been like the Chicago Bulls taking on a high school team. "I was scared," admitted Houck, who was slated for a $10,000 payday. "Chavez is so much better than me."

In a 1996 federal lawsuit (Jose) Venzor vs (Don) King, the plaintiff Venzor alleged the fight may have been fixed. While nobody in his right mind would have paid Houck to lose, Houck claimed under oath that Al Braverman, then King's director of boxing, wanted the stocky clubfighter to "go down."

"Ruin him, embarrass him," growled Braverman, referring to local promoter Jose Venzor, who had the audacity to try to get his one-fight contract with Chavez enforced. Braverman was angry, and so was King, because Chavez, who they regarded as their property, had signed a contract – on his own – to box Henry Hughes, a Cleveland clubfighter, in 1993.

Though Venzor, a wealthy restauranteur, loved boxing, he didn't have the remotest idea what he was doing. This wasn't the 1950s any more, when fighters or managers simply signed contracts. Now, promoters like King and Arum had "options" on their services. King's contract with Chavez was so tight that the Mexican legend couldn't shadowbox in public without King's permission.

Venzor claimed that he put $227,000 into the Chavez-Hughes mismatch, which never came off, but with Venzor's legal guns honing in on Chavez, *le Grand Campeon* "had to fight someone for Venzor, whether it was man, woman, or beast.

"This was the fight capital of the world," bellowed King when he hit Chicago. But Houck was quickly desposited on the canvas to a torrent of boos. Then Venzor filed a unique lawsuit against King, Don King Productions and others for fraud and breach of contract. In part, it read:

Defendant Houck holds himself out to be a profesional boxer. From 1989 to the present, Defendant Houck has fought at the professional level using his own name, using the alias 'Tim Bennett' using the alias 'Gary Meyers,' using falsified dates of birth, using falsified home addresses, and using falsified social security numbers … Defendant Houck, using fictitious identities and Social Security numbers, has participated in fixed fights in Oklahoma, Indiana, Iowa, Missouri, Illinois, and perhaps other states and countries as well.

Though Houck's compensation for his club fights sometimes included "gas money," according to his own deposition he usually got between $100 and $500 per match. Somehow Don King Productions had sold him to the appallingly naive Venzor for $50,000. Venzor had also agreed to pay Chavez $350,000, a $100,000 increase over the $250,000 he was due, if Chavez would do his best to publicize the show. Venzor, a wide-eyed guppy trying to swim with sharks, promised to pay the tempermental Mexican another $50,000 if the United Center was filled. In other words, a total of $400,000 to beat on a punching bag.

On 17 July 1995, this agreement was finally put into writing. What did Chavez do? He failed to attend "a July 19, 1995 appearence with Chicago's mayor and City Council." He ducked a training session at Matador's Restaraunt, and an interview with *La Raza*, the biggest Spanish language paper in Chicago. He also blew off an appearence at the Viva Mexico festial, which drew an estimated 50,000, along with other media interviews. Though it clearly was in Chavez's best interest to cooperate, and even King's, since he could always use a wealthy front promoter should he come back to Chicago, Chavez kissed off a public training session at the International Amphitheatre, and a meeting with local Mexican/American leaders. On July 28, Chavez again failed to show at Fiesta Del Sol, which drew an estimated 150,000 people.

The gist of Venzor's lawsuit was that King had breached his contract and perpetrated a fraud, not just because Houck was a bum, but because "a sustained number of ... Houck's 47 alleged wins were the result of fixed fights." Venzor asked for $1.5 million. He also contended that King had purchased other stiffs from the notorious "Oklahoma-Indiana Connection" and "on each of the 25 occasions, except one, a King-promoted fighter won." Venzor proved that Houck had boxed his housemate Marty Jakubowski five times under assumed names.

When Chavez did show up to finish Houck, the match was such a horrendous loser at the box office that Venzor, who owned a classy Mexican restaurant, was practically left washing dishes. Without television, Venzor never had a chance, and with Chavez, King, and Braverman doing everything they could to wreck the show, it was a disaster.

Though Sussens and Gibbons had no real money, Venzor sued them as well. "From at least 1989 and continuing to the present ... through the use of aliases and fixed fights [Sussens and Gibbons] sold these boxers ... to promoters in search of wins."

Houck, whose record was 47-6, typified the use of "opponents" who couldn't fight, but looked good on paper. From March 1989 through August 1990, "Houck, using the alias 'Tim Bennett,' fought Rocky Berg in Oklahoma. Rocky Berg's record reflects that he won all three fights ... Tim

Bennett's record record reflects that he lost all three fights ... All three of these fights were fixed at the direction of the Indiana-Oklahoma Connection."

In November 1989 and September 1990, "Rocky Berg, using the alias Rocky Vires, fought defendant Houck, who used his real name in Indiana ... Houck's record reflects that he won both fights. Rocky Vires' record reflects that he lost both fights. Both of these fights were fixed at the direction of the Indiana-Oklhaoma Connection."

On 19 February 1991, "Houck, using the alias Tim Bennett, fought Rocky Berg in Missouri. Rocky Berg 'won' that fight which initially appeared (on) record as a 'win' for Berg and a 'loss' for Bennett. In 1993-94, the Missouri Boxing Commission discovered the use of an alias in that fight, and has since reclassified it as 'no contest' in the records of both Berg and Houck."

When Venzor's attorney, Robert Orman, summed up "the careers of the two real and two fictitious fighters in question," Craig Houck's win-loss record was 54-11 by November 1996 and Rocky Berg's was 60-12. As for the fall guys: Tim Bennett was 5-22 by April 1996 while Rocky Vires was 4-28 by February 1992 – *though they never even existed.* They were just names.

There were actually a slew of different pugs using the moniker Tim Bennett, boxing at weights ranging from 136 to 190. There were at least two different Sussens and Gibbons boxers using the name Rocky Berg. In many ways, this was like the Harlem Globetrotters basketball team which, until it occasionally began playing real games again, always "beat" its travelling stooge team, the Washington Generals, who otherwise didn't exist. In essence, Tim Bennett and Rocky Vires were the Washington Generals of boxing. *They had to lose.* But with boxing having record keepers, the stooge boxing names have to show a few wins someplace, otherwise it's obviously phoney. According to Marder, Gibbons bragged that he called phoney fights into record keepers.

* * *

Though Gibbons and Sussens's scheme was one of the most outrageous scams in sports history, the only real money came when Sussens and Gibbons booked their winning fighters overseas. Houck was hoplessly thrown in against South Africa's Gary Murray, Germany's Michael Loewe and Denmark's Soren Sondergard. He should have been paid more than he got in places like Kentucky and Tennessee, but it was Sussens and Gibbons, the Butch Cassidy and Sundance Kid of professional boxing, who made all the bread.

According to subpeonaed contracts, Houck, through Gibbons and

Sussens, was supposed to get $12,500 for boxing Meldrick Taylor. He received less than $300. Houck was also supposed to get $10,000 for Chavez, but attorney Robert Orman concluded that Sussens and Gibbons "took essentially all the money." Though King had charged Venzor $50,000 to get Chavez an opponent, the Indiana-Oklahoma Connection "was paid approximately $10-13,000 for delivery" of Houck.

As for Rocky Berg, these two pimps sold him to England, France, Finland, Denmark and Australia. "I take just good enough care of them so they can be called bums," Sussens often told Gibbons.

Attorney Orman contended that Houck had not only faced title-contender Marty Jakubowski five times, "all of defendant Houck's fights against Jakubowski were fixed." In December 1992, Jakubowski was stopped in Las Vegas in a WBC title fight against Chavez. Incredibly, he got another WBA title fight against Kahlid Rahilou right after the scandal broke. Jakubowski is a slick boxer but not only is his 100-fight record bogus, he actually faced his brother Eric, who "fought under the name Dick Martin."

"Never let it be said Marty Jakubowski, a hard-nosed junior welter-weight from Whiting, doesn't give opponents a rematch," said the *Hammond Post-Tribune*, sardonically. "Jakubowski, in building his spectacular 98-3 won-lost record, defeated Verdell Smith at least 14 times. He beat Craig Houck five times, and he whipped Dwayne Swift on at least half-a-dozen occassions."

Orman concluded that there could've been "as many as 25 other boxers (who) may have been involved with fixed fights at the direction of the Indiana-Oklahoma Connection."

James Holly, who now has his own troupe, has been "Terry Thompson" or "James Roberts" for Sussens and Gibbons. Tim Bonds is also known as "Mark Hammon," while Tony Enna is "Anthony Montesoro and Anthony Saluto," alleged Venzor's lawsuit. "Rocky Berg has fought under his brother's name and social security number in Indiana," the suit continued.

The *piece de resistance* had to be a muscular southpaw named Reggie Strickland, who actually became Indiana super-middleweight champion after he had lost a documented 224 fights. "It don't bother me, why should it bother you," Reggie said, his pride injured. "As long as I got the ching-ching, I'm happy."

Strickland, a muscular southpaw, eventually got away from Gibbons and Sussens because he wanted to make some money. Under their proud banner, he had been "Reggie Raglin" or "Reggie Busse." Reggie's older brother Jerry was his role model, teaching Reggie all he needed to know as he slithered along the the sewer of professional boxing. Jerry Strickland compiled an awesome 13-117 log, but actually had more than 300 bouts and played the "name game" for years.

Reggie however, nearly ruined the family legacy. He could actually fight. "Reggie just tries not to get hurt," said one insider, who has used him on his cards. "Now, if you're a white boy though, who can't fight, Reggie will show some heart and beat your ass."

"Show me another place where I can make $600 for twenty minutes work," Reggie says, trying to justify his role as a travelling loser. Reggie even got his common-law wife, who boxes as Nicolyn Armstrong, into the act. She was stopped by Muhammad Ali's daughter Lailah.

Sean Curtin, who supervises boxing in Illinois, is against everything that Reggie Strickland represents. "If you're not coming into the ring to do your best, you have no business boxing."

Unfortunately, Venzor's federal lawsuit against King, Sussens, Gibbons, and Houck, was thrown out. But Randy Cook, a small-time huckster out of Kansas City who promoted at local casinos, also had a bitter fallout with Sussens and spilled his guts. Not only did he name names, investigators even laughed as he told them about a handsome heavyweight named Paul Presley, who billed himself as "the illegitimate son of the King."

In 1995, Tommy Morrison was banned from boxing in America after testing positive for HIV. He would eventually end up in prison, joining his boxing brother Tim. However, "the Duke" was allowed to fight in Japan. Morrison's set-up for the evening was slated to be Anthony Cooks, who turned out to be a fugitive from the law. Cooks, a bit player in the Sussens-Gibbons troupe, ended up in jail when he tried to leave the States.

"Who hasn't fought under an assumed name in the Midwest?" snapped Gibbons. "I did it. Mouse Strauss did it for a hundred years."

★ ★ ★

Bruce "the Mouse" Strauss was a sandy-haired Jewish boy with striking white teeth who married a schoolteacher. He claims his credo was, "The agony of victory, the thrill of defeat."

Strauss, who hailed from Omaha, Nebraska, had over 150 fights under a slew of names and jokes that he's been knocked out on every continent but Antarctica. Yet, on a deeper level, Strauss, who got into boxing when heavy-weight Ron Stander picked him up hitchiking, once admitted, "We trade our brain cells – and dead brain cells don't regenerate – so that we can feed out families. But most of us in boxing are fans at heart and we admire a [Donald] Curry or a [Marvin] Hagler. Secretly, they are what we all wish we could be."

On 30 September 1980, Strauss flopped down after he caught a right uppercut from Detroit's Danny Paul, who was the brother of Jimmy Paul, an IBF lightweight champion. "Hey," he announced, as he strutted around the dressing room, at the posh Mill Run Theatre in Niles, Illinois, "some guys don't know how to lose. That's why they get hurt."

With his straight nose and perfect teeth, Strauss looks like he's never taken a punch. By the early 1980s, his best routine was when he and an opponent like Billy Evans would "knock each down five or six times," in front of a screaming nightclub crowd, like the night they performed in Highland, Indiana. One disgusted boxing fan knew bullshit when he saw it, and angrily annouced, "I'm leaving."

In many ways Strauss was really the start of the Indiana-Oklahoma Connection, though Gibbons was too young to be involved then. Skip Nicholson reckoned the Connection had been around since 1989, but a simple look at Strauss's record proves it goes back to at least 1980. In October 1980, less than a month after Strauss took the easy way out against Danny Paul, he KO'd "Malcolm Gordon" in two in Indianapolis. Two days later, Strauss halted "Rocky Trampler" in five in Louisville, Kentucky. On November 1, "Charlie Sussens" went out in six in Wichita, Kansas. Though these names all went into *The Ring Record Book*, they were obvious ringers. It was a way for Strauss and company to give officials the finger, and laugh at the same time.

The real Malcolm Gordon was actually "Flash" Gordon, the irreverent boxing Rasputin who published a hilarious, muckraking newsletter out of his cramped New York apartment, and who Bob Arum reportedly tried to bribe by offering to purchase 4,000 subscriptions to get him off his back. At least, that's what Flash alleged in print.

"Rocky Trampler" was obviously a spoof on Bruce Trampler, a good friend of Strauss's who was also working for Fred Berns in Indianapolis at the time. As for "Charlie Sussens," how many people have the last name Sussens? Pete Sussens occasionally stepped in and boxed on his own cards.

By 1996, Sussens, and now Gibbons, had gotten incredibly sloppy. Not even Houck's revelations under oath seemed to daunt them. "They'd been getting way with this shit for so long," figured one boxing insider, "they didn't think anything would happen."

That July, at the sweltering St Charles Casino in St Charles, Missouri, ex-world champion James Toney out-fought clever Charles Oliver on national TV. Though it was 100 degrees, things were even hotter behind the scenes as Gibbons and Trampler argued with Tim Luckenhoff, who had just taken over the scandal-marred Missouri Boxing Commission. Days later, Luckenhoff wrote Bob Arum of Top Rank, who was the packager of the event.

On July 1, 1996, I was given the final list of boxers for the July 2, 1996 event. Included in this was Lee Cargle. I had previous information Cargle was suspended in Tijuana, Mexico, for a positive drugtest.

I informed Sean Gibbons, matchmaker, that Cargle could not fight unless I receieved a letter form the Tijuana Boxing Commission rescinding the suspension. I further stipulated that I wanted to be able to verify the leter, which would make it necessary to receive it in time to call the Tijuana Boxing Commission.

I was assured by Gibbons and Trampler that the letter was on the way … Top Rank paid for Gibbons' matchmaker's license as well as Trampler's at the event. Therefore, the Missouri Office of Athletics was under the impression that Gibbons was one of the two matchmakers at the event.

On July 2, 1996 I attempted to contact Trampler and Gibbons to determine the status of the letter. I received no reply. Although they indicated they had left a message at my room.

At 7:15 pm, after the fights had started, Trampler and an individual who introduced himself as an attorney for Top Rank, asked me to come to the side. (They had already heard that I was not going to allow Cargle to fight because of the suspension.)

This was the first contact I had with Trampler on July 2, 1996. Trampler then gave me a copy of the letter he said he received from the Tijuana Boxing Commission, which allegedly rescinded the suspension. I explained to Trampler that the letter had not been received in time to verify its authenticity. Trampler and the other indiividual continued to badger me because I would not allow Cargle to fight. They told me that I was hurting the show because Freddie Norwood (Cargle's opponent and the future WBA featherweight champion of the world) would not be allowed to fight in front of his hometown crowd.

After at least 15 minutes of badgering, Trampler said, "So let me get this straight. You would believe the Tijuana Boxing Commission before you would believe me?

"Yes," replied Luckenhoff, a former deputy sheriff who has a Bachelor of Science degree in Criminal Justice.

Trampler walked off in a huff. Luckenhoff didn't even see him at the casino that evening. On the surface, Trampler might've had a genuine beef. After all, a communique had arrived with the Tijuana Boxing Commission letterhead and logo. It read in block capital letters:

BY THIS LETTER I WANT TO INFORM YOU THAT LEE CARGLE IS ABLE TO FIGHT IN ANY PLACE. HE IS NOT SUSPENDED IN MEXICO AND HIS ANTI-DOPING RESULTS ARE NEGATIVE FROM HIS FIGHT WITH ERIK MORALES.

The next day, as Top Rank and the TV crew were preparing to leave town, Luckenhoff was stunned to learn that the letter was a forgery. Through a highly reliable intermediary, Ramon Espinoza Rivera, the president of the Tijuana Boxing Commission, was contacted, and swore that he never wrote the letter that bore his purported signature. But he did fax a previous commission letter, dated May 14, long before Cargle was slated to box in Missouri. It had the exact logo and letterhead, but when it was translated into English it read:

> *With the present letter, we inform you that the boxer from the United States, Lee Cargle, was positive for a drug test, which the Tijuana commission gave him in April after his fight against Erik Morales. For this reason we ask (you) to take further action against the fighter.*

There was even another June 13 letter from the Tijuana Commission that corroborated the authenticity of the suspension.

> *With the present letter we inform you that the boxer from the United States, Lee Cargle, has been suspended for one year commencing June 13, 1996 for being positive for a drug test that the commission gave him in April after his fight with Erik Morales. This suspension is valid too, for his cornermen of Lee Cargle. We hope you take action for any future matches.*

A copy of Cargle's drug test was sent, along with a note from Luis Escalona, a "liason" with the Mexican commission who vouched for the authenticity of the drug tests, conducted at a Mexican laboratory.

Now, if the Tijuana Boxing Commision didn't send the exculpatory Cargle lettter, just who did? "Fortunately, the fax number where the letter was sent from appears at the top of the letter," wrote Luckenhoff, in his complaint to Arum. "It apparently originated from a promoter in Tijuana."

That promoter, Fernando Beltran, not only handled Morales, he was a steady business associate of Arum and Top Rank. Trampler and Gibbons both knew Cargle was suspended and the only way to get him on the card was to get a letter to rescind the suspension. Why did Trampler go to a promoter from Mexico to get a letter from the Tijuana Boxing Commission? It would only seem logical that he contact the Tijuana Commission personally to get the suspension lifted. Why did Trampler hand over the letter at 7:15 PM on July 2, when it was originally faxed from Mexico at 12:47 PM on July 2? This left no time for the letter to be verified.

Luckenhoff politely asked Arum for an investigation, "and pray that you take the necessary disciplinary action involved." Arum is an attorney, and a former member of the United States Department of Justice. Ethically, he is still held to a higher standard than the average person because he is an "officer of the court." But the Missouri commissioner never heard from him.

Though Trampler and Gibbons were lucky to get away, Trampler, a childish, combative person with an intellectual facade, actually threatened a lawsuit in a letter to Audrey Zorn, who was Luckenhoff's boss. If that wasn't stupid enough, Trampler even faxed his embarrassing five-page harangue to boxing people, and to the *St. Louis Post-Dispatch.* "Trampler should be fired," promoter Cedric Kushner said, when he got his.

Never mind that Luckenhoff, not Trampler, is charged with the responsibility to safeguard boxing in Missouri. Forget that Lee Cargle had gone winless in his last twenty-eight fights, or that Norwood had already beaten him a couple of times. Trampler had passed off a fax, purporting to be from the Tijuana Boxing Commission, that even he later admitted came from promoter Fernando Beltran, who was "a client" of Top Rank's.

Though Trampler is lucky that Luckenhoff didn't have him, Gibbons and Beltran investigated for wire fraud. Trampler ludicrously tried to come off like they were the "victims" in his *bizzare* letter to Zorn.

> I've been a boxing matchmaker, manager, promoter, trainer, cut man, ring announcer, and worked in just about every other capacity in the fight game for 28 of my 47 years, in most states across America and in many foreign countries as well. Among my more prestigious positions were matchmaker at New York's famous Madison Square Garden for two years, and head matchmaker for the busiest promoter in the world, Top Rank, Inc., for the past 16 years.
>
> I've dealt with commissioners who were competent, and many who weren't. I've worked with those who were honest and forthright, and commissions who were corrupt and dishonest, but I always treat people with the same respect they treat me, and I try not to let matters get personal.
>
> I first encountered Tim Luckenhoff of the State of Missouri at a July 2, 1996 Top Rank promotion in St Charles. He has gotten personal with me over a match in which he's trying to punish a fighter because he doesn't like one of the boxer's handlers. Big Tim, according to one newspaper account, is 6' 5" and 240 pounds. It's amazing that a man so huge can have the brain the size of a pea. I made a mighty effort to explain the situation to Big Tim, but he just couldn't fathom what was going on.
>
> Big Tim proceeded to distribute and perpetrate a sordid series of lies and mistruths and to slander me and my reputation in the process … Big Tim, you see, refused to let boxer Lee Cargle fight in Missouri because the fighter was under suspension in Mexico, even though Big Tim had just re-licensed Cargle less than 24 hours earlier.

Of course, what Trampler didn't add was that he and Gibbons kept vouching for a fax that they had to know was phoney. But Trampler continued to make a fool of himself, in his diatribe to Zorn.

> In early April Cargle accepted a fight in Tijuana against unbeaten contender (and future world champion) Erik Morales, who is promoted by Top Rank. The booking agent was

> *a man named Miguel Diaz of Las Vegas, who since has been an employee of Top Rank. Cargle has a terrible record, but Morales was suffering from a sore hand and needed a relatively easy opponent. Cargle, the loser of dozens of fights, seemed to fit the bill, if he was approved by the Tijuana commission. To my surprise, he was.*
>
> *I went down to Tijuana for the fight, looking after he interest of our client, Morales. A clearly overmatched Cargle was not able to survive long with the hard-punching Mexican, and before the end of the second round, Cargle hit the deck … For some reason though, the Tijuana comission thought Cargle could do better … One of the commisson members commented that Cargle fought like he was on drugs.*

Though Trampler's complaint, if he had any in the first place, should have been directed at Tijuana, not Missouri, he kept trying to confuse the real issue, and threw in racism as well.

> *Told that Cargle does not drink, smoke, or use drugs, the commissioner remarked that 'all niggers do drugs.' Cargle, by the way is of African-American descent.*
>
> *On May 14, more than three weeks after that fight, the Tijuana board sent out a little letter stating that Cargle had tested positive for drugs. They must have access to the Psychic Friends Hotline, since boxers in Tijuana and elsewhere in Mexico DO NOT take drug tests, except in title fights. The Tijuana commission letter contained deliberately false and malicious information about the boxer, who was not put under suspension for his alleged offense.*

Of course he wasn't. The drug test results, which Trampler claims didn't happen, hadn't come back yet. Trampler actually had the gall to complain to Zorn, "Tim does not do any research or homework himself … Big Tim isn't so much interested in the truth as he is in covering his ample behind."

Then Trampler ranted, "I would peronally vouch for Cargle's drug-free status." Maybe Trampler would, but the State of Oklahoma won't. According to Skip Nicholson, Cargle was "released from the Oklahoma County Jail on January 24, 1997, after receiving a five-year suspended sentence for drug possession." After his release, "Cargle was immediately incarcerated in the Oklahoma City Jail on several traffic violations."

In his juvenile diatribe to Zorn, on Top Rank stationery no less, Trampler rattled on.

> *Big Tim, in his letter to my boss Bob Arum, 'prayed' that Bob would discipline me, like I'm a common criminal or fugitive? or something. Bob, who knows my integrity and allows me to handle millions of dollars for him every year just laughed at Big Tim's pitiful letter, wadded it up, and tossed it. Swish! Nothing but waste basket. My punishment is that Top Rank and I may not be doing fights in Missouri any more. All because of Big Tim, resident genius on your boxing commission.*

*Tell Big Tim that he had better apologize. He can't help being ignorant, but he can
start learning some manners and how to do his job in a professional manner, if he wants
to continue as boxing commissioner in Missouri.*

Luckenhoff never apologized. Neither Trampler nor Gibbons were stupid
enough to sue the State of Missouri, but this wasn't the first time Trampler
has tried to intimidate somebody when he doesn't get his way.

In 1982, Randy Gordon was fired by ESPN television after he
mentioned that one of the "opponents" on an Arum show shouldn't have
been licensed because he'd been stopped just six days earlier. After the
broadcast Arum, Trampler, and Akbar Muhammad angrily descended on
Gordon and demanded to know what the hell he was doing.

"I told the truth. I work for ESPN, not you," Gordon told them.

"Oh, we'll see about that."

Gordon, who'd been alternating as color man with Al Bernstein, got
bounced. Bernstein would go on another sixteen years. On the few occasions that Bernstein actually said anything journalistically, he'd preface it
with statements like, "The people inside the truck are going to get mad at
me." After he once said something controversial, he actually pleaded on air
to his then-partner Barry Tompkins, "Help me, I've got a career." In 1998,
when Bill Cayton became an adviser to ESPN boxing, one of the first things
he did was get rid of Bernstein. Arum also lost his exclusive with ESPN.

Despite Tim Luckenhoff seeing evidence of "fixed fights," he struggled
to do anything about it. He later wrote Senator John McCain, who had
passed the Professional Boxing Safety Act in 1996 and has done more than
anyone since Estes Kefauver to cleanse this sport: "I am saddened by the fact
that Skip Nicholson … and I gathered so much information … but we
could not discipline them because we did not have the authority under that
state law which was in effect at that time."

McCain was made of stern stuff. He had survived five-and-a-half hellish
years as a POW in Vietnam, where he was hung by his arms under the
scorching sun, starved, beaten into unconsciousness and was near death
numerous times. He would not accept re-patriation because it meant going
out of order, taking someone else's place, and embarrassing his father, who
was in charge of the bombing on North Vietnam. On 22 May 1997,
McCain opened a series of hearings into boxing in Washington, D.C.

I am interested in boxing not primarily as an investigator, nor as a regulator,
not as a critic. First and foremost I am a fervent, lifelong fan of the sport.

At its best, boxing is an unparalleled and riveting contest of courage, determination, and skill between athletes. I have followed professional boxing
closely for over four decades. I have taken great joy from its many triumphant

moments and from its truly admirable champions, one of whom (Floyd Patterson) is with us today.

I have also shared in the displeasure of millions of Americans who experience both sadness and dismay at the current scandals that mar the sport. Professional boxing has commonly been called the "sweet science" and the "red light district of sports." Both are accurate descriptions.

There are really *two* boxing industries in America, however. The first is comprised of famous and successful boxers, powerful promoters, and multi-million dollar revenues that startle even the most jaded sports fan paging through the morning paper. A single major championship bout may total over $75 million in revenue in the United States alone, with a purse exceeding $20 million for the victor. That is the premier side of boxing.

But those multi-million dollar spectacles have little in common with the great majority of profesional boxing events that are held across the United States each weekend. Most of the 740 boxing events held in 1996 featured unknown journeyman boxers plying their trade for extremely meager wages before a few hundred fans. This club circuit is in many respects the grassroots backbone of the sport. These boxers travel from town to town for years, earning only a couple of hundred dollars a night, with few advocates or benefactors to protect them against the ravages of their profession.

While my interest as a fan may be drawn to the most talented and exciting champions in the sport, my concerns as a public official are primarily focused on the journeyman boxers. They strive to succeed despite their often disadvantaged backgrounds, and they are dedicated and skilled athletes in their own right. Boxing is often the only way they know how to make a living. Their willingness to endure what is unquestionably a punishing profession may cost them their health, yet true club boxers are always ready to fairly compete and they fight to win.

CHAPTER ELEVEN

The Talmudic Scholar

O N 25 SEPTEMBER 1962, Sonny Liston unleashed his fourteen-inch fists on Floyd Patterson in Chicago's Comiskey Park and became the heavyweight champion of the world in just 2:06 of the first round. It wasn't a fight, it was a mugging, in front of 26,000 witnesses. "I think if people will just give Liston a chance, he can be a fine champion," said Patterson, showing enormous class despite being humiliated by the foreboding ex-con.

None of that concerned Robert Arum, a bright, thirty-one-year-old lawyer who worked out of the Tax Section of the United States Attorney's Office in the Southern District of New York. While Liston's glowering mug was on the front and back pages the next day, US Attorney-General Bobby Kennedy was ordering the fight receipts impounded, and Arum was the button-down whiz kid who tied up 263 closed-circuit outlets nationwide. Even with the disappointing gate of $665,420, the Feds swooped because the recent Kefauver investigation proved that Liston was owned by the Mob, and Uncle Sam was making sure he got his piece.

By 1965, professional boxing was virtually banned from American TV, and Arum had forsaken government service for the high-powered Manhattan law firm of Phillips, Nizer, Benjamin, and Ballon – but he couldn't get those millions out of his mind. He wangled an invitation, through pro football great Jimmy Brown, to meet Muhammad Ali. Madison Garden had been prohibited by court decree from extending its once iron grip, leaving the fight wide open, but without television, or Ali, you could not make any money in the States.

Enduring the anti-semitic taunts of the Black Muslims who surrounded Ali, Arum formed a company called Main Bout to promote the champ's fights. His first promotional venture came in March 1966, in Toronto, Canada, when Ali pummelled brave George Chuvalo over fifteen rounds. Ali's outspoken stance on Vietnam ("I ain't got nothing against them Viet Congs") forced him to take his title on the road, with defences against Henry Cooper and Brian London in England, and Karl Mildenberger in Germany, before he sent Cleveland Williams crashing three times in November in front of 35,000 at the Houston Astrodome. Ali-Williams, briefly, was the largest crowd ever gathered indoors to see a fight, though poor Williams, who had been shot point blank by a Texas Ranger two years earlier with a .357 magnum, was fighting with just one kidney – and he never got paid. His managers, Hugh Benbow and Bud Adams, both Texas oil millionaires, tied up his purse right before he stepped into the ring. "I still got my cheque from Bob Arum," claimed Williams's wife, Irene, years later. "It was no good. People laughed when I tried to cash it."

Before the reluctant Williams got into the ring, Arum was screaming, "Go out there and fight, you big, dumb sonofabitch."

Thirty years later, the once-magnificently sculpted Williams, who could hit so hard he broke sandbags, wrote a tragic letter to a friend, Rinzie Van Der Meer:

GOD, have given me the Pleasure, to sit here, and write you these Few lines. How are you doing, today? Well, and better I hope. As For me, I'm doing pretty good by the Grace of God, Rinze, as of this moment, I don't have any pictures, of Myself, as of todays Look, but since I have your address, I can have some Made and then I Promis to send you Two, or Three of them. I don't Look to much different now from I did when I Was Fighting, only two, thing, I'm older, and Sick, From that Gun, shot that I receive 31, years ago. I thank GOD, each Day, in my own way, for a Brand New day, that he gave me to see. You know I don't have any kidnies, the first one was Distroied, by that Gun shot. After that Gun Shot, It taken me two years to go From 157 Ibs back to 220 Ibs. After I got back in condition, I fought, 30, or 40, Fights, with that one Kidney, I got bang on it quite a bit, then I had to retire from Boxing. I got me a job driving one of Large 18, Wheeler Truck, then my Left Kidney, went bad, I had to leave that Job, because of Kidney Failire anyway. I'm a sick man, and can't get no help from no one, and that is the truth, so help me God.

Adams and Benbow claimed they paid for Williams's medical bills. Irene Williams, Cleve's wife, angrily disagrees. In 1999, the "Big Cat" died after being run down by a car on the way to dialysis.

★ ★ ★

On 28 April 1967, Ali refused to take the one step forward that would have constituted induction into the U.S. Army. The boxing authorities acted with indecent haste. Immediately, the brash twenty-five-year-old was stripped of his heavyweight championship, though U.S. Attorney Mort Susman said, "It will take at least thirty days for Clay to be indicted and it will probably be another year and a half before he could be sent to prison, since there'll undoubtedly be appeals." Despite his later iconic status, most of the public at the time was outraged at Ali's "conscientious objector" stance, and the heavyweight champion was facing five years in jail. He wouldn't fight again until October 1970. "The world never saw the best of Muhammad Ali," lamented his trainer Angelo Dundee.

Arum knew Ali's constitutional rights were being violated. That didn't stop him quickly meeting with ABC television and concocting a tournament with the WBA to determine a new heavyweight champion. An old Ali sparmate, Jimmy Ellis, was ultimately crowned after decisioning Jerry Quarry in April 1968, but everyone knew Ellis was just a pretender to the throne.

With Ali on the sidelines, American TV had little interest in boxing. Yet Arum sensed something. He left Phillips Nizer and formed his own firm but, having had a taste of the excitement and glamour of the sport, it was hard to go back to the musty world of corporate law. Arum finally dissolved his firm and jumped back into boxing on Ali's return.

On 28 June 1971, Ali's draft conviction was overturned. The public's mood on Vietnam had drastically changed. In the interim, Ali had regained his license and had stopped Quarry and Oscar Bonavena. Arum showed up to promote him, but to the Muslim brothers who still shadowed Ali, Arum was "a traitor Jew." Ali also railed against "Zionism" and regurgitated a lot of the crude anti-semitism he had been spoonfed. That didn't deter Arum, who somehow made himself innocuous enough to become Ali's closed-circuit promoter, and his attorney as well – a flagrant conflict of interest.

On 8 March 1971, Joe Frazier smashed Ali to the canvas and beat him on points in one of the great sporting spectacles of the twentieth century. This was the clash of titans, a fight so big it didn't have to be hyped. Only the second Louis-Schmeling clash, a metaphor for World War Two, and perhaps the Jack Johnson-Jim Jeffries bout, had more social significance. Yet Arum was out, and a Hollywood agent, Jerry Perenchio, was in.

Still, "I'm interested in anything that Ali does," Arum claimed. He shamelessly promoted a 1976 farce between the champ and Japanese wrestler Antonio Inoki, in which the giant wrestler stayed down like a crab and kicked Ali's shins till he nearly had blood clots. Arum also promoted Evel Knievel's daredevil jump across the Snake River Canyon in 1974, but gave

Knievel hell because he was drunk all week, and Evil wisely pulled the parachute halfway through, bailing out before he killed himself.

"Look, without boxing, Arum would've been just another lawyer in a cheap, walk-up office," sneered attorney Mike Trainer, who used to represent Sugar Ray Leonard, and who Arum called his toughest adversary.

Arum, who has a round, bland face, and thinning, reddish-brown hair, looks every bit the bland corporate attorney he was destined to be. Basically a shy man, it took him a good twenty years before he finally popped into the ring to get himself on television like his nemesis Don King. But behind the scenes, Arum had grown increasingly arrogant. He's a raspy-voiced whiner, with a New York mean streak.

Somebody once said, "Bob Arum is his own worst enemy."

"Not while I'm alive," said legendary fight manager Cus D'Amato, who was used to handshake deals even while fending off threats from the Mafia as he piloted Floyd Patterson to the heavyweight championship. "When Bob Arum pats you on the back," Cus used to say, "he's just looking for a spot to stick in the knife."

British promoter Mickey Duff says, "I'll shake hands with Arum, only I'll take off my ring first."

Dr Ferdie Pacheco, Ali's longtime cornerman-physician, called him, "One of the PhD liars of the world."

Arum claims he speaks in a straightforward, lawyerly fashion. This from a man who famously told sportswriter Bob Waters, "Yesterday I was lying, today I'm telling the truth."

Rival promoter Butch Lewis says, "Bob Arum comes across as meek and mild. Well, let me tell you, Bob Arum is treacherous. He's vicious. He has no morals at all. I worked with the man, putting together the first Ali-Spinks fight for CBS. We signed the contract, were walking out the building and Arum is snickering, 'We can really fuck them.' I looked at him, I said, 'Why do you want to do that? We just made a deal. The ink ain't even dry,' and he says to me, 'I know, but there's a loophole. We can fuck them if there's a rematch.'"

Arum brought the second Ali-Spinks fight to ABC. On the eve of the September 15 bout, Lewis was fired. Arum publicly branded him a thief for selling advertising at the New Orleans Superdome and supposedly not turning in the $25,000 he'd received. Arum claims stealing makes him very "uncomfortable," though he also says there's not much money in boxing unless you steal. Arum tries to maintain that fifty percent of his TV shows lose money, but if that's the case, how is he worth a conservative $30 million today?

"I really enjoy outwitting my adversaries," he often told his matchmaker, Bruce Trampler. His late publicity man Irving Rudd claimed he was a "prince," but for thirty-five years, this rather nondescript man with the Harvard education has used people and discarded them like paper cups.

In 1980, Ernie Terrell, the 1960s heavyweight contender, was trying to promote club fights in Chicago. His shows were constant losers. Arum came along brandishing a cable TV deal from the fledgling ESPN, and wanted to feature Terrell's shows once a month. Terrell was saved – or so he thought. Ernie, who was a terrible matchmaker, matched his ticket-sellers with complete stiffs, and there were seven one-round knockouts on one card. Arum was livid. He had two and a half hours of live TV to fill, and ESPN was so new it had no archive footage to fill in with. Arum hit the airwaves to apologize for the card; Terrell was finished.

In October 1981, Arum worked with Terrell again, reluctantly. Terrell had developed a good young heavyweight named James "Quick" Tillis, who some naively likened to Ali. Arum brought his WBA champion Mike Weaver to suburban Chicago to defend against him. Weaver won, but Arum blasted the Chicago press for not over-hyping the show, which also had Marvin Hagler defending against Mustapha Hamsho. Terrell got just $1,000 for being the front promoter. "Arum really humiliated Ernie," recalled the late Clarence Griffin, who ran the Windy City Gym. "He didn't even want Ernie at press conferences." Of course Griffin often said, "Ernie is the dumbest son of a bitch ever to piss over a pair of shoes."

Arum was the first promoter to really "package" boxing for an international audience, mainly because of technological improvements in TV. He was also brilliant in later exploiting the Hispanic market (in the 1950s and '60s, promoters George Parnassus and Cal Eaton made big money in Los Angeles with little Mexicans like Enrique Bolanos and Ruben Olivares; a Mexican-American, Art Aragon, was the biggest draw in California history, and never even bothered to fight in the Garden). In 1992, Arum signed the perfect TV hero in Oscar de la Hoya, who not only won a gold in the Barcelona Olympics but publicly dedicated his medal to his mother after she had died from breast cancer.

Before the "Golden Boy" came along, Arum grossed a then-staggering $30 millon for Sugar Ray Leonard and Roberto Duran. Duran, who was too crude and dark to really "cross over" into the Anglo market, was one of the greatest fighters of all-time, but years later, he was still using his body like an old streetwalker. After going through $50 million, he was broke, owing the United States $4.5 million in taxes. "It's not Roberto Duran," protested the one-time street urchin, "it's Don King and Bob Arum. Roberto Duran never took anything. He doesn't owe anybody any money. They were supposed to take care of his taxes."

At fifty, Duran was still fighting. Arum says, "I'm a businessman. Two guys in a ring, that has nothing to do with me. Fighters bore me."

Arum even warned Butch Lewis about getting too close to fighters. "Butch, don't you realise, fighters come and go. We'll be around forever."

* * *

It has been a long, strange journey for Robert Arum, this distinguished graduate of Harvard Law, Class of 1956. As a Jew, Arum knew all about being history's underdog. When a young, freshly-scrubbed Arum got his first job on Wall Street, he could only apply at firms that hired Jews, and then not too many. America called itself the Land of the Free but Jews couldn't join the most prestigious clubs. They couldn't live where they wanted. They were second-class citizens, and it's one reason why they have always been staunch supporters of black appeals for civil rights.

Growing up in New York City, Arum was just fifteen when he saw the horrifying newsreels of Auschwitz and Buchenwald. His father was an Orthodox Jewish accountant, and young Bob became a notable Talmudic scholar. Though the Talmud "is a document of faith, an expression of the soul," and the way "God should be served," (according to *Invitation to the Talmud* by Jacob Neusner), Arum never quite absorbed that. But he was brilliant at reciting the verse.

Somehow, a ghetto prodigy like Don King can almost be excused for his amorality, but how do you justify Arum, who didn't grow up father-less and poverty-stricken, amid junkies, whores and pimps? Boxing is a hustler's racket, and both Arum and King are predators, but if King uses a sledgehammer, forged in the Cleveland ghetto, Arum uses a velvet-sheathed stiletto, honed at Harvard. "We've done some terrible things to each other," Arum chuckled in front of the jury at Bob Lee's corruption trial. Arum admitted that it was wrong, but continued to smile as he savoured it. In 1988, Arum announced he was moving his headquarters to the Las Vegas desert. King cracked, "What better place for night crawlers?"

Arum tries to rationalize his behaviour as "street smarts" and has lasted longer than any packager in history. In 1980, he went to a one-trailer operation in Bristol, Connecticut, called ESPN, and ended up doing a weekly TV card for the next nineteen years.

"Arum is really the *accountant* of the major promoters," Philadelphia fightmaker Russell Peltz often told people. "ESPN made Arum and Top Rank. When ESPN signed the deal, Arum somehow managed to keep it for himself, and that's what really kept him on top. Top Rank Boxing was a profitable show, and I figure that Arum was making about thirty grand an episode. When you figure it runs forty times a year, that's $1.2 million he has to stick in his pocket. Maybe, that doesn't sound like much, but that pays for his office and salaries. Having ESPN gave Arum access to all the fighters. You put that in someone else's hands, and see how the power would change."

By 1998, ESPN had grown into a cable colossus, and cable television had re-shaped the cultural landscape. When Arum's exclusive contract was finally cancelled, he bellowed like a spoiled brat, "I'll sue. It's a monopoly." Of course, it wasn't a "monopoly" when Arum controlled everything. For nearly twenty years, ESPN had bankrolled Arum, giving him *entre* to nearly every good American prospect. "Sign with me or you won't get on TV," he told many managers, who faced an even worse alternative in Don King. Because of option contracts, Arum controlled a fighter's ability to fight. The game has changed enormously in the last twenty-five years, with Arum and King controlling the championships and access to TV. For all practical purposes, it was a restraint of trade. "The networks wouldn't deal with anybody but Arum or King. Occasionally, they might throw somebody like Russell Peltz a plum, but not often," said Nat Loubet in 1978, then editor of *Ring* magazine.

By the late 1970s, Marvin Hagler was the best middleweight in the world, but his managers could not go straight to network TV. "King showed up at Marvin's mother's house," recalled Goody Petronelli, who co-managed Hagler with his brother Pat. "King tried to steal Marvin, and gave his mother the usual 'black brother' crap: 'Us black people got to look out for each other, and you should help a black man.' But Marvin was loyal, and he told his mother, 'They've been good to me.'"

Eventually Hagler fought for Arum, and Arum would try to tout what he had done for Hagler for the remainder of his career. "We only got our title shot," swears Goody Petronelli, "because we complained to Tip O'Neil (Speaker of the House of Representatives) and he threatened to have Arum investigated for antitrust (monopoly) violations."

Vito Antuofermo, a crude bleeder from New York, held the middleweight title, but everyone knew Marvin was the king. In 1992, Mob stoolie Michael Franzese testified in Washington that some of Antuofermo's fights were fixed, but he claimed the Hagler fight wasn't. After Hagler pounded Vito on November 30, 1979, only to get a scandalous draw, you'd never convince skeptics.

By the 1990s, Arum so controlled his fighters that even the likes of Peter McNeeley and Butterbean couldn't fight each other, without his OK. McNeeley's manager Vinnie Vechione tried to make the match, but Arum bristled, "Do it the right way. Go to the promoters."

What were fighters paying a third of their blood money for? Under options clauses, which fighters had to sign, their own managers couldn't even manage their careers.

★ ★ ★

Don King labelled Arum "The Apostle of Apartheid" because of his promotions in South Africa during a period when that country was subject to worldwide trade sanctions. Arum didn't care about the international boycott; he was concerned about making money. Though Arum publicly called the WBA and WBC "two asshole jokes," by 1983 Flash Gordon was referring to the WBA as the WBArum, his ties were so close to that organization. Arum denied that, and claimed he had to bribe Pepe Cordero just like anybody else. Arum undeniably got behind the candidacy of Gilberto Mendoza when he was opposed for the WBA presidency by American Bob Lee. Rumours were that Arum and Mendoza's other backers used tactics that "border on bribery and extortion to sway votes from Lee," according to *Ring*. Arum angrily replied, "That's bullshit."

But Ron Hayter, who headed the Canadian federation, resigned from the WBA after its convention in San Juan, Puerto Rico, claiming that the presidential election was pushed back a day so Mendoza could fly in votes from "dummy" commissions in South America.

Surprisingly, Arum even told the *Ring's* Ben Sharav that Lee would have made a better president but it was Pepe Cordero who he really had to worry about, and he wasn't going to do anything to offend him. Arum admitted there were all kinds of payoffs, but claimed that the "bribes were actually worse in the WBC."

"Don't you think that [WBC boss] Sulaiman is Don King's partner?" Arum bristled, a charge he would make under oath before a Senate subcommittee in 1992. Arum reiterated to Sharav that Sulaiman had forced him to take on Don King as a partner, or there wouldn't have been a Leonard-Duran II. Instead of saying, "*No mas,*" as Duran did, Arum simply split $3 million with King. Though Arum continued to prosper, by claiming to pay the WBA under the table, it was a violation of American bribery statues, and the IRS non-profit laws.

For years, Arum had been saying, "Boxing is the most corrupt, poorly regulated big-time sport in the country," but when it really came to doing something, he'd snarl, "I'm not going on a crusade."

By 1988, Arum was publicly refusing to do any more business with the WBA, after a dispute arose over the santioning of the Iran Barkley-Sumbu Kalambay middleweight title fight. By 1988, Cordero was gone, trying to form the WBO, but Arum contended that if there had been a shift in power, the WBA still did business the same way.

By now, Arum was calling the WBA the "most atrocious" of the sanctioning groups, and an "intolerable organization." Though the WBA was tax-exempt in the States, this "non-profit" group somehow built themselves a "Taj Mahal" of a headquarters in Maracaibo, Venezuela. Arum even claimed that seventy to eighty per cent of all sanction fees were paid to the chairman of the Pennsylvania Boxing Commission, Jimmy Binns, who was also the legal council for the WBA. What Arum didn't mention was that Binns was also his attorney at the same time he'd done business with the WBA. This was clearly a conflict of interest, but Binns also represented managers, who came before the WBA — and expected to get their fighters rated.

Arum began calling for a congressional investigation, but he was also saying, "Bob Lee's a decent man, who's only concern is the fighter." Lee, boss of the International Boxing Federation, would later be jailed for corruption.

By 1988, Arum's marriage to the stunning Sybil was coming apart. They kept fighting about boxing, but Arum wouldn't leave the game. Despite the millions he'd made, Arum fashioned himself an "event promoter," not a guy just depending on networks like HBO. Arum actually tried telling critics that his bottom line on lucrative HBO shows was a "plus or minus fifty grand," which was preposterous. But if Bob Arum made so much with closed-circuit, or pay-per-view, why did TVKO, which was doing one show a month in the early Nineties, stop doing them regularly?

Arum, like other fight packagers, couldn't stay in business without HBO, Showtime, or casino site fees. Option contracts were the glue that held everything togther, but they were useless if TV wasn't bankrolling boxing.

One day, Arum, who was a man of moral pretensions, told Teddy Brenner, "I try to be as honest as I can be. But face it, this is a dirty, dirty business."

"Hey, it's not nearly as bad as when Carbo was involved," countered Brenner.

Maybe, but by 1991 Arum was predicting that the networks would get out of boxing, simply because of the constant scandals, most of which emanated from King. "Advertisers don't want to touch it," Arum said. But after network TV gave up on the sport, cable networks filled the breach, though the coverage wasn't nearly as widespread and that hurt the game.

* * *

As much as the lawyerly side of Arum decries the corruption in boxing, there's no question that he's clearly benefited from it. On 8 February 1992, he promoted an IBF middleweight championship bout between James Toney and challenger Dave Tiberi in Atlantic City, New Jersey. Tiberi was such an underdog that Las Vegas wouldn't even post a betting line. Tiberi was a handsome, moustachioed gent with dark brown hair, who looked like a *Playgirl* centerfold, but was so squeaky clean, he didn't even drink or smoke. Tiberi was actually a married to a Sunday school teacher, and came from a huge family of fourteen children, where he was the youngest of twelve boys, seven of whom boxed, with four turning pro.

Nobody gave him any chance to beat Toney, but "Tiberi, fighting on guts, raw courage and fierce determination, proved in the ring before millions of TV viewers, he was definitely the winner. But he got ripped off," wrote an outraged Matt Zabitka of the *Wilmington News-Journal*.

"There was a time when I had to borrow money from my family and friends to buy gas to travel to the gym and to eat. But I persevered, even though the life was a daily routine of ache and pains, of trading punches with fellow fighters who had the very same dreams," testified Tiberi in August 1992, before Senator William Roth's Permanent Subcommittee on Investigations.

"I watched when Dave fought James Toney on national TV, and I, along with thousands of others, was outraged at the decision, and still am," said Roth, a Republican from Delaware, who had begun an investigation into corruption in boxing.

"In 1991, after twenty-seven professional, fights and more than seven years of dedication ... I won the International Boxing Council world title, an achievement which I cherished," continued Tiberi, his voice quivering as he read from his prepared statement. "The rival and larger organization, the International Boxing Federation, claims the IBC was not a credible organization. Its officials insisted that I relinquish my crown, in order to accept the opportunity to fight its champion, James Toney for the IBF title.

"James Toney had fought twenty-eight fights in the middleweight division and he already had been scheduled for matches with Glenn Wolfe and Mike McCallum. They were to take place after his fight with me on February 8, 1992. In order for me to be allowed to participate in a fight with James Toney, Bob Arum, Top Rank promoter, 'convinced' me to sign a contract that I would belong to him for my next three fights, if I defeated Toney. It was like being bought at a slave auction. In fact, as a result of my first-hand experience, I sometimes find it very hard to still consider boxing a sport. For many promoters, it has become their private, legalized slave industry."

Tiberi also realized that he was brought in as a "patsy for James Toney ... as a warm-up fight that he could not lose." Since Arum had already signed Toney versus Wolfe, "an unexpected loss to the Delaware nobody would totally destroy their promotional plans."

Just two days before the fight, Larry Hazzard, the boxing commissioner in New Jersey, "replaced an experienced referee with an inexperienced one [Robert Palmer]. He also allowed two 'unlicensed' judges to officiate ... which was illegal under New Jersey boxing laws. All these hidden, illegal manoeuvres occurred without question," Tiberi maintained.

Though Tiberi clearly outboxed the sluggish Toney, and New Jersey judge Frank Brunette agreed, 117-111, Bill Lerch of Illinois and Frank Garza of Michigan appallingly scored it 116-111 and 115-112 for Toney. As boos rained down, even billionaire developer Donald Trump was incensed: "I think it's disgusting what happens in boxing. I watched something that made me nauseous. There'll be no more fights in Atlantic City until this disgraceful situation is rectified." Though an investigation was called for, neither the IBF nor the New Jersey State Athletic Commission did anything. Finally, Senator Roth jumped in because he felt that "allegations of corruption in boxing, were a legitimate concern of congress."

According to the report prepared for Roth, "Dave Tiberi was, in several ways, a victim of a system where the regulated have been allowed to rule the regulators. In apparent contravention of New Jersey boxing regulations, the judges who officiated at the Tiberi-Toney fight were selected by the IBF. Two of the judges officiated without a license to judge, or in any way participate in, professional boxing in New Jersey. These two out of state judges were not knowledgeable about New Jersey rules and, in fact, were under the impression that only the IBF rules were in effect during the Toney-Tiberi fight. Moreover, one of the unlicensed judges advised that two of the rounds which he in fact judged to be even rounds, he actually scored for Toney because of his understanding that the IBF rules do not permit the scoring of even rounds and that, in championship fights, it is the IBF policy that even rounds are to be scored in favor of the champion.

"The referee who officiated lacked any experience in refereeing world championship fights. He was selected as a referee despite having been poorly evaluated for his performance in a previous fight. His penalization of Tiberi for alleged low blows, and his failure to direct Toney to a neutral corner while Tiberi's gloves were being replaced were questionable exercises of a referee's discretion."

In a real blast at Hazzard, the report contended, "The lax enforcement of licensing requirements by New Jersey boxing authorities and their deference to private sanctioning bodies, and the failure of either New Jersey boxing authorities or the IBF authorities to investigate the Toney-Tiberi match, combined with a documented history of corruption in boxing in New Jersey, make it difficult to have faith in the fairness of the outcome of the Toney-Tiberi match."

It would be seven long years before the incredible corruption of Bob Lee was revealed. After this fight, the IBF president was asked, "Who do you think won?"

"I don't know. I wasn't watching. I was too busy talking."

Tiberi later protested, "I worked hard, sacrificed for years to attain my dream of winning a world title, and Mr. Lee . . . could not take thirty-six minutes of his time to oversee his organization's match?"

After the bout, in a chaotic post-fight press conference, Tiberi refused a rematch. According to the demoralized challenger, "Bob Arum threw a brazen-faced tantrum," but Trump bristled, "A rematch is not satisfactory. I think the decision should be overturned."

Tiberi had dreamed that he could win, and that one day his name would be placed in the record books alongside his idols, Jake LaMotta and Rocky Graziano. He eventually turned down $125,000 for a rematch. Arum's matchmaker, Ron Katz, a recovering drug addict, sneered, "Tiberi has got no bargaining power. This kid has got to get with the program or he's out."

Tiberi never boxed again. Yet he kept fighting, and went to Washington to plead for federal control of professional boxing. "For every fighter who climbs through the ropes in Las Vegas, there are a hundred more walking the streets with nothing to show for their efforts but a busted dream and broken bones. They are part of the homeless, the unemployed and the used and abused. Many are there because they had dreams and put their trust in those who do not deserve it."

★ ★ ★

The Tiberi scandal had barely died down before another of Arum's fighters, Iran Barkley, the IBF super-middleweight champ, testified, having finally yielded to a subpoena. Barkley was slated to defend his title against James Toney. Arum swore, under the threat of perjury at depostion, that he had to pay Lenny Minuto $125,000 from the the promoter's share of the purse.

Who exactly was Lenny Minuto? He wasn't Barkley's manager. Iran claimed that he had no manager, just an "adviser." But under oath, during convoluted testimony, Barkley was claimed that Minuto wasn't paid. Then, Minuto was paid, $100,000. Next, he said he owed Minuto $195,000.

In reality, Minuto received $295,000 from Berkley's purse, not counting Arum's $125,000. For what? When boxing manager Stan Hoffman was deposed by the Subcommittee staff, he admitted, "[Minuto] really knew nothing about boxing that I can tell." Barkley agreed.

"Minuto is not licensed as a boxing manager or promoter in any state," claimed the digest of the Subcommitee hearings.

Who the hell was Lenny Minuto? According to Alfonse D'Arco, the former underboss of the Luchese crime family in New York, Minuto was organized crime, an associate of the family. Arum knew this, even though he testified that there was no organized crime in boxing.

The Mob had its tentacles around Barkley. The bravest of warriors was scared for his life, and was being bled in and out of the ring. John Joseph

Conti, a soldier in the Luchese family, was also involved. "The Minuto-Barkley relationship illustrates how organized crime figures are involved in the boxing industry as 'unlicensed' advisors to boxers. The process of labelling oneself an advisor rather than a manager or co-manager, allows one to avoid state licensing, yet participate in the business of boxing," concluded the Subcommitte report.

Finally, Barkley admitted that Minuto negotiated his contracts, and served as his investment advisor. Lenny must've done one helluva job. Barkley earned an estimated $10 million from boxing. Currently, he faces blindness in both eyes and, at the time of writing, was so broke he was back living with his mother in the notorious Bronx housing project where he grew up. They even had to take up a collection for him so he could buy clothes.

★ ★ ★

In 2002, thirty-six years after he started, Arum was still one of the top three promoters in the game. While King controlled the heavyweights, and the Duvas briefly broke through, Arum had to be more innovative, and concentrated on smaller men and the burgeoning Hispanic market. "Boxing is really a cultural thing among Mexicans. It's like bull fighting. It's deeply ingrained in their culture, but Oscar De La Hoya will be the first cross-over superstar," Arum excitedly told Irving Rudd, who had been around gladiators since the Roman Coliseum.

Oscar was perfect for television, but was supposed to be locked into Shelly Finkel, an honest manager who did business exclusively with the Duvas. Finkel had quietly bankrolled Oscar's amateur career for years. He'd even paid for his mother's funeral. But Joel De La Hoya, Oscar's father, quickly forgot that when his son signed to turn pro with Steve Nelson and Robert Mittleman, a couple of fringe hustlers, for $1.2 million. The contract was for five years. Mittleman, out of Chicago, was quickly telling everyone, "The kid really likes me," but Joel De La Hoya forgot that too – and the $1.2 million that moved the De La Hoya clan out of the East Los Angeles barrio into a beautiful $500,000 house.

Mittleman and Nelson were forced out. Oscar was such a hot commodity, he didn't really need a manager – at least managers taking that kind of cut – unless it was Joel De La Hoya. Maybe the old man loved his kid but, like Pat O'Grady, he'd had his him in the gym since he was six, and Oscar was his his meal ticket. "He never told me I did good," Oscar once said, and it was obvious that Joel controlled his son by withholding his love.

With Arum packaging him, Oscar became the biggest non-heavyweight attraction in boxing. HBO loved him. When De La Hoya devoured a French pastry named Patrick Charpentier, 45,000 fanatic fans showed up.

Sultry young girls waved homemade placards that read, "Oscar, I want to have your baby." Oscar grossed $125 million with Arum by the time he was twenty-seven. In turn, Arum made more money with him than any fighter he'd ever had. But beneath his soft-spoken, boyish facade, Oscar was cold, and had little loyalty, just like his autocratic father. Trainers who'd worked with for years were fired by telegram.

In 1998, Oscar earned $35 millon, but the *Globe*, an American scandal sheet, reported that he had "paid out $2.5 million to an 18-year-old Cindy Crawford look-alike who claimed that she had a passionate affair with the boxer that began when she was just 15." Oscar's "Golden Boy" image was tarnished, but he wisely paid off, and the story was forgotten.

Finally, De La Hoya faced Felix Trinidad in a welterweight unification. Though Oscar had twice slashed his idol Julio Cesar Chavez into a bloody defeat, this would be his ultimate test as a fighter. In a storied match-up between a Mexican-American and a Puerto Rican, there were cultural bragging rights on the line. For the first half of the fight, Oscar boxed brilliantly, but in the last three rounds, he ran so badly, Don King, Trinidad's promoter, nicknamed him "Chicken De La Hoya."

After Trinidad copped a questionable verdict, setting off celebrations in Puerto Rico, King, ever the predator, sidled up to Oscar in the ring, and chortled, "See what happens when you've got a real promoter."

"You've got to win by a knockout to beat King in Las Vegas," Arum complained.

Oscar could really fight, but he still seemed more Madison Avenue than Stillman's Gym. De La Hoya had a slew of endorsements, but now he wanted to become a singer. Surprisingly, Oscar was nominated for a Latin Grammy, but De La Hoya's live-in girlfriend, a pretty blonde named Shanna Lee Moakler, claimed on American television that Oscar abruptly abandoned her one day, not leaving her enough money to even pay for their daughter's diapers. The fighter who had viciously cut Troy Dorsey and Chavez's faces to ribbons with his left hand, cut off her credit cards, cellphone and internet account as he tried to force her to leave his $5.5 million mansion in Bel Air. Moakler, a former Miss USA beauty queen and TV actress, claimed, "He's gone and abandoned us for no reason." Oscar left for the Latin Grammies and she spotted him holding hands with seductive Millie Carretjer, a top Hispanic singer, who he'd eventually marry. As Moakler described it, she barely held back sobs.

Arum was the next person to get the De La Hoya treatment. Suddenly, Oscar was being courted by Jerry Perenchio, who'd stolen the Ali-Frazier fight from Arum in 1971. Perenchio had never promoted another fight, but now he owned Univision, the largest Hispanic TV network in the States, and the billionaire wanted Oscar. Bye bye, Bob.

"The ungrateful bastard," roared the Talmudic Scholar. "Well, if he thinks I'm just one more of his bimbos, he'll find out. I'll get an injunction, and he won't be able to fight without me."

Though Oscar was signed to Arum till 2004, he contended through his attorney Burton Fields that Arum served as his defacto manager, which was a violation of California law. Under California law, Arum could be recognized as De La Hoya's manager if: he represented the fighter with respect to conducting or arranging matches; directed or controlled Oscar's boxing activities, or received or was entitled to more than ten per cent of Oscar's purse. "We believe Top Rank meets all three, but all they have to do is meet one," argued Stephen B. Espinoza, Oscar's lawyer. Arum also had a personal services contract. Under California law, it couldn't run longer than seven years. Arum's contract with De La Hoya was about to enter its ninth. In court, Arum got a beating. Judge Matt Byrne granted De La Hoya's motion for summary judgement. In essence, the judge stopped the fight before the bell actually rang. That's how bad Arum's contract was.

Byrne not only agreed with De La Hoya that Arum, the Hall of Fame promoter, hadn't complied with California procedures for promotional contracts; Arum didn't even have a California boxing license, figured Byrne. He agreed Arum was, in essence, Oscar's manager, and said he had violated California limits of three years for a promoter's contract, five for a manager's contract and seven for a personal service agreement.

"I'm shocked," sputtered Arum, who vowed to appeal, but never did.

By 2001, Bob Arum was seventy. He had made more money than he'd ever dreamed of, and kept saying, "I want to get out of this sewer," but the closest he came was when he tried to purchase a NBA expansion franchise in 1997. Unfortunately, professional basketball scrutinizes its partners, unlike the fight game, and Arum's attempts at $90 million in financing were deemed inadequate by the NBA screening committee. Naturally, Arum protested, but the NBA refused to play ball with him.

Arum wasn't happy unless he was chasing the next bloodstained dollar. He seemed to relish his public feuds with King, and the Machiavellian nature of the fight game, but after spending half his life in boxing, what has he done for the sport?

He paid $4,000 to ship Robert Wangila's body back to Africa, after the one-time Top Rank prospect was killed in a fight, though it wasn't a Top Rank promotion. After bantamweight Richie Sandoval was nearly beaten to death by Gaby Canizales, Arum gave the kid a one-year contract to work with Top Rank, providing he never fought again. But it's hard to find anything else.

Sure, Arum testified with some candour before congressional committees, and later praised Senator John McCain's seven-year effort to clean up boxing. "The enactment of the Muhammad Ali Reform Act bodes well for the sport," Arum told the *Boston Globe* in May of 2000, "The sanctioning organizations have suffocated the growth of boxing, but the question is not should those organizations disappear, but what to put in their place. With the proliferation of those organizations there are now dozens of champions and no sense to any of it.

"There are strict rules in the sport, but not in the business of the sport, The rules all involve the ritualistic functions like the weigh-in and the signing of contracts filed with commissions, that turn out to be completely different from the real contracts signed for a big fight. The fact is, these local commissions don't have enough people or money to police the sport. The reality is, where McCain is moving will be a hybrid of state and federal regulations, but on a national basis. Not a federal commission but a national commission using the Association of Boxing Commissions for an organization."

Yet if Arum was such a big fan of reform, why did he pay $10,000 – with Don King ponying up $50,000 – so Nevada Senator Harry Reid could block the Ali Act, before it was badly watered down? "The promoters were very afraid of the criminal provisions of the bill," said Paul Feeney, then a McCain aide, who drafted the bill and negotiated its final passage. Though the criminal penalties were left in, everyone knew that without them, the bill was useless.

While Arum blasts the Alphabet Boys and the state commissions, what has he done to clean his own house? Butterbean's fights have continually drawn cries of "FIX!" The Pulitzer Prize-winning *Miami Herald* ran an expose. It got fighters on the record claiming that they were paid to dive to the 350-pound hulk. Arum still promoted Butterbean on ESPN 2 – until Bob Yalen finally pulled the plug after *Boxing News* demanded a criminal investigation.

Sean Gibbons kept finding bums for Butterbean, and then worked their corners. Fighters told the *Herald* that Gibbons had arranged for them to lay down. Arum also knew that two states, Missouri and Oklahoma, had previously documented Gibbons's involvement in allegedly fixed fights with affadavits. Yet Gibbons still has his office at Top Rank.

Arum talks about reform, but his actions speak louder than his words. By 1999, the most educated major promoter in the history of the game was looking at prison. On 18 November 1999, he gave this sworn declaration to federal prosecutors in Newark, New Jersey in order to stay out:

In December, 1994 (Bob) Lee Sr, (Stan) Hoffman, and I met at the Mayfair Hotel in New York. During that meeting, Lee Sr, told me that he wanted a payment of $200,000 for the IBF to sanction the (George) Foreman – (Axel) Schulz bout. We agreed that I would pay one-half of the money before the bout, and one-half of the money after the bout. That would allow Foreman to fight an unrated boxer without losing his IBF heavyweight title.

During that December 1994 meeting, Lee Sr informed me that he would want four times as much (i.e. $800,000) for the IBF to sanction a fight between Foreman and former heavyweight champion Mike Tyson.

I later discussd with Stan Hoffman how I could pay Lee. Hoffman informed me that he knew a promoter in Europe, Peter Blaumert, who might be able (to) cash the checks. Hoffman later told me to draft the check directly to Blaumert.

In January 1995, I gave Hoffman a check for $50,000, made payable to Blaumert, based on the agreement that Hoffman would cash the check in Europe and deliver the proceeds to Robert Lee Sr. I later learned from Hoffman that he had delivered the proceeds of the check to Robert W. Lee Sr.

In or around April, 1995, I gave another check, also for $50,000. I made the check payable to Blaumert, as well. I later learned from Hoffman that the proceeds of the check were delivered to Robert W. Lee Sr.

I later learned that another IBF official had demanded $250,000 directly from Foreman for the IBF to sanction the Foreman – Schulz bout. As a result of learning that Foreman had paid $250,000, for the IBF to sanction the Schulz – Foreman bout, I paid Lee only $100,000. I later called Hoffman and told him to tell Lee that I refused to pay any more money. As a result of the agreement reached in December 1994, and the payments I made pursuant to that agreement, the IBF sanctioned the Foreman – Schulz bout and allowed Foreman to retain the IBF heavyweight championship.

Arum should have been kicked out of boxing after admitting to these felonies but instead of going to jail, he became a half-hearted witness against Lee. He didn't even lose his license to practice law.

In May of 2000, California attorney general Earl Plowman hinted that he might want Arum out of the promotion between Oscar De La Hoya and Shane Mosely. "If Bob Arum of Top Rank is the dirty does of this deal, then maybe Bob Arum would have to be out of the corporation before the fight could proceed. A lot of people could be hurt by this, Staples Center and a lot of others, I am a boxing fan, I do not want to see Oscar de La Hoya and Shane Mosely hurt by this."

Arum blustered back, "What the hell is this? I don't think California has any jurisdiction to look into this."

Arum, trying to play the victim, claims he wasn't indicted of anything, though he admitted breaking laws in his federal declaration. According to

Plowman, an attorney, and the chief law enforcement officer of the state, the California commisssion clearly had jurisdiction to investigate the promoters of a fight held within its border. Plowman cited Rule 391, which gave the state the power to discipline anyone that engaged activities that were "detrimental to the best interest of boxing."

Since Cedric Kushner promoted Mosely, and also sang for his supper and admitted paying off Lee, there shouldn't have been any fight – with these two corrupt promoters involved. But the California commission is gutless. Arum got just a piddling $2,500 fine, and the multi-million dollar bout went on.

Arum and Kushner were fined heavily in Nevada, and banned entirely in New Jersey. By then, Arum was calling boxing a "dying sport." If it is, who helped kill it?

"A lot of the troubles of the sport rest squarely on the shoulders of Bob Arum and others, who made millions, yet the good of the sport never crossed their mind," said fellow Harvard alum Lou DiBella, who dealt with Arum regularly at HBO. "He has never given anything back. Nothing. He has failed the sport of boxing, did nothing for its integrity. Remember, this is a man who already admitted in a court of law in New Jersey that he lied, cheated, and bribed people."

That's a helluva requiem for a Talmudic Scholar.

But Arum is a man with remarkable luck. After Perenchio abandoned boxing again, to concentrate on his new Hispanic television network, De La Hoya came back to Arum, for a much fairer contract. On 12 August 2002 Arum was riding in a small jet to Big Bear, California, to visit De la Hoya's training camp for his fight with Fernando Vargas, when the Cessna Citatione overshot the mountain runway, then crash-landed in a dry pond as its wings caught fire.

"The cabin filled up with smoke, and the co-pilot opened the door. By the time I got out, there was a wall of fire surrounding the door. It was amazing my clothing didn't catch fire," said Arum.

The plane was a charred wreck, just like the fight game.

CHAPTER TWELVE

The Humble Servant of Boxing

"I AM JUST a humble servant of boxing," says Jose Sulaiman Chagnon. While the bronzed, ruddy, seventyish president of the World Boxing Council manages to say that with a straight face, the record shows that this arrogant little man has done more to destroy the credibility of boxing than just about anyone else, with the exception of Carbo, Palermo and Don King. "He is clearly partners with King on fighters," testified Bob Arum to a federal probe called "Corruption in Professional Boxing" in June 1992. "This is King's own organization. There is no difference between Don King and Jose Sulaiman."

In hearings before the Permanent Subcommittee on Investigations in 1992, financial records provided by the WBC showed that in 1991, Don King Productions Inc. paid $535,000 in sanction fees to the WBC. That was nearly half of the WBC's total *reported* revenue of $1,176,000. Joseph Maffia, King's comptroller, swore in another deposition that King routinely paid the WBC *more* than the mandated sanction fees.

Why? That's a question the Internal Revenue Service should have been asking after the WBC was somehow declared a non-profit, tax-exempt corporation in 1982. There should have been a criminal probe. But while columnists such as the *New York Post's* Wally Matthews howled for a RICO (Racketeer Influenced Corrupt Organization) prosecution of King, Mary Jo White, the federal prosecutor in Manhattan, said, "I'm not going to try and clean up professional boxing."

Though the WBC has the facade of democracy, Sulaiman is dictator for life. Two decades after his ascension, with millions of dollars squandered, fighters don't even have pensions. One-time Puerto Rican whizkid Wilfredo Benitez won the world junior welterweight championship at just seventeen. Today, he's badly brain-damaged, is cared for by his mother and gets by on a $400 monthly stipend from the Puerto Rican government.

Former WBC middleweight champ Gerald McClellan ended up blind, brain-damaged and lost most of his hearing after his brutal fight with Nigel Benn in 1995. Emmanuel Steward once called McClellan "the best fighter I ever trained" but he is now trapped in a solitary world where there are no more cheers. He just sits and cries.

Yet there are WBC conventions held all over the world, at four-star hotels, with first-class air travel and all expenses paid, plus credit cards, for Jose's most loyal minions. There are also attorneys and publicity men, and a long list of vice presidents and board members for life. No wonder Randy Gordon, then chairman of the New York State Athletic Commission, could not get an answer from Sulaiman when he kept asking, "Where's all the money going?"

Though the WBC is tax-exempt, try getting a copy of its IRS forms. In 1989, the WBC's "total revenue," according to what it submitted to the IRS, was $1,823,646, with $946,446 in "net assets or fund balances at the end of the year."

One question on the form asks, "Did you engage in any activity not previously reported to the Internal Revenue Service?"

"No," was the WBC's answer. That would've brought some cynical laughs from boxing insiders.

"Did you receive donated services or the use of materials, equipment, or facilities at no charge or at a substantially less than fair rental value?"

"No," was the WBC's reply, sworn to under oath. So what were the plane trips and hotel rooms promoters are forced to pay for to have WBC officials work their fights?

Though the WBC has been in business since 1963, and still hasn't come up with a pension plan, in 1989 it wrote off $127,304 in "bad debts," spent $76,573 on "bulletins" and $140,635 on "office expenses" – when secretaries and rent come incredibly cheap in Mexico City. There was another $122,449 for "public relations" but just $27,150 for "boxers' life insurance" and a piddling $9,281 for "boxers' medical expenses." There was $203,538 for "legal fees," which comes as no surprise considering how Sulaiman ran the organization, and another $280,027 for "conferences, conventions and meetings."

In 1990, the WBC had a lean year. The "total revenue" was only $1,178,558, yet they had a "net assets or fund balance" at the end of the year of $538,494. Despite a vast decrease in revenue, the Humble Servant of Boxing spent a whopping $180,438 on "general office expenses," was which $40,000 more than the year before. Another $142,642 went for "public relations," $69,982 was for "trophies or belts," while $62,528 went on "bad debts." Contrast all this with "life insurance for boxers": just $35,000.

Naturally, the WBC had more bashes: there was $234,311 for "conferences" and a simply unbelievable $100,054 from "printing and publications." There was $116,952 for "legal fees," and $129,678 for "salaries and wages," though the WBC only had Sulaiman, one full-time aide, and a secretary. There was also another $21,165 in "office supplies." How an organization this small can have $142,642 in "general office expenses," then another $21,165 in "office supplies," makes one wonder who's working there: Imelda Marcos?

By 1992, the treasurer had quit, but in 1991, the WBC's "the total revenue" was $1,176,016. "Total expenses" were a mind-boggling $1,625,267. The WBC had carried $449,251 in "net assets or fund balances" at the beginning of the year, but though this is incredibly hard to believe, somehow the WBC lost money, nearly half a million dollars, and had just $89,243 in "net assets or fund balances at end of year."

Coming up to date, in 1999, the WBC had a terrific year. It took in $3,747,816. It had total expenses of $2,761,336. It made $986, 480, though Sulaiman spent money like a drunken sailor. This time management fees were $570,403. There was just $35,500 spent on boxers' life insurance, and $3,252 spent on the videotape library.

In 2000, the WBC had total revenue of $1,919,157. It's total expenses were $2,927,712. It lost over $1 millon! The annual convention was $533,123. Public relations was $100,345, which was more than the cost of life insurance for boxers ($66,856) and the video library ($6,430) combined. There was also a $2,478 for the national lottery. That's really helping the fight game.

In 2001, the WBC also lost money, though nobody in boxing understands how. The WBC's total revenue was $2,226,223. Expenses were $2,295,472. It lost $69,249. If you managed a McDonald's restaurant this way, you'd get fired, but the WBC spent $288,992 on "compensation for officers, directors, etc." There was $179,014 in legal fees, $71,270 for the telephone, a whopping $166,116 for travel, $291,300 for the annual convention, and a mind-boggling $446,337 in "management fees." The management fees gobbled up a third of the WBC's expenses. There was also $78,454 on public relations. Just $14,642 was spent on life insurance for boxers.

Though the WBC is based in Mexico City, for IRS purposes its mailing address was Miami, Florida. In all years available, the IRS requested: "Describe what was achieved in carrying out your exempt purposes. Fully describe the services provided; the number of persons benefitted ... " Every year it was blank.

***

One boxing insider, who has served as a right-hand man for one of the major American promoters says, "Sulaiman is a very proud man, but very arrogant. I've seen him strip off his shirt at weigh-ins and want to fight if he didn't get his way."

Former referee, Mills Lane, an ex-Nevada district court judge, agrees that "Sulaiman is not used to being told, 'no.'"

With 156 member countries, the WBC is the strongest boxing authority in the world, but critics have long claimed that its ratings make no sense. On a whim, according to British boxing expert Eric Armit, who served on the ratings committee, Sulaiman would simply come in and change things.

On 1 April 1993, the former underboss of the Gambino crime family in New York City, Sammy "The Bull" Gravano – who turned stoolie and got just twenty years for his participation in the murders of nineteen men, then ended up in the Witness Protection Program after doing five – testified in front of a Senate subcommittee that he tried to set up a fight with Francesco Damiani, who he alleged was handled by organized crime in Italy, and Renaldo Snipes, the fading New York heavyweight who had once come within seconds of winning the championship from Larry Holmes.

Gravano's plan was that Snipes would fight Damiani and lose. Damiani would ultimately face Mike Tyson, and then get annihilated for big money. Snipes wasn't told that he'd have to take a dive. The late Mark Ettes, billionaire Donald Trump's main man in Atlantic City, liked the possibility of Damiani-Snipes, but first the undefeated Italian had to beat Ray Mercer, while Ettes insisted Snipes had to get a world rating.

"Joe Watts, who is an associate in our family, told me that he had someone in Las Vegas who could help us get a ranking for Snipes," testified Gravano, whose cozy government deal could have been scuttled had he lied under oath. "Watts arranged a meeting for me with Joey Curtis, a boxing referee in Las Vegas. Joey Curtis had once visited our club, the Ravenite Social Club in New York City.

"So I went to Las Vegas with two of my friends and our wives. After we had dinner with Curtis, I took him aside and asked him if he could get Snipes moved up in the ratings. Curtis said he could move Snipes up in the rankings of the World Boxing Council, which was based in Mexico. Curtis said that this would cost $10,000, but because it was a favor for John Gotti (Gravano's boss and the most high-profile mobster since Al Capone), he might be able to get it done for $5,000."

Bob Lee, the corrupt founder of the IBF, contended long before he was convicted that he formed the IBF because a WBC rating cost five grand, then there'd be another five once the fighter got there.

Richie Giachetti, the thuggish ex-trainer of Larry Holmes, who reportedly had ties to organized crime in Cleveland, said, after attending one of the WBC's annual bashes, "The world is full of people who will shove an umbrella up your ass, but some of the people here will shove it up, then open it just for fun." Before he died, James Dusgate, an iconoclastic boxing journalist, covered the 1989 WBC convention in New York City, for *The Ring* and reported, "Money did most of the talking."

Sulaiman, like many third world tyrants, is big on pomp and circumstance and has a fetish for awards ceremonies honoring himself. Before the 1989 confab, there was actually a special ceremony at the United Nations honoring Sulaiman "for his valuable contributions as a sports person for the elimination of aparthied." While Sulaiman refused to rate South African fighters, and threatened other pugs with expulsion from his ratings if they had anything to do with the racist regime, his chief patron, Don King, did business with South Africa, and Jose said nothing.

Every year the WBC has a Medical Congress and various other workshops in the midst of their wining and dining. Dusgate, who knew boxing, "found most of the sessions very boring, rigidly controlled and having not even the slighest element of controversy of any kind." He did find that "there was simply oodles of glorious praise ladled out" for Sulaiman, who nodded, pursed his lips, and expansively beamed, like he was Juan Peron.

Unable to stand any more, Dusgate cornered him and asked, "Why do you think that the delegates have only good things to say about you?"

"It's because I live for boxers, to fight for them, so they are not used as objects as they have been in the past," said Sulaiman shamelessly, as a soft, reflective smile played across his heavily-furrowed face.

The first Medical Congress had taken place during a convention on the idyllic Caribbean island of Aruba in 1997. Two Welsh doctors attended as delegates from the British Boxing Board of Control. They had been behind the implementation of a scheme in Wales whereby a qualified anaesthetist – not just a doctor – had to be on hand at every professional boxing show, to act quickly in the event of coma or brain bleeding. So pleased were they with the sucesss of their scheme that anaesthetist Peter Fitzgerald addressed the 200 delegates and advocated it be adopted worldwide. His speech concluded:

> We believe the Welsh Area protocol for the ringside management of the
> acutely head-injued boxer provides for a cost-effective and logistically simple
> set of guidelines, allowing for immediate intervention by doctors who are
> skilled in controlled intubation and the management of raised intra-cranial
> pressure. We would ask the WBC to accept it as a mandatory safety require-
> ment that anaesthetists should be present ringside worldwide.

Fitzgerald's speech was met with stony silence, followed by as series of increasingly hostile questions from the floor. His life-saving recommendations were rejected.

★ ★ ★

On 11 December 1982, a game Bobby Chacon got off the canvas twice to defeat Mexico's Raphael "Bazooka" Limon over fifteen hard rounds in defence of his WBC super-featherweight title. Though Chacon, at thirty-one, was at least five years over the hill, he signed to defend against the WBC's top-rated challenger Cornelius Boza Edwards, who had stopped him in thirteen rounds a year and a half earlier.

Champions routinely duck top contenders, especially if they have already been stopped by them, but Chacon would fight King Kong. Suddenly, however, Jose Sulaiman stepped in and ordered him instead to face Hector "Macho" Camacho, who wasn't the top contender – but was controlled by Don King.

"I don't mind fighting Camacho," said Chacon, "but King is so cheap." He called Sulaiman in Mexico City to protest, but Sulaiman, who "lives for fighters," ordered Chacon to pass up a $400,000 offer to fight Boza Edwards and take just $150,000 to fight Camacho for King.

Chacon refused. King took him to court, but a Nevada judge ruled that King's promotional options weren't legal in Nevada, where the Camacho fight would take place. Still, with Sulaiman's assent, King tried to get a court order to stop the Chacon-Boza Edwards fight. He failed. In May 1983, Chacon beat Boza Edwards in a breathtaking contest. It should have been for the WBC title, but Sulaiman stripped him of the belt – for fighting the number one contender. Without King.

That was really the end for Bobby Chacon. He continued to fight on, but today, the handsome, curly-haired kid once dubbed "Schoolboy" because he had two years of college, is so punch drunk, he has to have written directions so he can find his way home. His speech is slow, he gets $500 a month for disability, and supplements his meagre allotment by scavenging LA's streets for discarded soft drink cans. On a good day, he might make ten dollars.

Chacon's first wife, Val, committed suicide. A son, Chico, was murdered in a gang war. The only friend Bobby had left was his chatty parrot, Pepito, who he'd had for twenty years. Then, one day, Pepito got stolen, just like his championship.

★ ★ ★

In one of the great upsets, a seven-fight novice named Leon Spinks shocked the world by thumping Muhammad Ali to win the heavyweight championship on 15 February 1978. "Ali's the greatest, but I'm the latest," bellowed Spinks, flashing his vampire smile. But Don King was worried. He had lost

Ali to Bob Arum after trying to steal Ali from his manager, Herbert Muhammad. Under boxing's feudal line of succession, Arum now had Spinks, for at least three defences. And Leon was twenty-four and might have a long future ahead of him.

So on March 29, Ken Norton was unilaterally proclaimed WBC heavyweight champion by Jose Sulaiman. Never mind that Norton hadn't won a title bout; Don King knew that if Arum controlled the heavyweight championship, it would be very hard for him to get back to the top of the heap. Though Sulaiman had no legal right to do so, and the heavyweight championship was sport's most important prize, he stripped Spinks of the WBC title and helped turn it into just another cheap trinket. He used the flimsy premise that Spinks had promised Ali a rematch and wouldn't immediately face Norton, the WBC's top contender (and controlled by King).

Ali had already beaten Norton two out of three times. The world didn't care about Spinks-Norton, but hungered for an Ali-Spinks rematch. As Spinks's title was in the process of being heisted, British promoter Mickey Duff told delegates at the WBC Madrid convention, "Boxing owes Ali," and he was adamantly against it. But the issue wasn't really Ali: it was Don King.

On 5 November 1977, the muscular California heavyweight with the funny, chin-low advancing style, defeated stylish Jimmy Young. Norton would lose his claim on the bogus championship in his next contest, against Larry Holmes, in June 1978. It was one of the great heavyweight fights and Holmes became a superb fighter. He would make eighteen defenses of the WBC title over the next six years, until he too, had to get away from King.

Holmes later claimed that King had robbed him of millions. According to Holmes, with Sulaiman looking the other way, promoter King grabbed a quarter of his purse as an undercover manager, while Giachetti got one-eighth as his trainer and Charles Spaziani got one-eighth as his lawyer, though it's hard to see what he did. Though the Nevada and New Jersey state athletic commissions were supposed to be protecting Holmes's purses, the embittered ex-heavyweight champ, who is still fighting in his fifties, swears he got just $150,000 of the contracted $500,000 he signed for, for his epic war with Norton.

Holmes also contends he got just $50,000 of the $200,000 he was contracted for after his March 1978 WBC eliminator with the dreaded Earnie Shavers. King would promise, "You'll do better next time," but the Don finally snapped, "God damn, Larry, you're lucky you're still not washing cars."

In October 1980, Holmes battered the sad remnants of Muhammad Ali, and cried after doing so. Jose Torres claims that Ali was on the experimental Parkinsons drug El Dopa, and the Mayo Clinic had a confidential report that strongly suggested Ali not go in the ring. Ali had to sue King, claiming

King had short-changed him by a $1 million in one of the most tragic sports events in history. Ali was on his way to the slurred, palsied wreck that he is today. Holmes says King cheated him of $2 million.

In June 1981, Holmes destroyed Leon Spinks (who had lost his rematch with Ali) in three rounds. Today, after earning $7 million in the ring, Spinks is lucky to get part-time work moving furniture. Holmes claims he also took it on the chin again from King, for another $250,000.

On 11 June 1982, Holmes won an ugly, race-baiting grudge match with Gerry Cooney, the latest Great White Hope. Though civil rights leader Jesse Jackson tried to knock down Cooney's purse on behalf of King, King was forced to agree that Cooney, as the most heavily-hyped challenger in years, had to get purse parity with champion Holmes. According to insiders who saw the records, Cooney, represented by astute managers Mike Jones and Dennis Rappaport, actually got $3 million more when all the closed-circuit revenue was tallied. Holmes later charged, "Gerry got his full share, but I didn't get mine. I had to sue Don over the accounting and auditing of the Cooney fight." Incredibly, Holmes also claimed, "I never saw a contract."

In November 1982, Holmes handed out a brutal beating to Randy "Tex" Cobb, a wise-cracking punching bag. Holmes contended that King slashed his purse from $2.1 to $1.6 million, then gouged him another $200,000 after the woefully one-sided fight. Cobb also swears his purse was cut by $200,000. A mysterious $200,000 was documentably paid to Cobb's manager, Joe Gramby, for "consultant fees" just days before.

In 1983, Holmes finally broke with the shock-haired ex-convict, and said bitterly, "I'm through being a whore for Don King."

What did Jose Sulaiman do? He put so much pressure on Holmes, Larry finally abdicated his hard-won WBC title, jumping to Bob Lee's new International Boxing Federation.

★ ★ ★

The WBC has no inalienable right to do business in the States. Any corporation that does business has to abide by American law. Yet the WBC's "rule book" must have been written in invisible ink. For two decades, Sulaiman performed countless sleights of hand that destroyed any pretence of fairness. Though great fighters like Mexico's Carlos Zarate and Wilfredo Gomez of Puerto Rico were comparatively small in the money sweepstakes, Sulaiman would let them go a year without making a "mandatory" defence. Once again, they were in bondage to Don King.

In August 1992, Sulaiman was hauled before the Permanent Subcommitte on Investigations that was probing Corruption in Professional Boxing. He was asked by Maine senator William Cohen: "Back in 1975, the WBC ordered

Luis Estobar to fight Raphael Lovera for the then vacant light-flyweight title, and it listed Lovera's record as twenty wins, one loss and one tie. Lovera then was knocked out … which didn't surprise a lot of people because, in fact, it was his first professional fight. Could you explain how it happened?

"I do not relate the fight, Mr Senator. Can you repeat the names, please?"

"Yes. It was Raphael Lovera and Luis Estobar," said Cohen, who had served as a young congressman on the Watergate impeachment committee that ousted President Richard Nixon.

"I do not recall those names in the WBC, Mr Senator, but I would like to check that."

Sulaiman knew exactly who Cohen was speaking about, though Cohen mistakenly called Luis Estaba, *Estobar*. Estaba had fourteen WBC light-flyweight title fights and was well-known to the WBC boss.

Pinning down Sulaiman is like trying to hit Willie Pep. When a question is too embarrassing to answer, he often lies, or his memory fails. Then he resorts to his old stand-by: politely answering in English, with brutally mispronounced words and syntax. Nobody can tell what the hell he's talking about. It's Jose's version of the dumb Mexican routine. It is so bad, you almost expect Sulaiman, who is actually half Lebanese, to amble into Washington on a *burro*. When Sulaiman is really pressed, and has no way out, he'll finally admit to "mistakes," and humbly beg forgiveness. But first, one has to wade through a swamp of lies, half-truths, obfuscations and noble-sounding cliches.

Cohen pressed on. "All right. Mister Arum, whose name has been taken in vain here this morning, has said that up until mid-1978 he was able to get you to rate his boxers who were not rated or upgrade his boxers who were rated to get them title bouts, but that in mid-1978, you stopped working for Arum and started doing the same thing for Don King. The question is, why did you switch and start dealing with Don King as opposed to Arum?"

"We do not switch," said Sulaiman, now sounding like someone who has a terrible cross to bear, but will nobly bear it. "We do not deal. Why Mister Arum has said those things, sometimes I do not understand it because he has done, I think, most of his biggest fights of his life with the WBC. The Thomas Hearns and Hagler, Hagler-Leonard, Leonard-Duran, those are Bob Arum's, but I think that I just cannot explain. I don't know. I'm sorry."

Of course, Sulaiman knew, but didn't say, that high-grossing fighters in the lighter weights like Leonard and Duran are financial aberrations. Pay-per-view figures prove that the big money is in the heavyweights. Though Sulaiman feigned ignorance of King's monopoly, why is it a gangster like Sammy Gravano knew who controlled boxing, yet he didn't?

With better research, Senate probers might have mentioned Julio Cesar Chavez, who wanted to fight Roger Mayweather without King. Sulaiman refused to bless the match until Chavez agreed King could be the promoter. It wouldn't have gone on in any other sport, but fighters are just voiceless minorities, and the public doesn't care, as long as it has bread and circuses.

* * *

Option contracts are the ball and chain that keeps fighters in servitude, and prevents them from making the best deal for themselves. Though options aren't legal in some states, like Nevada, boxing people fear being blackballed, and fighters simply lack the resources to sue. Sulaiman however, had the audacity to go before Senator John McCain's Senate Commerce Committee in July 1998 with a written distillation of the WBC rulebook, which ludicrously contended, "The evidence described, clearly indicates that the WBC does not support options."

The great Alexis Arguello, who won "world" titles at featherweight, junior-lightweight and lightweight, before being stopped twice by Aaron Pryor in bids for the WBA ten-stone crown, fought fourteen times under the WBC's banner. He claims that Sulaiman went out of his way not only to enforce King's options, but to make sure he couldn't unshackle himself from the ball and chain once the previous contract was fullfilled.

Arguello faced "Bazooka" Limon in Madison Square Garden in July 1979. "Right before the fight," he says, "they [King and Sulaiman] told me [if I want to fight] I have to sign the option. I look at the president of the WBC," Arguello said, emitting a raspy, disbelieving laugh, [and I said], "'Hey Sulaiman, you're supposed to be on my side. You my president."

"Sign the option," said Sulaiman gruffly.

Before the fight, King "offered me $180,000 in New York for 'Bazooka' Limon," says Arguello. "He gave me $95,000. [After the match] Sulaiman says that Don King lost money on the promotion, I said, 'I don't care.'" Arguello was forced to sign himself back into bondage – then got just half of what he'd been contracted for, he claims. He knows first-hand about Sulaiman and King, but said cynically in 1993, "There's nothing you can do about it."

Saoul Mamby was an artful ten-stone stylist who hailed from the notorious Bronx in New York. A black Jew, Mamby had a light-coppery complexion and delicate, almost pretty, features that he protected well with a deft left hand and a nimble pair of legs. Mamby personified the "sweet science" but it took him eight long years to get a championship fight. He was too good for his own good, and clever boxers don't sell tickets.

In October 1977, Mamby finally got his title shot, but had little hope of getting the decision over local hero Saensak Muangsurin in Thailand. The polite, softly-spoken globetrotter never got the protection he needed because he always had to fight in the other guy's backyard. He was so good that he could still win on the road without a knockout punch, but despite appearances in exotic locales like Curacao, San Juan, Kingston and Paris, his passport was getting a lot more action that his bank book. Then one day, Don King called.

King got Mamby a fight in February 1980, against Kim-Sang Hyun in Seoul, South Korea, for the WBC super-lightweight championship. There was a catch – he was forced to take on Carl King, Don's stepson, as his "manager." Carl didn't even bother making the trip to South Korea to see Mamby win in round fourteen. Not only was Carl in for at least a third of his purse, and perhaps half, Don King also took a fifth.

Mamby, an intelligent man, made four defences of the WBC crown, all of which were promoted by King. He won on the road against Maurice "Termite" Watkins in Houston and Obisia Nwankpa in Nigeria, but claims that, like so many others, he didn't get what the contract called for. According to Mamby, a gentleman outside the ring, Carl or Don King actually "managed" three of his opponents. Where the hell was Sulaiman, and his rulebook?

On 7 July 1980, Mamby scored his greatest win, halting Esteban DeJesus, who had been the first man to defeat Roberto Duran (and who would ultimately die of AIDS). Mamby discovered that DeJesus was officially "managed" by Connie Harper, Don King's girlfriend, who later went to prison in the 1980s after she and Don were indicted on twenty-three counts of income tax evasion.

When Mamby defeated Thomas Americo in Jakarta, Indonesia, he says he was supposed to get $350,000 for the fight. He got $135,000. He signed for $300,000 to face Nwankpa, but Saoul swears he got just $118,000. After all these tough matches, he finally lost to Irish Leroy Haley in June 1982 in Vegas. After the split-decison was announced, Carl King began to jump up and down in jubilation. Mamby suddenly realized that Carl "managed" Haley too. Despite all this happening in a state-controlled sport, Nevada did nothing about King's outrageous conflict of interest, which should have cost him his promoter's license, and neither did the Humble Servant of Boxing.

Still, Sulaiman cited the WBC rulebook, and rule 1.3, to Senator John McCain:

> No conflict of interest … no person is permited to act concurrently both as manager of and as promoter of a WBC championship contest involving the same boxer. To avoid any potential for a conflict of interest, and subject to rule

1.9, no contest will be certified by the WBC if any person acts in such a dual capacity.

By 1992, "Sweet" Saoul Mamby was forty-five and fighting from memory. He should have been set for life years earlier, but was heavily in debt to the IRS and not only had to risk his life every time he stepped into the ring, the former world champion had one of the most dangerous day jobs in the world: he drove a cab on New York's violent streets. Ten years later, at fifty-five, he was still trying to get fights.

* * *

Next to purse money, ratings are the most important thing in a fighter's career. Ratings are the path to big money, and Sulaiman, in his written presentation to McCain's committee, actually claimed, "We are sure that the ratings of the WBC are the standard in the business, as well as being the most respected in the world."

Mob killer Sammy Gravano had already vouched for the sanctity of the WBC's ratings, and virtually every boxing writer in the world just sneers. Boxer Hasim Rahman claimed before he knocked out Lennox Lewis, then was flattened in the return, that Don King had told him, "*I* make the ratings, and you'll never get a big fight if you don't sign with me."

While Sulaiman contends, "The amount of work that we do on ratings every month is overwhelming," for more than twenty years, the WBC's ratings looked like like they were compiled by the Make A Wish Foundation and tallied by King. Britain's Eric Armit, probably the most knowledgeable expert in the world, finally quit the ratings committee because Sulaiman "would come in on a moment's notice and put fighters in where they had no business at all." Armit would try to protest, "but Jose gets very angry and has tantrums when he can't get his way."

In 1992, Erik Podolak, a terribly limited white club fighter, rocketed up to number eleven in the ranks because one of Don King's chief serfs, Julio Cesar Chavez, needed an easy defence of his WBC super-lightweight title. The Nevada commission, however, refused to sanction that fight, despite the power of King. Shortly thereafter, Podolak was seriously injured in another bout and had to retire.

Gabe Ruelas was also looking for a fast payday. Though Ruelas was promoted by the Goosen clan, not King, the WBC obligingly served up Jimmy Garcia, a slow, methodical Colombian. Ruelas viciously pounded away with both hands, and by the sixth round HBO's Larry Merchant was sternly telling listeners, "This fight should be stopped."

As Garcia slumped on his stool, his brother pulled on his earlobes to revive him. Over in the other corner, Joe Goosen, Ruelas's manager/trainer, was bellowing in his face, "Hit the sonofabitch! I want you to go out there and knock this motherfucker out!"

Garcia had one fair round before the one-sided fight was finally halted by referee Mitch Halpern. Garcia seemed all right as he stood in his corner, but slowly collapsed. The little brown man never got up again. Garcia, aged twenty-three, was rushed to the hospial, where he remained in a coma, Ruelas would go visit him. With tears in his eyes, he'd whisper, "Get up, Jimmy, get up." But Garcia finally died. Ruelas was so tormented by the tragedy that he gave a big chunk of his purse to Garcia's family, so they'd be taken care of. But when Ruleas visited Garcia's mother and begged for forgiveness, she looked at him coldly and said, "You killed my son."

Referee Halpern was obsessed with his role. He knew he'd stopped the fight far too late, though an autopsy contended that Garcia had probably suffered his brain trauma somewhere in the third round. Garcia's death barely made the Sport's Briefs but both Ruelas and Halpern suffered tremendous guilt. Halpern was a real prefectionist and a chronic depressive. Five years went by before his marriage collapsed. Only days after behaving strangely in a TV interview, Mitch Halpern put a pistol to his head and blew his brains out. His young daughter was in the house at the time.

Sulaiman tried to con Senator McCain into believing that the WBC had magnanimously given Garcia's family $100,000. The WBC didn't dig into its own pockets; the money came from a standard WBC insurance policy, which should have been a helluva lot more. The truth is, Garcia never should've been in the ring. He wouldn't have been, if the "non-profit" WBC hadn't been trying to grab another sanction fee.

How then did Jay Bell, a tanktown clubfighter, get kicked up to number fifteen so he was eligible to be annihilated by the tragic Gerald McClellan, then WBC middleweight king? The televised atrocity, in August 1993, ended in just thirty seconds, an all-time middleweight record.

* * *

In August 1995, Mike Tyson whacked out Peter McNeeley in less than a round in one of the biggest pay-per-view bonanzas in boxing history. Though Tyson had just come out of prison after being convicted of rape, McNeeley, whose record was a pumped up 32-1, wouldn't have made a good sparring partner. At best – the very best – McNeeley might have been a six-round fighter.

His opponents were so bad that Massachusetts boxing commissioner Wilbert "Skeeter" McClure, who'd won a gold medal in the 1960 Olympics, finally stopped approving the bums being brought in to fight him. McNeeley was forced to campaign in the Deep South, where they barely had commissions. McNeeley signed with Don King in July 1994. Miraculously he vaulted into the WBC's ratings.

Prior to Tyson, McNeeley, who was white and therefore marketable, had faced a collection of ambulatory punchbags who between them had lost 301 times in 424 fights. They had been stopped a whopping 152 times. Building up fighters is nothing new, but this was incredible: McNeeley was simply one of the worst pugs ever to compile a record like this. *Boxing News* repeatedly blasted McNeeley's opponents.

Senor Sulaiman saw the reports in *Boxing News* but that didn't stop him from putting the hapless McNeeley into the WBC ratings, once he had agreed to be the human sacrifice for King. Eric Armit, then on the WBC's ratings committee, wrote a devastating piece that statistically summed up McNeeley's opponents in *Boxing News*. How did Sulaiman respond when reporters in Las Vegas suddenly started questioning the clubfighter's credentials?

"Well, Joe Louis had his 'Bum of the Month Club' didn't he?"

As for Armit, his days with the WBC were numbered. Nobody on the ratings committee would take his calls and he finally resigned about a year later. But poor McNeeley; he thought he could fight.

McNeeley was brave and charged out like a wounded rhino against "Iron" Mike, only to be rescued in the first. With Tyson set to destroy him, his manager jumped into the ring and waved off a fight that never should have happened.

Though McNeeley's purse was supposedly $750,000, what money he did clear – perhaps $200,000 – quickly went up his nose. "It was pretty blatant. People would see me in bars, sniffing cocaine in the open, and word travelled fast: he's a drunk, a cokehead. It hurt because I'd hear it and known it was true," admitted McNeeley, who speaks with a thick tongue but is highly intelligent and sensitive, and who was crucified by the national media.

In Boston, athletes are deities. McNeeley, who had wanted to be a hero, got so out of control that he busted one groupie in the face who claimed she was pregnant by him. He slashed another kid with a broken beer bottle at the Roxy nightclub, and ended up on probation. When McNeeley went to parties, toughs took swings at him. The lumbering kid who had belted out a motley collection of stiffs at the Whitman Armory ended up blowing all his money and sleeping in crackhouses. Manager Vinnie Vecchione, who cared about Peter in a strange sort of way, would get in his car and look for him, but the signs in Medfield, Massachusetts, that once said, "Good Luck, Peter. KO Tyson!" had long since vanished. McNeeley became an embarrassment, a tragedy, a college-educated kid who should have gone on to become a white-collar professional but instead tried to follow his father Tom into the fight game. He became an international joke and was in and out of drug rehab.

Five years after being served up to Tyson, he proudly celebrated the Christmas of 2000 by being clean and sober. He had been on the wagon four months. But on New Year's Eve, the old demons reappeared. He began guzzling champagne, "then I got popped for drunk driving." Peter had been roommates with actor/comedian Chris Farley at the Betty Ford Center. Not even Farley's fatal overdose could make him quit.

Finally, he called his father, Tom, who had been on the canvas twelve times when he fought Floyd Patterson in 1961 for the heavyweight championship. Alcohol had taken hold of him, too. Peter McNeeley returned to the gym. He still gets up and tells his story at the Alcoholics Anonymous and Narcotics Anonymous meetings he attends daily. "I find standing up and admitting I'm powerless actually gives me strength. So does letting go of my resentments," he told in the *Boston Herald*.

★ ★ ★

On 11 February 1990, Mike Tyson fought Buster Douglas in Tokyo. Though King had stolen Tyson from Bill Cayton, the fight film mogul who had been financially responsible for the troubled Brooklyn powerhouse and had helped spring him from a reformatory as a young teen, Cayton still had some "paper" on Mike, but no control. "I don't like the Douglas fight," Cayton kept saying to his long-time aide, Steve Lott. "Douglas is a boxer. Tyson has trouble with guys who are quick and who can jab."

Lott had watched over Tyson for two years when the fighter lived in his Manhattan apartment. Tyson fell asleep there after he had destroyed Trevor Berbick to win the WBC title in 1986, and Lott woke up in the middle of the night and put a blanket on him, incredulously thinking, *I've got the heavyweight champion of the world on my couch*.

Though a 42-1 underdog, Douglas repeatedly slammed his long, stiff jab into the much-shorter Tyson's face. By the eighth, everyone was astounded at the beating Iron Mike was getting. Suddenly, the battered Tyson lashed out with a vicious uppercut and Douglas crashed to the deck. As the huge crowd in the Tokyo Dome roared, an apopleptic Don King leaped out of his ringside seat and screamed at Jose Sulaiman, "Stop the fight! Stop the fuckin' fight!"

Douglas somehow wobbled up, survived, and finally resumed his beating. King, who could see his meal ticket slipping away, berated Sulaiman, snarling, "What kind of goddamn referee are you givin' me?" Unfortunately for him, one who could count.

In the tenth round, Douglas unloaded a vicious right uppercut followed by a brutal barrage, and Iron Mike became Scrap-iron Mike. The sight of the beaten champion, dazed and stupefied, groping drunkenly on the deck to put in his mouthpiece, was one of the most brutally poignant moments in sports history. When Octavio Meyeran counted Tyson out, even Sugar Ray Leonard, doing color commentary, lost his composure and stammered, "Unbelievable."

Tyson's $100 million future was in ruins. King immediately announced they were protesting the decision. The media went crazy.

"We saw the result," screamed *Boxing Illustrated's* Bert Sugar in print, "and the result is a knockout by Douglas. They cannot take that away from Douglas nor the boxing public. Once it was alright to try and fix fights by fixing the judges (and let it be known, the WBA and WBC tried even that, placing two incompetent Japanese judges at ringside, who, after nine rounds, had a throughly-beaten Tyson ahead on one card by one point and even on the other – both of whom should committ hari-kari by falling on their scorecards and never be seen again), the WBA and WBC have now gone that small scam one better: they even attempt to fix the results of fights, and of history. The word 'crooks' is too good a word for them!"

Sulaiman and King demanded that Meyeran overturn the decision, ludicrously claiming that Douglas had benefitted from a long count when Tyson had floored him in the seventh. Meyeran, with his pride and integrity at stake, and the world watching, refused. According to an affidavit later made by Meyeran, King threatened that if he didn't uphold his protest, King wouldn't pay his hotel bill. Sulaiman was right there with him, though the WBC's laughable constitution "regards the decision of the referee and judges as final."

With King and Sulaiman's hijacking in plain view, it was fiercely resisted by the media. King suddenly feared a congressional investigation. Finally, the ex-con backed down, and pressed instead for a rematch. What did King have to worry about? To get the fight, Douglas had to give up *six* options.

Boxing's credibility hit an all-time low. Advertisers fled the sport, never to return. Sulaiman later lied to McCain's committee that the "WBC does not support options." Meyeran's lucrative career as a referee was finished. Six years later, deposed under oath in Chicago promoter Jose Venzor's lawsuit against King, Meyeran even testified that his life had been threatened, but he was afraid to say by whom.

★ ★ ★

On 21 February 1990, Don King and his flunky stepson Carl arrived at the towering Mirage Hotel in Las Vegas. King, who just ten days earlier had tried to steal the heavyweight championship of the world from Buster Douglas, was now making sure that Douglas knew who his promoter was. He swept into the room like a monarch in exile. Douglas's manager, John Johnson, was there.

"Tyson's got to have an immediate rematch," King said heatedly to Johnson, a big man, who'd once been an assistant football coach at Ohio State.

"Look, Don, that's not in our interests," Johnson said, trying to be polite. "We've got other plans. I talk to Steve Wynn [the multi-millionaire who owned the Mirage hotel and casino] and he's gonna give $50 million for two fights."

"What? What?" shrieked King. "After what I did for you, you mother-fuckers are gonna try and cut me out? No motherfucking way. I done give that boy a-yours a chance. Buster was a dog. A yellow-bellied quitter. He quit against Tony Tucker."

Johnson tried to get a word in, and at the same time be diplomatic, but King is an overpowering presence, and a street bully. He doesn't dicuss things, he waves his arms, looks skyward as if divinely inspired, and melo-dramatically cloaks his greed in everything from the oppresion of the Black Man, to American justice, with plenty of "motherfuckers" in between.

Finally, Johnson said, "Look, Don, we'll give you $3 million to step aside."

"Chump change," sneered King. "After what I put into Douglas."

"You didn't do a goddamn thing but try and steal his title."

"Hey man, I been in boxin' for twenty years."

"Yeah, you run that fat, fuckin' Sulaiman and the rest of those thieves who give out the cheap belts."

"I don't control Sulaiman," King protested, now trying to be diplomatic. "Hey man, that shit after the fight was just B.S. for the press. Man, don't you understand I was tryin' to generate interest in a rematch."

"Bullshit. You tried to steal the title after Buster kicked Tyson's ass. Well, now it's his turn to cash in. I don't care what you say, Buster's fighting Holyfield for $25 million."

"Jesus, man," said King, now sounding contrite. "Y'all don't have to be greedy. There's enough bread for everybody."

"What did you ever do for Buster, except try and rob him?" Johnson asked.

"That sorry ass went from being a $50,000 fighter, to making $1.3 million. That's what I did."

King was getting hot. The overweight fifty-eight-year-old had to gulp pills for high blood pressure but couldn't contain his verbal abuse. He began hissing at Johnson and J.D. McCauley, Buster's uncle and trainer, "You're both a couple of stupid motherfuckers. Then, playing to McCauley, who was black, King resorted to his most successful tactic: the old racial divide.

Finally, Johnson furiously said, "Look, if you're gonna harp on that shit again, just get the fuck out." Johnson stormed into another room to call Steve Wynn. King looked at McCauley and said with a feigned mixture of sympathy and contempt, "How long you gonna be the 'house nigga?'"

Steve Wynn was not a man to be kicked around, even by King. The handsome, graying casino mogul, who looked like a movie star, was so big that he was re-making Las Vegas. As King continued to berate the two men, Wynn majestically strutted in.

"Helluva place you got here," King said, looking at Wynn. "Don't get too attached to it. I'm fixin' to own the motherfucker."

Wynn, who wanted to get into boxing, and had the muscle to do so, wasn't the least bit intimidated. "You are a lying, thieving, no good cocksucker," he spat, turning red. "You and Arum. You're dinosaurs."

King angrily got up and left. If Douglas went with Wynn, King was finished.

Bob Arum eventually realized it, too. He had quietly helped Wynn "venue shop," anticipating his lawsuit against King. Suddenly, Arum realized, just like King, that if fighters could go straight to casinos to promote their fights, what was the point of having a middleman packager like him?

A couple of weeks later, Douglas sued King to break his contract. Remember, options weren't even legal in Nevada. Yet King counter-sued Douglas and Wynn to make sure Douglas fought for him. King descended on Douglas's home town of Columbus, Ohio, and, after ensconcing himself at the classy Raddison Hotel, he stormed the black media. "I'm gonna kick that white boy's [Johnson's] ass," he promised.

He threw a lavish party for Billy "Dynamite" Douglas, Buster's father. Billy Douglas had been a good middleweight in the late 1960s, and early '70s. He was managed by a young Bruce Trampler, who used to send in "unbiased" accounts of his fights to *Ring* magazine. Few wanted to fight Billy because he could take your head off. Since American TV had abandoned boxing at the time, he never got a title shot and never made much money. A bitter, demanding man, he was also jealous of Buster, who had won the heavyweight championship after Billy had walked out on him for quitting against Tony Tucker in a fight for the vacant IBF title.

King swept into the party and started bellowing "Dyno-mite" as he got close to Billy. Getting tight with the beaming father, King began to coo, "Buster is the fruit of your loins. You should be reaping the rewards." Billy Douglas had one of the worst boxing stables in the country, with his divers going down almost on cue, and was obviously interested in money. Now his own son had signed for $25 million and he wasn't in for a thin dime.

Buster Douglas was estranged from his volatile father. Buster's brother,

Artie, was supposed to have been the hope of the family and won the national Golden Gloves, but at seventeen he was murdered. Buster reluctantly put on the gloves. The unmotivated kid who couldn't live up to his old man suddenly obliterated every expectation by winning the heavyweight championship. Buster's beloved mother, Lula, died suddenly, just three weeks before he KO'd Tyson. Years later, Buster would still cry at the mention of her name.

King trashed Buster all over Columbus for not giving Tyson a rematch (with King controlling everything, natch), and shamelessly played the race card with the help of the black media. Though Douglas had pulled off one of the greatest upsets in sports history, he was portrayed like a Judas for doing so.

In March 1990, King bombed into Buster's press conference shouting, "Man your battle stations! It's all gonna happen again!"

"I won't do business with King again," John Johnson swore.

With reporters present, it was J.D. McCauley, who had once been a hapless clubfighter, who spoke for pugs everywhere. With King listening just a few feet away, McCauley told the *Columbus Journal,* "Don King is a dirty, sneaking, lowdown leech. I've been around King for five-and-a-half years now. I watched what this man did. He talks about the black fighters he's helped and it's bull. The fighters he's helped, I can name them, and they're digging ditches right now. Tim Witherspoon, David Bey, Dwight Braxton (Dwight Quawi). None of them have a quarter to their name on account of Don King.

"All these guys made money. Who's got the money? Where's the money at? Tell me about Don King and what's he's done for black fighters. He ain't done nothing. And he's not going to do it to my nephew. I'll die and go to hell first."

At the end of the press conference, King lost his cool in front of the media. He screamed at Johnson, "You're sick, man. Get help."

Slavemaster King did everything he could to keep his quasi-monopolistic grip on heavyweight boxing. And it wouldn't have been possible without Sulaiman. But Sulaiman was nobody in Columbus. Benjamin Hooks, though, was the director of the NAACP, the most prestigious black civil rights organization in the country. He came to Columbus, for a fee, and had a profound impact on black opinion, strongly intimating that white racism was behind Douglas's refusal to give Tyson a rematch.

Hooks had a moral obligation to look out for the best interests of *all* black men. Records show that King paid him $25,000 on 5 May 1990. Another $12,500 went to the NAACP, and $12,500 went to Hooks's wife Frances. It wouldn't be the last time a prominent civil rights leader helped out Don King.

★ ★ ★

On 2 July 1990, King's lawsuit for breach of contract, which had been fast-tracked in New York City, came to trial. Boxing's pre-eminent monopolist wanted $24–27 million from Wynn, charging that he tried to break a valid contract. Millionaire developer, casino owner, and media darling Donald Trump testified on behalf of King. He tailored his testimony, in hopes that King would bring more fights to his slot palaces in Atlantic City. But Alan Townsend, a former deputy mayor of New York, once said, "I wouldn't believe Donald Trump if he had his tongue notarized."

Bob Arum also took the stand – on behalf of the hated King. He fudged his testimony, but it was either that or become a dinosaur if Wynn and the casinos started promoting. The most pitiful figure to swear in was Sulaiman. Despite the fact that jurors saw the February post-fight videotape, on which he announced that he was suspending recognition of Douglas, Sulaiman all but pleaded to the jury, "In the bottom of my heart I did not withdraw recognition. My embarrassment to the people of the world was in not having the courage and intelligence to say it openly."

On July 18, Wynn flew to New York, and by the wee hours of the morning, a compromise was reached. Douglas got rid of King's shackles, and was allowed to fight for Wynn, for $24 million. King and Trump got $7 million from the Mirage for their rights, with "The Donald" getting $2.5 million and King taking the rest. King tried to hail this resounding defeat as a victory, but had to pay the $100,000 he had promised Douglas if he beat Tyson. There was nothing Buster could do about the twenty-five tickets for friends and family that King had stiffed him on.

While boxing insiders were frustrated that the public didn't get a real look at King's monopoly and put him out of business, Wynn was wise to force a settlement. "Look," he told Johnson. "Sometimes, a courtroom is the last place you find justice."

On 25 October 1990, the most miserable seven months of Buster Douglas's life ended when he got nailed by a hard right cross from Evander Holyfield and lay on the deck like a beached whale. Don King jubilantly strutted around ringside, with a malevolent smile on his face, cackling loudly. Finally, he bellowed at Johnson, "I told you the motherfucker's a dog."

Douglas was beaten before he entered the ring. He weighed a whopping 246 pounds, fifteen more than when he halted Tyson. He was so soft that he didn't look like he had trained. Douglas then went into seclusion for the next five years. He was depressed, and angry, but pacified himself with food. He hit 400 pounds, and grew so obese that friends didn't recognize him. Douglas finally lapsed into a diabetic coma, and nearly died. "The doctors couldn't believe he came out it," said his assistant trainer, John Russell. Six long years later, Buster fought again.

* * *

Despite the settlement, Don King was out in the cold. Main Events, run by the Duva family, now controlled the heavyweight divison and threatened his hold on boxing. But once again, just like in 1978, Sulaiman came to King's rescue. "Justice must be served. Mike Tyson must get the next shot at Holyfield," claimed Jose, though new champions are customarily given the right to make an easy first defence.

At the Holyfield–Douglas fight, King had handed out communiqués purporting to be from the WBA and IBF that supported Tyson's claim, but those organisations repudiated that position. They said Holyfield could defend against George Foreman, who was enjoying a remarkable re-emergence as boxing's hard-hitting fat man, at forty-two. Sulaiman, however, stood firm. Though the WBC's constitution allows a title-holder to make at least one optional defence, Sulaiman insisted Tyson was the "mandatory" challenger. Yet Holyfield had been passsed up twice when he was Tyson's mandatory challenger. This was Sulaiman's latest ruse so King could break up the heavyweight title again, just like he'd done in 1978, when Bob Arum had new champion Leon Spinks.

On 22 July 1992, Holyfield gave a taped deposition, under oath, for the United States Senate, Committee on Governmental Affairs, Permanent Subcommittee on Investigations. Holyfield apologized for not coming before the committee in person, but a scheduling conflict prevented it.

"I am very strongly in favour of the federal regulation of boxing," he said. "I am no newcomer in calling for federal regulation of boxing in that I publicly issued such a call shortly after I became the undisputed heavyweight champion of the world."

Holyfield was asked, "In your career as a professional boxer, have you ever had any difficulties with any of the sanctioning bodies that you just mentioned?"

"Yes, I have; WBC."

"Could you explain the first time you had any difficulty with the WBC."

"The first difficulty I ran into with the WBC was getting the opportunity to fight for the heavyweight championship of the world."

"How were they denying you the opportunity?"

"Well, they wanted Buster Douglas to fight Mike Tyson once again, and I was ranked number one, and they was planning on stripping Buster Douglas from the title if he fought me."

"Is it true that the number one ranked boxer would be the mandatory challenger?"

"It's supposed to be," said Holyfield.

"Could you explain what you mean by 'it's supposed to be?'"

"Well, a lot of times you can be ranked number one. I was ranked number one for a year and a half and then didn't get the opportunity because the WBC kept passing me by and would give Tyson and them permission to fight other people."

"Do you know why the WBC was passing you by?"

"Well, I think because of Don King."

"Would you explain that, please."

"Well, a lot of times when a promoter had the heavyweight champion of the world, different governing boodies tend to come in cahoots together to turn different favours for each other."

"Do you believe that the WBC and Don King are in cahoots together?"

"I would think so."

"Please explain the second time you were involved in litigation with the World Boxing Council."

"After beating Buster Douglas for the undisputed heavyweight championship of the world and, in my first title defense, I was going to make it against George Foreman, and Don King wanted me to make it against Mike Tyson, and so he got the WBC to strip me of my title. I had to go to court for it."

"Why did Don King want you to fight Mike Tyson rather than George Foreman?"

"Well, Don King wanted me to fight Mike Tyson because more money would come to him and, when more money comes to Don King, then more money go to the WBC."

"What was the result of their attempt to strip you of your title?"

"Well, we won in the courtroom, and I got an opportunity to go ahead and fight George Foreman."

"What was the third time that you had to go to court against the WBC?"

"The third time is the fight that, the fight that's coming up, against Riddick Bowe. They didn't really want me to fight Riddick Bowe. They wanted me to fight, what's the cat's name?"

"Would you be thinking of Razor Ruddock?"

"They wanted me to fight Razor Ruddock, and I chose to fight Bowe. And they chose to go to court and try to strip me of my title."

"Why in your opinion, did they want you to fight Razor Ruddock rather Riddick Bowe?"

"Razor Ruddock is now managed by Don King, and Don King is affiliated with the WBC. And so, when it is more money for Don King, it's more money for the WBC."

"Have you had any similar problems with any of the other sanctioning bodies?"

"No, I haven't."

"Could you explain for us what sanctioning fees are that you have mentioned several times in your testimony."

"Well, sanction fees are, I guess, based on the percentage of a fight, but they usually have a cap of $150,000. And my last defence, the WBA charged $150,000, the IBF charged $150,000 and the WBC, $290,000."

"Would you be referring to your recent title fight against Larry Holmes?"

"Yes."

"In Las Vegas, Nevada?"

"Yes."

"Why did the WBC charge $290,000 whereas the WBA and IBF charged $150,000?"

"I figured they changed their rules regardless. They don't live by the rules, and they do what they feel is right for themselves."

"What would happen to a boxer if he did not pay the sanctiong fee that was charged?"

"They would be forced to give up their title," said Holyfield.

★ ★ ★

In 1993, with Tyson in prison for raping beauty contestant Desiree Washington, King's empire was foundering. He had just one fighter who could generate big money: Mexican idol Julis Cesar Chavez. In September 1993, Chavez faced Pernell Whitaker before 65,000 people in the "Alamodome" at San Antonio, Texas.

Before the fight, the excitable Lou Duva, who handled Whitaker, charged that Josc Sulaiman had handpicked judges to protect Chavez. Duva had once called Sulaiman a "crook" on national television after Whitaker had been robbed against Mexico's Jose Luis Ramirez. He knew that the Humble Servant of Boxing was not only close to King but was also a good friend of Chavez. He was such a good friend, he allowed Chavez to sign blank contracts with King.

Under intense media scrutiny, Sulaiman finally admitted that he had recomended certain judges to Texas officials, but had absolutely no control over their scoring. Yet when Britain's Mickey Vann and Switzerland's Franz Marti scored the fight a draw, it brought loud boos even from the flagrantly pro-Chavez Mexican-American crowd. Even Sulaiman later told the *Washington Post,* "I thought Whitaker won the fight." But he didn't order a rematch. Nor did he threaten to overturn the decision.

Sports Illustrated, one of the largest-selling weeklies in the States, would eventually give up on boxing, but before it did, it had a big cover picture of the Whitaker fight with the headline, "ROBBED!" According to long-time boxing scribe William Nack:

A check of veteran fight observers revealed that most of them had it eight rounds to four for Whitaker. *SI* had Whitaker nine rounds to three. Yet, Chavez got his wish. Everyone knew, going in, that Whitaker was in hostile territory, and all that remained to speculate about was how bold-faced the larceny would be if Chavez were to take a licking. It went as far as it could go without someone actually calling the police. Marti and Vann are fixtures at fights sanctioned by the WBC, an organization synonymous with Don King, Chavez's promoter and the man who put on the show.

Randy Gordon all but predicted this a year earlier, when he testified in Washington: "The sanctioning bodies would, in most cases, appoint the referee and the three judges themselves over the objections of the state athletic commission, under whose jurisdiction the bout was held … It's a game of poker. They want to see how many officials they can get by, and if they can get by with all four, the referee and the judges, they will do it." Gordon likened it to a "homeowner whose house was being robbed at gunpoint by a roving bunch of thugs," but it was his experience, as a former broadcaster, journalist and head of the New York State Athletic Commission, that if you didn't go along with it, there'd be no fight. Gordon, a "boxing junkie," favored its abolition if it wasn't cleaned up.

By 1996, after Senator William Roth's investigation into boxing had gone nowhere, Senator John McCain, who'd served on Roth's commmitte, had somehow got the Professional Boxing Safety Act passed. It meant the days of divers like Simmie Black were over. McCain was trying to clean up this cesspool of a sport, though there weren't ten votes in it. At one point there was a hearing with no spectators in attendance. Still McCain, who had fought hard for tobacco regulation, told a disheartened aide, "This is just as important."

The *Mexico City Excelsior* once ran a cartoon that depicted Don King walking a dog, and the dog had Sulaiman's face. Jose seldom yielded in his obedience to King. He had little problem submitting documents to McCain's subcommitte that said, "The WBC does not, never has, and never will receive from promoters any other compensation different from the corresponding sanction fees."

But in an affadavit from Joseph Maffia, dated May 1992, given under the penalty of perjury, he swore to a far different story.

I am a certified public accountant, and was Comptroller of Don King Productions (DKP) from on or about July 14, 1986, through September 28, 1991 ...

Whenever a fighter engages in a bout for the World Boxing Council (WBC), World Boxing Association (WBA), or International Boxing Federation (IBF) championship, he is required to pay a sanction fee. The fee is determined by a fee schedule (and) takes into account such variables as the size of the fighter' purse, and the weight class in which the bout is contested. On occasions a fighter's manager will negotiate a sanctioning fee, which is less than the scheduled amount.

However, for each championship fight that Mike Tyson fought with Don King controling his finances, Mr. King directed that Tyson pay sanctioning fees in excess of the scheduled amount. For example, when Tyson fought Frank Bruno, under the fee schedules of the WBC, WBA, and IBF, he was required to pay sanctioning fees totalling approximately $285,000. When Tyson fought Carl Williams, he was required to pay sanctioning fees totalling approximatety $236,000, and when Tyson fought Buster Douglas, he was required to pay sanctioning fees totaling approximately $319,000. But for each of these fights, Mr. King directed that sanctioning fees of $350,000 be paid. This resulted in an overpayment of approximately $209,000 by Mr. Tyson. Also, after the first Mike Tyson versus Razor Ruddock fight, Don King directed that Mike Tyson pay a sanctioning fee of approximately $100,000 to the WBC, even though the bout was not a world championship fight.

If these weren't payoffs, what were they? Yet the WBC is chartered as a non-profit corporation.

Evander Holyfield, who had worked as twelve-year-old selling programs at Atlanta Falcons football games, even had to pay for his own championship belt. Though Holyfield was gouged for a total of $590,000 in sanction fees, when he was asked by Senate probers just what Sulaiman and his ilk actually did for all that money, he replied, "I can't recall them doing anything but showing up and having judges to judge the fight."

By August 1992, Mike Tyson, who many still regarded as the number one heavyweight in the world, was prisoner number 922335 and the house guest of the Indiana Department of Corrections. Sulaiman and King however, kept trying to re-shape public opinion in hopes that it would result in an appelate court overturning Tyson's sentence. "Mike Tyson is not a criminal. He was raped. Psychologically raped. Women raped Tyson," Sulaiman claimed to one utterly repulsed woman journalist. King and Sulaiman also went on *Showtime* and repeatedly said that Tyson was a victim of "injustice."

Both tried the old racism ploy, but the jury in Indianapolis that convicted

Tyson was made up of blacks and whites. Tyson was obviously black, so was Desiree Washington, the beautiful eighteen-year-old who had met him when competing in the Miss Black America beauty pageant. She had confronted racism of her own to become one of the most popular students in her all-white, suburban Providence, Rhode Island, high school.

Washington's life never was the same after the attack. She quietly settled a civil suit against Tyson for $1 million and, unlike other Tyson accusers, ran from the limelight after doing the obligatory Barbara Walters interview. Her once-bubbly personality drastically changed. In college, she became a recluse. She wouldn't even wear make-up. She had taught Sunday School and wanted to be the first black president of the United States, but she painfully knew that notoriety would follow her wherever she went, and her ordeal with Tyson would never really be over. Her parents divorced, and Desiree and her mother took their name and number off the mailbox. They didn't want anyone to know where they lived. But every time Sulaiman and King got on *Showtime*, Desiree's problems started again.

★ ★ ★

In 1992, Riddick Bowe outpointed Evander Holyfield to win the undisputed heavyweight championship. King and Sulaiman had a new problem to deal with Rock Newman.

Newman was a short, stumpy ex-radio newsman from Washington, D.C., who became an insufferable egomaniac. Not only would he be involved in two boxing riots, on national TV he flagrantly pushed Ray Mercer's manager and called him a "coward." Newman was a racist too. His extravagant display of black pride and occasional dashiki came mostly from the fact that he suffered from a terrible lack of identity. He was the product of a mixed marriage and, up close, people were shocked to see that this "angry black man" was almost pink. Newman talked a good game, but for all his self-proclaimed racial pride he had no trouble sending Dwight Qawi to South Africa, despite apartheid.

Newman got into boxing by covering it, and was smart enough to ignore the conventional wisdom on Riddick Bowe, that he had "no heart," though he was "lazy." Knowing Sulaiman's ties to King, Newman knew it was impossible for Bowe to fight for the WBC. (Of course, Rock was a future monopolist, too. Alex Garcia claimed that he turned down a chance to fight Bowe for the title because under, Newman's onerous option contract, the most he could ever make was $1.5 million, while Rock would grab a fortune holding him in bondage.) Bowe infuriated Sulaiman by publicly dumping his WBC championship belt in the garbage. "Go in and get it," he challenged Lennox Lewis, who had stopped him in the 1988

Seoul Olympics. Instead of fighting for the WBC, Bowe hammered former King fieldhand Michael Dokes, who lasted just one round.

Trying to set up a line of succesion and get those sanction fees flowing again, Sulaiman, in a rare departure from King, suddenly annointed Lennox Lewis as WBC champ after he battered Razor Ruddock at Earls Court in two furious rounds. Jose then quickly decreed that Lewis had to face Tony Tucker, an otherwise colourless claimant who hadn't done anything since losing to Tyson back in 1987. Tucker was firmly shackled to King.

Four months later, in what should have been one of the most exciting nights in the history of British boxing, Lewis struggled to defeat Frank Bruno, who was the most popular domestic fighter since Henry Cooper. It was a cold, rainy, outdoor evening in Cardiff, Wales, and Lewis was even more dreary, till he bludgeoned Big Frank into submission.

Lewis was a brutal right-hand puncher, but the 6ft 5in ex-Olympian could be terribly lackadaisical and often just pawed with his jab. In 1994, in a sensational upset, a one-time Chicago burglar called Oliver McCall blasted him Lewis into defeat in round two. A Sulaiman-appointed Mexican referee quickly jumped in with Lewis wobbling against the ropes. After four-and-a-half years, "the (WBC) heavyweight championship was back where it belonged," exulted King.

In the spring of 1995, Tyson got out of prison. Despite predictions to the contrary, the broke, embattled twenty-nine-year-old foolishly went back to King, and became WBC champ again. With time eventually proving that Lewis was the best heavyweight in the world, King strenuously prevented Tyson from fighting him.

It took Lewis four years to win the WBC crown and he would go another five before getting a WBC title fight again, even after halting Lionel Butler in a so-called final eliminator. By 1997, with legal threats mounting, Lewis was finally the WBC champion again, but he was practically unknown to America's man on the street. King, with his power diminishing, conspired to pick up another payday. Of all the appalling things Sulaiman ever did to help him, this was one of the worst.

Oliver McCall had beaten Lewis in 1994, but by 1997 was not only washed up but was in drug rehab. In one of the most disgraceful decisions in boxing history, he was ordained to fight Lewis by Sulaiman. As McCall strode out for the bout behind Don King, he was so worked up that he was actually crying. Once the bell rang, he scurried around the ring, and absolutely refused to have anything to do with Lennox. McCall was having a nervous breakdown in front of the world.

After repeatedly imploring him to fight, referee Mills Lane stopped the disgusting travesty, with McCall meekly turning away. Shortly afterward, a

Boxing News reader named J.L Mullineux, from Merseyside, wrote a letter to the paper that summed up the prevailing mood:

> I have been a boxing fan and a regular reader of *Boxing News* for more than 50 years and it upsets me to see the once-noble art sinking into the depth of depravity. I can put up with the fireworks, the dancing girls and boxers being lifted in on a crane. But the Lennox-Lewis-Oliver McCall fracas was the last straw.
>
> How they can let a man so obviously disturbed fight for a 'world' heavyweight title is beyond me. I felt sorry for McCall. He should have been in a hospital, not a boxing ring. I am not a Lewis fan, but full marks to him for holding back. He could see the man wasn't well.
>
> I noticed the wire-haired Don King beat a hasty retreat. Perhaps he was looking for a quiet corner to count his money.

King and Sulaiman were harder to split up than Siamese twins, and teamed up again in Mexico City. Julio Cesar Chavez faced Miguel Angel Gonzalez for the WBC super-lightweight title. The once-great Chavez, who'd sworn under oath that he had signed blank contracts for King, was now getting by on name alone, but he still was a national hero in Mexico. In a light-flyweight "unification" bout on the same bill, Ricardo Lopez, another brilliant Mexican, took on his WBA counterpart, Rosendo Alvarez. He later claimed that he, too, signed blank contracts. Where was Sulaiman?

The Alphabet Boys hate unifications, because it means sharing the swag, but the bitterness surrounding this card was incredible. For two 105-pounders (about the size of twelve-year-old boys), there were *two* sets of judges – one official, one unofficial – at ringside. Both bouts ended in highly-controversial draws. They were aired on television in the USA on *Showtime* which, for once, made strong charges about what had happened – and backed them up. *Showtime's* Steve Albert told viewers:

> We have recently discovered that the scoring for both bouts was either dishonest, or at best, incompetent. In the Lopez-Alvarez bout, the WBA scoresheet shows judge Dalbey Shirley scoring the seventh round 10-9 in Alvarez's favor. Yet Shirley tells us he had scored that round 9-9 like the other two judges. This score would've given the fight to Lopez. Amazingly, his original ballot for the seventh round, taken by the WBA, has reportedly disappeared.
>
> The scoring for the Chavez-Gonzalez bout is equally suspect. Approximately an hour after that fight, two reporters, Graham Houston from the *Vancouver Sun* and Claude Abrams from Britain's *Boxing News*,

looked closely at Chuck Hassett's 115-115 scoresheet, and realized something
was not right. Abrams claims he and WBC representative Eduardo Lamazon
double checked Hassett's round ballots. And then, according to Abrams,
Lamazon realized the scores had been added wrong and turned to WBC president Jose Sulaiman and said, "There's been a big mistake."

Chavez's score did not add up to 115 on this photocopy of Hassett's offi-
cial scorecard. The round in dispute is round six, which reads nine points for
Chavez, ten points for Gonzalez. The final score should've been 115-114 for
Gonzalez, making him the new champion.

Instead of reversing the draw, and awarding a split decision to Gonzalez,
the WBC now claimed there was an error in the copying of the score, justi-
fying the draw. Judge Hassett tells us he cannot remember how he scored the
round.

"As of this taping," Albert said, closing solemnly, "the WBA and WBC stand
by their decision. However, it is apparent the scoring has been tainted, and
one can only ask: was it simply a confederacy of incompetence, or a conspiracy of thieves?"

As boxing approached the 21st century, there finally had been some
changes, but the blood-sucking King was still like a vampire you could not
kill. Three times the federal government had tried, and failed, to drive a stake
through his heart. After thirty years, King still cast a dark shadow across the
game. Mike Tyson finally blew up one day and furiously kicked him in the
face, after finding out he was broke again. Somehow, $65 million of Tyson's
money had disappeared.

Showtime reporter Jim Gray repeatedly asked King, "Did you steal Mike
Tyson's money?" King refused to answer.

After Tyson left King, his power diminished sharply. King had done
many shows bankrolled by *Showtime*, but without Tyson he quickly lost his
exclusive with the network and began to scuffle for "chump change."
Lennox Lewis, the best heavyweight out there, was a highly-intelligent guy,
who liked chess, and wouldn't be seduced by King.

The Don, however, got two mediocre light-heavyweights, Ricky
Frazier and Richard Hall, underserved title shots at Roy Jones, thanks
again to the Humble Servant of Boxing. Sulaiman had obscenely made
Frazier the "mandatory" challenger out of nowhere, simply because
Frazier had signed a promotional deal with Don King. Jones didn't want
the fights, and HBO actually apologized before the challenger got into
the ring. Frazier, a New York City policeman, was so bad he should have
been allowed to use his nightstick. Even his fellow cops jibed, "Ricky, you
better start selling advertising on the soles of your shoes." Jones quickly
demolished the outclassed clubfighter, who couldn't even get fights on

ESPN. HBO apologized again to its viewers, while Sulaiman, imperiously said, "I take all reponsibility."

Did he gave the sanction fee back?

* * *

On 23 July 1998, Sulaiman tried to justify his mandatory defences to Senator John McCain, who was holding hearings in Washington, D.C., on his proposed Muhammad Ali Boxing Reform Act. Sulaiman rightfully asserted that mandatory defences were necessary, otherwise there would be more boxers like Archie Moore or Jose Napoles, who had been ducked for years by gunshy champions. But the fiery McCain snapped, "And how many times, I must say to you Mr. Sulaiman, that the mandatory defence had to be conducted against someone no one ever heard of and never heard of again?"

"Not at the WBC," stumbled Sulaiman. "Your honour, we believe that the WBC have a very ..."

McCain angrily broke in. "I will be glad to send you some names."

Once the heat died down, there was more money to be made with this scam. Jones was generating the largest purses in light-heavyweight history, and Richard Hall was another Don King sacrifice to be served up. Carl King was his manager. Hall, however, was a lot better than Frazier. Shortly before the fight, in Indiana, Sulaiman tried to appoint WBC judges who would be beholden to him. Jones refused to accept them, so Sulaiman threatened to strip him of his title.

Jones's lawyer, Fred Levin, one of the smartest people in boxing, quickly got hold of McCain. With his colleague Senator Richard Bryan of Nevada, co-sponsor of the Muhammad Ali Act, McCain faxed a very strong letter to Sulaiman ordering him to apologise to the local boxing commissioner and not to break Indiana law again. Hall was predictably dismissed by Jones, then quickly forgotten.

Sulaiman had gone before the US lawmakers with a list of things he had done for boxing over twenty-five years. It was appallingly thin, even with the Mexican's penchant for grandiosity. It included "a modest pension for food and medicine" for damaged ex-champs Emile Griffith, Wildred Benitez, Saensak Muangsurin, Kid Gavilan and Jose Becerra "and many other donations in different countries of the world."

Despite the WBC grossing an easy $20 million, with an estimated ninety per cent generated in the States, Sulaiman wouldn't go into greater specifics. He did rattle off the name of Jack Cohen, whoever he was, the beneficiary of "a liver transplant," and threw in "a pension for Mrs Joe Louis for her retirement home, wheelchair, false teeth and her funeral; hospital expensies

for Jimmy Garcia for over $100,000, and a life insurance of $200,000 given
to his family." Sulaiman didn't provide any receipts to justify the Garcia
expenditures and his claims were, at best, highly misleading. It was the
insurance-carrier who paid the death benefit, not the WBC, on the WBC's
mandated insurance policy. One thing was undeniable: Garcia had no business fighting Gabe Ruelas in the first place.

As Sulaiman's list went on, he began looking like a harried tax-payer,
frantically trying to come up with deductions after the IRS had demanded
an audit. He offered up "a donation to the family of Esteban DeJesus, who
died of AIDS." He didn't admit that he had allowed the dead man to be
managed by Connie Harper, Don King's girlfriend, in an egregious violation of the WBC's "conflict of interest" provision.

"We have a Medical Foundation called 'Spar,' through which we have
donated $700,000," he claimed. Yet, six years earlier, on 12 August 1992,
Senator William Roth had asked him, "In the statement you submitted to
the subcommittee on August 4, 1992, you stated that the WBC has
contributed an amount of money to UCLA for sports medicine research.
Your letter is unclear. Do you say the WBC has contributed $700, or
$700,000, to UCLA?"

"I am not very sure about the amount," Sulaiman replied, "but it's from
$500,000 to $700,000. That's the contribution we have given."

"So, you say it is in excess of $500,000?" Roth asked.

"I would say so, yes."

Roth pounced. "Now, we have received a letter from K.G.Mayer, director of gift policy at UCLA, (which) states that the WBC has only
contributed $290,000 to UCLA, and that the last monies received were
some years ago, back in 1989."

Sulaiman also contended that the WBC spent "$100,000" to study the
"feasibility" of a pension plan. If so, it was never itemized on the WBC's
1989-92 tax forms. Everybody knows broken-down fighters need pensions.
Why spend $100,000? Why wasn't this money simply placed in a mutual
fund? According to a prospectus, $10,000 invested in 1971 in the American
Century Growth Fund would have been worth over $1 million by 2001.
So $100,000 back in 1971 would presumably be worth £10 million. There
would have been money for a pension fund, even if it was solely for ex-
WBC champions. How much of the WBC's revenue has actually gone for
the good of boxing?

Sulaiman got his hands on the WBC in 1973 and it didn't become a
non-profit corporation till the IRS gave it this charter in 1982. Sulaiman
contended in his written presentation, "We (have) constantly on-going
medical and ring official congresses and seminars, being the most important,
the WBC First World Medical Congress held in Aruba in 1997, with a total

cost of $494,866." Why was a half-million dollars squandered on a huge bash when you can get all the medical data you need on brain damage and research off the Internet? It doesn't take Einstein to conclude that repeated pounding to the head can cause brain damage. Studies show British footballers are even subject to it for heading a soccer ball. This was another $500,000 that should've gone into a fighter's pension fund.

As for ring seminars, the record proves that Sulaiman gets rid of good referees like Ocatavio Meyeran, and kept re-appointing hacks who toed the company line. All of the Alphabet Boys are adamantly opposed to using another organization's referees. Why? Because they can't influence their decisions?

"Look," claimed one former top aide to Cedric Kushner, who contends that he has heard of referees who have made $16,000 for just one fight, "I've had officials come right up to me before the fight, and say, 'You tell Ced I'm a team player.' These guys vote for the promoter who has the juice. Hell, they're paying them, which is outrageous in the first place, since the commission should be paying and appointing the officials. But these guys vote for the promoter with the power, otherwise they know they won't work again. Face it: there's a lot of money in officiating. Why the hell do you think these guys are lobbying for themselves at the conventions? The 'money fighter' almost always wins in Las Vegas."

Sulaiman recently announced that anyone now in the top thirty can fight for WBC crown. This guarantees that there will be more Jimmy Garcias. It also increases the likelihood of payoffs for ratings. Sulaiman was once asked by American lawmakers if he thought he was above the law. After hesitating a long time, he finally said no. Yet according to a 1993 ESPN video documentary, Sulaiman flat out said on tape, "This is not a court of law – this is the WBC."

Sulaiman though, had no problems availing himself of "due process" when he was indicted in Mexico and accused of smuggling pre-Colombian artifacts out of the country and illegally selling them abroad. On 18 December 1983, the Mexican Supreme Court upheld "a lower court ruling and dismissed all charges against World Boxing Council president Jose Sulaiman … by a 4–1 vote," said a wire report. The Court ruled "that Sulaiman had proven he was an artifact collector and was not engaged in illegally selling pieces abroad." Boxing writer Bert Sugar was no longer able to call him "The Raider of the Lost Artifacts."

Sulaiman was in Las Vegas, presiding over the WBC Convention, when he got the news. "I have never doubted my innocence from the very first moment that this happened, I had been in the past a known collectionist of archaeological pieces. I love my country, I admire its culture. I was confident and I must show my admiration to the system of justice in my country."

James Dusgate, who lived in Central America and knew a lot about Third World culture, wrote that Sulaiman "had been charged with the illegal possession of $200 million worth of archaeological treasure." $200 million. Where the hell did he get the money for this collection? Since Sulaiman presided over a tax-exempt corporation, the WBC, didn't the Humble Servant of Boxing owe fight fans an explanation? What about the IRS?

* * *

On 2 August 2002, Sulaiman launched suit against Mike Tyson and Lennox Lewis for injuries he supposedly sustained in a January 22 press conference to announce their upcoming fight. Though the WBC didn't get its non-profit tax exemption for attending press conferences, Sulaiman, who conducts himself like boxing's high potentate, had to be there. As both fighters strode out, Tyson kept walking and made a move on Lewis. Lewis slugged him back. All hell broke loose. There was punching and wrestling on the podium and security guards had to restore order. Sulaiman was caught up in the melee, and had a shocked looked on his face. In papers filed by his lawyer Tommy Deas in Manhattan State Supreme Court, the seventy-one-year-old Sulaiman claimed that Tyson knocked him unconscious. "When he got up after being knocked out, Tyson spat on him and threatened to kill him," said Deas.

Deas contended that Sulaiman needed several dental surgeries to repair his broken teeth and damaged bridgework. Though Sulaiman claimed he filed this lawsuit to be "true to his principles," he's actually asking $2 million in direct damages and $50 million in punitive damages. Jimmy Garcia lost his life and the WBC only had a $100,000 insurance policy.

In September 2002, Sulaiman's WBC lost a massive $31 million lawsuit because of the way he did business. "There's nothing that says boxing has to be like this. Mr. Sulaiman and all like him should be told that decent society won't stand for this type of behaviour," Graciano Rocchighiani's attorney Peter Schlam, told the jury after Rocchigiani was unfairly stripped of his WBC light-heavyweight championship. Rocchigiani had even come out of a German prison to win.

In 1997, WBC light-heavyweight champ Roy Jones, who behaves like an opera diva, renounced his WBC title, supposedly to fight Evander Holyfield. Jones, who indulged himself with this fantasy for a while, finally wised up. He wanted his title back. Meanwhile Rocchigiani had beaten Michael Nunn for the vacant crown. Schlam even introduced some devastating letters that Sulaiman wrote congratulating the new champion. But Sulaiman heisted Rocchigiani's title back because Jones's $3.5 million purses were much bigger and were guaranteed because of his HBO televison contract. Sulaiman tried to contend to Rocchigiani's attorney, after he'd grabbed back the belt, "what the TV announcers, the ring announcers or any other media called the fight was incorrect if it was called anything other than for the interim title." Of course, Jose collected the world championship sanction fee.

Rocchigiani sued. In February 2001, before the hearing could proceed, Judge Richard Owen, who ultimately presided, wrote, "The language in the written agreement admits of only one possible interpretation. The Rocchigiani-Nunn bout was for the WBC light-heavyweight championship. The word 'interim' is nowhere to be found within the four corners of the agreement. The WBC drafted the agreement utilizing its standard form, and is, and was, fully capable of explicitly designating the bout for the 'interim' title. However, it did not do so."

For once, the boxer was the clear winner. "Graciano Rocchigiani showed great character in fighting this," said Schlam. "But most fighters don't have the resources he did."

At the time of writing, the WBC was facing possible bankruptcy, or at least the removal of Sulaiman. It was one of the best things ever to happen to boxing. The Rocchigiani decision re-affirms that fighters are human beings with rights. Something even the fighters forgot a long time ago.

CHAPTER THIRTEEN

The Best Sanctioning Body
Money Could Buy

IN THE DARKEST days of the Depression, President Franklin Delano Roosevelt told Americans, "The only thing we have to fear is fear itself." In Chicago, gangster Al Capone ran free soup lines. At a time when "Hey Brother, Can You Spare A Dime," should've been the national anthem, and former millionaires sold apples on the street corner, a clubfight promoter in Cincinatti was charging just twenty cents to get into his shows. They were few takers.

In Brockton, Massachusetts, a quiet shoemaker named Piero Marchegiano excitedly told his son told his son about the Italian giant Primo Carnera. "I'm going to be heavyweight champion, too, Papa," his son, later known as Rocky Marciano, told him. In New Jersey, a twenty-seven-year-old ex-prizefighter named Jimmy Braddock, who had fought for the light-heavyweight championship of the world, had to go on relief. "We couldn't keep our lights on, and there wasn't any food on the table," said his young wife, Mary.

On 21 November 1933, in Scotch Plains, New Jersey, not far from the gritty urban sprawl of Newark, Robert Lee was born. Times were brutally hard for blacks. If things were better in the North, where blacks had less fear of the Ku Klux Klan and lynchings, Lee, the second of six children, was still a black child born into a white world. Lee's father was a hard worker. While many men abandoned their families and hopped freights in search of a better life, he gladly took the most menial jobs, and was smart enough to become a lumber yard foreman, road crew supervisor, and a hospital orderly.

By 1949, after President Harry Truman demanded civil rights for blacks and the US Army was finally integrated, Joe Louis had been heavyweight champion for twelve years but still couldn't even eat or sleep in most first-class hotels. Lee, a strong, athletic kid who loved baseball, avidly followed the exploits of Jackie Robinsom, the first black to integrate the major league. If you were black, you also had to be handy with your fists, so Bob learned how to box at the YMCA, and won his first four amateur fights before breaking a finger. He never donned the gloves again.

Lee graduated from high school and worked as a groundskeeper on a golf course and a blender in a plastic factory. He was an ambitious kid, however, and at a time when there was no affirmative action or racial quotas, became a trailblazer in September 1956 when he became the first black patrolman in Scotch Plains history. He had barely broken in his uniform before he was drafted into the army. He did his two-year hitch mostly in Germany, overlapping Elvis Presley's, and at twenty-five resumed life in Scotch Plains. He married Grace Hamlette and would have two children, Cheryl and Robert Jr.

For the next seven years, Officer Robert Lee patrolled the streets. With Martin Luther King's call for civil rights, the assassination of President John F. Kennedy, the murder of his brother, Robert, and the gunning-down of King, America had exploded. It was the most turbulent decade since the Civil War.

Lee was a guy who mumbled a lot, and seldom voiced his opinion, but he was smart, did his job well and joined the Union County Prosecutor's Office as an investigator in 1965. That August, the Watts riots broke out, leaving thirty-four dead in Los Angeles. By 1967, Detroit and Newark had also gone up in flames. With race, and the Vietnam War, the incendiary issues, President Lyndon Johnson's "Great Society" had blown apart at the seams.

In Newark, a fifteen-year-old boy named Marvin Hagler, cowered under the bed, while rioters burned the black ghetto down. Four four days later, all hell broke loose in suburban Plainfield, New Jersey. A white cop, John V. Gleason, confronted a black man, Bobby Williams, who was wielding a hammer.

"Put it down! Put it down!" barked the copper.

Williams refused. Gleason shot him dead. The furious mob of onlookers surrounded Gleason and stomped him to death.

It was a sensational case. Eleven defendants went to trial. Gail Madden, a huge, 300-pound black woman, was quickly implicated because of her bright orange dress. Prosecutors contended she finished off the screaming policeman with either a meat cleaver or a butcher knife. But her case was so rife with bias that Madden and another defendant who had been convicted got their cases overturned.

"It was a very tough case for me," recalled Lee. "Racial sentiments were high, and people wouldn't help me." Instead, they'd hiss, "Uncle Tom," and, "That cracker mutha-fucker had it coming," or ask, "Why you arrestin your own people? That pig down shot Williams down like a dog." Many would even spit as Lee drove by.

While many from his community embraced black militancy, Lee still believed in law and order. Hard work and achievement could set you free. Lee was actually a Republican, though the last time a Republican had done anything for a black man was arguably when Abraham Lincoln freed the slaves. In 1971, Lee campaigned for Republican office-seekers and drew tight, disbelieving smiles wherever he appeared. He was out of step with most blacks, though some whites called him "a good nigger."

Lee ran for county sheriff, but lost. Needing a job, he joined the New Jersey Division of Consumer Affairs. He worked fraud cases till 1976, when he was moved into boxing regulation for three months. The casinos hadn't yet arrived in Atlantic City, and Jersey's former holiday resort was just a faded old dowager. But there was boxing there, and Lee quickly became friendly with trainers Lou Duva and Al Certo. They showed him how the sport really worked. Lee was surprised to learn that Rocky Marciano had been a front for mobster Frankie Carbo, who ran a New York restaurant. Duva was good friends with Anthony Giacalone, who was said to be the Detroit captain of the Mafia and "a ruthless tough guy," according to the *Associated Press*. Giacalone was notorious as a suspect in the 1975 disappearence and probable murder of national labour leader Jimmy Hoffa.

The volatile Duva, pushing eighty, now has something of a lovable, grandfatherly facade, but he served his apprenticeship at Stillman's Gym in New York. In 1965, as an aging Joey Giardello tried to squeeze one more payday out of his middleweight championship, he turned down his buddy Duva's advice to defend against unbeaten Nino Benvenutti in Italy.

"We'll get robbed over there," protested Joey.

"Yeah," agreed Duva, "but we'll bring 'em back here for the rematch, and just rob 'em back."

As for Certo, he became best known as the trainer/manager of Buddy McGirt, the artful stylist who would win the IBF championship at junior-welter and the WBC title at welterweight. According to New Jersey State and federal investigators in 1992, Certo was a known "associate" of organized crime who even visited mob boss John Gotti.

In 1977, Lee went to work full-time in the office of Jersey Joe Walcott, the former heavyweight champion, who was the New Jersey boxing commissioner. By 1980, Atlantic City had been resurrected and gambling was booming. Gangster Nicodemo Scarfo actually ran the town from his social club on Fairmount Avenue. Bodies began showing up all over: Scarfo, dubbed "Crazy Nicky" by his associates, was on a killing spree that even frightened New York's five criminal families. But if you wanted to do any business in Atlantic City, you had to go through him. Boxing flourished in

"Joi-sey," with more than 200 cards a year. Not even Nevada did that many. And somewhere along the line, Bob Lee became a crook.

By 1981, the FBI had begun a sting operation dubbed "Crown Royal," and heard, among other things, that Walcott and Lee were shaking down prospective promoters trying to get licenses. On 19 December 1981, at a meeting at the Playboy Hotel, the FBI got a conversation on audiotape. A "cooperating witness," Reginald Barrett, played the part of a would-be promoter with a criminal record who was willing to pay off to get a state license.

"That's for Christmas. That's for Christmas," Barrett said, handing Lee money. "Well, told you I was gonna take care of you, I meant it."

"Yeah, yeah," said Lee.

"I want you to know I'm for real," insisted Barrett.

"Yeah, I, I, believe you."

"All right."

"I always did."

"I'm for real," insisted the stooge, who was overplaying his hand.

"Okay," said Lee. " ... I have to [have] a little something for Joe [Walcott]."

"What, you want some more for Joe?"

"No, no, this is for Joe," insisted Lee.

"All right, that's three thousand ... do you want me to give Joe some more?"

"No, no ... I'm gonna give this to Joe. Joe is my man, and I got to take care of him."

In August 1982, an undercover FBI agent named Victor Guererro, posing as a drug baron who wanted to launder his money through boxing, sat ringside next to Walcott, who was supervising a fight on national TV.

"Did you get all of the money, all right?" asked Guererro. "Are we going to get our license?"

"Yes," replied Walcott, whose image was that he was a fine family man, religious and civic-minded.

The next day, Guererro and Special Agent Juanita Ward, posing as his secretary, met Walcott and Lee at the boxing commission office in Trenton, New Jersey. Guererro later swore in an affidavit, "I entered the office of Walcott and handed him $1,000 and stated, 'This is for you, Joe.'"

Walcott, who had been the oldest man ever to win the heavyweight championship, was very polite. "Thank you, thank you very much," he said.

Minutes later, the undercover Fed went into Lee's office. They discussed the license again, and Guererro handed Lee another envelope stuffed with another ten one-hundred dollar bills.

"You didn't have to do that," Lee said.

Bob Lee and Jersey Joe Walcot, the former champion of the world, had officially become whores.

★ ★ ★

Though Lee was a novice in boxing administration, in 1976 he had joined a dissident movement and helped form the United States Boxing Association, which was afflliated to the WBA. Lee was not given to a lot of talking, so he didn't make enemies, and eventually became a second vice-president to ruling oligarch Gilberto Mendoza.

In 1982, he boldly challenged Mendoza at the WBA convention in Puerto Rico, but the Latins had sworn they would never let "another fucking gringo be president." Lee's candidacy was also torpedoed by Don King and Bob Arum, who were worried that he was not someone you could do business with. "Americans are generating all the money, yet we've got nothing to say," complained Bill Brennan, a retired Navy man who ran the Virginia commission and had urged Lee to run.

In April 1983, Lee founded his own organization, cumbersomely called the United States Boxing Association, International. Though traditionalists scoffed, many Americans applauded Lee's move, and the former New Jersey cop said piously, "If boxing had been run fairly, we'd have never come into existence." He promised "fair and honest ratings."

In May, 1984, Lee wisely changed the name of his organization to the International Boxing Federation, or IBF. It was supposed to be the antidote to the corrupt WBA and WBC, whom writers called "the banditos." Jose Sulaiman and Mendoza were so worried that they contemplated merging their fiefdoms.

Middleweight Marvin Hagler became the first IBF champ. Sulaiman, who was looking for any excuse to steal his belt and stymie the IBF, threatened to strip him if he fought another fifteen-rounder like his one against Roberto Duran – the WBC had just adopted twelve-round bouts, ostensibly for safety but really to meet TV requirements. Though some of their other "champions" were a joke, Larry Holmes, who was also being emasculated by Sulaiman and Don King, accepted the IBF heavyweight title.

The façade of probity soon cracked. In 1983, the New Jersey State Commission of Investigation began probing boxing and issued a scathing criticism of Walcott and Lee. "How could Lee possibly grant state licenses while heading his own organization?" it asked. Clearly, Lee couldn't possibly be fair to the WBA and WBC in his capacity as a state official while at the same time running a rival boxing body.

Though the Feds had caught Lee taking that payoff in 1981, he had

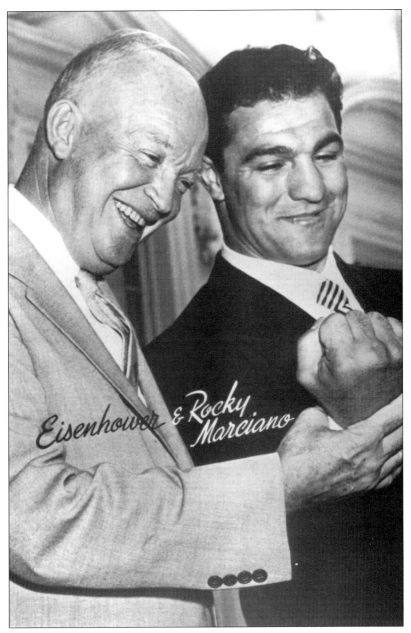

Eisenhower & Rocky Marciano

President Dwight D. Eisenhower greets heavyweight champ Rocky Marciano and quips, "I had no idea you were so small." He also had no idea of Marciano's links to hoodlums.

Bobo Olsen

Bobo Olson won the vacant middleweight title against Britain's Randy Turpin, but his purses were carved up in an undercover deal between his manager and mega-rich promoter Jim Norris. Olson ended up owing $127,000 in taxes and working as a fruit picker, factory worker and security guard.

Welterweight champion Johnny Saxton was another of the numerous boxers manipulated by Carbo. He ended up destitute and homeless in Florida and died in a mental institution.

The fearsome Sonny Liston destroys Floyd Patterson inside a round in Chicago to win the heavyweight crown. Liston was completely controlled by organised crime. Patterson later served as head of the New York State Athletic Commission, even though he had trouble remembering his own name.

Senator Estes Kefauver (centre), flanked by fellow senators, was a progressive man who attacked the Mafia vigorously and championed federal control of professional boxing. He was also an alcoholic, and died suddenly in 1963 after helping to clean up the game.

Busted! Carbo, the infamous Mr Gray, is finally taken into custody. He served a long stretch and was one of the few senior Mafia figures to die of old age.

Jim Norris, the wealthy tycoon who headed the monopolistic International Sporting Clun and who "just had a thing about gangsters," according to fight manager and film collector Bill Cayton.

Muhammad Ali may have been "The Greatest" but that didn't stop promoter Don King, manager Herbert Muhammad and the Nevada Boxing Commission putting him in with Larry Holmes, even though he was already suffering from brain abnormalities.

A young Don King, arrested for beating Sam Garrett to death. King killed two men during his reign as a Cleveland numbers czar. He emerged from prison with an unstoppable thirst for power – at any cost.

King became the dominant power in world boxing and a truly malign influence. According to the FBI, and Senate testimony, he was hooked up with as many as four organized crime families.

Jose Sulaiman of Mexico, oligarch of the World Boxing Council and self-styled "Humble Servant of Boxing." © *Press Association*

Jerry Quarry, perennial White Hope of the 1960s and 1970s, who was pushed into boxing by his brutal father. After suffering from acute brain damage, Quarry eventually lapsed into a coma in the late 1990s and was taken off life support by his family.

"Boxing's biggest upset": 42-1 underdog Buster Douglas belts Mike Tyson into submission in Japan. The WBA and WBC frantically tried to overturn the result, to media and public outrage.

Julio Cesar Chavez, Mexico's *Grand Campeon*, earned more than $100 million yet ended up broke. According to testimony in a fraud trial, he signed blank contracts with Don King.

Oliver McCall surprisingly halted Lennox Lewis to win the WBC heavyweight title, but was hauled out of drug rehab for the rematch and had a "nervous breakdown" before millions of TV viewers worldwide.

Jersey Joe Walcott in his prime. The respected former heavyweight champ later became corrupted as head of the New Jersey Athletic Commission.

Former detective Bob Lee, once involved with Walcott in taking kickbacks, became president of the IBF, the third most powerful governing body, before he was spectacularly brought down by an FBI corruption probe. © *Associated Press*.

Bitter enemies Bob Arum (left) and Don King smile daggers at each other before the Oscar De La Hoya-Felix Trinidad superfight. Money was the only thing that could make the sport's two dominant promoters bury the hatchet – temporarily. © *Press Association*

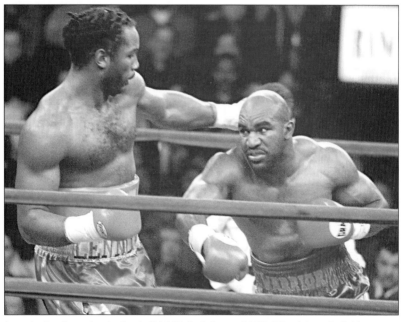

Lennox Lewis outboxes champion Evander Holyfield in the first heavyweight title fight, only to see the decision inexplicably declared a draw. The outrageous verdict provoked a raft of investigations into boxing. © *Press Association*

escaped with a reprimand when he should've been fired and indicted. Now the NJSCI asked Lee under oath whether WBA officials had sweaty palms.

"I think some of them may be capable of being bought," testified Lee, "and I just think that they have no regard for what's right and fair, and that's what hurts so bad. When I first came into boxing, I was told that in order to get a fighter ranked in the WBA or the WBC, it costs $5,000, and it costs another $5,000 if they fight for a world title."

Amazingly, in February 1984 Lee was given Walcott's old job on a temporary basis, after the former champ was quietly forced into retirement. Though the NJSCI had called the New Jersey commission "a particularly flagrant example of inept administration," and claimed that safety issues were "skirted" to get lucrative fights," Lee was still given the job by Governor Thomas Kean.

His honeymoon didn't last long. Soon the State Commission on Ethical Standards had begun another probe of Lee for allegedly taking money from promoters – the same promoters he would regulate in New Jersey – for his WBA candidacy. Finally, with organized crime making a run on Atlantic City because of the fabulous riches generated by casino gambling, Kean realized that he couldn't have a corrupt boxing commissioner. Lee's nomination was put on "hold."

"I'm tired of the tactics they're using against me," railed Lee. "I've been investigated by everyone. It appears to me that the Executive Commission on Ethical Standards is attempting to exclude a black from the position of commissioner. They're attempting to force a black to abandon his philosophy and principles." This wouldn't be the last time Lee would hide behind racism.

The Ethics Commission charged Lee with soliciting money from promoters at the 1982 WBA convention, and claimed that Lee got two $5,000 cheques, though he quickly returned the money after the news broke. Lee also panhandled the casinos. "That was the only way I was going to win the election," he pleaded. "I'm not a man of means. I didn't have the resources. So, friends of mine helped me with contributions." Lee, as a state employee, knew better than that, and was roundly criticized by a New Jersey judge for the flagrant conflict of interest.

Records proved that Don King paid $262 for a USBA dinner, and another $4,437 for three USBA cocktail parties. Lee was so shamelessly greedy that he even sent Bob Arum, a legendary tightwad, a $6,900 bill for the IBF's photocopier. "Look, politicans do it all the time," Lee claimed.

The hearing judge recommended that Lee be suspended by the state of New Jersey for six months, and fined $600. Lee quit his state job and concentrated on the IBF, where there was big money to be made.

★ ★ ★

The IBF was corrupt virtually from the beginning. In April 1985, bantamweight champ Satoshi Shingaki lost his cardboard crown to Australia's Jeff Fenech. Shingaki, who turned pro in 1982 and won the IBF title just a year later, should never have fought for a "world title" in then first place, but after he was stopped by Fenech in nine, Shingaki's promoter, Hisashi Ikeda, requested a rematch. Benjamin Franklin, whose picture is on a hundred-dollar bill, vouched for him ten times: Lee got a $500 bribe to run the rematch through, and so did Bill Brennan. Fenech, who went on to become a great fighter, stopped Shingaki in three. Though both fights were held in Australia, the Japanese Boxing Commission, which is actually run by Japanese promoters, refused to do business with the IBF.

Lee's newsletters touted fairness, but this is the way the IBF really worked. On 29 May 1997, Doug Beavers, the IBF's ratings chairman, met with Roland Jankelson, who managed a flabby American Indian named Joe Hipp. Jankelson had just taken $50,000 out of a bank account to pay off. He had paid $20,000 once before. Though Hipp was very tough, he was a terrible bleeder who blocked everything with his face. Despite that, with the right rating from Lee, a mediocre heavyweight like Hipp could still be in line for a big payday. Jankelson wanted Hipp high in the IBF's Top Ten, with a guaranteed title shot.

On May 30, Beavers had a morning meet with Lee, his son Bob Lee Jr, and an unidentified male, to plan how much they'd shake down Jankelson for.

"I talked to Jankelson," said Beavers, "and he says he went over the ratings anyway, he wants Joe Hipp."

Both Lees began to mutter, but Beavers continued over their quiet objections. "I realize there ain't much room, 'cause these other guys above him have been active," but he quoted Jankelson when he said, "I'd like to leave here with (Hipp) at least in the Top Ten."

Beavers went on, "Now, I looked at the ratings and the only thing that I could see was, maybe (Tony) Tucker going down, 'cause there ain't no other room."

"Tucker's getting ready to fight for the (WBO) title. That's the spot," figured Bob Lee Jr. They could use the fact that he was fighting for a rival organisation to demote him.

"Well, when he's fighting?" asked his old man.

"Tucker's fighting on, uhm, I think June 28. He's fighting uh, the British guy … "

"Akinwande?" asked Lee Sr.

"No, Henry Hide," piped in Jr.

"*Herbie* Hide," interjected Beavers (Henry Hide was the US congressman who lead the impeachment fight against President Clinton, in the Monica Lewinsky affair).

Suddenly, Junior said, "(Tucker's) fighting (for) Hide's WBO title, so win or lose, he (Hipp) can take that spot."

"What's he talking about?" asked Lee Sr, who wanted to know how much Jankelson would pay.

"He didn't, he didn't say," stammered Beavers. "He says, 'I like for you to talk to Bob'"

"Well, you think ... you think you can work it?" asked the president of the IBF.

"I think I can ... But I don't know, you know, just going into like eight or nine. I don't know what to work it for ... "

Suddenly, the droll, mumbling Lee said, "Thirty to fifty thousand."

Beavers began to chuckle at Lee's stupidity and greed. "I don't know if you can get that."

Even Junior agreed: "I don't know if it's worth that much. I don't think you're going to get it."

"I don't think he'll pay that much," added Beavers.

"I think it's twenty," suddenly proclaimed Lee Jr.

"Maybe twenty dollars," wryly cracked his old man.

"Twenty," repeated number one son.

"Twenty?" asked Beavers, looking to his boss for confirmation. "So tell him twenty?"

Beavers finally added, "and he's a whining sonofabitch."

At 10:30 AM, Jankelson arrived at Beaver's room.

"Roland, come on in," Beavers said heartily. "Have a seat there," he added, motioning with his hand. "I spoke to Bob, and he says that you know, there's posiblility that you can get in the Top Ten ... but there's a lot of other people jockeying for the position. You're not the only one here ... He needs twenty-five to get you in the Top Ten ... Then he said, later on, there'd be an opportunity to move up. But he said he couldn't do it for less than twenty-five thousand."

"That's too much," protested Jankelson.

"I, I'm just the mesenger," replied Beavers. "I can get back to him."

Jankelson tartly responded, "We've been there before."

There was an awkward silence for a moment, before Jankelson suddenly worried about what the boxing media would say if the tough, clumsy Hipp were given a favored slot. What was the point of paying twenty grand, reasoned the manager, if it wasn't going to result in a lucrative title shot?

"I mean," said Jankelson, "if he can put Joe in the Top Ten ... and then show me that there really is a, a uhm, you know a future. But to have just a Top Ten rating ... doesn't hack it."

"I know."

"Gotta come out of my pocket," added Jankelson, who sounded like he was trying to talk himself out of the whole thing. "I can't go back to the fighter," though both men knew that wasn't true. Many of the flesh peddlers in this business simply would have told Hipp that it cost $75,000, or maybe a hundred grand, and stolen the rest for themselves if a lucrative fight came around. But Jankelson ended this attempt to buy an IBF title shot for Hipp by muttering that Bob Lee was "not gonna have any respect for me ... if I say, 'Here's a lot of money for nothing.'"

Jankelson wouldn't pay off – at least for now.

* * *

At an earlier meeting with the Lees, Beavers had broached a scheme that proved how corrupt they were.

"Now, I got a fucking retirement plan, we can do it," babbled Beavers, barely able to contain himself. "I mean, this is some serious shit. You remember Glen Thomas? That (promoter) Butch Lewis had? About five years ago."

"St Louis," nodded Lee, trying to jog his memory.

"I don't know, he was living in Delaware, I think at the time," said Beavers, "but he's originally from the Midwest someplace. He fought for our title, he was undefeated. You had him like one or two or something, right? He went to jail, alright? He's out of jail, and he's in Kentucky. Now a guy called me and left a message on my voicemail, the guy that's training him ... he *hookayed* up with some drug dealers. Now, this guy, the guy I know, is from the army ... He said these guys [the drug dealers] are young, but they've got Lexington, Louisville, Frankfort, and he said they got all the fuckin' drug trade ... They want this kid to get a title shot."

"What weight is he?" asked Lee.

"He's 168 pounds now, he's had two fights, I think ... since he's been out of jail, he's been out of jail six months or so. He's scheduled to fight again next week, and they got another scheduled fight someplace else, but these hip-hop fucking guys, they not only are managers, but they want to promote a fucking title fight of some kind. They're paying this fucking guy that I know fifteen hundred dollars a fucking week, under the table, just to train the motherfucker. He says that they bought a fucking dump truck company."

Bob Lee broke in: "With the [drug money]?"

"Cash fucking money," said Beavers. "In excess of three million dollars.

Mike says he can get him a title shot, you know. A few more wins and shit like that … He says these guys don't know a fucking regional title from a fucking world title."

Lee Jr again muttered, but he was drowned out by the sheer greed and excitement in Beavers guttural, hillbilly voice: "A half a million dollar. A half a million fucking dollars."

"They gonna pay up front … for us to see this guy?" asked Lee Sr, who once took an oath under God to uphold the law.

"He says … these motherfuckers will bring it *and* the motherfucking brown shopping bag."

Lee Jr was so stunned, he kept moving his lips inaudibly. But Beavers issued a strong warning: "These are some violent motherfuckers, so if we make the deal, we gotta do the deal, or they'll kick your motherfucking door in and kill everybody in your motherfucking house." He chuckled. "They want to meet with us."

"Well, where the guy from?" Lee asked.

"They're Kentucky, they're all Kentucky."

The old man was thinking out loud and mumbled, "Fly … "

" … Meet with 'em out in the sticks someplace," added his dutiful son.

"Roanoake [Virginia] ain't that far from Kentucky," piped in Beavers. But Lee said, "I'm not gonna be there."

"Okay," said Beavers, who seemed chastened till Lee added, "But … I'm gonna … talk to 'em … this is not done overnight."

"No," agreed Beavers

"It takes time for me to get a guy in position to challenge for a world," explained the elder Lee.

"Right."

"But if you get the right support …"

"Got the right feel," interjected Junior.

"If you're really serious about it," Lee said, directing his comments to Beavers, but really speaking to the drug dealers, "you guys ain't serious about this, don't waste our time. Don't waste your time, don't waste my time."

As the plot took shape, Beavers pondered what titles Thomas could fight for. Junior asked, "We have him anywhere in the ratings?"

"No, I mean he's only had two fights since he's been out of jail."

"You could slip him a USBA fight?" Lee Jr asked.

"We'll talk about moving him somewhere else," said Lee. "But if these people expect this is gonna be a six months or a year program, to get 'em to fight for a title, it's not gonna happen … They gotta know that up front."

"Yeah," agreed Beavers, "because I don't wanna be fucking with these guys. I don't want 'em kicking my door down in and start shootin'."

"No, you can't build Rome in a day," commented Lee.

With the project a go, Beavers said, "I'll get to work on it."

* * *

On 9 June 1997, in the late afternoon, Lee, Beavers and an unidentified man met in room 426 at the Holiday Inn in Norfolk, Virginia, supposedly to discuss ratings.

"Jimmy Adams. There's another one of fuckin' [Don] King's people," sneered Beavers, describing the manager of former WBC heavyweight champ Oliver McCall, who had halted Lennox Lewis in 1994, then had a mental breakdown in their rematch after being hauled out of drug rehab. "There is sure enough a bad guy. He's a hood," claimed the garrulous Beavers. "Supposedly he used to be in [the] Southern Mafia bullshit, up and down the Tennessee border."

"Ah huh," nodded the bored Lee.

"He's sure enough supposed to be a bad guy."

Lee, however, didn't want to hear any more. He called his daughter Cheryl, who was in hospital for minor surgery. Then he quickly called his second wife Shirley. He was trying hard to get out of Norfolk at 7:15 in the morning. "If I don't get that flight out, I can't get a jet until 5:45 tomorrow afternoon," he complained to his wife, "and I ain't riding on them prop planes."

Finally, they got around to the ratings. They began with the heavyweights. That was where the money was.

"Now, do we put this Ibeabuchi in, or whatever the fuck his name is?" asked Lee, speaking of Ike Ibeabuchi, the mentally-deranged heavyweight who had just upset the touted David Tua but who was subsequently charged with raping a sexual escort and was committed to a mental institution till he was well enough to stand trial.

"Yeah, we gotta put him in, 'cause he's 17-0 now, and he beat the number six guy."

"We, do we have, who ahh, we don't owe anybody, do we?" asked Lee, speaking of the favoured promoters whose fighters had to get preference, even if they were bums.

Beavers then asked, "Did you ever find out what happened to this no-fightin' Lee Gilbert, on how he pulled out of this fight with [Francois] Botha?"

"Nah, I never did."

"If you're scared of Botha, you're in the wrong goddamn business."

Lee was amazingly ignorant when it came to fighters. He had basically become a flunky for Don King, who he often referred to by the nickname "Fuzzy Wuzzy" or "Fuzz," a reference to King's spectacular hairdo.

"Listen, a guy that Fuzzy's interested in is a guy that you got in the intercontinentals," said Lee.

"Steve Pannell," said Beavers.

"Yeah. Can he fight?"

"Now, he's got a lot of natural ability, but he's got a pissant's heart. He ain't got no balls at all." Pannell was from Roanoake, Virginia, which was Beavers's country. "But he's a big, impressive looking sonofabitch. He's about six feet."

"Yeah," nodded Lee, who wasn't interested at all in a boxer's ability but simply the politics of the situation and who was paying off.

"Good-looking kid," continued Beavers, labouring the point, but who did actually love the sport. "A nice straight jab … I mean they got him fighting four-rounders."

"Yeah," muttered Lee, who didn't care.

"I mean against guys that never had fights," persisted Beavers. "This (Jimmy) Adams has got him, and they're in Nashville."

Suddenly, Lee remembered that it was him who had given Pannell a rating.

"Yeah," rattled on Beavers, "he fights once a week, but he's fighting guys that ain't never had fights."

* * *

The ratings are supposed to be based on merit, but by June 9 Beavers was still trying to get Lee to go along on the $25,000 scheme to put Joe Hipp into title contention.

"Now this Jankelson. This motherfucker ain't batted an eye about $25,000," lied Beavers.

"The best we can do is a number six and then he's gonna have to challenge a couple of these guy ahead of him and move up," said Lee. "Ya know, that's the best we can do."

"But don't you think we should get … the twenty-five before we put him in (at) six."

"Yeah, yeah."

Doing the ratings was a juggling act, because certain promoters like Don King couldn't be offended. For the first decade or so of its existence, Don King wasn't much of a factor in the IBF. He obviously tried to buy influence, but Lee got cozy with rival promoters Dan Duva, of Main Events, and Cedric Kushner, and King regularly denounced him as an "Uncle Tom," a "traitor to his race," and a "black man who's forgotten the colour of his skin." All that would eventually change, and King became the most influential IBF promoter.

"Do you think Fuzzy Wuzzy would be friendly about that?" Beavers asked, after Steve Pannell, the heavyweight who supposedly lacked courage and was facing four-round stiffs, was drop-kicked into the number fourteen rating in the USBA's heavyweights, while former WBC heavyweight champ Tim Witherspoon, who had successfully sued King and settled for $1 million, was removed.

"Yeah, I imagine he would," figured Lee. "Besides, Witherspoon ain't done nothin' for us."

Deep down, Beavers's sensibilities as a former fighter, were offended. "There's three no-fightin' motherfuckers in there," he cursed, describing the USBA's ratings. "[Lee] Gilbert, [Mark] Randazzo and Donny Steele."

Lee wouldn't take responsibility for that. He blamed King for heeding stupid people who couldn't judge talent.

Beavers, who knew boxing but not as well as he put on, was mystified "that Fuzzy is so interested in fucking Lee Gilbert, 'cause that prick can't fight a taste. He's worse than Botha." Francois Botha had won the vacant IBF heavyweight title in December 1995 on a scandalous decision in Germany against Axel Schulz. Lee had then been forced to defrock him after he tested positive for steroids. King reportedly paid Botha's fine.

Lee figured that manager Al "Bonami sold [King] a bill of goods" on Gilbert. Yet Lee was so ignorant of fighters, he asked, "Is he a white boy?"

"Uh uh."

"Bonami sold him a bill of goods," repeated Lee. "But that's what I said about Fuzzy. Robbie and I both said, 'Man, how come this guy ain't a better judge of fighters?' I mean, I'm surprised at some of the people he signs. If I worked for him, I'd tell him, 'Don, you don't need to sign this guy.' And I told him that on the phone."

"Dumb motherfucker," Beavers muttered, shaking his head. "Who knows more about fuckin' boxers than me?" But what difference did it make, when Lee was *selling* ratings?

Beaver's eventually shifted tack. "Let's talk about our two drug dealers from Kentucky."

"Who's that?" asked the sixty-four-year-old Lee, who at times seemed almost senile.

"Yeah, we'll meet with them someplace," piped in Robbie, who wanted to do it in the sticks. "So I figure, because they're from Kentucky ... "

"Yeah," nodded his father.

"My guy from the army says that these motherfuckers have 'fuck you' money," said Beavers. They control, all the dope in fuckin' Louisville, Lexington, Frankfurt ... they got shit cans full of money ... The one [thing] that Kelly says is these young motherfuckers are crazy."

"Yeah," muttered Lee, taking it all in.

"So don't tell 'em nothing," warned Beavers, that "we can't do, because they be kickin' the door in and comin' with knives and shooting."

Finally, Bob Lee agreed that Glen Thomas, purportedly managed by a deadly Louisville drug syndicate, could fight for the USBA regional title.

"Because they don't know what the fuckin' regional fight is anyway," chortled Beavers.

"No, but it's glamorous with the belt," said Lee.

"I figure if they all come up with fifty thousand, for a fuckin' regional fight, if we get 'em in position for a fuckin' USBA or a world title title fight ..."

"Yeah, they come up with more," grasped Lee.

The founder of the IBF quickly added this caveat, mouthing to Beavers the message to be given to the drug lords: "You cannot tell anybody that we helped you. All you do is deal with me direct, one on one, we do what we have to do, and get it done, but don't go to other people in boxing."

★ ★ ★

Lee had no trouble helping his new "friends" and no qualms about sticking it to his enemies.

Promoter Dan Goosen was trying to put together an IBF middleweight title fight for Bernard Hopkins, but the mooted challenger wasn't rated. Hopkins had also dumped promoter Butch Lewis, and later sued him. Lewis was a longtime favourite of Bob Lee.

"I damn sure don't think that we should let Goosen go outside the fuckin' ratings. Fuck him," blustered Beavers.

"No," agreed Lee. "I'm gonna tell him, 'Hey man, I've had some talks with our championship chairman and he's opposed to us having a rating of convenience.'"

Lee then began getting angry. "I mean, he's the motherfucker that tried to go for our jugular."

"And it caused us a whole bunch of fuckin' problems," added Beavers, suddenly steamed himself.

"And he tells me how HBO loves Hopkins," sneered Lee. "In a pig's ass."

At junior-welter Kostya Tszyu was trying to get a non-title fight with IBF champ Vince Phillips. Akbar Muhammad, Phillips's manager, had called Lee.

"Akbar is a fuckin' tough hog, man," said Lee, "A piece of shit. Akbar came to my office, him and Bilal (Muhammad) and Bahu Muhammad, and they wanna talk about ... letting Kostya Tszyu have a bout against Phillips."

Lee didn't want to do that because he loathed Phillips's promoter, Bob Arum, and was worried that Phillips would get so busted up "he won't be able to fight for four months because [of] the cuts that he's sustained." If that happened, it meant Phillips would be on the shelf, and no sanction fees. "Now Arum is the same son of a bitch that forced us to have Terry Norris vacate his title [because he wasn't fighting his mandatory] … You go in to court, what you gonna tell the judge? 'Well judge, we didn't mean it?'"

Lee claimed with relish that Akbar Muhammad "walked away with his tail between his legs."

With enough intrigue to satisfy Machiavelli, Beavers and Lee finally got down to rating the lightweights.

"Somebody told me Shane Mosley was gettin' ready to fight somebody," said Lee.

"Getting ready to fight [Phillip] Holiday isn't he?"

"When is that?" asked Lee, who was so ignorant, he didn't grasp that Holiday was his own IBF lightweight champion.

"Damned if I know. We may have a new champion, 'cause this fuckin' kid Mosley can fight."

"Well," concluded Lee, who didn't care about boxing, just money, "that's both Cedric's [fighters], so he can't lose."

There was treachery afoot with the IBF featherweight championship. Don King was trying to steal Prince Naseem Hamed from Frank Warren, but Sky Television refused to buy the Prince fighting Hector Lizarraga, a tough, ex-California fieldhand who was one of the few fighters who had punched his way up without a major promoter. Duke Durden was ostensibly Lizarraga's manager. He was the first black man to serve on the Nevada State Athletic Commission, but he had a reputation as a stooge for Don King.

"They got a little argument going between Duke Durden [and King] and he's got Lizarraga. He wants him to fight Naseem Hamed. Now, there's some machinations again, made by King's people. I don't know what the deal is but they don't deal with Duke too much now."

Lee added, "King socializes with him and [will] have a drink with him, but he don't want the motherfucker working for him, ya know."

"He's another fuckin' drunk," sneered Beavers, taking a shot at both Durden and King.

"Yeah," agreed Lee, "but I don't know, some bad shit musta went down between him and King."

When they got down to the bantams, Lee's ignorance of fighters again reared up, though he knew all the gossip and politics involved. "Now, the number five guy, John Michael Johnson. That's not … John Michael Johnson [a former WBA world champion]?

"Yeah it is," confirmed Beavers.

"Somebody told me about him, who was it?"

"Hey, you the one who put the motherfucker in there."

"I told you to put him in there?" said Lee, not quite believing it.

"Yeah."

"That must have been one of Fuzzy Wuzzy's."

"It is Fuzzy Wuzzy's guy. He was our USBA champion, then he fucked us and fought for the WBO. The little cocksucker can hang himself before I put him back in the ratings, 'cause he ain't loyal."

By the time they'd gotten down to the junior-flyweights, both mens' interest flagged. There wasn't a lot of shakedown potential in a small fighters' ratings. American television wasn't interested in their fights.

"We don't even need to talk about that shit," Beavers said. Lee agreed, but Beavers continued to rattle on anyway. "This guy Jesus Chong just won. The number eight guy, he just won the WBO title, and he knocked out the number ten guy to win it. So, we're through with both these assholes, correct?" Fighting for a rival title could rule a boxer out of the IBF's ratings.

As for lesser titles, like the USBA, a sanctioning body is supposedly set up to determine the proper champions and challengers. But the IBF was just a money-making scam, and the promoter was actually telling the ratings officials who would be fighting for the title.

"Now, who is fighting for the USBA heavyweight title?" asked Beavers, who should have had some clue, since he was the IBF's ratings chairman, and on the championship committee. "Have we made the fight?

"Yeah," said Lee. "Cedric [Kushner] gave me … the names."

"Who the hell is it?" Beavers asked "You could let Lee Gilbert fight Mark Randazzo. That'd be the worse fuckin' USBA championship fight in history!"

Then both took a swipe at Kushner, who was paying off to make sure his fighters got rated.

"Have you ever ridden with Cedric driving?" Beavers asked.

"I rode to his house from his office and he, he, they tell me he's a piss-poor driver," Lee stammered, not wanting to say it.

"He can't drive a fuckin' lick," sneered Beavers, who was jealous because he could barely pay his home mortgage and drove two junky cars, while Kushner had gotten so wealthy from boxing that he collected automobiles, and bragged to fringe promoter Mike Acri that he "had $4 millon tucked away." Kushner had a Rolls Royce, a Masserati and a cherry Corvette that he'd bought from Jimmy Binns. Maybe he couldn't drive "worth a shit," but when the 350-pound Kushner wasn't compulsively stuffing his face, he was also buying buildings, while his fighters struggled to survive. An embittered Beavers knew this wouldn't have been possible if he hadn't helped fix the IBF's rankings.

Beavers wanted more, but so did Kushner. According to Bob Lee, "Walter

[Stone, the IBF's lawyer] said he talked to Cedric, Cedric asked him, 'What do I have to do? I've been very good to the IBF. It's shocking that I've never been Promoter of the Year. How come King is recognized as Promoter of the Year?'"

Beavers quickly answered the rhethorical question. "King's the only one who hasn't sued us."

★ ★ ★

Though judges are also supposed to be fair and impartial, in the IBF that was just another noble theory. Lee and Beavers discussed the recent case of a promoter who had vociferously criticised a female American judge for not voting for her fellow countryman.

"I heard Murad Muhammad showed his ass. Was it Lynn Carter that he jumped on?" asked Beavers.

"Yeah, he jumped her ass," nodded Lee.

"Crazy motherfucker," sighed Beavers.

"I mean, he shouldn't have said that," agreed Lee, "but what he was sayin' was right, from where he was comin' from, but he shouldn't have opened his mouth."

Beavers wondered what exactly was said.

"Well," said Lee, drolly, "he was sayin' shit, that, 'Here's an American coming to South Africa … the American oughta be voting for the American fighters.'"

"Well, that ain't right," figured Beavers, who still had a smattering of integrity about the game.

Lee gave him a cynical laugh.

"But that shit ain't right," persisted Beavers.

"But ya know, that's what them foreigners do," explained the all-knowing Lee. "You got a Jap [judge] comin' here with a Jap fighter, you know what that motherfucker gonna do."

"Yeah, he had his scorecard filled out before the fight started," agreed Beavers, a bit sadly.

Finally, Lee mentioned that they needed to get together.

"You wanna try to get into Richmond, instead of coming down here to Portsmouth?" asked Beavers.

"Well … "

"Easier on Bill [Brennan, another member of the IBF hierarchy]. Whatever ya wanna do."

"Well, I'm just, I don't wanna exclude Bill," said Lee, struggling to explain what he really did want.

"Right."

"But I'm just wondering," mumbled Lee, not wanting to say it.

"Come in and not tell him," Beavers interjected, trying to get to the point.

"Shit, he'll find out and be mad as a wet hen." Finally, Lee said, "The reason I'd like to come to Norfolk is … "

Now Beavers knew *exactly* what Lee wanted. A woman.

"Alright, you gonna come Monday, then I need to get her lined up, right? You like that college shit."

Lee gave a salacious laugh.

* * *

On 10 July 1997, Beavers called the office for another rigorous discussion on the merits of fighters.

"Hey Beavers," Lee exclaimed, greeting him warmly. "My man."

"I'm ready to do this stuff."

"Alright," Lee said, fumbling around, "let me just get my paper together."

Finally, Lee got organized. "Listen to me, we'll go with the IBF first."

Naturally, they started with the heavyweights. "The major change that we have to make is Tony Tucker's got to go." Tucker had just fought for the WBO title.

"Yep, he's out," agreed Beavers.

They got to Lee Gilbert, the glorified clubfighter. "Gilbert's gotta move down," said Lee. "Who do you have to put in there, man?"

"Well, let's see here."

"Oh shit," exclaimed Lee, "we back to David Tua again." Tua was the deadliest young puncher in boxing, but he had to get buried since he wasn't promoted by King. "How about Mark Randazzo?" asked Lee. Randazzo was a white stiff out of Chicago.

Beavers got so angry at the mere mention of Randazzo's name, he began sputtering. "He makes fuckin' Botha and Lee look like Superman. I mean, this guy is absolutely fuckin' awful."

Steve Pannell's name came up again. "I think he's lost every fuckin' ten [rounder] he's ever been in. Goddamnit," pleaded Beavers. But since he was "one of Jimmy Adams's guys" – a front for Don King – Lee quickly countered, "See if we can move him to number eight."

Lee however, would not give any rating to huge Michael Grant, who some boxing writers were calling the next great heavyweight. Grant had won the worthless IBO title and eventually was destroyed by Lennox Lewis for the real world championship, though many Americans predicted he would win.

After Lee had wreaked enough havoc on the heavyweight division, they got down to the super-middleweights.

"Ya got [Charles] Brewer as champion," said Lee, as is if he was trying to confirm it to himself.

"Right," said Beavers, "and [Gary] Ballard needs to go so far down you can't find him."

"Yeah, well, put Ballard behind Joseph Kiwanuka."

"Let's don't leave him that high, Bob. Did you see this fuckin' fight?"

"Yeah, I seen it but … "

"Motherfucker looked like he never had gloves on before."

"But aah, you know he's one of [King's] guys."

"Alright," shrugged Beavers, knowing he was fighting a losing battle. "That's okay. But what in the fuck's he gonna do with this no-fighting mother fucker?"

"Well, your guess is as good as mine."

★ ★ ★

The IBF's ratings were a joke and its awards were a sham. Even the regional titles were compromised by Bob Lee's greed. In early 1996, Lee suggested that "Antonio Barerra" be put in the USBA ratings at 122 pounds for his February fight with Kennedy McKinney, a former IBF champion.

"Antonio Barerra?" Beavers had never heard of him. "That's Marco Barerra?"

"Yeah," Lee said, struggling to name the superb fighter who would eventually become the first man to beat Prince Naseem Hamed.

"I got no problem with that," said Beavers, enthusiastically, "that's a helluva fighter."

Lee had already sanctioned the fight, to be promoted by Murad Muhammad.

"For what?" asked Beavers, knowing neither was a "world" champ anymore.

"For the, ahh, ahh, USBA title," stammered Lee, almost embarrassed.

"How the fuck can they fight for the USBA title? This motherfucker's from Mexico City."

"He's livin' in the States."

"He's a lyin' motherfucker," shot back Beavers.

"So he is."

"He's a lyin', no good, bean pie-eatin' motherfucker," bristled the profane Beavers. "He ain't livin' in no fuckin' States."

"Yeah."

"Maybe ten days before a fight," Beavers sneered.

"But he goes in before he fights," countered Lee slyly, looking for any loophole he could possibly find to justify calling this a United States Boxing Association title fight, so he could grab a piece of Barerra's purse.

"He ain't livin' in a hotel on the Boardwalk," snapped Beavers. "That lyin' motherfucker. That motherfucker [promoter Murad Muhammad] ain't no good, is he?"

"Shit, tell me about it."

"Fuckin' Muslims," muttered Beavers, who was so angry, he was becoming tongue-tied, "boy, you can't goddamn ... "

"They the crookedest motherfuckers you ever seen," agreed Lee.

"Livin' the fuckin' States, my ASS. The motherfucker goes to the University of Mexico City. Fuck, that's a hell of a commute every day for school, isn't it?"

"No shit."

Finally, Beavers asked, "Where do I put him from, California?"

"Yeah. Is that where's he from?" asked Lee, who not only was ignorant and corrupt but sometimes comically slow on the uptake.

"Bob, what the fuck, aren't you listening to me? I said the motherfucker's from Mexico City. He goes to the University of Mexico City. This motherfucker don't live in the United States."

"Well then, put him from California," replied Lee, who didn't care if he came from Mars so long as he got his sanction fee.

On 5 February 1996, Home Box Office television kicked off its new series *Boxing After Dark* with Barerra-McKinney. It turned out to be one of the great fights of the 1990s, for an utterly bogus title.

★ ★ ★

On 8 August 1997, the great minds at the IBF were at it again, tortured by the momentous decisions they had to make.

"Hey, listen, in the middleweights," said Bob Lee, "can we get Simon Brown in the IBF?"

"Ahh," I guess," replied Beavers, reluctantly. "Do we need him in the IBF?"

"Yeah, I need him in there."

"Okay, I got a magic motherfuckin' pencil, boss."

They got to the junior-middleweights. "Robbie called me the other day about this guy Carl Daniels," said Beavers. Daniels was a former IBF champ now hooked up with King. "I was told the motherfucker was going to jail..."

"Well, how high can we get him?" asked Bob Lee.

On 5 January 1998, the two were doing the ratings by phone again.

Though it was a new year, time for resolutions, nothing at the IBF had changed.

"Can we make [Britain's Henry] Akinwande one-A?" asked Lee.

It was a shocking request. Six months earlier, Akinwande had "fought" one of the most stinking championship fights ever before he was disqualified in the fifth round against Lennox Lewis for the WBC heavyweight title.

"Ah, you think we need to do that shit?"

"Well, he belongs to you know who." Don King.

As for tough no-names like cruiser Jakob Mofokeng, who was trying to fight his way out of poverty in South Africa? "Now Mofokeng, didn't Ced [Kushner] say to get rid of him?" asked Lee.

"He said take his title," replied Beavers.

"Alright, then we gotta move him down."

Beavers, who knew what it was like to sweat and bleed in a boxing ring, tried to stall, and finally said, "Let me see if I can get ahold of Ced, and see if he still wants to do that."

Lee went on, "Now you can get rid of this Jaime Quinonez from Ecuador? He's not gonna fight for us."

Former light-heavyweight champion Virgil Hill, who made a record twenty-two defences in two different incarnations as WBA and IBF champ, also hit the tobaggon because he "getting ready to fight for the WBA [and] we don't owe Hill nothin'," figured Lee.

King got Kenny Bowman kicked up, while Jimmy Adams did the same for Lincoln Carter. Neither light-heavy could carry Hill's foul cup.

Another King pug who got preferential treatment was Byron Mitchell at super-middleweight. "Can we upgrade him, about eleven?" asked Lee.

"Hmmm. Let's do him to about twelve or something."

"Okay."

Beavers added, "He's from fuckin' Alabama, so the chances are he can't fight a lick."

As for Britain's noble warriors? "Dean Francis just beat the number thirteen guy, so he can take his place, but this kid Robin Reid from Great Britain, who was the WBA champion or something, he just got beat by Malinga, so probably should go."

Lee barely nodded. These fighters meant nothing to him. They weren't connected.

"Now Ryan Rhodes, number six, didn't he just get beat?" asked Lee.

"Yeah, he lost for the WBO title, so he can get the fuck outta there."

In another move, far more absurd, Lee mentioned Abdullah Ramadan. "Shouldn't he go up there?" asked the president of the IBF.

"Now, the motherfucker ain't but like twelve and ten."

"Huh?" asked Lee.

"His record ain't but like twelve and ten," repeated Beavers.

Lee laughed. "Well, let's move him to number two then, not number one." And Jason Pappillion, who "was fighting and winning?"

"Kill him," said Beavers.

Papillion's manager had been calling for weeks trying to get him to number one, but Papillion no longer was with King. The IBF was afraid to kick Papillion right out of the ratings because they feared a lawsuit.

"I mean we step on a dick if we do that," figured Beavers, again expressing himself so eloquently. "Papillion, there's nothing we can with shit. We're stuck with him. I mean, he's way too high."

"Yeah," agreed Lee. "But he was put there because he was Fuzzy's."

"Yeah, and now we're stuck with the motherfucker," concluded the ratings chairman.

When they got to junior-welterweight, Lee asked, "Now who's got Virgil McClendon?"

"Fuzz," replied Beavers.

As for Diobelys Hurtado, who had nearly stopped the great Pernell Whitaker?

"Who, who's got him?" asked Lee.

"Damned if I know, but why do we owe him anything. He's never done nothin' for us."

"Alright, leave him out then."

"Fuck him," chortled Beavers.

France's Bruno Wartelle hadn't even had a ten-round fight, but he was one of "Fuzzy's guys," so Lee said, "We'll put him on next time, make a note of that."

At 130, Britain's Barry Jones bit the dust for committing the unpardonable sin of fighting for the WBO title. According to Beavers though, at featherweight, "This fuckin' kid [Angel] Vazquez is a bad bitch."

Lee simply dismissed it, though American fight experts figured Vazquez would probably behead Prince Naseem. Lee nominated Dramane Nabaloum instead.

"Where the fuck is he from?" asked Beavers. "Let me run the motherfucker. I never heard of the fuckin' guy." Neither had Lee, who painstakingly had to spell out his name.

At bantam, Beavers asked about USBA bantamweight champ Ancee Gedeon, a Haitian refugee who was parentless and had slept on the dangerous Miami streets before he was allowed to crash at night in his trainer's gym. They were going to strip him of his hard-earned title.

"Did you put this fuckin' Ancee Gedeon [on notice] this cocksucker's so far overdue?"

"Yeah, we gotta," agreed Lee.

"Yep, get him off his ass," added Beavers.

At junior-bantam, Julio Gamboa could be put in, though Lee had to spell his name to his ratings chairman.

"Alright, that Fuzz's?"

"Yeah," said Lee.

When they got to the number fifteen flyweight, from Thailand, Lee began to giggle as he tried to spell his impossible name. Mercifully, it was aborted when Lee suddenly realized that he was a WBO titleholder. But first, Lee warned him to double check; King might've given him the kid's name.

Rugged Carlos Murillo was put in at number ten, but Beavers didn't want him to go any higher: "On two different occasions, he fought for the WBA and lost. I don't feel we owe that prick nothing."

But Lee, who was Mr Racial Sensitivity, disagreed. "Move him in between the two Japs."

★ ★ ★

On Monday, January 5, Beavers called again after getting a ridiculous message to put "a typical fuckin' New England fighter," Sammy Gerard, into the ratings, so he could fight Sugar Shane Mosley, who many said was the new Sugar Ray Robinson. Beavers couldn't believe it.

"Did I say Shane Mosley?" asked Lee, whose ignorance of boxing was downright dangerous. "Oh shit." He meant Israel "Pito" Cardona, which was bad enough.

"I can tell you this, he ain't gonna beat this fuckin' kid Cardona," said Beavers.

"Cardona's pretty good, huh?"

"This little motherfucker can fight."

Lee then related how "Rob Murray was in here pissing and moaning," trying to get an IBF light-heavyweight title fight for Philadelphia's Will Taylor against a supposedly reformed ex-drug baron from St Louis called William Guthrie. According to Beavers, Taylor had no business fighting Guthrie, because he had only "twelve fights or some shit."

Lee agreed. Somehow though, Taylor was going to become "the fucking mandatory," even though Beavers figured Guthrie will "kill this kid Will Taylor."

"Well, Will Taylor wants to fight him," said Lee.

"He may fight him, cause he's a street kid, but he's gonna get the country dog shit beat out of him." Realizing it was no use, Beavers just shrugged, "If he can get a payday, let him fight."

★ ★ ★

On 7 January 1998, Beavers called Bill Brennan, who was a father figure to him. Brennan was a grizzled ex-Navy man who looked old enough to have sailed with Lord Nelson. He had got Beavers involved in boxing regulation after Beavers himself had retired from the Navy. Brennan had been a president of the WBA and of the Virginia commission, and had encouraged both Beavers and Lee to get involved in boxing politics. He was now pushing ninety and Lee had far eclipsed his mentor.

"Brennan was a tough old bastard," according to one boxing figure. In 1965, the legendary Willie Pep mounted a comeback after six years out of the ring. At forty-three, he had blown all his money on "fast women and slow horses." He won nine in a row against second- and third-raters, then agreed to box an exhibition with speedy Calvin Woodland in Virginia.

At the weigh-in, Brennan told him, "This fight's for real."

"I agreed to an exhibition," protested Pep, who was old enough to be Woodland's father.

"If you don't box, I'll get you suspended all over the country," Brennan told him.

Pep reluctantly got into the ring and got a hiding for a piddling $500. Luckily, it was only a six-rounder. Pep never fought again. Still, he says, "I got a wife and a television – and both of 'em are working."

Brennan complained to Beavers on the phone, "Man, it's been a long dry summer." No payoffs had been coming his way.

Pancho Fernandez was due up from South America, and would be bringing something, since he was trying to get his pugs rated. But after three weeks, Beavers was still re-arranging his schedule and there was no Pancho.

"He never tells you where he's gonna stay. He calls and says, 'I'm at the Holiday Inn.'"

Brennan gave a gruff laugh. Beavers began to chuckle too. "I mean, goddamn, there must be forty Holiday Inns in Tidewater. You gotta start lookin' around for the sonofabitch."

"I don't know why Bob puts up with him," said Brennan.

"He's crazy. But fuckin' Bob, this shit with him is outta control. Me and him talked about ratings. Never said a word about anybody's fighters but King's. Every fighter he had mentioned, we gotta move this guy. Don't make no difference whether they can fight or not."

King had just signed an ex-WBA champ, Quincy Taylor. Lee "wanted to put him in the top five of our fucking ratings and the motherfucker hadn't fought in fourteen months. He hadn't fought since Keith Holmes knocked him out. I said, 'Bob, we can't put this motherfucker in.'"

"Well, I don't know," shrugged the old man. "But I'll tell you one thing, it ain't like it used to be."

Beavers bitched that so little money was coming his way. "Fuck. I can hardly even pay my motherfucking bills. I'm still working the fucking warehouse at fucking night and trying to do this shit during the day, this shit is killing me."

Beavers had a contract with the Commonwealth of Virginia to run a privatized version of the state boxing commission, which he called the Virginia Boxing Association. "The first fucking quarter, I got sixteen hundred dollars. You can't live on that."

"That's crazy," agreed Brennan.

Beavers was sick of Lee's stinginess and greed. "Bob and Robbie and all them motherfuckers are getting big salaries, and this fucking Weitzel [the IBF's money man] was getting rich."

Beavers, who still had some corroded feelings of right and wrong, finally said, "I don't know how come we ain't getting sued on a weekly fucking basis." Lee's ratings had gotten so corrupt, complained Beavers, that there was a promoter in Thailand who was calling for a world title fight and so some mystery fighter suddenly got put into the world ratings by Lee, even though "nobody's got a record on him."

Still, Beavers's biggest bitch was money: "The minute King got involved in shit, me and you get cut out, you know that."

"Yeah, shit," replied Brennan, sadly, "I been cut out so long." He began to moan about a recent trip to Thailand: "It wasn't any money. Come to payoff and they run out of money."

Beavers said, "You come back with a suitcase full of that shit, you ain't got but twenty dollars."

Beavers was sick of everything. With Senator John McCain's reform law coming in July, things had gotten so dire that he was contemplating getting out of boxing and getting "a full-time fucking job."

He complained, "Bob's fucking me and you so much," and ripped into Lee's drug-addled son, who he felt was the bagman when it came to payoffs from King. "Fucking Robbie might as well open an office up down in fuckin' Florida, as much time as he spends down there with King … He's down there on a weekly fucking basis."

"Maybe, he's, uh, what do you call him, a mail carrier or something."

"Sure he is, but the mail ain't coming south, is it?"

Finally, Beavers got philosophical. "The handwriting is on the wall, Bill."

"I know it, I can see it," agreed the battle-scarred old man. "I just been sitting up here being quiet. I ain't doing nothing."

Media criticism of the IBF had risen to the point where Lee had become paranoid about the FBI and wiretaps. That's why King was

"Fuzzy" and Cedric Kushner was "the Fat Man." Payoffs were "turkey" or "ginseng."

Beavers obviously got into the IBF because of the power it promised. Payoffs were also a big factor. But because of Lee, who threw nickels around like they were manhole covers, Beavers, who was fifty-four, ended up "humping these fucking carpets at night."

"Damn," moaned Beavers, "this is physical motherfucking labour, Bill. I be so nasty and tired. I don't get home till about six-thirty, seven-thirty in the morning. I be so motherfucking tired, I can hardly get out of the car."

Maybe Beavers did sweat, but nobody was trying to batter him into unconsciousness. "I gotta pay the bills," he said, self-righteously. "I gotta family to feed." But "financially, I'm fuckin' ruined."

Beavers had become so haunted, he even mentioned the possibility of prison. "If the Feds are looking at us, the shit that he's doing, and the way people talk about him, that he's fucking Don King's punk ... There's only one thing that can happen."

"Well, that's what I'm thinking," replied Brennan. "I don't even talk to people any more."

"How the fuck can you? I mean, the shit he does is so fucking ridiculous. Ray Charles could see that he just works for fucking King."

"Well, that's the word," replied Brennan, a slick old Navy vet who didn't last a lifetime by stirring up rebellions.

Beavers was a mutineer, despite his two decades in the service. "If me and you knew how much money this motherfucker had took, *shit*. If we would have got our fucking end, we would have been sitting on Easy Street."

Beavers also bitched about little things. A guy named Acada sent him the names of six fighters – all named Acada, after him. "They ain't got no records because they change their names. You don't know who the fuck they are."

"They do that in Thailand too," complained Brennan. "Dutchboy Jim ..."

"They must have got that shit off the paint cans," figured Beavers, who was in a lousy mood.

Brennan agreed. "They're a bunch of thieves over there. I mean, some lulus."

"Ain't as many as there is in New Jersey," sneered Beavers, taking another shot at Lee.

Brennan didn't like the gist of the conversation, but he admitted, "Well, something's got to blow. I just got that feeling. I've had it for a little while, too."

"Bill, listen to me," Beavers said, firmly. "I'm not going to jail for this motherfucker."

"I'm not either."

★ ★ ★

On 12 January 1998, Beavers called Brennan again. It was 11:32 in the morning. Doug began another harangue about how cheap Lee was. He bitched that he was driving a car with 150,000 miles on it, and that his wife Susan's had another 130,000. Both cars had tyres balder than Yul Brynner's head.

"It don't even bother [Lee] that I'm starvin' to death."

Though Lee was one of the most powerful boxing figures in the world, both men agreed that when they rode with Lee, he never talked about boxing. He just wanted to talk "about pussy."

One of the prostitutes Beavers lined him up with "was as big as me … I mean a nice old girl, but goddamn, she was forty years old. I carried her ass in there to him. I mean a big, healthy motherfucker, must of weighed two hundred pounds. It wasn't as bad as the motherfucker with the watch. You didn't know whether was a boy or a girl."

"She didn't have no teeth," recalled Brennan.

"To this goddamn day," marvelled Beavers, "I don't know [whether] that stinky motherfucker was a boy or a girl."

On January 20, Beavers called Lee at the IBF's office in New Jersey.

"Listen, you gonna be home tomorrow morning?"

"Yeah."

"Thought I might bring a little ginseng up to help you get through the winter."

Brennan chuckled. "Sounds good to me."

On January 22, Beavers excitedly called again. "Hey, did you guys hear the news?"

"What news? Mike [Tyson] shot himself?"

"No, Clinton just announced that he did fuck that broad [Monica Lewinsky]."

"There ain't nothing wrong with that."

"But *he didn't come*," exclaimed Beavers, laughing like hell.

★ ★ ★

A lantern-jawed Puerto Rican named John Ruiz would eventually become the first Hispanic to win a version of the heavyweight championship after hooking up with Don King. But for a long time he couldn't get any sort of rating with the IBF.

"This Ruiz is not with Fuzzy, so we just leave him alone," ordered Lee.

Another time, Dan Goosen, one the main honchos at America Presents, called Lee and complained that his fighters were being ignored.

"I don't know what's wrong," Lee said, mimicking and mocking Goosen at the same time. "'We can't get any of our guys taken care of. I don't know if Beavers has a hard-on for us. We want to work with you guys, but we just can't seem to get you to take care of our fighters.'"

Goosen was talking about Britain's Robert McCracken and the Ruelas brothers, both of whom had been world champions, with Rafael once holding the IBF lightweight championship.

"Fuck the Ruelases," spat Beavers. And Goosen? "Fuck him. He sued us."

Dan Goosen was trying to pitch David Reid, who had won a 1996 Olympic title with one punch but who turned out to be a ratings disaster for HBO television.

"Where's Reid going to be able to fight," asked Beavers. "He got that droopy goddamn eye. His eye looks like it's going to fall out on the floor every time he fights."

"Yeah. He's going to wind up blind, man," figured Lee.

Beavers asked, "Why are we letting Hasim Rahman be the Intercontinental and the USBA champion?"

"Well, because he didn't lose either title."

"I know, but shouldn't he give one of them up? Because that costs us sanction fees."

"Yeah, well it does," agreed Lee, "but he wants to hang on."

"Oh yeah, Mittleman, that greedy motherfucker," sneered Beavers.

In April 2001, Rahman won the *real* heavyweight championship of the world by knocking out Lennox Lewis in one of the biggest upsets in history. Bob Mittleman was no longer his manager. Don King had tried to steal Rahman, and did so briefly, telling him, "I make the ratings, and you'll never get a big fight without me," but Cedric Kushner won him back. Stan Hoffman was his new manager and by then, Kushner and Hoffman didn't need Lee.

On 6 March 1998, Beavers called Brennan and was joking with him about the 1-0 Thai, who had just won by knockout and was both the WBU and the WBF titleholder, too.

"Those guys are a trip," laughed Beavers, speaking of the conniving Thais. "Hey, being the championship chairman, I have to tell you something."

"Oh good," replied Brennan, who dreaded hearing it.

"Okay, your Intercontinental middleweight champion is Lanasamba Dejole or some shit. This motherfucker's got eight wins and fourteen losses."

Brennan gave a sad, disbelieving laugh. Beavers also informed him that Lee "wanted to take an interim championship and just hand over a world title to him. I told Bob, 'No way in hell.'"

"He needs to be slapped," sighed Brennan.

"It's the laughing stock of the whole European situation," said Beavers. "I'm going to catch him as soon as I get off the phone with you. I'm going to tell Bob, 'Fuck off!' I can't put no motherfucker that's got an eight and fourteen goddamn record in the world ratings. I mean, this shit is out of control."

"I don't know what's causing this," said Brennan.

"Well, Bob is so motherfucking greedy."

When Beavers called Lee eleven days later, he was singing a different tune.

"You fucked up."

"What happened man?"

"You didn't fax me the number for the big [lottery] game."

"Oh yeah."

"But nobody hit it," Beavers said. "This motherfucker's forty million dollars."

Lee gave a greedy little laugh: "I better jump on this motherfucker."

"They pull Tuesday and Friday ... Forty million *fucking* dollars."

"Boy, if I had that," sighed Lee, "I'd be pissin' in high grass."

Beavers also gave his boss the bad news that the USA Network, which had run the longest televised weekly boxing show in history, was throwing in the towel after seventeen years, despite the fact that it was reportedly the highest-rated show on the cable network.

"Yeah, they tell me that the guy who bought USA is a fag and he don't like boxing," said Lee.

"That's what I heard."

"He likes to be cuddled and squeezed," mocked Lee.

"Ain't that some shit."

"Hey, the fags are running the motherfucking world," said Lee, firmly setting him straight.

On April 7, Beavers again called Lee and talk turned to another huge lottery. Beavers wanted Lee to fax him the numbers that he wanted to play. "In case you hit, I don't want to have to run away with your money."

"Yeah," said Lee, laughing.

"The fucking temptation," said Beavers, thinking out loud.

"Boy, temptation is a bitch, ain't it?" said Lee.

"[It] be a mutherfucker," Beavers agreed. "Fifty-million dollars ... *Hey Bob, I'm in Afghanistan — me and your money*."

Lee began to hoot again, before speaking with surprising intimacy, "Listen, did you see where some guy up in New York bailed out with seventy three million dollars, man?"

"No."

"He done hauled ass," said Lee, giving a wistful sigh. The ex-cop began to fantasize what he'd do with all that stolen money. "I'd get me an island with young bitches."

"Real young," cooed Beavers, conspiratorially.

"Don't even know how to pee good," laughed Lee.

On 30 April 1998, Beavers spoke to Lee three times during the day. Don King was on trial again, this time for insurance fraud. The Feds were trying to lock King up for the third time, contending that he'd ripped off insurers Lloyds of London for a large sum. The fight game has its own grapevine, and it's a lot faster than CNN.

"What did you hear about Fuzzy Wuzzy's … court case?" asked Beavers.

"It's in progress right now. You know, ain't nothing exciting happening, and nothing new."

"Have you talked to him?"

"I talked to him the night before last. I called around ten minutes to twelve. I got ahold of him and he was sleeping. You know … we only talked a couple of minutes. He said, 'I'll get back to you tomorrow' … and I [haven't] heard a word."

"Motherfucker trying to put you in jail, you ain't got time for chit-chat," figured Beavers.

"He's fighting for his life, man," said Lee.

"I mean that fucking organization would go *ka-poot* if he goes to fucking jail."

"Oh man, tell me about it."

"Goofy motherfuckers that he's got working for him."

"Oh boy," sighed Lee.

"Drunks and fools."

"Yeah," agreed Lee. "He got people down there that need head examination, man."

★ ★ ★

On May 15, Lee told Beavers, "Duva called up and he wants to come in here to see me."

"Maybe gonna bring you a present," figured Beavers.

"Yeah, he's coming with his father [Lou]."

"That ain't no present," cracked Beavers. "Maybe they want to do something with that fucking heavyweight Michael Grant. Maybe they're gonna … give up the fucking IBO title and bring you a suitcase."

On June 2, Beavers spoke to Robbie Lee, and trashed Walter Stone, the IBF attorney who had testified before Senator John McCain's Senate Commerce Committee and made an absolute ass of himself trying to defend Bob Lee.

"Hey, did you see an ad from Walter Stone in the [IBF] book?"

"Should have been one," slowly said Lee Jr.

"Well, I must not be able to find it and I looked."

Robbie claimed he'd called him, and Stone had promised to buy an ad. "And the motherfucker still owes me $175 from last year for a box of cigars," sputtered Robbie, now getting mad.

"Now how much did we pay him this past year?" asked Beavers.

"Half a million dollars."

"*MOTHERFUCKER*," exclaimed the poverty-stricken Beavers.

On a more serious note, Beavers had talked to Stone about McCain's new federal law, which prohibited members of a state athletic commission from serving with a sanctioning group. Beavers was trying to find a way around it.

"Like if I withdraw my [IBF] membership."

"Yeah," nodded Lee Sr, all ears.

"Because there's a stipulation, it says you can't be compensated."

"But now," said Lee, who grasped exactly what Beavers was saying, "if you withdraw from being ratings chairman."

"Right."

"And we worked it through the back door with Darryl [Peoples, Lee's nephew] ... and let Darryl put in for expenses."

"Is he gonna bring me cigarettes when I go to jail?" replied Beavers, half-joking.

In June, Pancho Fernandez from Colombia arrived in Norfolk, Virginia, and spent two days running around trying to find Beavers, who was out of town at a boxing show. "Why doesn't this motherfucker tell somebody when he's coming," cursed Beavers jovially.

When he did make contact with Beavers, Fernandez was in a noisy hotel room and the American could not understand his broken English. Beavers told Lee that Fernandez and his boys had the TV on so loudly that he couldn't hear them clearly. The IBF president opined, "You know how they are man. Five or six of [them] suckers in one fucking room."

"Forty Mexicans live in one house!"

"Yeah," agreed the droll Lee.

"They family-oriented."

Finally Beavers asked, "Do you have any idea what the fuck Pancho wants?"

"Probably ... something with some of those old dog-ass fighters that they got in the ratings."

"Goddamn."

"He can't bring us that shit he be bringing us, man."

"No," agreed Beavers.

"I mean," elaborated Lee, who had formed the IBF on a promise of honest, competent ratings, "we shouldn't even have them fucking guys in [the] ratings."

The IBF had made millions of dollars claiming their rankings were the standard of the industry, but one junior-bantam was rated despite having only four pro bouts, none of them in the past eighteen months. Insiders kept bitterly complaining that there were too many Colombians in the IBF ratings.

"Well, when I go see this silly motherfucker, I won't commit to nothing," said Beavers. "Now, what if he brought a little something?"

Lee advised him to tell Fernandez that it would be very difficult to justify ranking his "cannibal fighters".

"You have to play that shit by ear," instructed Lee.

"Okay."

"See what you might be able to shake out the tree."

Beavers finally met with Pancho and his band of Colombians.

"Did he give you a list, of names?" Lee asked afterwards.

"Well, they were just talking about Moises Pedroza, primarily. He's a junior-lightweight that we had in the ratings ... The guy that was with him, that's his fighter, and he brought a little something."

"Yeah, well, what about some of the other sorry fighters that they have?"

Beavers didn't readily reply. He just began sputtering, "I mean, four and oh [four wins and no losses], and ranked number two in the fucking world. What sense do that make?"

"None at all, man," agreed Lee, who'd put him there.

The real news was that the Colombians had paid off, and Doug quickly asked what should he do with their "funny money."

Lee told him to hold on to it, adding, "Do that for me, 'cause I may have to take a hop down there in a month or so and sit down and talk with you about a few other things."

On June 29, Lee and Beavers spoke again.

"Well, listen, uh uh, you still holding that thing from Pancho?" asked Lee.

"Yeah, absolutely."

"What ... he was needing, is there a possibility of it being done?"

"Can be done," replied Beavers, as he agreed that Moises Pedroza's rating in the IBF could be improved for money. Neither crook had any respect for Pancho Fernandez, the Colombian who came bearing gifts. "You know, this motherfucker's an order of french fries short of a Happy Meal," said Beavers.

* * *

On 21 July 1998, Beavers called and spoke to Robert Lee Jr, wanting to know if he was going to get some money from Don King.

"When you going to make a run?" he asked, in IBF code.

"Damned if I know. Spoke to him last week for a hot minute." Junior then began to cough. "Excuse me. I don't know when I'm gonna get down there. I may see him in a couple of weeks, but I like to see him sooner."

"And that be nice," purred Beavers, who frequently used black street slang in order to form more of a rapport with the Lees.

"It's been a lean year," sighed Junior.

"You ain't shittin.'We have to wait … No motherfucking Thanksgiving, no motherfucking turkey now." The word turkey was code for a bribe.

"I know … and no real turkey either."

Lee's son had no trouble taking the blood money that came with the fight game, but admitted, "I don't watch the fights."

On August 21, Beavers called Lee Sr and bitched about having to oversee a small-time card in Lexington, Virginia. "I mean the motherfucking only restaurant in town is the Tastee Freeze."

"That's the local eatery?" replied Lee, who loved food as much as money and illicit sex.

"Yeah. The Tastee Freeze. If you don't like soft fuckin' ice cream, you're in deep shit."

Finally, Beavers got down to business. "I'm still holding the shit from Pancho. You gonna make a trip down here?"

"Yeah, but you know, I'm so tight right now. But I will."

"Maybe this time that you get down here, maybe we'll have something from Fuzz."

"Yeah, that's what I'm … bankin' on," said Lee, "and maybe it can be a double exchange."

"Oooh, I like that shit,"

On August 31, Beavers spoke to Lee four times. The boss had been away.

"You bring anything back?" asked Beavers.

"Well, I … managed to do a little of that, you know," Lee replied, warily. The ex-cop was cautious about how to send Beavers his cut. "I don't know whether to settle Fed Ex or whether to hold it until I can … "

"Why don't you just hold it until you come down?" interrupted Beavers. "Maybe you'll have something else."

On September 8, Beavers spoke to Lee again on the phone as they did the monthly world ratings. Young men who made the daily sacrifice of blood, sweat and pain had their futures on the line.

"Now, can we put Saul Montana in at number two?" Lee asked of the battle-scarred Mexican cruiser.

"Sure [we] can do whatever the fuck we wanna do, can't we? I book the fucking ratings.'

Upon reflection though, Beavers asked, "You don't think nobody'll say nothing, 'cause he wasn't [in the rating previously]?"

"I hope they don't remember. Who gives a shit?"

Though the IBF would sink to almost anything, some matches were too one-sided even for them. In one call, Beavers spoke to Darryl Peoples, Lee's nephew, who was now masquerading as the new ratings chairman. A flesh peddler from Roy Jones camp called the office, desperately trying to get a hapless white club fighter rated so that Jones could annihilate him for $3.5 million on HBO.

Peoples told Beavers that he had instructed Jones's flunky to "call the [W]B-A and the [W]B-C."

"That's who the fuck you need to talk to," shot back Beavers.

"I couldn't believe they said that," said Peoples.

"They got balls, man," sighed Doug.

Peoples had been given the sham title of ratings chairman to allow Beavers to continue working for a state commission. But the latest ratings chart almost gave the game away.

"You still got me as fuckin' ratings chairman," said Beavers, after he got a preliminary fax with the IBF rankings.

"Oh!" laughed Peoples.

"Well fuck me! You are trying to send me to fucking jail?" Beavers said, laughing back.

"I don't want you to go to jail," Peoples replied, suddenly contrite.

Beavers chuckled again, but nervously. "And not down [here], cause they don't bullshit in prison down South."

The *real* IBF ratings chairman ordered Peoples, "Change my name off there, put yours on and let's get the motherfucker printed."

★ ★ ★

Beavers spoke to Lee about Butch Lewis, the black promoter who is a dead ringer for fifties pop music legend Little Anthony of Little Anthony and the Imperials, and who had long had influence with Lee. Lewis's unheralded heavyweight Vaughn Bean stunned the boxing world by almost beating champion Evander Holyfield. Named as mandatory challenger, Bean had accepted money to step aside so that Holyfield could fight Michael Moorer, a common practice in boxing.

"Why the fuck do we owe Bean now?" asked Beavers

"We don't owe him," said Lee, "especially when his ... manager is being a real pussy."

"I think there's some short-memory motherfuckers."

"Ain't they, though?"

"I mean, when he makes $350,000 step-aside money, he should've sent a fucking turkey."

"Shit," sneered Lee. "Yeah, yeah, he should have, man."

"Cause we didn't have to let him do that."

"No. He had 200,000 on the table with [promoter Dino] Duva … and we went to the meeting, and I pushed the championship committee to give him three-fifty."

"Right," chirped in Beavers, outraged.

"So they give him three-fifty, Pat English [Main Events' lawyer] balked at it, but it was a very mild balk…. What's his name, John Davimos [Michael Moorer's promoter] said he wasn't paying it. But the Holyfield people, in order to get the thing done, Holyfield split it down the middle. Holyfield paid one-seventy-five and Moorer paid one-seventy-five."

"That's when Holyfield fought Moorer?" Beavers asked.

"The step-aside was so Holyfield could fight Moorer," explained Lee.

Bean had been ranked the IBF's "mandatory challenger" and had priority, but he'd faced an outrageous collection of stiffs

"I don't know where Moorer is now," bristled Beavers, angry that there was no kickback. "I don't think that we gotta fuck with him, we can start dropping his ass."

"Yeah," agreed Lee.

On 21 October 1998, Beavers met with Bill Brennan and Bob Lee in a room at the Portsmouth, Virginia, Holiday Inn. After Beavers and Brennan left, there was a rap at the door. Lee answered. It was Special Agent Theresa Reilly of the FBI. She was an attractive, frizzy-haired brunette, with a young, earnest, chiselled face. She told the startled Lee that she had audio and video proof that he had taken bribes, and asked to come in.

"We explained we were conducting an investigation into corruption in the boxing industry and the meeting had just been taped," Special Agent Reilly later testified. "We were looking for his cooperation."

Lee wearily invited the agents in. No soon had Reilly's partner started to play the tape than Lee's phone rang. Since this was a crime scene, Richards grabbed the phone. It was an emergency call for Lee: his thirty-three-year-old daughter, Cheryl, had just been rushed to intensive care in Newark, New Jersey, suffering from sickle cell anemia. She died that night.

The agents tried to give Lee privacy to call his wife, but Lee was told he couldn't go any further than the bedroom to get his medication for diabetes and heart disease. They quickly confiscated the $1,000 payoff from his natty blazer.

After Lee got word that his daughter died, Reilly went over to the funeral home.

"Did Don King pay for the funeral?" she asked

"No," said the attendant, who thought the question was in very bad taste.

★ ★ ★

On 5 November 1998, Beavers drove to the parking lot at Northern Neck Seafood, a country store along the Rappahanock River at Naylor's Beach, Virginia. There he met Bill Brennan, and climbed into the old man's pick-up truck. It was 1:52 PM.

"We're in trouble."

Brennan didn't say anything.

"Deep trouble," reiterated Beavers, solemnly.

"Yeah, I was kinda scared it was coming to that," Brennan finally said.

"Too goddamn reckless," Beavers sighed.

"I know."

"But they got, they got that meeting, that meeting that me, you and Bob had, that shit's on tape … passing the money and everything."

"Yeah," said Brennan. The cagey old Navy man was scared to say anything.

"I don't want to go to jail," said Beavers.

"Well, you know, you got to take care of yourself."

"I told you a long time ago, when this shit got outta hand . . . I didn't intend on me or you … going to jail."

"I ain't gonna talk to them," Brennan said abruptly, cutting right to the chase.

"Huh?" said Beavers, who couldn't believe his ears.

"I ain't gonna talk to them," repeated the gnarled old man. "If they come see me, might as well save their time, 'cause I ain't gonna talk to them … I don't trust them any more than I do Bob or you. I've seen some of the things they have pulled."

By now, Beavers was all but pleading. "If you cooperate, they won't do nothing, 'cause me and you ain't who they're after."

Brennan mulled it over.

"We gotta cooperate," wheedled Beavers.

"Well, I don't know that."

"I mean, we gotta fucking cooperate with them."

"You mean, we gotta tell them we accepted money?"

"They already know that," said Beavers, who wanted to scream.

Brennan shook his ancient head.

"They know every fucking thing," shrieked Beavers. "Did you know Junior's got strung out on fucking drugs again? Have you seen any championship reports? They're not letting him work. He's been missing for fucking, six or eight weeks."

Brennan weighed his options while Beavers insisted, "Right now, what we gotta do is stay the fuck out of jail. You know he ain't done right by me and you."

Brennan agreed.

"Let me tell you something," went on Beavers, trying to justify his treachery, "me and you've done all the fucking work, and they're all getting fucking rich and don't know a fucking thing about boxing. You're the one who struggled with the championship fights. I'm the one that's sitting looking at the goddamn tapes, and then the people that should've been rated never got rated anyway."

"Well, here's the thing," moaned Brennan, about the lack of honour among thieves. "The last goddamn fight that I handled, they still owe me over seven hundred dollars."

"Bill, listen to me," Beavers said, staring at him intently. "You're like my daddy. That's the way I've always looked at you for the last fifteen years. I told you … when this shit started getting outta hand, me and you talked about what was gonna happen in the fucking end. We knew this shit was gonna happen, and I told you – distinctly told you – that I'd make sure that me and you didn't get into trouble. Well, we in trouble. But we're gonna have to cooperate with these people. 'Cause, like I mean, they got us."

Beavers then began to laugh strangely. "You can't argue with a fucking videotape."

Despite the fact that the FBI had Beavers "passing the fucking envelopes out, and Bob passing envelopes to me and you," Brennan still wouldn't roll over.

"Why should we take the fall for this fucking guy?" Beavers asked of Bob Lee.

"He's the guy that got rich, too," mused Brennan, who appeared to be thinking about it but did not want to go in front of the world as a crook and a snitch. "I haven't got any money in over a goddamn year, except this," Brennan finally said.

"You know I love you like a dad," said Beavers.

"Yeah, I love you, too," said the old man.

"I've suspected the phones were fucking tapped for three or four years,"

"Well, I have too," agreed Brennan.

"You could never get Bob to shut the fuck up on a phone call."

Finally, Beavers asked, "How much money did you get the other day in the envelope? I got $4,000."

Before Brennan could say, Beavers broke in and added, "FBI counted it for me." Both men then laughed, but it was sad laughter. "Not only that," added Beavers sarcastically, "they got the hundred dollars for the fucking haircuts . . . Least it wasn't [for Lee's] hooker."

Beavers then began to bitch about the way Lee cut up the swag. "Who the fuck does a $16,000 bribe? I mean, that doesn't make no goddamn sense . . . Don King didn't give him $16,000."

". . . Millions," muttered Brennan, who seemed stunned over what had come down.

"I mean, he probably gave him thirty or forty or fifty, and who the fuck knows what he did? But he gives . . . you and me four and he keeps the fucking rest . . . Surely, he's not giving none to fucking Junior now with Junior's fucking drug problem."

Finally, Beavers emitted an almost primal moan. "This is fucking self-preservation. If we cooperate ... nothing fucking happens. If we don't cooperate, who the fuck knows. They got us dirty."

Beavers began a fast litany of what the Feds had: "They know about the hundred thousand that we got from Cedric that I picked upon the Interstate in New Jersey. They know about ... Robbie coming in a fucking red convertible, to get him and Bob's half."

"I didn't know about that," Brennan said, as if telling Beavers could somehow extricate himself from this whole mess. "Hundred thousand?"

"Yeah, we got twenty-five thousand apiece for the rematch for Schulz and Foreman."

Finally, Brennan asked Beavers what he wanted him to do.

"Tell them everything we know."

"We do that, then they'll know as much as we know," protested the old man lamely. Despite the evidence, Brennan just wouldn't roll over. "I'll tell you why. They might put me in a position where I get a fucking heart attack. I'm an old man, and I ain't got as long to live as you have."

Beavers got out of Brennan's pick-up truck. As Beavers walked sadly away across the parking lot, he knew it was over.

Theresa Reilly, the FBI agent who had busted Lee, appeared and approached the old man. After she flashed her credentials, Brennan discovered that Beavers had sold him out. The ratings chairman had been wearing a body wire for nearly a year and a half, and had recorded all his conversations with Brennan and Lee. There were 200 of them. The old man didn't know whether to curse or cry. Though he was dying slowly of congestive heart failure, and had a ninety-one-year-old wife, Bill Brennan was one tough, old bastard and would not roll over.

★ ★ ★

One year later, on 3 November 1999, Bob Lee, Robert Lee Jr, Bill Brennan and Francisco "Pancho" Fernandez, the IBF's South American representative, were charged with conspiracy, racketeering, money laundering and tax evasion in a thirty-two-count indictment in Newark, New Jersey. "In the IBF, ratings were bought, not earned," contended US Attorney Robert F. Cleary. "The defendants completely corrupted the IBF rating system."

After a two-year investigation, the Feds charged that Lee had shaken people down for $338,000, with the bribes encompassing every weight division. Though Lee had promised integrity when the IBF was formed, the Feds claimed, "A culture of corruption has festered at the IBF virtually since its inception."

The Government subpoenaed all records from as far back as 1982, including fight contracts, cancelled cheques, telephone records, invoices and ratings lists. In addition to the criminal defendants, there were twelve unindicted co-conspirators, including Don King, Bob Arum, Cedric Kushner and Dino Duva. The most devastating pieces of evidence were the eighty-three video and audio tapes. There were 7,000 pages of wire transcripts.

There had been rumours of indictments for months after the initial arrests, but for twelve months nothing had happened. When the indictments finally came down, Bob Lee was allowed to surrender, then was released in $100,000 bail. Robbie was rousted out of his Scotch Plains, New Jersey home, and handcuffed after cops found fifteen glass vials of crack cocaine. His bond was also $100,000. In an obvious bid for sympathy, Robbie's lawyer, John DeMassi, tried to locate a bed in a drug treatment facility. Lee Sr was angry and defiant.

"For almost three years," he said, fiddling with his wire-rimmed glasses as he read a combative statement, "I have been the target of malicious gossip and vicious rumours . . . spread by people in the boxing industry who stand to benefit from the prosecution. They shall not prevail." At sixty-six, Bob Lee was looking at twenty years in jail; Robbie, or Junior, was also facing twenty. Brennan would not go on trial with the Lees because of his age and health.

On 11 April 2000, the criminal trial began in Newark, New Jersey. Bob Lee was joined by his morose lump of a son at the defendants' table. In day-long opening statements, prosecutor Joe Sierra tore into the attack, alleging that Lee and his son stole fighters' futures by selling the ratings. This was "about men with dreams, about young men who sweat and the men who make millions of dollars without breaking a sweat – the men who control boxing and boxing's ratings," he said. "It's just not about the boxers who benefit from the bribes, but the boxers who get left behind."

Sierra, who often prosecuted organized crime, meticulously detailed what he planned to prove in his opening statement. The thin, thirtyish prosecutor, with black curly hair, drove home his point: "Time and again, you'll hear defendant Lee discuss the ratings and see how little the ratings have to do with the fighters' wins and losses." Don King "practically owns Lee Sr . . . Don King's fighters are routinely favoured over other fighters without regard to their record." But Lee was on trial, not King, and Sierra quickly added: "Lee demanded bribes for one reason and one reason only – because he could."

Lee's attorney was the slick, likeable Gerald Krovatin, a white-haired mouthpiece with a theatrical flourish, who had a mountain of evidence to contend with. "Just because somebody calls it a bribe doesn't make it a bribe," he argued in his ninety-minute rebuttal. "It's showbusiness." Playing to the jurors' prejudices, he even likened boxing to professional wrestling. Payoffs were simply the way boxing was run. Krovatin claimed the money Lee got was like the sponsorships in beauty pageants. Appealing to the irrational anger many felt at the time for Big Government, Krovatin finally asked, "What business does the FBI or federal government have in telling Mr Lee how to run a private business?"

Opening arguments are crucial. Most attorneys feel that four out of five cases are won or lost here. Jurors are supposed to wait until all evidence is in, but they are twelve human beings, not robots. Still, the Feds appeared to have a devastating case, including the videotape of 21 October 1998 that showed Lee accepting $1,000 in suite 379 of the Holiday Inn in Portsmouth, Virginia.

Agent Reilly's testimony was very believable, but Krovatin pounded away on cross-examination and claimed that the FBI was pressuring Lee at a terribly vulnerable time. Both agents, however, testified that Lee insisted on continuing their interview after this arrest. Maybe the ex-homicide investigator did, but he was still human. With a daughter dying, Lee elicited the jurors' sympathy. Because the evidence against Lee was so strong, Krovatin had little to work with but raw emotion. He tried to claim that Beavers became a rat because "his own schemes were collapsing," but in many ways, Beavers wanted to get caught.

In May 1997, FBI agents had walked up to Beavers in the garden of his Virginia home. Agent Reilly told Beavers that she had a tape that implicated him in bribe-taking. She showed him the tape in her hand. Beavers simply asked, "What took you so long?"

Incredibly, Beavers never asked to see the contents of the tape. Had he done so, the investigation might have collapsed before it had properly begun. It was a bluff; the tape was barely audible. It had been recorded by Dan Duva of Main Events, who had been arguing with Beavers about Frans Botha's ridiculous ascent in the heavyweight ratings. Duva claimed

Lee was being bribed by Don King. Duva had since died and the tape had been given to the Feds by Pat English, Main Events' chief attorney. That started the investigation of the IBF.

Normally, when the FBI comes knocking, a prudent man asks to speak to a lawyer, but Beavers was more worried about getting the agents out of the house before his wife and daughter could see them. He quickly agreed to become a snitch – as long as he didn't go to prison.

By the second week of trial, the prosecution began laying the ground-work for eight of Beavers's undercover recordings, plus the damning cheques that the Colombians had paid, purportedly to get their fighters into the ratings. The Colombians gave sworn affidavits that they had paid off.

There was the case, for example, of tiny Felix Naranjo. A mini-flyweight, he bounced into ratings at number five in June 1990, even though he was still fighting six-rounders. Somehow, he became the IBF's top contender. In 1992, he was halted in two in an IBF title fight in Thailand. He dropped to fifth in the ratings but should not have been there in the first place. Less than two years later, without having fought a single contest in the interim, he was back up to number one.

However, Steve Farhood, a boxing writer/broadcaster, hurt the Government's case when he testified as an expert witness. There's no question that Farhood is one of the most knowledgeable fight journalists in the world, but after speaking in tepid, nasal *New Yaawk* euphemisms about the low quality of some of Vaughn Bean's opponents, he cracked, "The value of a world championship belt is equivalent to what you might find in a Crackerjack box." Aesthetically, maybe, but that quip only served to under-score Krovatin's theme that boxing was show business – and trivialised Lee's selling of the ratings.

On April 19, chief witness Doug Beavers took the stand. Bob Lee showed no emotion as his burly nemesis was sworn in. Beavers had a rather flat, rugged face, with a heavily-sunburned nose. He was gray and tired-looking, appearing much older than his fifty-six years, though he dyed his hair, beard and moustache black. He was highly intelligent but not formally educated. Despite his nineteen years in the Navy, he still came off as a good ol' boy. He had a strong, robust voice, with a slight Virginia drawl.

The prosecution wanted him to look as good as possible, and shep-herded him through some basic biographical information. Beavers was a retired Navy corpsman (medic) who had delivered babies and saved lives when in Vietnam. He claimed to "love boxing," and supposedly had some professional fights in Mexico under assumed names. He had been involved in regulating boxing in the state of Virginia for nearly two decades. He had formed his own corporation, the Virginia Boxing Association, to surpervise the sport after the state disbanded its commission. But the federal Government made a big mistake when they signed their deal with him.

For a snitch to have credibility, he has to look repentant to a jury. He has to look like he has at least suffered. Yet Beavers was still supervising boxing and wrestling in Virginia, on a state contract, despite signing a fifty-six-page affidavit admitting his own corruption in the IBF! It wasn't until Pedro Fernandez, an Internet boxing scribe, called Virginia officials, that his contract was abruptly terminated. By then it was too late – he was already on the stand. It was sloppy work by the FBI; Beavers should've been forced to resign every affiliation he had with boxing, or no immunity deal. Instead, Doug's wife Susan had even fronted for him when their fighter Sean Fletcher boxed.

Under oath, Beavers readily admitted the IBF ratings were a sham. "I didn't think president Lee would trust me if I didn't take the bribes," he told the courtroom. Money was the criteria, admitted Beavers, but it was Lee, not him, who had the final say.

By the third week of the trial, the themes were unquestionably money, greed and betrayal. Looking cool and collected, Beavers testified that he had participated in bribery from 1985 to 1998. Both men began fearing their phones were tapped, hence the nicknames employed.

Once "turned" by the FBI, Beavers had worn his first "wire" at the 1997 IBF convention. He was always bitching about being broke, but Bob Lee handed him $8,000 and joked, "This will keep the wolves from the door for awhile." It didn't. Beavers had to turn the big wad of cash over to his FBI handler.

Initially, Beavers was against the payoffs, he told jurors. His first taste of dirty money had come in 1985, when he took five $100 bills to set up the rematch between Australia's Jeff Fenech and Japan's Satoshi Shingaki. Lee reportedly got greased by manager Hisashi Ikeda.

In his slow, deep drawl, Beavers said he grabbed another $5,000 from Don King, supposedly to improve the rating of one of his heavyweights. But there was a screw-up, and King demanded his money back. "I'm thinking, Don King's a street guy … If you're running an illegal business you don't ask for a bribe back. I told Bob Lee, 'What's Don King going to do, sue me?'"

With ratings being hawked like it was a Turkish bazaar, and the IBF's credibility swirling down the toilet, Beavers also admitted extorting $20,000 from Roland Jankelson so that Joe Hipp, his unranked, grossly fat heavyweight, could vault up to number five at heavyweight. Earlier, Jankelson had paid to get Francois Botha into the IBF's rankings.

In 1997, Jankelson approached Beavers again at the IBF convention. Hipp had dropped in the ratings. He was never more than a very tough

journeyman anyway, but with Jankelson promising more swag, Beavers
went to both Lees to see if big Joe's standing could be improved. Only now,
he was wearing a body wire.

"I think I can work it out," Beavers said on tape, as the jurors followed
along with a prepared transcript of the meeting. "But I don't know. You
know, just going into like eight or nine. I don't know what to work it
for . . ."

Lee finally muttered: "I don't know ... thirty to fifty thousand?"

"I don't know if I can get that."

Lee Jr then popped in: "I don't know it it's worth that much, I don't
think you're going to get it."

It was devastating evidence, *taped*, so everyone could hear. Beavers went
on, "I don't think he'll pay that much."

"I think it's twenty," interject Junior.

"Twenty," agreed Juniour.

But Lee Sr was the man in control. He finally decided $25,000.

Beavers went back to Jankelson. He was almost embarrassed by Lee's
greed. "He said he couldn't do it for less than $25,000."

"That's too much," replied Jankelson.

"I'm just the messenger," Beavers said flippantly.

Krovatin jumped up and asked for a mistrial. He claimed Lee's rights
were prejudiced because Beavers had gotten into areas of "uncharged
conduct," but Krovatin was desperate. With that one tape, the Government
had devastatingly proven its case. Mistrials are seldom granted, but Krovatin
was trying to protect the record for a possible appeal.

As the case moved on, Beavers admitted that he usually took bribes of
less than $1,000 to move a fighter, but there was a gentleman's agreement
to split most swag four ways, between the two Lees, Brennan, and himself.
He also claimed that Larry Vallace, a former New Jersey boxing commissioner, once got $2,000.

The prosecution wanted the jury to believe their star witness. In many
ways, he had plenty of downhome charm, but once Krovatin got his chance
at cross-examination, he did his best to turn him into a Judas.

"Mr. Beavers, do you tell lies?"

"If there's a reason," replied Beavers, suddenly wary.

Krovatin made jurors grasp that it was Doug Beavers who led his "second
father" Bill Brennan into a government trap. It was Beavers who had set up
the Lees, though Bob Lee had once loaned him money to keep his house
out of foreclosure. Bob Lee may have been a crook, but the sly, beguilling
Beavers was now coming off as a double-crossing bastard.

Beavers was forced to admit that he misled his wife Susan about being
a snitch for the Government. He had lied to Lee about the Kentucky drug

dealers who had wanted to do a deal with the IBF – that was an attempted sting and Lee, the ex cop, sensed something and pulled out. Beavers even admited he didn't tell Virginia authorities about his criminal involvement with the IBF, despite the fact that his company, the Virginia Boxing and Wrestling Association, continued to tax and oversee ring activities in his state.

Trying to vaporize his credibility, Krovatin asked if Beavers lied to the grand jury, which resulted in the indictment of the Lees. He hammered away, even though the evidence was so overwhelming that at times the feisty defense lawyer seemed overwhelmed.

Beavers also testified that in 1995, George Foreman won a terrible split-decision over Germany's Axel Schulz in Las Vegas. Nobody but the two judges thought Foreman won, but with George bringing all the fans and TV money, there was almost no way the rugged German could get the decision.

There had to be a rematch, but Beavers told jurors that Lee wanted $100,000 before it could happen. Cedric Kushner, who was Schulz's American packager, was furious, but finally agreed to pay off, and German businessman Wilfred Sauerland put up the cash. Beavers left his home in the early hours for Kushner's posh East Hampton, New York, estate. Kushner gave him a manila envelope bulging with $100 bills and Beavers divided the crisp, green booty into four equal packs. He excitedly drove for a couple of hours till he rendezvoused with Bob Lee Jr at the Vince Lombardi rest stop on the New Jersey Turnpike, in Ridgefield, New Jersey. Beavers waited awhile, then Bob Lee Jr suddenly roared up. He was driving a fire engine red convertible, and was wearing a canary yellow sports jacket, with slews of jangling gold jewelry.

Beavers told the jurors, "I was afraid someone was going to jump out of the bushes thinking we were drug dealers." Beavers testified that he gave Junior $50,000 for him and his old man. The other $50,000 was for Beavers and Brennan.

The IBF ordered the rematch, but Foreman refused to fight Schulz a second time. The Feds maintained that promoter Bob Arum had also paid the IBF $100,000 for a "special exemption" for the first fight. Prosecutors also felt that the Revered George had a made a love offering of $250,000, so Butch Lewis could lobby the IBF. Surprisingly, Foreman never testified. Publicly, he denied paying a bribe. But what was all this money for?

Things got even worse for the Lees. As an expectant hush fell over the courtroom, a grainy black and white video was played. The prosecution had entered eighty audios and three videos into evidence, and this was perhaps the most damning.

On 18 December 1997, at the Holiday Inn in Portsmouth, Beavers was shown slowly untaping a thick cellophane packet from his trouser leg and handing it to Lee. Lee had been talking on the telephone to his sick daughter Cheryl.

"Christmas cheer," said the IBF bagman.

"What . . . how much is this?" asked Lee, like getting a big wad of cash like this was the most natural thing in the world.

"This $5,000," said Beavers, who was intentionally taken a long time so the hidden FBI camera could catch everything.

"You got a piece," Lee mumbled.

"We got twenty-five hundred apiece. We got ten thousand total," said Beavers.

"Five grand for me and Rob, for Robby," mumbled Lee, doing mental calculations.

Beavers began to explain about the $5,000 cheques from Pancho.

"So did you clean them?" Lee asked. Beavers had been laundering them through his boxing club.

After perfunctorily going through the ratings, the men alluded to Don King.

"I hope Fuzzy sends us a Christmas turkey," Beavers said.

"Hey man, it wouldn't be Christamas without a turkey," chortled Lee.

Initially, during pre-trial, Judge Bissell had not allowed the tape in, but the prosecution vociferously protested, and he reversed himself after the Government argued that he was gutting their case. This video was the best single piece of evidence the Feds had. If this wasn't a bribe, what was it?

Four days after Christmas, on December 29, Lee sent a Federal Express package to Beavers. After tearing it open, Beavers found $4,000 in cash. Beavers claimed this was bribe money from King, and the FBI immediately confiscated it.

★ ★ ★

After weeks of anticipation, Bob Arum took the stand. He immediately rocked the defense by claiming that Lee "had tried to shake him down" for $500,000 to sanction the Foreman–Schulz fight in April 1995. Arum called Lee's demand "totally crazy," but Lee also wanted an $800,000 payoff – in addition to the IBF's normal sanction fees – if Foreman faced Mike Tyson.

Arum testified that he agreed to pay Lee $100,000 before the Schulz fight, and another $100,000 after, but his ruddy face suddenly got redder as he told jurors, "I refused to make any further payments. I was outraged by what these bastards had did to George Foreman."

As prosecutors led Arum through his testimony, he did well on the stand, till he got too self-righteous and told jurors he had come forth without any offers of immunity. "I felt it was time to do what I could to end the corruption in boxing," Arum said, piously. Arum only came forward because he was worried about being indicted. Months after Lee's trial, Arum paid $10,000, along with Don King's $50,000, to help block passage of the Muhammad Ali Act, which greatly would've cleaned up boxing.

Though Arum smiled on the witness stand, and tried to make jurors laugh, once Krovatin began to cross-examine him, the man who coined the phrase, "Yesterday I was lying, today I'm telling the truth," began coming apart.

Arum had no choice but to admit money laundering when he paid Dutch promoter Peter Blaumert a total of $100,000 in cheques, then had them "washed" through Stan Hoffman's bank account. Hoffman swore that he paid the swag to Lee. Hoffman eventually testified that he got Arum's first cheque of $50,000 in January 1995, then began writing out sums of less than $10,000 to avoid IRS scrutiny. At one luncheon, Lee supposedly got $9,000, and Hoffman swore he got more in cash at other meetings between March and April 1995, just before the Foreman–Schulz fight. Finally, two cash packets of $25,000 apiece were turned over to Lee after Hoffman had a meeting with Blaumert in Holland.

These payoffs were crucial to the Government's case, and Arum's signed affidavit proved that he knew exactly what he was paying for. Yet on the witness stand, the Harvard law graduate suddenly claimed, under Krovatin's cross-examination, that Hoffman never gave the $100,000 to Lee! It was bizarre: Arum had just sandbagged the Feds' case. Arum's claim was like listening to President Bill Clinton proclaim, "I had never had sex with that woman."

Arum didn't care. He was trying to protect his promoter's license, and the Feds could go to hell. The prosecutors only had themselves to blame; Arum should have been indicted and forced to sing for his supper or go to jail. After Arum was met in the corridor following his contentious testimony, he justified his actions by snarling, "Boxing is a dying sport anyway."

Inside the courtroom, with jurors becoming confused, a contrite Dino Duva testified strongly. In December 1998, one day after Fernando Vargas had halted Yory Boy Campas to win the IBF light-middleweight title, Dino went into a shop near the Taj Mahal Casino in Atlantic City and purchased some candy. He also slipped $25,000 in cash in the bag and handed it to the Main Events site coordinator, Dennis Dueltgen.

"Make sure this gets to Bob," he insisted.

Duva swore that Dueltgen knew nothing of the payoff. "While I didn't say what was in it, I was very, very adamant: 'Make sure Bob Lee gets this bag.' I didn't want to hand the cash over to Bob Lee personally."

Lee apparently took this money six weeks after the FBI busted him. Duva knew nothing of that, and obviously wouldn't have paid if he had. He testified that Beavers had told him in June 1998 that he had to pay or Vargas wouldn't become the IBF's mandatory challenger. "Doug Beavers made it clear to me I would have to take care of Mr Lee, and Mr Lee reminded me of that," swore Duva. "It was made very clear they were expecting to get paid off."

Unlike Arum, or the rest of the rogues gallery, Dino Duva came across as a decent, vulnerable human being. He was forty-one but had never got out of his family's shadow: a trained accountant, he had never wanted to go into boxing but was pushed by his domineering father, whom he strongly resembled, though he was nearly forty years younger and 100 pounds thinner. Dino admitted on the stand that he'd been in drug rehab for cocaine abuse and was taking medication for clinical depression. After his older brother Dan died, Dino became the Main Events front man, but Kathy Duva, Dan's widow, wanted control of the family business, and bitterly ousted the entire Duva clan. With Dino's promoters, license about to be pulled in New Jersey for the admitted payoff, he told jurors, "Look, I made a mistake, but I did it, and it's something I have to live with."

In late June 2000, 350-pound Cedric Kushner waddled into court and became the third American promoter to swear that Bob Lee had shaken him down. According to Kushner, Lee demanded $100,000 to sanction the Foreman–Schulz rematch, which never happened. "I used some foul language and suggested that he was crazy," swore Kushner, who had a droll South African accent and a walrus mustache, and reminded people of the old character actor Sidney Greenstreet. "It seemed an absurd amount of money. I remember him, Mr Lee, saying at ringside, my fighter [Schulz] had been robbed, then to come back thirty days later and demand $100,000!"

Kushner vigorously complained to Beavers, but the IBF's bagman simply replied, "You know how the game's played."

In his earlier testimony, Beavers admitted that he picked up and passed on Kushner's payoff after driving to Cedric's house. Wilfried Sauerland, the German promoter, also testified that he funded Kushner's $100,000 bribe. But Krovatin scored one of his best shots of the trial when he got Sauerland to admit that Schulz's purse was $350,000 – not the $75,000 Kushner had told Lee. Since the IBF legally got a percentage of the fighters' purses, Kushner had obviously lied to Lee. Kushner was trying to recoup the alleged shakedown, but Krovatin argued that Beavers' pick-up was just a "sanction fee." It was a ridiculous argument, but from the jurors' perspective, everyone began looking like a thief.

Kushner swore that he had been paying off Lee since 1987. Initially, the bribes were small, $2,500 to $10,000, but Kushner claimed he had no choice if he wanted to stay in boxing's fast lane. "I always knew I was second fiddle, or fourth," he complained on the stand. "No matter what happened, King came first.

* * *

With Bob Lee getting chopped to pieces inside the courtroom, Jimmy Binns, lawyer for both the WBA and Don King, got involved. Binns flagrantly tried to play the race card. "There's a grave injustice being perpetrated in that federal court in Newark when you have a snake like Arum admitting to bribery and money laundering and he isn't facing prosecution. If they're not going to do anything to Arum, how can they lynch Bobbby Lee just because he's a black man?"

It was obvious that Don King was getting nervous: the Feds had offered Lee a chance to roll over on King. Suddenly, in the middle of July, two more hired guns showed up: the Reverend Al Sharpton and Martin Luther King III, who staged a made-for-TV press conference on the steps of the courthouse. With the evidence against the Lees so overwhelming, and much of it on tape, Sharpton (who had earlier been nailed on tape in the 1983 so-called "Crown Royal" boxing sting) asked the racially-charged question: "If you have people on the stand admitting crimes, why aren't they on trial?" The Feds left themselves open to this by not indicting Kushner or Arum, who were white.

The *New York Post* has called Sharpton a "racial arsonist." Investigative journalist Jack Newfield says he's a "street hustler," "mob front," "social activist," and "media manipulator," and old FBI tapes have Sharpton bragging he once quashed a criminal indictment of Don King.

Marty King, whose father Martin Luther King was one of the great men of the twentieth century, joined in. "There seems to be a double standard," he opined. With black/white suddenly the issue, not how the Lees, who were black, repeatedly sold out minority young men, the Feds now had to deny that this trial was about selective prosecution and had anything to do with race. "All bribery roads led to the IBF, so we prosecuted the IBF," insisted prosecutor Marc Agnifillio.

Yet, after Sharpton and Marty King worked their magic, a hung jury for the Lees seemed a distinct possibility. Evander Holyfield, who had castigated the Alphabet Boys eight years earlier in a Senate deposition, even rallied around on behalf of Don King, now his promoter. He was mobbed entering the courthouse, but intentionally sat next to Lee's sobbing first wife, Cheryl, so the Lees looked like the victims.

"There's no doubt who was a calling the shots when the IBF was looking to make illicit money," argued Agnifillio, in his final summation to the jury. "It's Robert Lee Sr. The tapes make that abundantly clear. This was about greed." Yet though the prosecution showed the videotape of Lee taking money, and even had a giant blow-up of him taking dirty swag, this trial was now about race.

Krovatin, who did a masterful job considering the massive evidence he had to contend with, pleaded for his client with tears running down his eyes. "Race is as much an issue in this case as any other ... We're in a situation now where some people have gotten a free pass, and two people, a man and his son sit at that table. That's not fair. That's not right. Some people are bothered by a successful black man." He even added that there was a "white conspiracy" to run the Lees out of boxing. While Krovatin didn't cite any cross burnings, some of the seven men and five women jurors had tears in their eyes. Wisely, the Lees never took the stand in their own defense.

The marathon trial ended on August 17. After fifteen days of agonizingly slow deliberations, the Government looked in big trouble. A hung jury looked almost certain, after what should have been a slam-dunk conviction. Finally the jury of nine whites, two blacks and one Hispanic came back with an obvious compromise verdict: Bob Lee was convicted on six criminal counts, but aquitted on twenty-seven others. Incredibly, Robbie was absolved of everything. "There's no evidence linking Robert Lee Jr to anything whatsoever," said jury foreman Gerard Brand, a plumber, when later interviewed. Apparently, under the mountain of taped evidence, jurors forgot that Bob Lee Jr joined right in as Beavers and Lee Sr discussed how much to shake Jankelson down for. It's right there on the tapes and in the transcripts

In a confusing, wildly contradictory verdict, Lee was exonerated on the charge that he took $338,000 in bribes, but convicted on two counts of filing a false income tax return (on the money he supposedly didn't take). Nevada chairman Luther Mack, who is black, and had been reading the court transcripts daily, couldn't fathom how Lee Sr possibly beat the bribery charges. "This is amazing. I can't believe that. They caught him taking the money on tape." Lee was also aquitted of racketeering, but found guilt of three counts of interstate travel in aid of racketeering, and one count of money laundering. Jurors, however, said after the trial that they didn't believe Arum gave Hoffman $100,000 to bribe Lee. If that was the case, why would Arum, a Harvard educated attorney, risk disbarment and losing his promoter's license? The jurors' logic was preposterous. There was so much evidence, they simply couldn't see the forest through the trees.

Gerry Spence, the legendary Wyoming lawyer, didn't coment on this case, but as one of the best criminal lawyers in the country, he firmly believes, "Every case has to tell a story." This was a saga about incredible greed, but jurors looking for "perfect justice" didn't like Arum, Beavers, Hoffman or Kushner.

"We all felt many of these people were just as guilty as Mr. Lee," said juror Aileen Smith.

Juror Sean Frierson, who was black, said, "There just wasn't enough evidence," despite the damning video that showed Lee taking money after Beavers untaped a wad of cash from his pants leg. Maurice Glasser didn't believe Beavers because he had a government deal. Brand, the jury foreman, felt Beavers was simply a liar and claimed that Beavers had stolen Kushner's $100,000 New Jersey turnpike payoff and kept it in a "strong box."

"We don't believe Mr. Lee got that money," Brand insisted. "We don't believe Robert Lee Jr met Beavers on the New Jersey Turnpike. Unanimously, we felt that Beavers used the deal to his advantage and booted the money."

The Feds had enough evidence to convict ten men but in the aftermath of the O.J.Simpson acquittal, they forgot how deadly race can be. Lee knew it. Shamelessly playing the race card again after he left the courthouse, temporarily free pending sentencing, he said, "If you're white, you're right. If you're brown, stick around, but if you're black – get back."

* * *

"Everything I did was because I was a man who tried to make a difference," Bob Lee told Judge Bissell six months later, as he awaited sentencing. Lee had made up to $268,000 a year legally, yet he gave boxing the most documentably corrupt sanctioning body in history. Though federal guidelines called for a sentence of around forty-six months, and the probation department recommednded six years, Bissell gave Lee just twenty-two months. Lee was banned for life from boxing, and fined $25,000. He also agreed to pay the IBF $50,000 in compensation, while appealing his criminal conviction.

"Those seeking to clean up boxing won another round," proclaimed U.S. attorney Robert J. Cleary. But two years after the trial, the IBF's ratings were still a cancer on the sport. Lee's picture still graces the headquarters. None of his underlings was removed. The IBF was under federal monitor, but instead of TV ignoring it, it followed up with one of its most successful years, with $1.79 million dollars in sanction fees, said IBF lawyer Linda Torres.

It's doubtful the ailing Lee, freed on appeal bond, will ever see the inside of a prison. Brennan was never prosecuted because he was too old.

"We did some bad shit," admitted Doug Beavers, before he dropped dead one day.

CHAPTER FOURTEEN

The Don

O N THURSDAY, 20 August 1931, Colonel Charles Lindbergh, the man who first braved the Atlantic in his rickety plane, was forced down in the fog-bound Keyoi Islands, off Japan. In Geneva, Switzerland, with Germany's financial condition perilous, a war debts parley was scheduled to meet. In New York City, with the Depression worsening, a forty-two-year-old milliner was jailed for stealing a five-cent can of milk.

In Cleveland, Ohio, a squalling black child named Donald King was born.

It was a time of soup lines and Hooverville shanties and the Communist Party screaming, "Bread for the people!" Don King painfully came of age during World War Two in Cleveland's notorious East Side ghetto. Rib shacks and blues joints dotted the streets. Dice games and shootings were common. Negro spirituals blared from storefront churches and Bible thumpers tried saving souls on every corner, but it was hard to compete against drug dealers and pimps and a whore's cheap perfume.

America the Free? *That's* what they told you in history books. Blacks were sick of Southern lychings, of the Klan, and having to sit at the back of the bus and give up your seat to "Whitey" while they seethed but politely smiled and said, "Yahsuh."

On 7 December 1941, Japan sneak-attacked Pearl Harbor. The War became America's war – and nine-year-old Donald King's father disappeared after falling into a vat of molten steel. It was a horrifying accident, but the family couldn't even grieve. There was no body. At least the people who died in the streets got a funeral.

After that traumatic experience, young Donald King became someone who buried his real emotions. On the surface, he was loud and gregarious. He laughed, jived, slapped palms and acted the fool on the streets. With four brothers and one sister, the family struggled to survive. Donald King however, was going to get his.

King was bright and developed a remarkable facility for figures – though he didn't learn it at school. The "players" who drove the big-finned Cadillacs called him "the Kid," or "Donald the Kid," and he became a numbers runner. Hitting the number was a staple of life in the black community. Maybe you couldn't pay the rent, or you didn't have food, but a quarter could buy you hope in the illegal lottery. King didn't dare carry slips with people's names on them. He memorized them all, lest the cops grab him and shake him down.

Young King answered to black gangsters, but the Jewish mob, led by Moe Dalitz, was the ultimate power behind the numbers racket in Cleveland. Shortly after Sonny Liston won the heavyweight championship, he nodded to Dalitz in Las Vegas, cocking his hand like a pistol. It was a gesture of respect, but Dalitz turned on Liston and hissed, "Lay one hand on me, nigger, I'll make a phone call and you'll be dead in twenty-four hours."

Though Don King rose fast in the numbers, and eventually took in $15,000 a day in poor people's money, in a rare moment of reflection years later he had some regret about the choices he made. "Our motherfuckin' schools were shit," he drunkenly confessed to Duke Durden, his one-time flunky on the Nevada State Athletic Commission. "You couldn't even stay in a hotel or get served downtown. Sure, I went into the rackets, but shit, what was I s'posed to do? Shine those crackers' shoes?"

By 1951, Donald the Kid was a skinny, double-breasted, stick-pinned sharpie, who always carried a big "flash roll." King would wrap fifties and hundreds around a wad of dollar bills. He loved big cars, and was constantly speeding. By the 1960s, King developed his persona as a swaggering loud-mouth who dressed like a pimp, strutted like peacock, and invoked the name of the "Almighty God" like the radio huckster "Reverend Ike." Cleveland cops say King was also a snitch, a young man who would "drop a dime" on his rivals. He survived two murder attempts. He also learned that his dirty money gave him a lot of influence with corrupt cops and politicians.

In May 1954, the Supreme Court declared "that separate is not equal" in the historic Brown versus Board of Education case that finally began to integrate the nation's schools. While brave men like the NAACP's Thurgood Marshal fought for civil rights, on December 1954 the twenty-three-year-old King shot Hillary Brown to death after Brown and two other thugs from Detroit tried to stick up one of King's gambling dens on East 123rd Street. County prosecutor Bernard Conway ruled it "justifiable homicide" and King wasn't prosecuted.

By 1966, the call for civil rights rang out all over America. Dr Martin Luther King was spat upon and hit with a brick as he called for open housing on Chicago's Southside. In Birmingham, Alabama, black protesters who peacefully demanded their human rights had been met by snarling police dogs and firehoses. In 1963 racists blew up a black church and four little girls died. Meanwhile, in Cleveland, Donald King was swaggering around the ghetto sporting a .357 magnum and infuriating his customers by winning his own lotteries.

On 20 April 1966, King loudly barged into the Manhattan Tap Room for an early drink. Sammy Garrett, a former King flunky, was sitting nearby. The two had been friends, but Garrett owed $600 after King had laid down a bet with him on number 743. Garrett was a nondescript man, with short hair and a bland face, and like so many players in the ghetto, he was a junkie. He also had TB, and had just lost his left kidney.

King bounded up to the sickly man and began to bellow, "Sammy, where's my bread? Where's it at, man?"

Garrett tried to protest. He was tapped out, but King began bullying him, and the two ended up outside on litter-strewn Cedar Avenue. A crowd watched, hooting at the spectacle, as King began to brutalize the little man. He smashed Garrett to the pavement with either his pistol or a punch, then began to kick him in the head. Garrett's features contorted with the impact. Some in the crowd of fifteen or so began to plead, "C'mon, Donald, he's had enough," but Garrett's head continued to crash against the pavement and ooze blood. King's pointed, shiny shoes left indentations in Garrett's cheekbone. Nobody stepped in because King was in a frenzy and still waving his pistol.

King weighed 245 pounds but later claimed the 135-pound Garrett threw the first punch. He was just defending himself.

At 12:30 PM, recalled Detective Bob Tonne thirty-five years later, "We were on patrol, April 20, on Cedar Avenue. We saw a crowd of people ... and I saw a man laying on the ground, his head bouncing off the ground, and a man kicking him. We immediately sped up to the area, pulled onto the curb and jumped out of the car. We said, 'Drop the gun.' He took the gun, threw it over the trunk, I turned to grab the gun, and he goes over and kicks the guy right in the head. I mean a kick.

"That's when I grabbed his hands, put 'em behind his back. The victim, I could see blood coming out of his mouth and ear. I bent over, to see If he could say anything but the only thing he said was, 'I'll pay you Donald. I'll pay you.'"

The cops put King in handcuffs. He sneered at them, "I'm Donald King."

Garrett died of massive head injuries. King was facing a murder charge. According to reports in the *Cleveland Plain-Dealer*, King had also pistol-whipped Garrett with his illegal gun. After the street thug was read his rights, he refused to speak to police. Lieutenant Carl De Lau headed up the homicide squad and had known King for fifteen years. De Lau claims King routinely gave up other policy operators to stay out of jail, but now King was looking at life behind bars.

The charge was second degree murder. Four eyewitnesses disappeared quicker than a policy slip in a March wind. De Lau had seen fixes before, but the word on the street was that King was making payoffs. De Lau says Tonne, who was a devastating witness against King, was twice approached to change his testimony. "I was approached two different occasions, somebody trying to bribe me," confirmed Tonne. "Offers of money, Don King can help me."

Herman Roberson, a local bail bondsmen, stopped Tonne's car and made one offer. On July 18, the detective bumped into Milton Firestone, a Mob-connected shyster, who offered him $10,000 to change his testimony. On August 2, 1966, Tonne filed a confidential memorandum with the Intelligence Division of the Cleveland Police Department.

By February 1967, authorities still felt they had a strong case, but on February 21, when the trial began, all four witnesses developed amnesia or were gone. Rosa Wrines, aged fifty-three, had seen the brutal beating from her window, but she didn't come to court, nor to work, nor was she hone. According to affidavits, King's men simply ran her out of Cleveland. The state's other three witnesses, Jack Owens, Charlie Johnson and Danny Howell, were in the numbers rackets themselves.

At 11:45 AM, on February 22, as King's murder trial was in its second day, Fred Mollenkoff, the city editor of the *Plain-Dealer*, called Sergeant Mike Haney of the Cleveland Police Department, and told him that he'd gotten an anonymous call that Don King was bragging on the street that he'd spread $30,000 around, and "I ain't gonna do one motherfuckin' day behind bars."

The confidential informant turned out to be Garrett's nephew, who obviously wanted King in jail. But on February 17, just five days earlier, a friend of Rosa Wrines's had been shot. Tracy Smith, who ran a neighbour-hood shoeshine parlour, was reportedly blasted because he couldn't get Wrines to change her testimony. In all shooting incidents, the police have to be notified, but Smith filed a bogus robbery report, claimed Garret's nephew, because he didn't want to say what really happened.

Detectives Tonne and Johnny Horvath swore they saw King kick Garrett in the head repeatedly. At around four o'clock on February 23, King's jury of eight women and four men began deliberations. In just four hours – including dinner – the swaggering predator was convicted of second-degree murder. Though King was looking at life behind bars in the Ohio State Penitentiary, Judge Hugh Corrigan waived sentencing while King's mouth-piece, James Willis, announced he was filing for a new trial. Incredibly, Corrigan did this in the privacy of his office, not in open court. There were no prosecutors present. There wasn't even a stenographer to compile a court record.

As De Lau stormed around, he swore to Tonne, "The judge's in the bag. It's got to be a fix." Corrigan was a former police officer. On 24 July 1967, the *Cleveland Plain-Dealer* screamed, "Judge Cuts Hood's Murder Penalty." According to a confidential FBI report of June 1965, later unearthed by investigative reporter Jack Newfield, the late Judge Corrigan was on the payroll of James Licavoli, one of the top Mafia leaders in Cleveland. King and Licavoli even shared the same lawyer.

King was eventually remanded to Marion Correctional Institute, a tough joint but much easier than the Ohio State Pen. Corrigan had worked more magic; he outrageously dropped King's charge to manslaughter, and King got out on 30 September 1971, after serving just three years and eleven months. King later chortled, "I listened to the first Ali-Frazier fight on the radio behind bars, then promoted the third one."

He didn't forget Corrigan, who put him there. In 1976, when Corrigan ran for the Ohio Court of Appeals, King, just five years out of the joint, shanghaied Muhammad Ali to campaign for him. Though Black Muslims were prohibited by sect leader Elijah Muhammad from being politically involved, Ali recorded radio commercials that aired on black stations like WJMO and WABI, saying, "I'm endorsing Corrigan for judge 'cause of what he did for my man Don King."

* * *

Inside the walls, King descended on the prison library. Shakespeare, Voltaire, Tolstoy, Sartre and Thomas Aquinas became his intellectual sparring partners. Reporters would later laugh at his malapropisms – Thomas Aquinas became Thomas A-quine – and though King became something of a self-educated man, his use of big words was more artifice to compensate for his raging inferiority.

Later, he'd crow, "I've whipped the Harvard graduate's ass," speaking of Bob Arum. "Nothing against Harvard – it's a helluva school – but there I was, twenty-five yards behind, wrapped in legs irons, and I beat him."

Though sportswriters have continually downplayed his treachery, and little is written about King's financial dealings, Irving Rudd, the white-haired publicity gnome, claimed in 1990, "King learned nothing from his time in prison. It didn't change him one bit."

In June 1972, just nine months after getting out, King conceived the idea of staging a benefit boxing show in Cleveland to help the Forrest City Hospital, which served the poor black community. King called his long-time friend, Lloyd Price, the rhythm and blues singer, who knew Ali. Once he had got an audience with Ali, who had lost his crown to Joe Frazier, King went into his routine. "You got to do it champ. It's for the people. The little people." King bellowed, cajoled and pleaded and Ali, who was always a soft touch, agreed.

King knew nothing about promoting boxing, though he'd had four amateur fights as the world's skinniest flyweight in 1949. He wasn't much of an athlete. During high school, he somehow managed to flunk physical education. But he quickly latched on to Don Elbaum, a tanktown promoter and matchmaker with a Runyonesque reputation. The wily King gave him the treatment: "My man, we can't let the poor suffer and die."

Elbaum, who had a prematurely old, furrowed face, looked at him and said, "Five grand."

"Agreed."

Ali hit town at his inimitable best. He promised at a press conference, "Terry Daniels is going to get a whipping. He wants plane tickets, I'm here for free." He even visited the local jail. As inmates pressed their faces to the bars, Ali roared, "Put me in there! Put me in that cell with three of your baddest – and see who comes out." The jailbirds laughed like hell.

Ali boxed Daniels, Alonzo Johnson (an old opponent and now sparring partner), and Amos Johnson (who had beaten him in the 1959 Pan American Games). As he feigned a knockdown, the crowd of 8,000 at the Cleveland Arena hooted in delight. Price also got Lou Rawls, Marvin Gaye, Wilson Pickett and Johnny Nash to put on a concert.

It was a helluva bill but, come payoff time, Elbaum got just a grand. Joe Fariella, who handled Johnny Griffin, a promising local fighter, swore that King tried to beat his kid out of his $1,200 purse. For weeks King had been laying on the bombast, but even as he schmoozed the media, Elbaum saw big wads of cash, and it was obvious to him that King was still in the numbers business.

Though the Cleveland papers proclaimed the benefit a success, it's questionable how much the inner-city hospital ever saw. Supposedly, Forrest City was to get 40-50,000 but Elbaum claimed he got just $1,000, Ali got $10,000 and King gobbled up the rest. In September 1972, Clarence Rodgers, one of the accountants, claims Forrest City cleared $17,000. Roger Saftold, another accountant, insisted that King got nothing, but if you believe *Boxing Illustrated*, a 1993 article by investigative journalist Rick Hornung contended that the greedy King grabbed $30,000 – while the dying hospital got just $15,000. King later proclaimed, "We saved that hospital!" But by February 1978, Forrest City Hospital was as dead as Sammy Garrett.

King however, had "made his bones." Paddy Flood, one of the legendary thieves in boxing, looked at his partner Al Braverman, and said, "Man, that's some nigger."

* * *

On 22 January 1973, George Foreman gave Joe Frazier one of the worst beatings in the history of boxing, knocking Frazier down six times before the slaughter was stopped in round two. As a mob enveloped the ring in Kingston, Jamaica, jubilantly trying to congratulate the new champion, King pushed his way through in his zeal to gladhand Foreman.

"I told you, George! I told you!" King kept yelling. That night he rode back in Foreman's limo. He'd arrived with Frazier. "I came with the champion, I left with the champion," King gleefully howled years later.

Foreman was one thunderous puncher; Earnie Shavers was another. "Earnie Shavers hit so hard, he makes you piss gasoline," remembered a latter opponent, James Tillis. In February 1973, the menacing Alabama banger KO'd artful Jimmy Young in one round, and in June, Jimmy Ellis, the former WBA champ, bit the dust in the first at the Garden. The brawny, balding Shavers had hand grenades for hands.

Shavers was co-managed by Dean Chance and Blackie Gennaro. They were in dispute with each other, and King had designs on their fighter. To woo Shavers, he employed what would become one of his standard business methods: he dumped a huge bag of cash ($20,000) in front of the fighter. He also offered Chance $8,000 for Earnie's contract. Chance, an Ohio promoter who once won the Cy Young Award as baseball's best pitcher, was a smart businessman and saw right through King. He took the cash.

King next sat down with his new "partner," Joseph "Blackie" Gennaro, the money man, and Gennaro's ally Don Elbaum. Though Gennaro should have known better, King conned him out of the $8,000 he'd paid Chance, claiming he had to be "reimbursed."

"I gotta have another eight thousand to really get Earnie's publicity campaign rolling," King said, gladhanding Gennaro, who was an Ohio road paver. As Gennaro took out his cheque book, Elbaum, who had separated countless boxing groupies from their money, marvelled. With King invoking the name of God, Jesus Christ, and the awesome power of Earnie Shavers's fists, even Elbaum was almost convinced. "We can make it happen!" King thundered. "Don Elbaum, your boxing insights are legendary. You'll pick the opponents, while I'll pilot this ship to the Promised Land. Mr. Gennaro, your money is the mother's milk that eases the way."

When King descended on New York, he had a flunky handing out autographed pictures, but not of Shavers ... of King. A mug shot would have been more appropriate. King laid down money and bribed some New York sportswriters, though he always made good copy.

After the sensational Ellis knockout, neither Gennaro nor Elbaum got paid. King even billed them for rooms, airfare and pocket expenses for his friends and relatives. Gennaro meekly tried to protest, but King battered him down by not letting him get a word in. Gennaro wanted to believe he had a potential champion in Shavers, but King, who knew he had a mark, demanded another $2,000 because he'd "entertained" sportswriters.

By now, Elbaum's relationship with King was strained. In 1991, Don Elbaum briefly went to prison for income tax evasion, but King, who could've taught Machiavelli a few things about treachery, fought with the naive Gennaro, then poisoned Shavers' mind against that "racist white man."

On 14 December 1973, Shavers bombed Jerry Quarry in the first round, but Quarry not only survived, he transformed Shavers into a sweaty heap before the round was over. Come payoff time, Shavers's contracted $75,000 turned into just $3,000, according to FBI man Joe Spinelli. But Shavers, a disarmingly high-pitched bomb-thrower, would still have to fight for King, as the indefatigable ex-con ruthlessly took over boxing.

Jeff "Candy Slim" Merritt was a handsome, 6ft 5in blaster and one of the hardest hitting heavyweights in memory. He broke Shavers's jaw in the gym. Merritt, who had a stylish part cut into his big Afro, was also a convicted rapist and armed robber with a rap sheet longer than his right arm. He possibly had the talent to be a champion, but was doing life on the instalment plan. In March 1973, Merritt was arrested and charged with burglary after pulling a job on Manhattan's fashionable West Side. King got Merritt's charge plea-bargained down to time served in jail, and in September 1973, Merritt annihilated former WBA heavyweight champion Ernie Terrell in one round.

With Merritt needing a license, King told the New York Commission, "I love boxing and really want to do something for the sport." He parroted some more psycho-babble, threw his arm around Jeff, looked at him with staged concern and told anyone who'd listen, "All Jeff needs is a little bit of love."

Ron Stander, who had fought Joe Frazier for the heavyweight championship, eventually faced Merritt, now was being built-up by King. "Candy Slim was the hardest puncher I ever fought," marvelled Stander, shaking his battered old head, which once resembled Elvis Presley's. "He was the only guy to ever knock me out." Stander actually lived with Merritt in Cleveland when they fought.

Despite King's grand design, Jeff would mutter to Stander, "Man, all I need is a hit of heroin, a couple of bitches on the street, and a can of tuna."

In March 1991, the late Harry Mullan, then editor of *Boxing News*, was in Las Vegas to cover Mike Tyson-Razor Ruddock. As he entered the Mirage, he spied a dirty, dishevelled man who was obviously homeless. "Don't y'all motherfuckers know who I am?" the derelict rasped, "I'm Jeff Merritt, Don King's first fighter. Give me some money." King heard about it, and quickly had security remove him. Guys like Merritt were bad for his image.

* * *

On 29 January 1974, Muhammad Ali beat Joe Frazier in their Madison Square Garden rematch in front of 20,748 people, generating a record indoor gate of $1,053,688. When the closed-circuit revenue was counted, both fighters were looking at a possible total of $5 million, the same as they had received for their amazing first fight.

Meanwhile, Don King's fighter Earnie Shavers had been destroyed by Jerry Quarry in one round. Ali called King to offer his condolences, but King immediately began to pitch him about promoting his next fight. "Champ, we're both black. Black is beautiful, but what chance does the ordinary black man have? Ali, you've got to help me. We've got to show the world what a black team can do."

Bob Arum was one of Ali's lawyers and had promoted his most recent fights, including Ali-Frazier II. Arum had laughingly denied King the closed-circuit rights in Ohio, but he didn't have an promotional exclusive on Ali. Ali's manager, Herbert Muhammad, was bombarded with King's pleas: "You gotta help a black man. Your own father, the honorable Elijah Muhammad says, 'If you see a black man can do the job, ya got give him the job before the white man.' Hey now, that's what your daddy teaches."

King berated him about slavery, segregation and racism. Finally, Herbert offered a compromise. "Why don't you and Arum co-promote?"

"No," bristled King, stiffening. "This is a *black* thing. Arum's a Jew who hates brothers." The Black Muslims were terribly anti-semitic, but Herbert Muhammad refused to believe that Arum hated blacks.

After two weeks, King wore Muhammad down, but after tentatively inking Ali for a challenge against champion George Foreman, Herbert insisted, "You've got to get Foreman's name on the contract." Nobody figured King would come up with the money. "That's nigger's crazy," Ali told his flunkies.

Arum was pitching Ali to fight Jerry Quarry a third time for $850,000. But in February 1974, Video Techniques, the closed-circuit firm that King ostensibly worked for, paid Ali $100,000 for signing to face Foreman. Ali also got another $100,000 ten days later, but King had to provide a letter of credit of $2.3 million at Chicago's Guarantee Bank and Trust by March 15. Another $2.5 million was due to Ali ninety days before he stepped into the ring. If King didn't meet the deadlines, Ali kept the money.

King had two days to sign Foreman – or the entire deal was dead. Arum chuckled about it. It seemed impossible.

King anxiously dialled his partner, Hank Schwartz from Chicago. "Did you sign Foreman?"

"Can't get to him."

"*Gawd damn!*" King raced for O'Hare Airport and caught the first plane for California, where the troubled heavyweight champion was training in Oakland to fight Ken Norton.

Foreman, who had proudly waved the flag for his country after winning a gold medal in the 1968 Olympics, had become a bitter young man. At twenty-five, he was not only labouring in Ali's shadow, but his rolypoly manager Dick Sadler had sold pieces of him on the way up, looking for fast money. With George now the champ, investors kept coming out of woodwork, trying to attach his purse. Sadler also held back $25,000 every time he fought, claiming he had to take care of the referees.

Leroy Jackson, who had attended the Job Corps, a military-like organization that teaches job skills to disadvantaged youth, had hustled his way into a gig heading up the George Foreman Development Corporation, but the company was $175,000 in the red, and Jackson was always going behind George's back. Foreman, who was young, naïve, surly and volatile, was also going through a divorce. Into this chaos swept Don King.

Jackson loathed King and never forwarded his messages, so finally King descended on Foreman in person. Using bluster, flattery, and loud appeals to his racial pride and insecurities, King preached and pleaded, invoking the name of God and money, for nearly two hours. King was so desperate he nearly went hoarse.

"George, you and Ali are both magnificent black man, standing on the threshold of history. Don't deny yourself this moment in time!"

Foreman nodded.

"I can get Ali for you," King continued, using his familiar ploy of not giving the other man time to talk or even think. "I know you been gettin' screwed. Ain't been gettin' paid what you're worth, but my brother, I'm givin' you a chance to make *five million dollars!*"

"Five million!" grunted a startled Foreman, shaking his bushy Afro. "Where you gonna get that kinda money? Ali ain't gonna fight me."

But King managed to leave with a blank contract, signed by the heavyweight champion. In March 1974, Foreman bludgeoned Ken Norton into defeat in two murderous rounds in Caracas, Venezuela. The stage was set for Ali.

Though King and Schwartz now had both fighters signed on the dotted line, they had no more money – and no venue. In February, Schwartz flew to London, trying to get Jack Solomons and two brothers in the film business to back them. But when Schwartz said they were committed for $10 million, the ancient Solomons, who had always used his own money, gasped, "Bloody God!" and that was the end of the meeting.

Schwartz slunk out and called King, who frantically tried to snare Jerry Perenchio, promoter of the first Ali-Frazier fight, to bail them out. Nobody, not even Teddy Brenner at Madison Square Garden, would touch it. Finally, the rain-drenched, bedraggled Schwartz happened to pass a building signed "Hemsdale Films." The name vaguely rang a bell. Schwartz remembered that he had once given Hemsdale some advice about pay-per-view video. On impulse, he made a call to John Daly, president of the firm, who surprisingly saw him without an appointment. "I don't know if you even want me to stay long enough to have tea," Schwartz joked, as his shoes squished and he left puddles wherever he stood, "but I've got Muhammad Ali signed to fight George Foreman, and I got to have $400,000 in a couple of days."

Daly, whose father was a fighter, loved the idea. He made a couple of phone calls to the States, and miraculously the lawyers were working on contracts within hours. Unfortunately, there was a power cut in London, but like something out of Charles Dickens, everyone worked by candlelight.

Schwartz was ecstatic, but the fight nearly collapsed again a week later. Schwartz and Daly had a big disagreement after the Londoner had wired $200,000 to each fighter. Fred Weymer, a notorious drunk and one-time member of the American Nazi Bund, who had international financial contacts with the fugitive American financier Bernard Cornfield, heard about it. He was also an adviser to murderous dictator Joseph Mobutu of Zaire, and handled Mobutu's secret Swiss bank accounts. On impulse, Weymer called Schwartz. Mobutu had wanted to stage a huge extravaganza for international prestige. Why not the Ali–Foreman fight?

Though Zaire was one of the poorest countries in Africa, with a brutally repressive dictator, it had nearly eighty per cent of the world's diamonds. Mobutu reasoned Ali-Foreman would put Zaire on the map. Weymer met with Schwartz, King, John Daly, and Mobutu's other financial guru, Mondunga Bula, in Paris. Weymer was prohibited from coming back into the States while Bula was not allowed to go into Zaire without special permission from Mobutu. The bloodthirsty dictator feared plots on his life and always travelled with his entire cabinet. Normally Bula, a potential rival, would have been killed, but he had a remarkable ability to scare up money.

In Paris, Bula attended the meeting with his Swiss lawyer, Raymond Nicolet. Nicolet represented a Swiss corporation called Risnelia Investments Inc. Risnelia was incorporated in Panama but was really just a shell corporation bought by Mobutu. It allowed the dictator to stash his cash after he stole his impoverished countrymen blind.

In the midst of this cloak and dagger intrigue was the Barclay Bank. Barclay had a Paris bank manager who was such a racist that Bula actually sprang at him and knocked him to the floor during another tumultuous meeting. Finally, it was agreed that Risnelia would provide letters of credit of $4.8 million apiece for Ali and Foreman. For tax purposes, King and Schwartz would pick up the letters of credit at Barclay's main branch, then get them confirmed in New York, so the money wasn't paid from France or Zaire.

King and Schwartz were manically excited at this deal of a lifetime, but for two agonizing days in Paris they kept going to the Barclay's branch, only to find, in King's words, "the motherfuckin' bread ain't here." Mobutu had guaranted the letter of credit but it had to arrive from Kinshasha, Zaire. Finally, a furious Mobutu heard about the delay and ordered his troops to find Barclay's Zairean bank manager, who had been enjoying a vacation with his girlfriend. After he was found, roughed up and thrown into a filthy cell, the head of Barclay's had to fly to Zaire and beg for his release. The Parisian manager of Barclay's who had been so obnoxious to King and Bula earlier, imperiously spat out, "I don't have to take treatment like this." Bula hauled off and belted him to the floor again. As Bula pummelled the man, in the normally sedate, moneyed environs of the Barclay Bank, King and Schwartz were frantic. The letter of credit hadn't been issued, yet Bula was beating the hell out of the man who'd do it.

Next day, the letter of credit did arrive. King and Schwartz broke into broad smiles, and met their deadlines to Foreman and Ali. But the backers' contracts showed that Risnelia would get forty-two per cent of the "gross proceeds," since Mobutu had put up $9.6 million. Hemsdale got twenty-eight per cent because it had fronted $1.5 million. Almost all of the remainder went to Telemedia de Panama and Video Techniques, Schwartz's companies, with Video Techniques also providing its usual technical and broadcast services. King, who conceived the promotion, and still takes credit for it today, got just 4.33 per cent.

King was furious about the percentage. "I was just one more nigger on the plantation," he told Schwartz bitterly.

The "Rumble in the Jungle" was delayed for five weeks, till October 30, after Foreman received a cut brow in training, but Mobutu wouldn't let the fighters leave the country. And on the eve of the epic contest, he did some house cleaning of his own. He had all the petty criminals in Zaire rounded up and had some of them shot at random, as a warning to the others: he didn't want them robbing the international media.

A few hours before dawn on 30 October 1974, in a vast, ramshackle arena under a brilliant African moon, the fighters entered the ring. Sixty thousand Africans chanted, "Ali, boom-a-yay!" – which meant, "Ali, kill him." Though the brooding Foreman was an overwhelming 7-1 favorite, and there were even fears that he might kill his challenger, he was left spiraling to the canvas in the eighth round when Ali opened up with a flurry, having repeatedly lain on the ropes to tire out the younger champion. "The great man has done it," shouted one British broadcaster. But Mobutu didn't go to the stadium to see it. He was afraid his countrymen would turn on him.

* * *

In March 1975, Ali battered a pale, hopelessly outclassed clubfighter named Chuck Wepner into submission in the fifteenth round in Cleveland. The flabby, balding Wepner kept missing with wild, roundhouse swings, while Ali surgically stabbed and countered. Wepner's story gave rise to the *Rocky* movies, but if the subtext was " hapless loser tries to find personal redemption by just trying to go the distance," Mob money was actually responsible for the fight.

"King wanted to stay in the heavyweight picture," Bob Arum told Thomas Hauser, who did a fine biography of Ali in 1991. "He wanted to control Ali, so he went to some Mob guys in Cleveland and got financing from the Mob. That enabled him to offer more for the fight than anyone could afford. I know for a fact, because some FBI people told me, that the interest he owed on the loan from the Mob kept building and building, and King wasn't able to pay it off until after [Larry] Holmes and [Gerry] Cooney in 1982."

Arum also told Irving Rudd, "Without that dough, I doubt whether there would have even been a Don King. The bastard would've stayed where he belonged – in the numbers racket."

Financially, Ali-Wepner made no sense from the beginning. Why would anyone put up $1.5 million just to pay Ali, when nobody in their right mind wanted to see this fight? *Sports Illustrated* may have put the homely, battle-scarred Wepner on its cover, but the "Bayonne Bleeder" had already been stopped by Liston, Foreman and a young Joe Bugner. King, who was frantic to stay in boxing's big time, had tried to get John Daly to back the fight. Daly stood him up after King had flown all the way to London, then never showed for a second meeting.

Teddy Brenner, at Madison Square Garden, thought he had a deal for Ali to fight Ron Lyle, the heavy-handed Denver contender, on March 24. But once King proved he had the money – however he got it – Wepner became the designated punching bag in Cleveland. Arum, Brenner, Rudd, and Don Elbaum all swear that King used Mob money to put on the fight, and sources in the Cleveland Police Department agreed.

Ali-Wepner was a bad fight and reportedly lost $1 million. The offical attendance at the Cleveland Coliseum was 14,900, but King heavily "papered" the 22,000-seat house. The closed-circuit sites were a disaster, only a third full. Suddenly, King was in trouble in Cleveland, because Ali-Wepner had lost so big.

Teddy Brenner told Irving Rudd in the early 1980s, "They were gonna kill that goddamn King. King went to a guy I know, and begged, *begged* I'm tellin ya, this guy to call off the contract they had on his life. Hey, the Cleveland people were sending a guy to New York to hit King 'cause he hadn't paid back the dough on the Ali-Wepner thing."

In 1986, the late Dan Duva, a lawyer who then headed Main Events, told the *New York Daily News*, "Don King is a damn sleazebag. King is nothing but a strongarm man. He has taken his gangsterism and put it into boxing."

On 1 October 1975, Ali met Frazier in the "Thrilla in Manila." The match was one of the most brutal heavyweight title fights of all time. "What you saw was next to death," gasped Ali, who didn't think he could come out for the fifteenth, before Frazier's trainer, Eddie Futch, abruptly halted it as an exhausted Joe spat a stream of blood while on his stool.

Though the first Ali–Frazier fight was a primal masterpiece, Dave Anderson of the *New York Times* likened their third epic encounter to "two old bull moose who had to stand and slam . . . because they couldn't get away from each other."

Moving on weary legs, Ali began to measure Frazier in the 13th with a flurry of punches to Frazier's face, which resembled a squashed chocolate marshmellow. In the 13th the champion quickly knocked out Frazier's mouthpiece with a long left hook, then landed a left-right combination. Frazier was shaken now, wobbly on his stumpy legs, but his heart kept him going. But then Ali's straight right hand sent Frazier stumbling backward to the centre of the ring but somehow the former champion kept his feet. His mouthpiece gone, Frazier kept spitting blood as he resumed his assault.

In the fourteenth, Joe bounded out fast, but before 25,000, indoors in the cauldron-like heat, Ali began to sharpshoot and jarred him badly with flush combinations to his puffy face. As Joe tottered back to his stool, Futch, who genuinely cared about his fighters, said softly, "Sit down, son. It's all over. But no one will ever forget what you did here today." Both gladiators were ruined. Joe's speech is badly slowed, while Ali suffers from horrible tremors and paralysis.

Phillippine dictator Ferdinand Marcos put up the money up for this fight. Imelda Marcos, the Phillippines' first lady, was ringside, though she's best remembered for her 2,000 pairs of shoes. Though the Marcos' raped their poor countrymen, King conned them with his over-priced fight. But after King fell out with his old partner Hank Schwartz, he had to have someone handling close-circuit TV. He turned to Arum, who claimed he was supposed to get $300,000, plus a percentage of the expected $20 millon gross, but Arum later told Brenner and Rudd that King was playing games with the letter of credit and was planning on cooking the books.

Arum, in his own difficult way, refused to co-sign any documents. Finally, as King ranted and raved, Arum just sold King his interest. Bob Arum, the Harvard-educated tax attorney, was petrified that King, just four years out of prison, would get both of them murdered by ripping off Marcos.

* * *

By 1976, King was again struggling. Maybe he had a sumptuous black marble office in New York's RCA Building, but he'd lost Ali. King had tried to doublecross Herbert Muhammad. He'd tried a coup, and wanted to take over as his promoter/manager, but Ali began to shriek, "You dishonored the Messenger's son!"

A struggling New York actor came into King's suite and asked him to bankroll his film, which had a boxing theme. King quickly turned Sylvester Stallone down. But *Rocky* was a brilliant portent of the future. That summer in Montreal, the 1976 Olympics showcased Sugar Ray Leonard and a superb American team, and network television suddenly re-discovered boxing.

King put together his scandalous U.S. Boxing Championships with ABC TV's money, but even after ABC pulled the plug in 1977, they didn't drop King. Over the next twenty years, he'd dominate boxing the way no man had since the darkest days of Carbo. Using network money and the "option clause," King even appointed fighters' managers, though it was illegal.

On the surface, King had grown more colorful and bombastic, but it was just a refinement of his TV act. Mangling his speech, King made TV viewers drop their guard. He was fairly entertaining, with his wild, straight-up Afro, and came across on television as a human cartoon. Even now, thirty years after he sprang to prominence, it's not common for the audience to grasp that a black man is a helluva smarter than his white counterparts. Bob Arum described King's routine as "con man as a buffoon," but it's much deeper than that

King might bellow, "When you can count your money, you ain't got none!" but in a world where people don't really read any more, television is reality.

"King gives you this 'bro' stuff and tells you that the white man did this and we should stick together," said the half-crazed heavyweight Mitch Green, who once chased King around a table at a press conference and tried to dismember him. "Then he starts cutting your purse. I was with him six years. You put your head in a noose when you sign with Don King."

In 1975, in Scranton, Pennnsylvania, King was given the key to the city. "Since then, we've changed the locks," claimed Mayor James McNulty.

Larry Holmes dominated the heavyweight division from 1980 to 1985, but he cried after he gave the ghost of Ali a savage beating. Ali's speech problems became much worse shortly thereafter. How did Don King repay the nan who gave him his big chance to be a promoter? By shorting him $1.1 million.

Ali sued the "world's greatest promoter," but King got hold of Jeremiah Shabazz, a Muslim minister, and ordered him to go see Ali. He handed Shabazz a briefcase with $50,000 in cash. "Show this to Ali, but don't give it to him, until he signs off on the suit," King insisted.

King realized that Ali was basically unsophisticated about money. Knowing that $50,000, in hard, cold cash, meant more *psychologically* than an abstract figure of $1.1million, he got Ali to sign away his rights. When Ali's Chicago lawyer, Michael Phenner, heard about it, he cried.

By the 1980s, King controlled most of the top fighters in the sport because of the money he generated with the heavyweight championship. He was also always eager to gobble up any pretenders to the throne.

In August, 1982, King pressured Tim Witherspoon, a promising boxer/puncher out of Philadelphia, into signing a slave-like agreement whereby Carl King, Don's flunky stepson, would be his "manager." Don King Productions would have exclusive promotional rights. As usual, King dispensed plenty of "fatherly" advice as he put his arm around Tim, but once they met at King's posh 69th Street office, the real Don King emerged: the jive-talking hustler whipped out four different contracts for the bedazzled fighter to sign.

One was an exclusive contract with Don King Productions; a second was an exclusive managerial contract with Carl King, which called for his stepson to receive a third of Witherspoon's purses; a third called for Carl to get half of Tim's purses, though fifty per cent deals were illegal in fight capitals like Las Vegas and Atlantic City (Witherspoon always claimed that King filed a 33.3 per cent contract with the commission while taking fifty); a fourth contract that Tim was ordered to sign was blank.

On 20 May 1983, Witherspoon got a shot at Larry Holmes, who'd made thirteen defenses of his WBC crown. Boxing beautifully, Witherspoon fought the fight of his life as he banged the fading heavyweight champion throughout the twelve rounds, only to get stuck-up by the judges when Holmes was given a split decision. Months later, Tim finally got his purse: $53,000. Scott Frank, a podgy white clubfighter controlled by the Duvas, got $350,000 for getting destroyed by Holmes.

By now, Holmes himself was bitterly rebelling against King's control, but if he thought he had certain rights under the United States Constitution, he was sadly mistaken. In November 1983, Holmes practically beheaded Joe Frazier's son Marvis in the first round, but the WBC refused to recognize the fight and Jose Sulaiman threatened to strip Holmes, if he didn't go back to King. "I'm through being a whore for Don King," he replied angrily.

After fifteen defenses, the most any heavyweight had made since Joe Louis, Holmes was robbed of his WBC title. Sulaiman, that shameless stooge of King's, quickly annointed the winner of the Witherspoon–Greg Page match as new champion. Naturally, Don King controlled both fighters. After a dreary contest, Witherspoon finally was a "champ," but according to a devastating article Jack Newfield wrote in *Details* magazine, the $250,000 King promised him turned out to be just $41,498. Carl King supposedly got $125,000.

Though King's business practices were flagrant violations of the antitrust laws, not one state boxing commission did anything. Later in the year, Witherspoon defended against Pinklon Thomas, which brought more sneers from insiders. Don King promoted while Carl King "managed" both fighters. By now, Witherspoon had grown angry at his mistreatment, but when he requested $350,000, Don King demanded half for his son. When has a promoter ever negotiated on behalf of a manager?

As the Kings ruthlessly exploited him, Tim simply stopped training, and lost a majority verdict to Thomas. It made no difference to Don King. There were always more bodies like Michael Dokes, Tony Tubbs, Trevor Berbick, and Page, whom Carl also "managed," in what was a terrible period for the heavyweight crown. Seth Abraham kept looking the other way as he bankrolled the operation on behalf of HBO.

On 21 September 1985, Michael Spinks shocked the world by upsetting Holmes to win the IBF heavyweight championship. In January 1986, Witherspoon was recycled again and decisioned the flabby Tubbs for the WBA title. In Britain, muscular Frank Bruno was being groomed for the crown. Mickey Duff thought Bruno was best British heavyweight ever, and the stiff, immobile puncher had won twenty-seven of his twenty-eight fights, most of them against nonentities.

In July 1986, Witherspoon stepped into a hysterical, flag-waving crowd of 55,000 at Wembley. It was the biggest fight in Britain since the second

Ali-Cooper clash in 1966, with a live gate worth over $2 million. HBO television paid $1.7 million for the American TV rights. Micky Duff claimed $1 million had been set aside for Witherspoon's purse, but Tim claims that with Carl negotiating on his behalf with his stepfather, he was promised $550,000.

The Witherspoon-Bruno fight was a brutal affair. Bruno, the European champ roared on by his countrymen, was slightly ahead until Witherspoon, his left eye almost closed, his paunchy brown body throbbing with pain, suddenly connected with four looping rights and finished him in the eleventh. Witherspoon had retained the WBA title but "Terrible Tim" was so badly beaten up, he had to be helped back to his hotel room, and hurt for weeks after. In a rare moment of compassion, Don King promised him a bonus, but weeks later, Tim's $550,000 turned out to be just $90,000.

Duff, Britain's longest-reigning promoter, figured King made a couple of million dollars. Carl King got $250,000 according to deductions. Bruno cleared six times what Witherspoon, as champion, received. By now, a furious Witherspoon wanted out of his contract with the Kings, but HBO wanted boxing to build its subscriber base, and Don King resurrected a forgotten contract Tim had signed for a rematch with Tubbs. Days before the fight, Tubbs angrily pulled out after King hastily renegotiated his purse down to a pitiful $25,000.

King immediately threw in James "Bonecrusher" Smith. Witherspoon didn't want the fight. Bonecrusher, so nicknamed because he hit so hard, had halted Bruno in 1984. Smith was a college graduate, but he was forced to take on Carl King as his manager to get the shot. Carl King wasn't even a licensed manager in the state of New York. Though "unlicensed managing" is what got Frankie Carbo and Blinky Palermo in trouble, incredibly Carl King was allowed to represent both contestants in a heavyweight championship contest, promoted by his stepfather, and Jose Torres, the former light-heavyweight champion and then-boxing commissioner, did nothing. According to Witherspoon, Don King threatened him with forfeiture of the title when he protested. Torres, who is always proclaiming how much he has done for fighters, allegedly told Tim, "You'll never fight in New York again if you don't get into the ring."

On 12 December 1986, at Madison Square Garden, Smith sledgehammered Witherspoon to the canvas three times and the fight ended in the first round. Tim slumped on a chair in his sombre dressing room afterwards. "I'm glad I lost," he said. "Maybe I can get my career straightened out and a manager who can help me."

Witherspoon figured he was finally done with the Kings. According to Jack Newfield, who saw the contracts on file at the New York State Athletic Commission office, Witherspoon was guaranteed $300,000, with accountable training fees up to $100,000. Out of a potential $400,000 gross, Witherspoon glimpsed just $129,826. After deductions, that shrank to $99,000. Carl King, who supposedly held just a minority percentage, got $97,900 off the top, and $30,000 was supposed to go to Tim's trainer, Slim Jim Robinson. Carl stiffed him. Witherspoon paid Robinson out of his share, which left him with $69,000. Though the contract had also provided for $100,000 in training expenses, Don King forced Tim to train at his lavish Ohio farm at $1,000 a day. This $28,000 was part of the $75,594 that Don King deducted from the gross purse.

Suddenly, the IRS got involved, and hit Tim for $66,000 in back taxes. Witherspoon was left with $3,000 after supposedly earning $400,000. By Christmas, just thirteen days later, Witherspoon couldn't even afford presents for his family. He was on the verge of eviction from his $500 a month apartment. His telephone had been disconnected, and his car had been repossessed.

"Don hurt me real bad," he told Newfield. "He made me sign blank contracts, he made me use his son as my manager. He warned me never to talk to a lawyer. He never gave me copies of anything I signed. I had no rights. I had no one I could appeal my case to. Don messed me up real bad. Let me tell you, I hate that motherfucker."

After a Witherspoon lawsuit and nearly a decade of legal manoeuvres, Don King finally came up with $1 million. But Witherspoon never fullifilled his promise as a fighter and, at the time of writing, was still risking his health at forty-four. He was so broke, he had to ask *Boxing News* correspondent Jack Hirsch for $20.

On May 12, 1992, Don King's former comptroller, Joseph Maffia, gave a sworn affadavit that shed light on Don King's sweetheart business relationship with his stepson Carl.

Under Nevada law, the maximum percentage a manager can take from a fighter's purse is 33⅓ percent. Yet in many cases, Don King promoted fights in Nevada in which one or more of the fighters was managed by Don's son, Carl King of Monarch Boxing Inc. Oftentimes, in these instances, the fighters were required to pay Carl King a fifty percent management share, and false declarations were filed with the Nevada State Athletic Commisssion. Monarch Boxing was financed and controled by Don King, and the bulk of all money received by Monarch was paid in turn to DKP (Don King Productions) as a 'loan repayment.'

As Don King pillaged his way through professional boxing, it finally came to the attention of the FBI. Joe Spinelli was a thirty-one-year-old agent who had loved boxing since his grandfather took him as wide-eyed six-year-old to see Rocky Marciano bludgeon Archie Moore at Yankee Stadium. Spinelli began asking around about King, and concluded that he was still mobbed-up in Cleveland. In January 1981, Richie Giachetti, who had trained Larry Holmes, surprisingly turned over five tape recordings of King, and one of Holmes, he had made between 1973 and 1980 that supposedly proved King was guilty of crimes,

Giachetti was a tough guy, who knew how the system worked. He told Spinelli he was willing to testify if he was subpoened in front of a grand jury. Giachetti's phone tapes supposedly showed that King paid off Sulaiman and some journalists. King, however, allegedly sent a "hit man" to Las Vegas, who supposedly warned Giachetti that he had better back off. Giachetti had stupidly told Holmes of the recordings, and Larry blabbed to King.

According to two other FBI informants, Spinelli concluded that Don King was actually arranging for the portly trainer's murder. Philadelphia mobster Frankie "Flowers" D'Alfonso was going to be involved. D'Alfonso had gotten closed-circuit TV rights for Holmes-Ali in Atlantic City, and would later grab Holmes-Cooney, before he was gunned down in a hit in 1985.

In May 1981, Giachetti was warned that King had allegedly put a contract out on his life. Though Giachetti is a hard-ass, he publicly babbled to Mike Marley of the *New York Post*, "I'm fearful of my life. I think they would try to make it look like a mugging. A bombing, an outright killing, would be too obvious. The Mob guys have come to see me. My family is very scared and my two kids are upset. I make sure I don't go out alone."

Though Don King has constantly draped himself in the flag, by 1982 he was openly seen having dinner with some of the leading mobsters in New York. On September 14, King dined with John Gotti at a restaurant it Little Italy, three years before Gotti murdered his way to the top spot in organized crime. On September 29, two weeks later, King was seen at Abe's Steakhouse in Manhattan with Genovese family *capo* Matty "The Horse" Ianello. On December 6, Gotti, Ianello and King were again at Abe's. An FBI informant claimed King and Gotti had a "heated discussion" and it appeared "King was in serious trouble with Gotti." Ianello was overheard saying, "King's got to be taught a lesson, and John will take care of it." Rumours are that either Gotti, or Paul Castellano, then New York's Godfather, slapped King in the face.

Ten years later, when King was subpoenaed to testify in front of a Senate Subcommittee investigating boxing, King took the Fifth Amendment against self-incrimination when asked if he ever met with Castellano or Gotti. King also pleaded the Fifth about meeting Michael Franzese, though Franzese's meeting was recorded by the FBI. King was playing a deadly game with Gotti, but by November 2001, the gangster was dying of neck and throat cancer in a hospital in Springfield, Missouri. The "Teflon Don" was doing life without parole in a cage with extraordinary security measures. According to the *Globe*, an American tabloid, Gotti eventually "made peace with God" and admitted to twenty-five hits.

Franzese, a boyish-looking former *capo* in the Colombo crime family, who sported gold chains and hip clothes, testified under oath in front of a Senate subcomittee in Washington that he was present when King met with Castellano and Colombo family crime boss Thomas Dibella back in 1976. Franzese, who also had a small piece of Davey Moore, a former eleven-stone king, swore that both mobsters "berated" King for not telling them who was going to win a fight between two pugs he controlled. King then assured the mobsters that they would "never lose money on any deal they had together," testified Franzese.

Since the FBI had audio and video tapes, there was no question that King was familiar with organized crime. "Don King is not with my family. He is with some cousins," Franzese damningly said on one monitored tape.

Franzese also had some startling insights about the 1982 Holmes–Cooney mega fight. "[Cooney] knew that he just couldn't win that fight, and he passed that information along," testified the so-called "yuppie mobster," who won $30,000 after getting Cooney's tip. Franzese also told Senate probers that Vito Antuofermo, the former middleweight champion, was controlled by a Colombo capo named Andrew Russo. Supposedly, the Mob knew that some of his fights had allegedly been fixed.

Al Certo, the manager/trainer of Buddy McGirt, the WBC welter-weight champion, was also alleged to have had links to the Genovese crime family, and McGirt's purses were allegedly cut up between New York and Buffalo crime families. John DiGillio, a pro fighter who had been trained by Certo, was a lieutenant in the Genovese crime family – until he was found floating in 1988 in the Hackensack River with two gunshots in the head.

* * *

In March 1982, the FBI approved a brilliant "sting" operation called "Crown Royal," conceived by Joseph Spinelli to clean up professsional boxing. A phony company, TKO Productions, was set up near Madison Square Garden. A posh apartment was rented near Lincoln Centre, and a Rolls Royce was leased. Victor Quintana, a fifteen-year veteran of the FBI, played the role of a South American drug trafficker looking to launder $4 million in drug money but needing the right contacts. Quintana began hanging out with Franzese, bragging that he was worth $50 million. Quintana wanted to meet Don King, but Franzese wouldn't violate Mob protocol.

"Look, you don't think I'm for real, call this number," Quintana told him.

It was a bank in Illinois, where the FBI had set up $15 million in a bogus account. Franzese then called Corky Vastola, who allegedly controlled King through the Cleveland mob, and the DeCalvalcante crime family in New Jersey. In November 1982, Quintana and Franzese met with Vastola and Jimmy Rotundo, two New Jersey mobsters from the DeCavalcante family (the real life prototype of TV's *Sopranos*) at Gargulio's Restaraunt in Coney Island. Quintana was asked if he had the money to do business with King. Quintana cooly told them he had $4 million in cash – right now. A couple of days later, Franzese was told by Vastola that the Cleveland family had approved Quintana's meeting with King.

In March 1983, King's long-time ally, the Reverend Al Sharpton, one of the most powerful black leaders in New York (and later the country), met two undercover FBI agents purporting to be drug traffickers. Sharpton was flanked by Danny Pagano, the son of a top *capo* in the Genovese family. Pagano was tight with Sharpton because of their involvement in the black music industry. Franzese, who'd been promised half of the so-called promotional company, for setting up the meeting with King, had sent word to Pagano and got him involved.

After the two agents told Sharpton and Pagano they had $4 million in cash, Sharpton stammered badly, "That's all in cash, cash money?"

"Whoa, whoa," Paguano said, "What you wanna do is you want to make the deal with Don but you want somebody there so he can't [fuck] nobody. I'll go with you."

Later, the undercover Fed, trying to get something incriminating on tape, said, "I'm sure Don is going to want to know what our relationship is . . . 'cause first we came with Michael. Now [we] are with Danny."

"No," said Sharpton, this devout man of God. "He ain't gonna worry about that 'cause he knows I'm with Danny."

Finally, Pagano explained Mob protocol to the supposed drug-money-rich promoters: "As far as [Franzese] goes, [he] really don't have anything with Don King. It's through, it's through us."

The meet with King was eventually made in King's Manhattan office in 1983. Franzese warned Quintana to be very careful; King was under a lot of pressure from the Feds. Franzese also told King that he couldn't completely "qualify" the drug dealers, and that he should speak carefully to them. They could be FBI. But Franzese also discussed what the percentages would be, and which family would get what.

During the meeting, Franzese forgot his own advice and stupidly asked if King could get the "drug dealers" licenses to promote? "King told me not to worry about licenses because he could get them in any state," testifed

Franzese in 1992. Afterwards, if Franzese is to be believed, the four men – King, Franzese, Pagano and Quintana – shook hands on the deal.

By now, Spinelli was positive that King was mobbed up. Spinelli's sources told him that King was "connected" with crime families in New Jersey, Philadelphia, Cleveland and the five families in New York City. He figured that one reason King ruthlessly exploited his fighters was that organized crime was his hidden partner.

On 30 June 1983, Sharpton was kibbitzing with Quintana at TKO's $2,400 a month company apartment when Spinelli and another FBI agent, Ken Mikionis, burst in. Without a word, they inserted the video casette of Sharpton offering to call Pagano about a so-called drug transaction. The Reverend Al quickly said, "I'll do whatever I have to do to stay out of jail."

Sharpton was quickly passed over to FBI agents making other Mob cases. He helped John Pritchard gather evidence against Morris Levy, the Mob's main man in the record industry. He supplied "probable cause" for a wiretap on Danny Pagano. He helped nail Franzese on his gasoline and tax swindle, which was reputedly a $35 million scam, one the Mob's biggest ever.

Not only did Sharpton survive, he talks about being a black candidate for President. As for Crown Royal? The Justice Department aborted the investigation, ostensibly after Duk Koo Kim died after his televised fight on American TV. Once again, Don King's incredible luck continued.

Don King is boxing's ultimate survivor. He has for thirty years dominated a racket that is supposedly regulated by the states, even though two of his most prominent fighters, Larry Holmes and Mike Tyson, publicly claim he stole a staggering $75 million dollars from them. "I estimated that he took twenty, thirty million dollars from me," figured Holmes.

In his prime, when Holmes was boxing's best heavyweight, he talked about defecting to Bob Arum. "You go to Bob Arum," King suppoedly told him, "I'll break your legs."

"I told him I'd kill him: You come toward me, I'll shoot you," Holmes says. "Don King is the devil, man," sighs Holmes, now a slope-shouldered old man still trying to fight at fifty-plus. "The hair sticks up to hide the horns."

"Don King is probably one of the most despicable people on the face of the earth," said Bill Cayton, stifling a hiss. "He's a con man that makes Svengali look like an amateur."

"Animal-like. Really, really barbaric," agreed Cedric Kushner, probably the fourth or fifth biggest promoter in the world.

King is shameless, amoral, but oh so cunning. He does whatever it takes, and because he is flamboyant and adept at TV soundbites, he is never held accountable. And whenever the Government attempts to go after him, King immediately screams, "It's because I'm black."

★ ★ ★

On 22 November 1986, Mike Tyson left Trevor Berbick lurching around like a drunk to become the youngest man, at twenty, ever to win a heavyweight championship. King bolted into the ring, flashing his pearly barracuda smile, to hug him and raise his hand. Like Ali, like so many young men before, Tyson was a commodity, and King had to steal him: this murderous brown youngster with the pronounced lisp was the future of boxing.

In January 1988, Tyson left Larry Holmes flat on his back in the fourth round, after King had conned his former champion into making a disastrous comeback. On February 9, Tyson married a beautiful TV starlet named Robin Givens, who had lied to Mike that she was pregnant. On March 20, Tyson destroyed Tony Tubbs in Tokyo. Awed Japanese kept following him around, like he'd descended from war gods.

In New York, however, Tyson's co-manager Jim Jacobs was dying of leukemia. Tyson was inconsolable. He had never been close to his other co-manager, Bill Cayton, though Cayton is a kind, decent man when you take the time to know him. King knew just how to play this young black kid from the Brooklyn ghetto who been patiently nurtured by Jacobs and Cayton, two paternal Jews. Jacobs had loathed King, but King crashed his funeral in Los Angeles and began making his moves on Mike. Meanwhile, Givens and her mother, Ruth Roper, refused to attend Jacobs's service at all. Though Tyson was in tears in LA, in New York Givens and her mother descended on Merrill Lynch in the Pan Am building at 200 Park Avenue, and demanded that Tyson's money, $1.9 million, be transferred into a joint account held by Tyson and Givens at Citibank. Givens now had power of attorney and demanded that this $1.9 million be put solely into an account in her name at the European-American Bank. European-American refused, and Givens exploded.

"I want my motherfuckin' money!" she screamed. Givens called her husband in Los Angeles. Tyson, overwrought from Jacobs's death, instructed Merrill Lynch to do whatever Robin wanted. Two months later, she angrily closed Tyson's $10 million account, and deposited it into the United States Trust Company.

Tyson was soon living with Robin and her controlling mother on a gorgeous $4.5 million estate in Bernardsville, New Jersey. "I really liked Robin at first," recalled Steve Lott, the junior member of the Jacobs/Cayton team. Tyson had lived in his apartment for two years, and the worst Mike had ever said to him was, "What? You ate all the vanilla ice cream?" Though Lott was white, he loved Tyson like a little brother.

The lean, fit, ex-handball prodigy began to cry as he remembered how

Tyson's life just careened out of control. "I thought Robin would be good for Mike," he recalled slowly. "I really liked her in the beginning. I thought she really loved him. Bill was for the marriage too. He thought it would settle Mike down. But one day Robin said to him, 'Hey Mike, what's with all the white people?'"

Though Tyson had been a guy who carried old ladies' groceries across the street (a far cry from his ghetto days when he was mugging them), Lott claims that Tyson was having sex with five or six groupies a day. And the Tyson-Givens marriage made the War of the Roses look like puppy love. In May, Tyson had a fender-bender in New York City. The newly-wed heavyweight king was so frazzled, he popped out of his $183,000 Bentley and gave it to the two startled cops who had arrived on the scene.

By June 17 Givens, who was playing the greatest role of her life in front of a tabloid-obsessed country, went public with her tales of beatings at the hands of Tyson. Even Tyson laughingly told Jose Torres that he once back-handed Robin so hard, she bounced off all four walls in their house, before she went down in a heap. But Rudy Gonzalez, Tyson's chauffeur, claims that Robin was an imperious woman, who didn't want to spend any time with her husband.

Once, Gonzalez was sent to fetch Tyson's old Brownsville buddies to a party that he was having at the mansion, but Robin shrieked from the upper staircase, "I don't want those niggers using my bathrooom!"

Though Tyson had worshipped her, he barked back, "Only nigger here is you, bitch! Shut the fuck up!"

In June 1988, Tyson annihilated Michael Spinks in just ninety-one seconds to cement his claim as "the baddest man on the planet." Earlier in the day, with King pulling the strings, Tyson sued Cayton to break his contract. Trainer Kevin Rooney, who had brilliantly perfected Tyson's vicious bob-and-weave style, was also finished after the explosive fight.

The following month, Tyson acquired Donald Trump as his so-called adviser. Trump, a fabulously wealthy developer, loved young women and the limelight. Tyson went with him because he was still wary of King. King, deftly trying for total control, was trying to shove Givens and Roper out too, since they posed the greatest threat, but King knew just how to handle Trump.

One day, after Tyson was being difficult, King bellowed to him, "I'm tired of your shit with Trump. Goddammit Mike, while you're out with Trump on his yacht, why don't you ask him why he's fucking your wife?"

As King stormed out, Tyson exploded, and fired the remote from his giant fifty-inch TV against the screen. Gonzalez, his driver, got scared because he had never seen Tyson go off like this. Fifteen minutes later, Robin came in, and chirped, "I'm home."

As usual, she was laden down with expensive packages from shopping. Moments later, Gonzalez heard a loud smack. Robin was on the ground, her packages scattered all over, when Gonzalez came in. The chauffeur tried to pick her up, but she was hysterical. Ruth Roper walked in. "I can't take this anymore," Givens screeched to her mother.

Just sixteen days later, Tyson settled with Cayton out of court. Cayton, who'd financed this "hopelessly incorrigble" street kid out of reform school, was cut down from a third to twenty per cent. Cayton was now a manager in name only. For months, according to Gonzalez, King and "the women," as Cayton bitterly called them, had been bombarding Tyson with a never-ending race rap. "Why you allowing all these white people to control your career and money?"

At one point, King even said to Cayton, "I poisoned his mind against you, I'll unpoison it if I have to."

Cayton, a man of principal, would not deal.

* * *

At four o'clock one August morning, Tyson was in Harlem when he was suddenly confronted by Mitch Green, the crazed heavyweight, who had run like a thief when they boxed two years earlier. Tyson was standing in front of Dapper Dan's, a clothing store, when Green, a one-time gang leader, confronted him, stinking of alcohol,

"Don King robbed me," grunted Mitch.

"Don King robs everybody," countered Tyson, trying to brush him off.

Green persisted, demanding a championship rematch. Words were exchanged, then things got crazy. Tyson, the highest-paid fistfighter in history, broke a bone in his right hand, while Green's face ended blown up like a balloon.

With Tyson's once carefully orchestrated world now a tabloid nightmare, he became so unhinged, one day at home he hopped into his expensive Bentley and drove straight into a tree. It made screaming headlines in the *New York Post* and *New York Daily News*. Both called it a "suicide attempt." As Tyson was wheeled into an emergency room, Givens finally revealed the first glimmer of public concern she ever showed for her husband by telling cameramen, "Give the guy a break."

The media was now claiming that Tyson suffered a chemical imbalance that made him violent and irrational. Lott and Cayton figured Givens and her mother were behind those stories to get a better divorce settlement. With the media haunting his every footstep, and King working his black magic behind the scenes, the twenty-two-year-old boxer had no one he could trust. With the instincts a tiger has for a boa constrictor, King knew what Givens and Roper were after, and did everything he could to keep them away from Tyson's money.

In September 1988, Givens figuratively castrated her husband on national TV. With Tyson sitting zombie-like beside her, she unflinchingly spilled her marital difficulties to Barbara Walters, a glorified gossip monger who poses as a journalist. According to Givens, who never completed college despite her fraudulent Harvard claims, Tyson supposedly was a manic depressive, and she was afraid of him. "It's been hell, absolute hell," she said of her marriage.

Tyson, normally a volcano of emotions, meekly sat like he had been sedated. When he got back home after being eviscerated in front of the country, his "friends" John Horne and Rory Holloway came up to him and shook their heads: "Man, that bitch sure dissed you. She made you look like a punk."

For months Holloway and Horne had burrowed themselves into Tyson's marriage. Gonzalez claims they were on King's payroll. Holloway was Tyson's close boyhood friend, while Horne was a failed stand-up comic and a friend of Rory's. Horne and Holloway were street punks more than anything, always referring to Givens as a "bitch" or a "ho" in front of Tyson, and he took it. After the Walters interview, Tyson went berserk.

On October 2, Tyson started heaving $10,000 pieces of furniture out the window of his Bernardsville mansion, while Givens and her mother ran for their lives. The police were called. Tyson was subdued, but five days later Givens filed for divorce. He filed for an annulment, claiming he was tricked into his marriage because Givens was never pregnant. On October 26, Trump billed Tyson $2 million for "service rendered." All that did was push him more desperately into the clutches of King, who was now publicly claiming that they were partners.

Givens sued Tyson for $125 million because of a *New York Post* story in which the furious fighter called her and and her mother "the slime of the slime." By now, Givens was being booed in public because people thought she was a shameless gold digger. With Tyson's life in chaos, King, the master puppeteer, had Tyson re-sue Cayton to get him permanently out of the picture. An earlier audit demanded by Givens, after she publicly questioned Cayton's honesty, proved that Cayton had actually overpaid Tyson $168,000.

Givens got a multi-million dollar settlement. The writing had been on the wall from the beginning. On their first date, Givens had brought three publicists with her.

With the spotlight now blinding him, Michael Gerard Tyson, who in two years had gone from relative anonymity to one of the most famous men in the world, was sick of his role as poster boy. "I'm just Anna Mae's son from Amboy Street," he protested.

King continued to play his public role as benevolent father figure, always making sure that he was especially close to Tyson whenever photos were snapped. Neither Cayton, Jacobs, Lott, or Tyson's real mentor, the late Cus D'Amato, were there anymore. In Givens's wake, all sorts of women came out of the woodwork demanding outrageous sums of money because Tyson had grabbed or patted them in nightclubs.

Sandra Miller sued because Tyson allegedly grabbed and propositioned her inside a club. She was awarded $100, which barely covered filing fees. That same day, Tyson was sued by Lorrie Miller after he allegedly grabbed her by the buttocks. By now, it looked like Tyson had testosterone on the brain. In January 1989, during a deposition in his suit to oust Cayton as manager, a flustered Tyson suddenly began making blatant sexual gestures with his hands and talking dirty to an attractive female attorney who was trying to question him. The following month, on St Valentine's Day, Tyson and Robin Givens were given a quickie divorce in the Dominican Republic.

Two weeks later, Tyson easily dispatched Britain's Frank Bruno. His private life, however, had become a staple of the tabloids. In a sport starved of media attention, he was now one of the most publicized people in the world. In April 1989, in Los Angeles, he was accused of striking a parking lot attendant three times with an open hand because he was asked to move his Mercedes Benz from the club owner's parking space. In July, the fearsome young Tyson had his last great fight, blasting out Carl "the Truth" Williams in one round. He was weeks away from his twenty-third birthday.

With King firmly in control, Tyson was slated an easy defense in Tokyo against James "Buster" Douglas, who'd once fought for the IBF title but was considered lazy and lacking in heart. Just two years after Jim Jacobs's death, Tyson was shockingly knocked out by Douglas, a huge underdog in the betting. Tyson, with Rooney no longer there to train him (just hacks King provided like Jay Bright and Aaron Snowell), no longer slipped and rolled; he stood straight up, and Douglas's long jab kept harpooning him in the face. By the seventh round, Tyson's left eye was closing. Incredibly, there wasn't even an Endswell in the corner to ease the swelling.

In the eighth, Tyson finally connected and dropped this modern Cinderella Man, but Douglas lurched to his feet. Tyson couldn't finish Douglas in the ninth, but nearly went down along the ropes himself. With the huge crowd yelling for an upset, Douglas was inspired, and finally sent Mike down in the tenth from a vicious right uppercut. As the once invincible Tyson groped drunkenly on his knees, groggily trying to put his mouthpiece in, but clumsily placing it upside down, it was one of the most poignant scenes in the history of sport.

The shameless attempt by Don King and Jose Sulaiman to deny Douglas victory has already been described (see Chapter Twelve). Nearly a year later, a financial statement in a civil court case revealed that King still owed him $2,097,000 from the disastrous fight.

On June 28, 1991, Tyson had a brutal clash with Donovan "Razor" Ruddock. "Pardon my French," Tyson exclaimed after it was over, " But man, that motherfucker hits hard."

Rudy Gonzalez claims that King was so worried about losing Tyson and his millions, he brought in LA gang members to make sure nobody broke his stranglehold. Horne and Holloway were still spying for King, while according to Jack Newfield, King's most persistent critic, "In 1991 when I was in Vegas covering Tyson's fight with Ruddock, King would send the gang guys around and [they'd] say, 'Get outta town, Jack. We're going to kill you.'" Newfield was a portly, bespectacled, gray-haired man in his early fifties.

On another occasion, an infamous thug called "Death Threat" told grandfatherly Jack, "We'll kill you. Get out of town."

Gonzalez saw the gangbangers, who dealt in drugs and murder, and says that Death Threat was actually a leader of the notorious Crips in South Central LA, and that Tyson had walked into the ring flanked by this punk.

Six years after Ruddock, Tyson was disqualified for outrageously biting off part of Evander Holyfield's ear in their rematch. Gonzalez, who saw the intimate side of Tyson, figured that Iron Mike "had been living in total, total fear. That was his way of saying, 'Enough is enough. I gotta get out of here.'"

* * *

King's publicists have tried to fashion a benevolent, colorful image, and the media has no problem whoring for access or a few drinks, with some notable exceptions. In August 1987, the *Chicago's Tribune's* Sam Smith covered a King double bill in Chicago, featuring Edwin Rosario versus Juan Nazario for the WBA lightweight title. Chicago's Alfonzo Ratliff, who had come out of prison, was also defending his cruiserweight belt.

Nearly fifteen years later, Smith wrote:

Ratliff also was the textbook example of how boxers are ruined by promoters like King. There are no organizations for boxers. The international symbol for the various alphabet organizations is an outstretched hand in a field of dollar bills. In basketball agents are licensed and can get paid no more than 4 percent on a contract.

As Ratliff's promoter, King extracted one-third of the fighter's purse. Then King installed his son as Ratliff's manager. Right, another 33 percent. Then there was another dodge King had going. He'd have his fighters train at his

Ohio 'farm.' For that honor, his boxers were assessed a fee of $1,000 per day. And sometimes they wouldn't even get the bottom bunk.

It's why when Ratliff 'made' $250,000 far his championship victory over Carlos DeLeon, he came home with about $25,000, before taxes.

Smith also wrote about the impending ripoff the day of the fight. When this brave reporter, all too rare in boxing, tried to take his ringside seat at the University of Illinois Circle Pavilion, "King and his goons were waiting. Yes, he has goons."

One thug confronted Smith, and bellowed, "Leave. Get the hell out."

Smith still tried to take his seat, but a huge, nasty man came up menacingly behind him, when Smith sat down. "You wrote some motherfuckin' stuff," he growled, so close to Smith that he could feel his breath. Then King "came over and took my chair away. He invited me, somewhat unpleasantly, to leave and then ripped my telephone out."

Smith was about to leave when Gordon Volkman, chairman of the Illinois Boxing Commission, stepped in. As King towered over Volkman, shaking his finger in his face, Volkman argued back. Finally, the fifty-six-year-old, who was also treasurer of nearby Kane County and had a reputation for honesty, got up and gave Smith his seat. "Use our telephone. If you interfere," he said, spinning around to face the furious King, "I'll forfeit your bond with the state."

By 1992, Tyson was in prison for raping Desiree Washington, a Miss Black America contestant, in Indianapolis, Indiana. This was one case King couldn't fix. Tyson liquidated the trust fund Cayton had set up that would have paid him $250,000 for life, simply to pay his appelate lawyer Alan Dershowitz, hoping to overturn his conviction. Dershowitz had the best appeals record in the country. It was double the national average: two per cent.

After Tyson's indictment, the greedy King tried to set up one last fight: a November 8 match with Evander Holyfield in Las Vegas, but that fell through, and the King's meal ticket was now on ice.

Tyson's father, Jimmy Kirkpatrick, who was white, died while he was behind bars, but Tyson didn't even request to go to his funeral. Lott, his old roommate, wrote him "hundreds of letters," pleading with him to turn his life around, but never got an answer. Ironically, when Tyson "was at the lowest point in my life," fellow jailbird Reggie Kray, once Britain's most powerful mobster and one of the notorious East End twins, wrote Tyson a letter. "I was very grateful for that," said Iron Mike.

In March 1995, Tyson was released from the Indiana Youth Centre. He had done his time in a minor league prison; he could have gone to the walled fortress in Michigan City, or the new "Super Max," one of the most secure joints in the country, at Westville. Suitors like Rock Newman had been to see him. Now that Tyson was supposedly a Muslim, Newman, who managed Riddick Bowe, was shamelessly wearing a kaftan and throwing down a prayer shawl.

Yet as rumours abounded that King was out, nobody became more devout than the Don. According to Wally Matthews of the *New York Post*, King literally prostrated himself at Tyson's feet and begged for him to come back. Though Tyson was broke, after somehow going through $100 million, he stupidly re-signed with King, who couldn't have maintained his blood-sucking control of boxing without him.

In his first match back, Tyson demolished Peter McNeele in a round. Eventually he vanquished Bruce Seldon for the WBA title with a punch that clearly missed. In July 1997, however, the Nevada State Athletic Commission unanimously revoked his boxing license for biting off part of Evander Holyfield's ear and spitting it out. The MGM also terminated its contract with Tyson and King after Tyson fans went on a rampage, breaking up the casino, after the barbaric ending.

By now, the public was so disgusted with Tyson, a New York jury even ordered him to pay Mitch Green $45,000 — even though they agreed that Tyson had been provoked into their long-ago Harlem street fight. After Green heard the verdict, he began to bounce in front of the jury box, crazily shadow boxing and whooped, "I whipped Michelle Cicely Tyson." Then he began chanting at Tyson: "Homo! Homo!"

On October 29, the nomadic thirty-one-year-old was cruising on a Connecticut highway when he suddenly hit a patch of sand and careened off the road. Tyson could have been killed; he did break some ribs on the right side. Five days later, he apologized to Holyfield for biting him, on the nationally televised news program *20–20* but added ruefully; "I'll probably be banned for life."

Tyson had become a man who trusted no one and "expected to be betrayed." He had, however, remarried. Monica Turner was a highly intel-ligent, softly-spoken pediatrician with long black hair, who at first blush seemed an unlikely mate. After all, Tyson was a rapist, a "cannibal" and a two-fisted destroyer who had once terrorized the prize ring. "I don't care," she said firmly. "He's not perfect, but nobody is. He's a nice guy."

Tyson seemed like a gentle, playful puppy around her, but it was nothing like his crazed infatuation for Givens. "I thought she was just another girl I was going to score with," Tyson said of the good doctor.

On TV, Tyson openly snuggled his children, in the fabulous mansion that his fists provided. But if Monica was finally getting him to question his rela-tionship with King, she seemed to be living in a fantasy world when she told her questioning friends, "I've got him wrapped around my finger." Tyson was never there. He actually lived in a Las Vegas mansion, a good 2,500 miles from his wife.

Mike Tyson, who once wore cardboard in his shoes to keep out the snow, and who survived cruel taunts of "fairy boy," and "big-headed Mike," earned a staggering $112 million in six fights since being released from prison. But in late January 1998, he suddenly discovered that he was bust again, and owed the dreaded IRS $7 million. He kept crying, "How could they do this to me?"

Tyson's mood vacillated between killing fury and deep depression. He had brought Horne and Holloway in to protect him, then fired them and dumped King. Tyson was remarkably ignorant about his affairs. He got a phone call from the World Wide Wrestling Association. They were going to pay him $3.5 million for appearing in their annual burlesque, "WrestleMania," and officials said that King had collected $300,000 for the rights to Mike's likeness. Tyson had been sweating and bleeding as a pro since 1985, but under King, he didn't even own the rights to his own face. Tyson descended on King outside the swank Hotel Bel Air in Los Angeles, swearing loudly and demanding, "What happened to my motherfucking money?"

King was frightened, but quickly assumed his father/protector pose. Tyson would have none of it. He threw off King's arm, then slapped him in the face. After furiously pushing King away, he walked briskly toward a waiting car. King, knowing he was in big trouble if Tyson left, bounded after him. With dozens of onlookers present, King pulled Tyson's limo door open only to get kicked hard twice in the face. As the crowd gasped, King fell back, stunned. The "World's Great Promoter," hadn't been beaten this badly since he arrived in Jamiaca in 1981, and tried to claim Trevor Berbick's promotional rights before Berbick's fight against Muhammad Ali. A group of Jamaican heavies set about him and gave him a thorough hiding.

This wasn't the first time that Tyson had confronted King about "financial irregularities." In May 1991, Tyson had collared King, with Gonzalez at his side. This time King was so shaken, he went out and paid $850 for a bulletproof vest.

Though Tyson was committed to four more fights with King, he'd been calling around and asking, "Is it customary for a promoter take fifty per cent of a fighter's money?" Of course, it isn't.

As Tyson prepared to sue King, an audit showed that King was flagrantly double-dipping from the manager's end. Though Horne and Holloway were supposed to be his managers, King was getting thirty per cent, while they were just getting ten per cent apiece. He, not them, had the major control of the fighter. King was also Tyson's promoter. In essence, he was illegally negotiating with himself. King was also receiving a huge promoter's fee.

Despite the banner headline in the *New York Post* of "Tyson says Don owes him $45 million," and a lawsuit for $100 million, claiming King cheated him, the Reverend Jesse Jackson, America's foremost civil rights leader, kept calling Tyson and telling him to go back to King. It was not the first time Jackson, confidant of presidents, had come out fighting for King.

Tyson's new legal team had prepared a massive fraud suit against King and also sued his former friends and so-called managers, Horne and Holloway, claiming they were actually "King's puppets acting in the interest of the promoter and his companies." King reportedly took $45 million of Mike's $112 million, claimed the lawyers. He got $9 million for just one of the Holyfield fights. After a forensic examination of the books, Tyson's accountants contended that King used Tyson's money to pay Julio Cesar Chavez's purses.

By now, with the mainstream press trumpeting these allegations, even toadies like Jim Gray, the *Showtime* reporter, were forced to ask King on air, "Did you steal Mike Tyson's money?"

King was obviously nervous, but wouldn't deny it.

Black civil rights leaders like Sharpton and Jesse Jackson continued to act shamelessly for King. Kwesei Mfume, the head of the NAACP, which had bravely fought black exploitation throughout the century, actually went on television and embarrassingly gushed, "I *love* Don King." Jackson, who was also at the microphone at one more award ceremony meant to counter the disastrous publicity, actually looked upward and said reverentially, "Boxing is finally in the hands of its children."

* * *

On the very day Tyson sued Horne and Holloway, two young women named Sherry Cole and Chevelle Butts sued him for $22 million, claiming they were insulted and and physically abused at a Washington, D.C., nightspot. With controversy also swirling because Tyson was playing a stooge in the upcoming "Wrestlemania," even Peter McNeeley, now battling crack addiction, said sadly, "It's a real comedown for him."

With his money problems mounting, he tried to get his boxing license restored, and choked back tears in front of the New Jersey commission. But by the end of his thirty-five-minute appearence, Tyson was sputtering and cursing in front of the somber regulators. Shelly Finkel, his new manager, wisely withdrew the application.

Beset by King, money problems, personal demons and ravaged by the media, Tyson foolishly gave an interview to *Playboy*. Vacillating between rage and self-pity, he said, "I'm really bitter and defensive. I'm just always ready to attack. I'm a very hateful motherfucker, right now, a hateful individual. I'm really angry at the world.

"I'm always trying to be cool, take care of my children, not kill anybody. I'm always doing my best to be cool. I really feel bad about my outlook, how I feel about people and society, and that I'll never be a part of society the way I should. I expect the worst to happen to me in my life. I expect people to fuck me and treat me bad.

"I expect that one day, somebody, probably black, will blow my fuckin' brains out. My life is doomed the way it is. I have no future. I know I'm going to blow one day. But I'm going to make sure that when I blow, my kids are fine. There's not much more of this I can take."

In August 1998, Tyson finally went berserk after a minor traffic accident in Maryland. Richard Hardick rear-ended Tyson's Mercedes driven by his wife Monica. Under the law, there's no question that Hardick was wrong, but Tyson bolted out of the beautiful vehicle and kicked Hardick in the groin, while Abmiela Saucedo claimed the former heavyweight champ slugged him in the face as he talked with another man. As Monica screamed for him to stop, Tyson was so out of control he had to be restrained from going after Hardick again. Both victims were aging men, fifty and sixty-three years. Criminal charges were filed. Tyson still had three years to do on parole, and was facing prison again, because of his Indiana rape conviction.

Tyson denied all charges, but the Nevada Athletic Commission demanded a complete psychiatric evaluation before he could even hope to box again. At Massachusetts General Hospital in Boston, one of the finest medical centers in the country, the inner workings of Mike Tyson's mind began to emerge. He was prodded and probed for five days.

Dr Jack Singer, a Las Vegas-based sports psychologist, who had nothing to do with his examination, insisted that there's never been any test devised that can predict with any degree of probability where someone will be violent. He also maintained that these tests were culturally biased against African-Americans, who often came from violent, drug-ravaged, crime-ridden ghettos. Singer figured that since the tests were devised by mostly white, middle class males, "somebody who came from a socio-economic background that's different from the people used to develop these tests might look deviant when they're not."

Six renowned psychiatrists, psychologists and neurologists examined Tyson. Considering that Tyson might have taken too many punches and that might be precipitating his violent acts, they gave him regular medical tests and neuropsychological evaluations, which consisted of an MRI of the brain, EGG and drug screening. Dr Ronald Schouten, the psychiatrist who headed up the Massachusetts General Hospital law and psychiatric program, was in charge.

Tyson, who suddenly became a devout Muslim again, was seen praying in a suburban mosque, and wearing a skullcap. He was besieged by autograph hounds when he made a brief foray outside the hospital. He was also very worried about his situation. He had been on Zoloft, an anti-depressant, but it had done no good. He told his doctors he was embarrassed, humiliated, and furious that he was on public display. According to the extensive report, which was made public over Tyson's strong opposition, this gifted athlete, who had made around $200 million, felt hopeless and sad "all his life." He trusts no one, feels terribly alone, and expects to be betrayed. He was consumed by pent-up anger, and repeatedly tried to hurt himself with self-destructive behaviour.

In 1988, he briefly took lithium after being erroneously diagnosed as manic depressive. He didn't want to be on Zoloft because it made him slow and sluggish in the ring. The good doctors found that Tyson showed symptons of a learning disability, hyperactivity and attention-deficit disorder. He had been repeatedly attacked with bricks and baseball bats and was knocked unconscious at least five times as a child. Tyson was obviously an articulate, intelligent human being, but he felt inferior intellectually and flat-out refused to take reading or spelling tests because he was so embarrassed. When doctors tried to prod him, Tyson snapped, "I feel like I'm in a concentration camp."

He also said, "People look at me like I'm a psycho."

Though he was one of the world's biggest celebritities, "Mr. Tyson reported that 'I have no self-esteem but the biggest ego in the world.' Upon further explanation, he was aware that his inflated ego was a psychological defense to his poor self-esteem. He stated that he was uncomfortable with his celebrity status, indicating, 'I don't want super stardom.'"

As for his temper, "Mr. Tyson's changes from normal to anger seem to be triggered by his belief that he is being used, victimized and treated unfairly. When this occurs, he becomes defensive and uses anger to push people away."

Tyson "reports being deeply embarassed that everyone knew he was here and at the possibility that people would think he was 'psycho.' He expressed his frustrations at being required to undergo this evaluation, which he believes to be unprecedented. In spite of this degree of humiliation and frustration, Mr. Tyson did agree to proceed with the evaluation, and cooperated with the process. There were times, particularly early on, when his anger over the process made it difficult for him to continue."

Still, in many ways Michael Gerard Tyson was the Golden Child. He had been plucked from a life of crime by Cus D'Amato at just thirteen, nurtured by Cayton and Jacobs and had earned more money than any athlete in history. Yet, twenty years later, "Mr. Tyson reported that he has experienced feelings of sadness, hopelessness and helplessness 'all my life.'"

Did he ever contemplate suicide? "He reported that he has struggled with thoughts of self-destructive behaviour for his entire life ... He stated that he has not wanted to kill himself, but recalled engaging in passively self-destructive behaviour, such as intentionally antagonizing 'bad people' so they would harm him."

Once the report was released, the *New York Past* summed it up with a huge, front-page headline: "Shrinks say Tyson's crazy, but he's FIT TO FIGHT"

* * *

In January, Tyson knocked out Francois Botha with a freight train of a right hand, but struggled first. And he had been so profane during one pre-fight radio interview, the announcer told him, "Show some class, fella," then cut the power.

During the hype, Tyson was so anxious, so whacked out, you would have thought it was pro wrestling, or his first pro fight. But tickets weren't moving at the MGM Grand in Las Vegas. The joint only filled up when two-for-one tickets were offered the last two days before the match.

On February 5, a month later, Tyson was in a Rockville, Maryland, courtroom conservatively dressed in a three-piece suit. There was a packed house of about 300, which included a loud contingent of his supporters, as well as the two men he had slugged, who were urging that he be given a pass. Tyson had paid them off. Dr Monica Tyson, who Mike felt was "embarrassed by him," was also there to plead for mercy.

As she stood before Judge Stephen Johnson, tears running down her pretty mocha face, she swore Mike was "a good husband and good father" to their four kids. Tyson came apart after the minor traffic accident because he was "under a tremendous amount of stress." Tyson had also not been taking his anti-depressants and was worried that he'd never be able to box again. Monica pleaded, "The IRS was sending letters that they were going to take away our house ... My husband is a good, kind-hearted person and he doesn't deserve one minute of incarceration."

Judge Johnson wasn't moved. Tyson had assaulted two men old enough to be his father. He was the former heavyweight champion of the world. He had bitten off part of Holyfield's ear. He had made a complete ass of himself in Vegas just weeks earlier. When was it going to stop?

Tyson got a year in jail. As Johnson banged down his gavel, Mike looked stunned. He was led away in handcuffs.

Two weeks later, Tyson was watching television when a prison guard barked at him, "Your TV time is up."

Tyson got up and hurled his twenty-five-inch Sanyo against the bars. After it shattered into pieces, Tyson was confronted by an angry squad of hacks and was locked down in a tiny cell. He was allowed out just one hour a day for exercise. He would spend the next twenty-four days in the "hole."

★ ★ ★

As Tyson languished behind bars, all hell broke loose in Madison Square Garden on March 13.

Britain's Lennox Lewis had proven too big and strong for Evander Holyfield and finally won the heavyweight championship of the world, after being exiled to the fringes because he wouldn't sign with King. Or rather, no he didn't. This one-sided contest was declared a draw and Holyfield, who was King's fighter, kept his belts. There followed such a furore that New York governor George Pataki called in the Government and demanded that they crack down. "I don't want to tell the federal government what to do, but part of the problem is that when you have governing bodies choosing the judges, I think you need some sort of regulation, and the states aren't in a position to govern world boxing organizations."

Larry Merchant, HBO's color commentator, said on the taped replay that this outrageous draw had "the smell of an organized fix."

In 1990, King took his cards to *Showtime* because HBO wouldn't fire Merchant, but Merchant was so incensed by what had happened to Lewis, he bristled: "I'm ashamed as a boxing fan and an American … because [Lewis's] great moment of glory was taken away."

Jim Lampley, doing the blow-by-blow, called the decision "a tragedy," "a Brink's job," and "highway robbery." He added, "Once again, at one of the most critical and propitious moments possible, boxing's cesspool opens to emit an unconscionable odor."

Light-heavyweight king Roy Jones, also working the broadcast, said, "Tonight I am upset because Lennox Lewis didn't lose, and it wasn't a draw – but anytime Don King's involved, you can expect a draw to come from somewhere."

Even Robert Shapiro, who had defended O.J. Simpson, called it, "A miscarriage of justice."

With the biggest stink in boxing since Tyson–Douglas, New York State Attorney General Elliot Spitzer announced that he was probing the fight. He relented when Manhattan District Attorney Morgenthau convened an investigation of his own. City Council Speaker Peter Vallone called the fight decision a "travesty" and demanded that Morgenthau impound the receipts, but the $30 million in letters of credit had already been released. Muhammad Ali sent a letter to Senator John McCain, who had been trying to clean up the sport, calling it "the biggest fix in fight history."

Michael Gee of the *Boston Herald* cynically contended:

> The only surprise about the result of the Lennox Lewis–Evander Holyfield bout is the enormous amount of surprise it generated.
>
> The governor and the mayor of New York, prominent editorialists and civilian big shots are appalled that a title fight results in a questionable decision. This reaction speaks more to their own naive ignorance that to the nature of boxing ... Chicanery in boxing is only the oldest tradition in sports.
>
> The only difference between boxing today and its alleged golden era of 30 years ago is that its most prominent leader is now Don King, a flamboyant African-African motormouth thief, rather than a reclusive Sicilian mobster thief like Frank Carbo or Blinky Palermo.
>
> If anything, King gives his fighter victims larger crumbs off the table.

TV sports columnist Phil Mushnick, of the *New York Post*, also dove in:

> Last year a guest column appeared in the *New York Times* providing suggestions on how to clean up boxing. This column's author, by invite of the *Times*, was Don King. That defies belief.
>
> The man who tried to have Mike Tyson declared the winner after he was knocked out by Buster Douglas, the man who brought you Tyson vs Peter McNeeley, a first round DQ on pay-per-view, the man who for thirty years has done endless dirt to boxing fans and boxing was extended a forum in the New York *Times* on how to cleanse the sport!

As the *New York Post* screamed, "Fix the fixing," Larry O'Connell, one of the judges, who lived in Kent, England, incredibly announced, "I was wrong," after declaring it a 115-115 draw. O'Connell, who had a fine reputation, was vilified when he returned home. His life was threatened and many British fans apparently held him responsible for denying Britain her first real heavyweight champ since the days of Bob Fitzsimmons 100 years ago.

Fellow judge Stan Christodoulou, of South Africa, had called it 116-113 for Lewis. Even that seemed ridiculously close, but the veteran referee and judge told the South African Press Association, "I thought Lewis definitely dominated, especially the first seven rounds."

But it was Eugenia Williams, an obscure New Jersey judge who had been appointed by the corrupt Bob Lee, who drew the most outrage with her unfathomable 115-113 score for Holyfield. Williams was such a mystery women, even Jose Sulaiman and Gliberto Mendoza had protested her appointment. "I didn't make any mistakes," insisted the forty-eight-year-old Atlantic City government clerk. "I got paid to do a job, and I did it the best I could. I stand by what I scored."

The TV tape showed a fifth round so lopsided for Lewis, he landed forty-three blows, while Evander tallied just eleven. Yet somehow, Williams gave this round to Holyfield, though now she claimed she couldn't see the punches from where she was sitting. "I heard punches, but I didn't see them. How can I give him [Lewis] credit because I hear noise?"

* * *

By the time Don King was seventy, he was still the most powerful man in boxing.

He had bought a huge oceanfront mansion in Manalapan, Florida, an exclusive enclave south of Palm Beach, for $7.8 million. The glorified street hustler who had killed two men, was just two houses down from the Vanderbilt palace, where Winston Churchill used to vacation in the final years of his life.

Always wary of being sued, King again had the deed put into his wife Henrietta's name, just like he'd done with his other estate in Delray Beach, or the 400-acre farm in Ohio.

This flag-waving patriot has been indicted three times since 1986, despite his extensive political protection, but the authorities can't get a conviction. "Some of my greatest promotions have come when I was under indict-ment," he cackles. "Indictment is my middle name."

King was charged with allegedly bilking Lloyds of London out of $350,000 after he supposedly submitted a fraudulent claim for training expenses for Julio Cesar Chavez, who was slated to fight Harold Brazier. The 1991 fight never took place and in 1995 Chavez swore under oath that he never saw the money. Most people hate insurance companies. It's easy to see how King walked, despite a strong government case. The 1995 trial ended in a 6-6 deadlock, before it was finally declared a mistrial. In the retrial, King was acquitted.

By now King, like his Mafia acquaintance John Gotti, was dubbed the "Teflon Don" because nothing stuck to him. His former secretary and mistress, Constance Harper, was convicted of income tax evasion in 1986. Harper and King were indicted for conspiring to divert $1 million in corporate receipts for their own private use. Harper was convicted on three counts, while a beaming King walked free. Harper was a plump, dependant woman who had worked for him fifteen years and loved King. She'd also served as a front for him in the "management" of fighters like Esteban DeJesus..

While the workaholic King has wrecked countless fighters' lives, his own family has also suffered. "I'll never forget when I was in his home with his family," recalled former IBF light-heavyweight champ William Guthrie, whose career was nearly ruined by King. "His wife walked in. His children walked in, and his grandchildren were there. They were running, but I never saw him smile. But now, if you mention money … he laughs, he smiles. That, to me, is a man you should never ever trust."

His daughter Debbie, an attractive forty-year-old who bears a striking resemblance to her father, succumbed to her demons and became a crack addict. Though King reportedly paid her $100,000 a year and bought her a $500,000 house in Boca Raton, she was actually selling her furniture to buy crack cocaine. King had made her vice-president of Monarch Boxing, which dealt exclusively with the fighters he promotes. Tom "Boom Boom" Johnson protested this obscene arrangement in a British court, claiming under oath that he couldn't get the lucrative Prince Naseem Hamed fight unless he took Debbie King on as his "manager."

Eric King, Don's oldest son, is forty-eight at the time of writing. Though as handsome as a male model, he's a self-pitying mortgage broker in Texas, after falling out with his old man. Continuing the family's fine moral tradition, Eric King is one of America's foremost "deadbeat dads." He was finally arrested after owing $300,000 in child support.

Carl King, who is really Carl Renwick, was fathered by Henrietta's first husband, John Renwick. Carl is president of Monarch Boxing. He's so dependant on Don, when the FBI raided King's Deerfield office in June of 2000, Carl's files were there too.

Don King has been called many things. He claims he's a victim of racism, but Rudy Gonzalez, Tyson's chauffeur, noticed how thoroughly King studied Hitler and the Nazis. He has a big collection of Nazi memorabilia and documentaries, and read meticulously about how Joseph Goebbels, Hitler's minister of propaganda, spread the Big Lie. According to Gonzalez, King firmly believed that if you told somebody something long enough – they'd believe it. Once King even chartered a private jet and took everybody to Auschwitz. Tyson cried as he witnessed the crematoria where millions died, but "King seemed absolutely fascinated … at the most gruesome death camp in the history of mankind." King even dropped down to pick up some dirt and rocks to add to his collection.

For some reason, King is a man who doesn't feel other people's pain. It probably takes *Abnormal Psychology and Modern Life*, a college textbook, to clinically define what he is:

King is Paranoid: which is "suspiciousness and mistrust of others; tendency to see self as blamelesss; on guard for perceived attacks."

He's also Narcissistic: which is "grandiosity; preoccupation with receiving attention; self-promoting; lack of empathy.

He's Sadistic: which is "intimidation of others through infliction of pain, humiliation, embarrassment or cruelty.

Most of all, this loud, bombastic man, who has been misperceived by the general public as some sort of amusing human cartoon, is Antisocial: which is "lack of moral or ethical development; inability to follow approved models of behaviour; deceitfulness; shameless manipulation of others."

Antisocial Personalities "continually violate the rights of others ... without remorse or loyalty to anyone. Some antisocial personalities have enough intelligence and social charm to devise and carry out elaborate schemes for conning large numbers of people." What better sums up King?

"I could never understand it," sighed former Cleveland detective Bob Tunne, "how a man who committed a murder, even got invited to the White House. Knowing who he is, what he is, a murderer, a numbers man, a racketeer, you wonder how they get away with these things, but he has."

AFTERWORD

Free At Last?

AFTER MORE THAN 100 years of black eyes, the IBF corruption trial and the scandalous Holyfield–Lewis fight finally created enough outrage for boxing reform. Senator John McCain, a maverick Republican war hero from Arizona, led the fight for seven years, and the Muhammad Ali Boxing Reform Act finally passed on 26 May 2000 after King and Arum tried to sabotage it.

Though Arum should have lost his promoter's license after admitting to money laundering, he quietly gave Nevada senator Harry Reid $10,000 to block passage of the Ali Act. It seemed certain to pass on 19 November 1999, and would have been signed by President Bill Clinton into law. Don King, however, also gave Reid $50,000.

Reid, who had been a guest of King's at the first Lewis-Holyfield fight and feted at the lavish Patroon Steakhouse, along with twenty-five other corporate, political and casino insiders, was openly critical of the criminal penalties in the bill. Of course, it threatened to put his benefactors into prison. "Promoters did not want any criminal provisions at all," insisted McCain's aide, Paul Feeney, who drafted the bill. "They were adamantly against it."

That would've made the Ali Act useless. A weakened version was finally passed, which became McCain's second piece of boxing law in four years. (In 1997, the Professional Boxing Safety Act set national standards for health and safety.) The Ali Act basically set limits on exclusive contracts between fighters and promoters, in an effort to break up monopolies.

"This is an anti-Don King law," blustered King, who set out to destroy it, but finally lost his hold on the Congressional Black Caucus. It also prevented promoters like King from having financial connections to managers like his stepson Carl, though Carl still manages Tim Austin and he fights only for Don King.

The law mandated that the Alphabet Boys establish objective ratings criteria, which gives fighters the right to appeal. These tax-exempt buccaneers can no longer receive any compensation, outside normal sanction fees and expenses. Promoters can no longer compel a mandatory challenger to sign an "option contract," at the expense of a title shot.

There are also strong financial disclosure requirements, so fighters can't be robbed as easily, but critics like former trainer and fight broadcaster Teddy Atlas say, "It doesn't nearly go far enough. We need a national commission."

In September 2002, the McCain/Dorgan Bill was approved by the U.S. Senate Committee on Commerce, Science and Transportation. The bill will have to go to the Senate floor for a full vote. It would then need to be passed by the House of Repreentatives before President Bush George Bush would sign it into law.

The proposed federal body would be the United States Boxing Administration, and the administrator would be appointed by the President. It would be part of the Department of Labor. The administrator would have to have experience in pro boxing, or a related field, and would serve for four years. The administrator would be able to select his or her own assistant and legal counsel. The proposed USBA's basic functions would be enforcing the current federal laws (the Ali Act), and developing guidelines for all boxer, managerial and promotional contracts. The USBA would develop guidelines for the ratings of fighters, and would have the authority to investigate and hold hearings on any possible violation of the law. Sanctioning bodies would be licensed and regulated. Fighters would have a national medical registry. Health insurance would also be established. The USBA fees incurred would not tax club shows, but would be borne by television, sanctioning groups and the big promoters. Top fighters would bear the smallest part of the load.

For the last quarter century, the Alphabet Boys have plundered boxing. They have taken out millions; now it's time to give something back. The big question is: will this bill pass?

The tragedy of September 11, and the war drums against Iraq, have stymied lots of domestic U.S. legislation. McCain has also had health problems, suffering skin cancer after the North Vietnamese let him broil in the hot sun.

But there has been a change in boxing. King is still the most powerful predator in the sport, but Cedric Kushner, who was the fourth most powerful packager in the States, is on the verge of bankruptcy. Not only have his cheques been bouncing, but his production company owes millions of dollars, according to a filing by the Securities and Exchange Commission, which regulates all public companies in the United States.

If Kushner didn't have enough problems, Buster Mathis Jr won a $650,000 fraud judgement against him, and bankruptcy is not an option when the law determines that Kushner, not his company, was personally at fault, claims Mathis's attorney. Kushner was also sued in New York by his former partner Rodney Berman, who contends Kushner defrauded him out of millions.

Mike Tyson is just about finished after his destruction at the fists of Lennox Lewis. In some ways, it was tragic seeing him flat on his back, bloody and dazed. It signalled the end of an era – and symbolised much that had gone rotten in the sport. Tyson, despite his box-office appeal and compelling presence, had become a terrible liability for boxing. At least he still has his $100 million suit against King, which the Don can't get him to drop.

When John McCain first started scaring King, during the formative stages of the Ali Act, the shameless conman descended on the senator who nearly grabbed the Republican nomination for president, and bellowed, "John McCain, my friend! We're going to clean up boxing together!"

McCain laughed. King offered him $1 million for his financially strapped presidential campaign. Though there weren't ten votes in boxing reform, McCain, who was hideously tortured for more than five years as a POW, turned him down. King, who descends on people with loud, evangelical fervour and has so much energy he sucks the air out of a room, was shocked to find somebody he couldn't buy. But after seven decades, King still keeps moving, like a shark that can't stop swimming, lest he sink to the bottom and die.

In Nevada, Assembly Bill 446 was awaiting a hearing in the state Senate. Dr Elias Ghanem, the chairman of the commission, decided before his recent death that it was needed so they could finally regulate the Alphabet Boys. "Until now, they have had a free hand in doing what they wanted to do," said Ghanem, who once served with the WBC. He contended that the so-called sanctioning bodies refused to give Nevada the information it wanted as to ownership, non-profit, or for-profit status.

"What this gives us the ability to do, if there is an egregious act by a sanctioning organization, we can pull the license," says Dr Flip Homansky, who is a doctor with the commission.

Nevada already had all the power it needed, but when has its commission ever disciplined King for his front managers or flagrant double-dipping from Tyson's purses? According to the Nevada Attorney General's office, there were 124 "championship fights" from 1996 to 2000 in Nevada, which generated $8.85 million in sanction fees. "Boxing is big business. One fight can gross $100 million," says Mark Ratner of the Nevada Commission, yet fighters were nothing more than bodies that drew the high rollers, while they risked brain damage and had no real protection under the law.

In the United States of America, indeed anywhere in the world, this is an outrage and a disgrace. Boxers are not fighting cocks or racehorses, they are human beings.

Sources

Selected Book Bibliography

Allison, Dean, and Bruce B. Henderson. *Empire of Deceit, Inside the Biggest Sports and Banking Scandal in U.S. History.* Doubleday, New York, 1985.

Anderson, Dave. *In the Corner: Great Trainers Talk About Their Art.* William Morrow, New York, 1991.

Boxing Update Bullet. Volume 7, 2001. Brenner, Teddy, with Barney Nagler. *Only the Ring Was Square.* Prentice-Hall INC., New Jersey.

Carson, Robert C., James N. Butler. *Abnormal Psychology and Modern Life (Ninth Edition).* Harper Collins, New York, 1992.

Fleischer, Nat. *Fifty Years at Ringside.* Fleet Publishing, New York, 1958.

Fleischer, Nat. *Ring Record Book and Boxing Encyclopedia* (numerous years).

Fleischer, Nat, and Andre, Sam. *A Pictorial History of Boxing.* Bonanza Books, 1959

Fox, Stephen. *Blood and Power: Organized Crime in Twentieth Century America.* William Morrow, New York, 1990.

Fried, Ronald K. *Corner Men.* Four Walls Eight Windows Publishing, 1991.

Gonzalez, Rudy and Martin A. Fegenbaum. *The Inner Ring.* The Oliver Publishing Group, Miami, 1995.

Hammer, Richard. *Playboy's Illustrated History of Organized Crime.* Playboy Press, Chicago, 1975.

Hauser, Thomas. *The Black Lights.* McGraw-Hill, New York, 1986.

Hersch, Seymour. *The Dark Side of Camelot.* Little, Brown, New York, 1997.

Heyman, C. David. *R.F.K.* Dutton Books, New York, 2001.

Kahn, Roger. *A Flame of Pure Fire: Jack Dempsey and the Roaring Twenties.* Harcourt, San Diego, New York, 1999.

McCallum, John D. *Encyclopedia of World Boxing Champions.* Chilton Boook Company, Radnor, Pennsylvania, 1975.

MaCambridge, Michael. *The Franchise: A History of Sports Illustrated Magazine.* Hyperion, New York, 1997.

Mingo, Jack. *The Juicy Parts: Things Your History Teacher Never Told You About the Twentieth Century's Most Famous People.* Berkley Publishing Group, 1996.

Mullan, Harry. *The Illustrated History of Boxing.* Hamlyn Publishing Group, London, 1990.

Mullan, Harry. *The Book of Boxing Quotations.* Stanley Paul Publishing, London, 1988.

Mullan, Harry. *Boxing – The Last Twenty-Five Years.* W.H. Smith, London, 1991.

Nagler, Barney. *James Norris and the Decline of Boxing.* Bobbs–Merrill Company, New York, 1964.

Newfield, Jack. *Only In America: The Life and Crimes of Don King.* William Morrow, New York, 1996.

Nicholson, Skip. *Special Report to the Oklahoma Labor Commissioner.* 1996.

Roberts, Randy. *Jack Dempsey, the Manassa Mauler.* Louisiana State University Press, Baton Rouge, 1979.

Roemer, William F. *Accardo, the Genuine Godfather.* Ivy Books, 1996.

The Ring 2001 Boxing Almanac. London Publishing Corporation, Ft. Washington, PA, 2001.

Rudd, Irving and Stan Tischler. *The Sporting Life.* St. Martin's Press, New York.

Sammons, Jeffrey T. *Beyond the Ring: Boxing in American Society.* University of Illinois Press, Urbana, Ill., 1988.

Solomons, Jack. *Jack Solomons Tells All.* Hamilton, London, 1956.

Summers, Anthony. *The Arrogance of Power: the Secret World of Richard Nixon.* Phoenix Press, 2001.

Summers, *Anthony Official and Confidential: The Secret Life of J. Edgar Hoover.* Putnam Pub. Group, 1993.

Tosches, Nick. *The Devil and Sonny Liston.*

Selected Newspapers:

Boston Globe
Boston Herald
Boston Herald-American
Chicago Daily-News
Chicago Sun-Times
Columbus Journal
New York American
New York Daily Mirror
New York Post
New York Sun
New York Tribune
New York Herald-Tribune
New York Times
Washington Post

General interest magazines:

Look
Life

Boxing publications:

Boxing News
Boxing Illustrated
Boxing and All-Star Wrestling
The Ring
True Boxing Yearbok, 1962

Selected Television and Radio:

Ali, Through the Eyes of the World
Ali, Reputations
Boxing, A Bloody Business
Boxing, Hall of Fame interviews, Carmen Basilio, Marvin Hagler, Jimmy
    Carter, Ike Williams, Archie Moore, Willie Pep, Gene Fullmer
Boxing, In and Out of the Ring
Boxing, the Last Round
Carmen Basilio – Fighting the Mob
Unknown George Chuvalo documentary
Sonny Liston, The Mysterious Life and Death of a Champion
Sonny Liston, Biography
Outside the Lines (ESPN)
Sugar Ray Robinson, Pound for Pound
Sugar Ray Robinson, Bright Lights, Dark Shadows
Real Sports – Bobby Chacon, Reggie Strickland
Real Story – Max Schmeling, Joe Louis
Mike Tyson, Nevada and New Jersey Relicensing Hearings
Randy Turpin, 64-Day Hero
Selected BBC interviews, Jack Dempsey, Jimmy Wilde
On the Line, BBC Radio 5 Live, for Harold Smith and Bob Lee

Selected American radio broadcasts

Fight films: too numerous to list, from James J. Corbett – Peter Courtney,
    to Lennox Lews – Mike Tyson

Selected legal filings:

Declaration of Robert Arum, United States of America v. International Boxing Federation, et al., nominal defendants and Robert W. Lee Sr., et al, defendants

Declaration of Stan Hoffman

Recorded conversations, Douglas Beavers, Bob Lee Sr, Bob Lee Jr, others, 1997-98, IBF, Bob Lee trial

Corruption in Professional Boxing, Report prepared by the Permanent Subcommittte on Investigations, 1994

Corruption in Professional Boxing Hearings, August 11-12, 1992

Corruption in Professional Boxing, Part II, hearings before the Permenant subcommitttee on Investigations, of the Committee on Governmental Affairs, March 10 and April 1, 1993

Business practices in Boxing, hearings, March 24, 1998, U.S. Senate Committee on Commerce, Science and Transportation

Oversight of the Professional Boxing Industry, Hearings before the Commerce, Science and Transportation Committee, United States Senate, May 22, 1997

Subcommittee on Antittrust and Monopoly, Hearings on Professional Boxing (Frankie Carbo), 1960

Other:

FBI (Federal Bureau of Investigation) files on Charles "Sonny" Liston, Jim Norris, Frank Carbo, Frank Palermo

Internal Revenue Service, income tax filings: various years, from 1980-2002 for International Boxing Federation, World Boxing Association, World Boxing Council